I NEED
THEE
EVERY HOUR

BOOKS AVAILABLE BY BLAINE M. YORGASON

I Need Thee Every Hour

Angus Austin's Rising

Girl at the Crossing

Courageous Defender of Truth—John Taylor

Humble Servant, Spiritual Giant—Harold B. Lee

From Orphaned Boy to Prophet of God—Joseph F. Smith

One Tattered Angel

Gabriel's Well

Hearts Afire, Book One—At All Hazards

Hearts Afire, Book Two—Fort on the Firing Line

Hearts Afire, Book Three—Curly Bill's Gift

Secrets

Spiritual Survival in the Last Days

The Soderberg Saga

The Shadow Taker

Chester, I Love You

Charlie's Monument

I NEED THEE EVERY HOUR

THE JOY OF COMING TO CHRIST

BLAINE M. YORGASON

DESERET BOOK

SALT LAKE CITY, UTAH

Portions of this book were previously published as
Spiritual Progression in the Last Days

Visit us at deseretbook.com

Library of Congress Cataloging-in-Publication Data

Yorgason, Blaine M., 1942-
I need Thee every hour : the joy of coming to Christ / Blaine M. Yorgason.
p. cm.
Includes bibliographical references and index.
ISBN 1-59038-230-7 (alk. paper)
1. Salvation. 2. Church of Jesus Christ of Latter-day Saints—Doctrines.
3. Mormon Church—Doctrines. I. Title.
BX8643.S25Y67 2003
234—dc22 2003019509

Printed in the United States of America 72076-7176
Publishers Printing, Salt Lake City, Utah

10 9 8 7 6 5 4 3 2 1

For Sheri, a dear friend
who regularly pushes me
to new heights

CONTENTS

INTRODUCTION

Nine years ago this past spring, I finished a manuscript I had titled *Spiritual Progression in the Last Days.* I was very excited about this, for during the previous few years I had discovered, and was endeavoring to follow, a scriptural theme that seemed to outline a divinely organized pathway of progressive spiritual growth. Of course, this growth followed an upward path, denoting increasing difficulty as one moved forward; nevertheless, the journey was bringing me much joy and great peace, with the ultimate destination, clearly evident in the scriptures, a glorious reunion with Christ and the Father that it seemed was to be experienced in both this life and the next.

With high expectations I watched the manuscript's publication and introduction, and then two things happened that still seem remarkable. The first was that the book sold very slowly and, in fact, never got beyond the first printing. Added to this was the surprise that many who normally enjoyed and praised what I had written either said nothing to me about this book, or responded that they had found it either incomprehensible, or—and this was the most startling—understandable but suggesting a far more difficult life choice than they were interested in pursuing.

The second remarkable occurrence began shortly after the book's publication and has continued steadily ever since, even though the book has for many years been out of print. Every month or so a letter has arrived from someone who is unknown to me. Many of these letter writers give their names but many do not; they thank me for illuminating and defining the very journey they have found themselves passing through. A very few have asked questions; most have simply shared in humble brevity their own experiences with, and insights into, the personal spiritual growth that the Lord is giving them. These letters have become a treasure to me.

Meanwhile, my own spiritual learning curve has taken all sorts of unexpected twists and turns, particularly during two major life events. These were the almost eight years spent with our now-exalted daughter, Charity; and shortly following her death seven years ago today, June 26, 1996, my several years of service as a bishop. Despite my feeble attempt to describe what I learned from our adopted, angelic daughter (see *One Tattered Angel*), I now know, because sweet insights continue to surface in my thinking, that I will never in this life fully grasp all she came to share. It is proving to be the same with my bishopric, during which tenure I gained far more in spiritual growth than I can ever hope to give back. It was not that I was involved in much personal study during those years, for bishops rarely have time for such luxury. Rather, I was led through an unending series of events and experiences, constantly overlapping, that were both amazingly sweet and terrifically painful. As my wonderful ward members allowed me into their hearts and homes, I gradually realized that my eyes were being opened in all sorts of ways. And though the particulars of each incident, including in many cases actual identities, seem to have been thoroughly expunged from my memory, overall views have remained and, through the impressions engendered by the Holy Ghost, continue to enrich and bless my thinking.

When Sheri Dew, president of Deseret Book Company, called me a few months ago with the suggestion that I consider updating and republishing *Spiritual Progression in the Last Days,* I thought the task would be fairly simple. Hardly! At every turn and on every page, I found myself rewriting, adding to, reconsidering, clarifying, and occasionally even discarding what I had once said, with the past nine years of study, letters, and personal experiences casting everything in what seems to me a clearer, brighter light.

While the general theme of a rigorous lifelong spiritual journey toward our Savior remains the same, for I am more convinced than ever of its scriptural veracity, the changes and additions have been so substantial that in reality I have written an entirely new book. In so very many ways and circumstances I have been brought to understand, and so to echo the phrase, "I need Thee every hour."

For those who may feel earnestly drawn upward to Christ

and His incredible "peace in this world, and eternal life in the world to come" (D&C 59:23), my prayer is that they will read, ponder, and hopefully, enjoy.

BLAINE M. YORGASON
June 26, 2003

Part One

TROUBLED TIMES, GLORIOUS BLESSINGS

Chapter One

A MANTLE OF LOVE

Four days after I had been ordained and set apart as a bishop, I had one of the most remarkable experiences of my life. As my stake president had set me apart, he had promised that the mantle of a bishop would fall upon me, and that I would then understand what the Lord desired of me in my calling. Four days later I was still "swimming," trying desperately to figure out what I was supposed to be doing for the approximately four hundred ward members who had so abruptly become my responsibility. Neither had any sort of mantle fallen upon me that might give me direction.

All week I had been worrying about it, wondering why I didn't feel any different than I had before the ordination. I had spent Tuesday evening with the youth and had a good time getting acquainted, but there had been no spiritual moments or feelings that I could discern. Wednesday I had given some temple recommends and with my counselors had issued several calls, for we were organizing a new ward. But still there had been no sign of what I might call a mantle.

A SENSE OF RESTLESSNESS

That day, Thursday, I had been working at home, but shortly after lunch I started feeling restless. I couldn't focus on what I was doing, but I had no idea what else to do. I continued my effort to work, but the feeling of restlessness grew until finally, around three o'clock, I at last gave it up. I climbed into my car and started driving aimlessly around the ward, praying all the while that Heavenly Father would teach me what I had to do to be a righteous bishop.

Suddenly, as I was driving through one of my ward neighborhoods, I was filled with the most amazing feeling I have ever experienced! It was a warm feeling, wonderfully pleasant, but in an instant I found myself awash with tears of joy and love, and it was all I could do to keep from stopping my car, running up to the nearest door, and hugging whoever opened it.

That was a surprise, for I am not by nature a "hugger." From that instant, however, no one in the ward was safe from my exuberance! No matter who in the ward I thought of—old or young; man, woman, or child; active or inactive, and even nonmembers—tears of joy and love flowed anew, and I was overwhelmed. *I loved my ward!* More, I felt compelled to tell them of this love, to show them! I really did want to hug everyone I could think of, and I couldn't imagine any of them asking anything of me that I wouldn't drop everything to do.

LOVE MADE MANIFEST

Moments later, still inching along and trying to drive through my tears, I turned into a cul-de-sac, saw a home ahead of me whose inhabitants I had never met, and knew in that instant that I had to stop and meet them. Cleaning my face as best I could, I rang the bell and was soon visiting with an inactive family that I found myself loving with all my heart. An hour and a half later I was in another home under similar circumstances, with the same overwhelming feelings of love, and so it continued from house to house until long after dark, when I finally found my way home. While the visits I had with the various families were remarkable to me, what is really amazing is that even now thoughts of those precious ward members still engender within me that same sweet and overwhelming feeling of love.

Just as remarkable to me was that as I told my wife of my experiences, I found myself weeping again, that sense of love once again enveloping me as with a mantle. Later, as I knelt to thank Father in Heaven for this remarkable blessing, the sensation of love returned with great force—only with a major difference. Now I found myself trembling and weeping and in a measure feeling as if I might be consumed with an amazing love for God and His Beloved Son. It was like a fire within me, and as my mind jumped from one aspect of the life and ministry of Christ to another, but particularly as I reconsidered His suffering, death, and resurrection, I was overwhelmed with the wondrous thing He had done—not just for me but for every single person in my ward! In fact, a familiar verse of scripture finally became "mine" that night, one I have thought of innumerable times since, almost as a litany: "God so loved the world, that he gave his only begotten

Son, that whosoever believeth in him should not perish, but have everlasting life" (John 3:16). Always I had believed that the Father and the Son loved all mankind; now I was overwhelmed with the love I felt for them because of it.

A day or two later as I was sitting in the temple reading in the Book of Mormon, a verse from Nephi's vision that I had read many times before but paid little attention to leaped out at me with great force: "[The angel] spake unto me again, saying: Look! And I looked, and I beheld the Lamb of God going forth among the children of men. And I beheld multitudes of people who were sick, and who were afflicted with all manner of diseases, and with devils and unclean spirits; and the angel spake and showed all these things unto me. And they were healed by the power of the Lamb of God; and the devils and the unclean spirits were cast out" (1 Nephi 11:31).

As I read that verse again and again, the feeling of love consumed me once more, and I *knew* that Christ's ministry of blessing His beloved people had not ended. Rather, the multitudes of "sick and afflicted" included my wonderful ward, with all their diverse strengths, weaknesses, trials, problems, tribulations, and blessings, and I had been called to continue His loving ministry among them!

Within my mind words had formed, more faint than a whisper but clear and unmistakable: "Go, my son, and do thou likewise." Again, my love for Him—as well as His children who were my friends and neighbors and to whom I now *knew* I was being sent by Him to minister—felt as if it might consume me!

SOME STUDIES

In the weeks and months that followed, as I had a minute here or there, I began looking for an explanation for my almost constant flow of emotion—of love. One of my first discoveries came as I was striving to make the numerous meetings I had to conduct more effective, and I turned to Elder M. Russell Ballard's book *Counseling with Our Councils* for some guidance. In that book Elder Ballard related the experience had by a newly called bishop who also felt an immediate "profound sense of love for the people he was being called to serve." The bishop concluded his increased capacity was a fruit of the spiritual keys he had received when ordained and set apart (pp. 117–18). I was having that same experience!

Carrying the issue a bit further, and putting it in words that I could clearly understand, Elder Merrill J. Bateman has stated that the mantle "is a very strong feeling of love for all the people in your jurisdiction" ("Merrill J. Bateman—A Pioneer in Building the Kingdom," *Church News,* July 4, 1992).

President Gordon B. Hinckley has added, "As we look with love and gratitude to God, as we serve him with an eye single to his glory, there goes from us the darkness of sin, the darkness of selfishness, the darkness of pride. There will come an increased love for our Eternal Father and for his Beloved Son, our Savior and our Redeemer. There will come a greater sense of service toward our fellowmen, less of thinking of self and more of reaching out to others ("And the Greatest of These Is Love," *Ensign,* March 1984, p. 5).

THE GREATEST COMMANDMENT

In the context of another of Jesus' mortal experiences, what I was feeling finally became understandable: "Then one of them, which was a lawyer, asked him a question, tempting him, and saying, Master, which is the great commandment in the law? Jesus said unto him, Thou shalt love the Lord thy God with all thy heart, and with all thy soul, and with all thy mind. This is the first and great commandment. And the second is like unto it, Thou shalt love thy neighbour as thyself. On these two commandments hang all the law and the prophets" (Matthew 22:35–40).

The mantle I had been given, I could now see, was not from me but was God's gift—His pure love for my neighbors, His children within my ward boundaries—enabling me to keep these two greatest commandments so I might have sufficient righteousness to be a blessing to them.

CHARITY—THE PURE LOVE OF CHRIST

Of course, what I was experiencing and learning about, I now understand, is charity, which, as Mormon puts it, is "the pure love of Christ" (Moroni 7:47). For a bishop (or anyone else called of God to minister in His kingdom) to obtain by the laying on of the hands this mantle of love is consistent with the scriptures, which, according to Elder Bruce R. McConkie, teach that "charity is an essential qualification for the ministers of Christ (D&C 4:5); no one can assist in the Lord's work without it (D&C 12:8; 18:19); and the Saints of God are commanded to seek and obtain it. (D&C 121:45; 124:116; 2 Ne. 33:7–9; Alma 7:24; 1 Cor. 16:14; 1 Tim. 4:12; 2 Tim. 2:22; Tit. 2:2; 2 Pet. 1:7). . . . Above all the attributes of godliness and perfection, *charity* is the one most devoutly to be desired. Charity is more than love, far more; it is everlasting love, perfect love, the pure love of Christ which endureth forever. It is love so centered in righteousness that the possessor has no aim or desire except for the eternal welfare of his own soul and for the souls of those around him. . . .

"'Above all things,' the Lord says, 'clothe yourselves with the bond of charity, *as with a mantle,* which is the bond of perfectness and peace' (D&C 88:125; Col. 3:14)" (*Mormon Doctrine,* p. 121; italics mine).

Charity. Christ's pure and perfect love. The mantle that overcame me that Thursday afternoon consisted, primarily, of impressions and feelings of love—pure, sweet, and holy, that I knew in that instant came directly from heaven. It came not from me or through any virtue of mine but was a gift from the Lord so I could more appropriately serve as a common judge in Israel. How? By letting me know in no uncertain terms exactly how the Lord felt about my ward members, for it was His love for each and all of them I was constantly awash with (insofar as I was righteous enough to feel it), given that I might strive to minister in the same way He would minister were He here to do so.

No wonder it seemed so remarkable! It was! In fact, it was divine! The sweetness of it—the tenderness and patience and mildness and compassion that almost consumed me whenever I prayed about or interacted with any members of my ward through the next several years—was overwhelming and astounding! Yet through it I gained a powerful witness that Christ's pure and perfect love for each of us, in its beauty, majesty, and glory, is much more vast and encompassing than any of us can imagine or comprehend.

QUALITIES OF CHARITY

Neither can Christ's love be adequately described. In fact, the effort to do so (and I have made numerous pitiful attempts) puts me in mind of what the Nephites said of Christ's words when they were privileged to hear Him pray: "No tongue can speak, neither can there be written by any man, neither can the hearts of men conceive so great and marvelous things as we both saw and heard Jesus speak; and no one can conceive of the joy which filled our souls" (3 Nephi 17:17). Despite their loss for words, these blessed Nephites obviously felt of His pure and perfect love as keenly as have I.

Nevertheless, there are descriptions, inspired by the Lord and given through the power of the Holy Ghost, of what a person's behavior should be like if he or she is possessed of this pure love. According to the Apostle Paul, "Charity suffereth long, and is kind; charity envieth not; charity vaunteth not itself, is not puffed up, doth not behave itself unseemly, seeketh not her own, is not easily provoked, thinketh no evil; rejoiceth not in iniquity, but rejoiceth in the truth; beareth all things, believeth all things, hopeth all things, endureth all things. Charity never faileth. . . . And now abideth faith, hope, charity, these three; but the greatest of these is charity" (1 Corinthians 13:4–8, 13).

Mormon, following the whisperings of the same Spirit, used essentially the same phrasing when he declared, "Charity suffereth long, and is kind, and envieth not, and is not puffed up, seeketh not her own, is not easily provoked, thinketh no evil, and rejoiceth not in iniquity but rejoiceth in the truth, beareth all things, believeth all things, hopeth all things, endureth all things. Wherefore, my beloved brethren, if ye have not charity, ye are nothing, for charity never faileth. Wherefore, cleave unto charity, which is the greatest of all, for all things must fail—but charity is the pure love of Christ, and it endureth forever; and whoso is found possessed of it at the last day, it shall be well with him" (Moroni 7:45–47).

Speaking specifically to those called in our day, as was I, to minister through priesthood ordination or setting apart to His people, the Lord has declared by way of reminder, "No power or influence can or ought to be maintained by virtue of the priesthood, only by persuasion, by long-suffering, by gentleness and meekness, and by love unfeigned; by kindness, and pure knowledge, which shall greatly enlarge the soul without hypocrisy, and without guile—reproving betimes with sharpness, when moved upon by the Holy Ghost; and then showing forth afterwards an increase of love toward him whom thou hast reproved, lest he esteem thee to be his enemy; that he may know that thy faithfulness is stronger than the cords of death" (D&C 121:41–44).

A COMMANDMENT TO ALL LATTER-DAY SAINTS

What I experienced as a bishop (and this was troubling to me when I finally realized it) came not because of any great endeavors toward righteousness or repentance or seeking after Christ that I made. It was, in fact, a gift that came because my stake president had recommended me as a bishop, the Brethren at Church headquarters had approved his choice, and my stake president had then ordained me and set me apart. In other words, the Lord was honoring them, not me, and He was also blessing my ward members.

It was a mantle that had come with my calling, and it would leave when that calling was ended.

It was this unhappy realization, finally, that impelled me to seek further understanding. And with that understanding came the realization that I, of myself, still had a long way to go. Yet—and this fact thrilled me when I understood it—I did not have to lose with my release that love for God and my ward members that had so enhanced and blessed my life! In fact, I had been commanded, scripturally speaking, *not* to lose it. In other words, this pure love of Christ—for His Father in Heaven and for *all* His Father's children, myself included—is not merely for Church leaders to feel. As Elder McConkie said, all the "saints of God are commanded to seek and attain" this love (*Mormon Doctrine,* p. 121). President Hinckley confirms this, saying, "To love the Lord is not just counsel; it is not just well-wishing. It is a commandment. It is the first and great commandment incumbent upon each of us because love of God is the root from which spring all other types of love; love of God is the root of all virtue, of all goodness, of all strength of character, of all fidelity to do right. Love the Lord your God, and love His Son" (Ricks College Regional Conference, Rexburg, Idaho, October 29, 1995). Then "there will come a greater sense of service toward our fellowmen, less of thinking of self and more of reaching out to others ("And the Greatest of These Is Love," *Ensign,* March 1984, p. 5).

This divine love is chief among the gifts of the Spirit that each of us must obtain if we desire salvation. As Moroni puts it, "There must be faith; and if there must be faith there must also be hope; and if there must be hope there must also be charity. *And except ye have charity ye can in nowise be saved in the kingdom of God;* neither can ye be saved in the kingdom of God if ye have not faith; neither can ye if ye have no hope" (Moroni 10:20–21; italics mine).

To Moroni the Lord also said, "Behold, I will show unto the Gentiles their weakness, and I will show unto them that *faith, hope and charity bringeth unto me—the fountain of all righteousness.* And I, Moroni, having heard these words, was comforted" (Ether 12:28–29; italics mine).

This great prophet and son of a prophet then replied, "I remember that thou hast said that *thou hast loved the world, even unto the laying down of thy life for the world,* that thou mightest take it again to prepare a place for the children of men. And now I know that *this love which thou hast had for the children of men is charity; wherefore, except men shall have charity they cannot inherit that place which thou hast prepared in the mansions of thy Father*" (Ether 12:33–34; italics mine).

TO BE ENERGETICALLY PRAYED FOR

If this marvelous gift of love for God and man, made gloriously manifest by Christ through His atonement, is required to be manifest in and through all of us before we can enjoy salvation, then how are we to obtain it? Turning once more to the scriptures, we learn that we must first live for it; and second, we must pray for it. Again, according to Mormon, "None is acceptable before God, save the meek and lowly in heart; and if a man be meek and lowly in heart, and confesses by the power of the Holy Ghost that Jesus is the Christ, he [will] have charity; for if he have not charity he is nothing; wherefore he must needs have charity" (Moroni 7:44).

How do we become meek and lowly of heart? Through

constant repentance and sincere prayer. Again quoting the prophet Mormon, "Wherefore, my beloved brethren, *pray unto the Father with all the energy of heart, that ye may be filled with this love,* which he hath bestowed upon all who are true followers of his Son, Jesus Christ; that ye may become the sons of God; that when he shall appear we shall be like him, for we shall see him as he is; that we may have this hope; that we may be purified even as he is pure. Amen" (Moroni 7:48; italics mine).

WE MUST COME UNTO CHRIST

Humble Amaleki, descendant of Jacob and one of the subjects of righteous Nephite kings Mosiah and his son Benjamin, wrote movingly as he neared his own death, "exhorting all men to come unto God, the Holy One of Israel, and believe in prophesying, and in revelations, and in the ministering of angels, and in the gift of speaking with tongues, and in the gift of interpreting languages, and in all things which are good; for there is nothing which is good save it comes from the Lord; and that which is evil cometh from the devil. And now, my beloved brethren, I would that ye should *come unto Christ,* who is the Holy One of Israel, and partake of his salvation, and the power of his redemption. *Yea, come unto him,* and offer your whole souls as an offering unto him, and continue in fasting and praying, and endure to the end; and as the Lord liveth ye will be saved" (Omni 1:25–26; italics mine).

Come unto Christ! This counsel from Amaleki, I believe, is the key to obtaining charity, or the pure love of Jesus Christ. To feel the Lord's pure love, we must come to Him. Literally, we must seek diligently until we find Him.

Repeatedly, we hear the Savior's injunction, "Come unto me" (Matthew 11:28–30; 16:24–27; 19:14; Exodus 24:12; Isaiah 55:3). We are also told, "No man can come unto me, except it were given unto him of my Father" (John 6:65). Lest we be confused by the meaning of these things, Moroni explains, "And again I would exhort you that ye would *come unto Christ, and lay hold upon every good gift,* and touch not the evil gift, nor the unclean thing. . . . *Yea, come unto Christ, and be perfected in him,* and deny yourselves of all ungodliness; and if ye shall deny yourselves of all ungodliness, and love God with all your might, mind and strength, then is his grace sufficient for you, that by his grace ye may be perfect in Christ; and if *by the grace of God ye are perfect in Christ, ye can in nowise deny the power of God.*

"And again, if ye *by the grace of God are perfect in Christ,* and deny not his power, then are ye *sanctified in Christ by the grace of God,* through the shedding of the blood of Christ, which is in the covenant of the Father unto the remission of your sins, that ye become holy, without spot (Moroni 10:30, 32–33; italics mine).

In other words, it is only by the grace or goodness of God—through Him—that we can in any way be perfected and sanctified through coming unto Christ. Jesus adds, "He that believeth these things which I have spoken, him will I visit with the manifestations of my Spirit, and he shall know and bear record. For because of my Spirit he shall know that these things are true. . . . *Come unto me, O ye Gentiles,* and I will show unto you the greater things, the knowledge which is hid up because of unbelief. *Come unto me, O ye house of Israel,* and it shall be made manifest unto you how great things the Father hath laid up for you, from the foundation of the world; and it hath not come unto you, because of unbelief. Behold, *when ye shall rend that veil of unbelief which doth cause you to remain in your awful state of wickedness, and hardness of heart, and blindness of mind, then shall the great and marvelous things which have been hid up from the foundation of the world from you—yea, when ye shall call upon the Father in my name, with a broken heart and a contrite spirit, then shall ye know*" (Ether 4:11, 13–15; italics mine).

To come unto Christ through the Father, then, we are to "repent of all [our] folly, and clothe [ourselves] with charity; and cease to do evil, and lay aside all [our] hard speeches" (D&C 124:116); and we are to "be humble, and be submissive and gentle; easy to be entreated; full of patience and long-suffering; being temperate in all things; being diligent in keeping the commandments of God at all times; asking for whatsoever things [we] stand in need, both spiritual and temporal; always returning thanks unto God for whatsoever things [we] do receive. And see that ye have faith, hope, and charity, and then ye will always abound in good works" (Alma 7:23–24).

Sanctifying, or purifying, ourselves through diligent repentance, obedience, patience, long-suffering, gratitude, service, and prayer, which are all "good works," is the process through which, by the grace of the Father, we come unto Christ, and through the power of His Spirit are made partakers of charity, His pure and perfect love. And each of us must do this in the exact manner prescribed by the Lord and His prophets if we are going to come to Christ in this troubled world and obtain His true and living peace.

Chapter Two

POWER FROM ON HIGH

We really do live in a troubled world—a world vastly different from that in which our parents and grandparents were raised. I will never forget a conversation I had with my father, who served as a bishop some fifty years before I received my call. I had just encountered my first marital crisis within the ward, which caught me completely unawares, so afterward I had called Dad to ask how he had handled such difficulties when he had been bishop. After a significant pause, he replied thoughtfully, "You know, I don't think I ever encountered a marital problem." Stunned, I then asked how he had dealt with moral issues and transgressions, of which I had already encountered several. Again Dad paused, thinking back. Then, "Blaine, neither do I remember ever dealing with a moral issue." "My word, Dad," I pressed, feeling truly amazed, "what *did* you do?" "My memory of my bishopric experience," he responded quietly, "besides refereeing a few neighborhood squabbles, is of a constant, rigorous effort at fund-raising for a new chapel. Aren't you grateful you don't have to spend time doing that?"

Indeed I was! And as the years of my calling passed, with almost constant serious issues, problems, and crises within the ward consuming both my time and attention, my gratitude that the Church has assumed that financial burden grew apace.

A CHANGED WORLD

Understanding of that bit of freedom also helped me become more conscious of the fact that indeed our world has changed over the past generation or so—and not for the better! Truly we are living in tumultuous, troubled, fearful times—times that the Lord has designated as the last days before the coming of Christ in His glory (D&C 1:4; 20:1). Economic stability has been taken from the earth as the devourer does its work (Malachi 3:7–11). New and previously unheard-of diseases such as SARS sweep the earth, leaving desolation in their wake (D&C 45:31). The hearts of men and women are failing them in record numbers (Luke 21:26). Nations and kingdoms, including our own, are rising against each other in violent and unending war, while famines, pestilences, and earthquakes occur on all parts of the earth (Joseph Smith–Matthew 1:29).

THE EARTH IS IN COMMOTION

As the Lord proclaimed, "The whole earth [is] in commotion" (D&C 45:26) as we hear "the voice of thunderings, and . . . the voice of lightnings, and . . . the voice of tempests, and . . . the voice of earthquakes, and great hailstorms, and . . . the voice of famines and pestilences of every kind, and . . . the voice of judgment" (D&C 43:25), "and the voice of the waves of the sea heaving themselves beyond their bounds. And all things shall be in commotion; and surely, men's hearts shall fail them; for fear shall come upon all people" (D&C 88:90–91). Peace has been "taken from the earth, and the devil [has] power over his own dominion" (D&C 1:35). Elder James E. Talmage noted, "This is the day of shaking, when everything that can be shaken shall be shaken, and only those things which are established upon an eternal foundation shall endure" (Conference Report, October 1918, p. 59). Literally, as the Lord declares, "the day has come, when the cup of the wrath of mine indignation is full" (D&C 43:26).

More significantly, in these last days the very natures of men and women will be changed as wickedness and iniquity abound and the love of people for each other waxes cold (D&C 45:27; Joseph Smith–Matthew 1:30). Elder Neal A. Maxwell writes, "In today's relativistic society, we see indulgence masquerading as tolerance. We see the primacy of 'politically correct' substituting for righteous indignation and for moral outrage. Instead of genuine and pervasive concern for the public good, we see intense devotion paid to niche causes. People are often viewed as advocates of causes rather than as neighbors, being stereotyped because of their interest groups. It is anemic enough to know neighbors and others only as functions but worse still to regard them so much more narrowly. Because all others are actually the spirit sons and daughters of God, the new math of the new morality is even more disturbing than it is fuzzy" (*The Promise of Discipleship*, p. 9).

It is exactly as the Apostle Paul prophesied nearly two thousand years ago: "This know also, that in the last days perilous times shall come. For men shall be lovers of their own selves, covetous, boasters, proud, blasphemers, disobedient to parents, unthankful, unholy, without natural affection, trucebreakers, false accusers, incontinent, fierce, despisers of those that are good, traitors, heady, highminded, lovers of pleasures more than lovers of God; having a form of godliness; but denying the power thereof: from such turn away. For of this sort are they which creep into houses, and lead captive silly women laden with sins, led away with divers lusts, ever learning, and never able to come to the knowledge of the truth" (2 Timothy 3:1–7).

TROUBLED TIMES—MORE PERSONAL THAN WORLDWIDE

What I believe all of this is saying—and it certainly proved true in my own little ward—is that while we are bound to be affected to one degree or another by tumultuous and destructive world or natural events, ofttimes even dramatically, the real troubles of these perilous times—the potentially destructive troubles—will occur within our own hearts, our own souls. My experiences as a bishop have caused me to believe it is these potential calamities, at least as much as adequate food storage and other temporal precautions, for which we should labor most diligently to be prepared!

After relating the New Testament account of Christ calming the storm, Elder Robert D. Hales recently taught,

"We are living through turbulent times. A great storm of evil has come upon the earth. The winds of wickedness howl about us; the waves of war beat against our ship. . . . It is true that ominous clouds gather around us, but just as the Savior's words brought peace to the apostles in the boat, they bring peace to us today: 'And when ye shall hear of wars and rumours of wars, be ye not troubled: for such things must needs be; but the end shall not be yet' [Mark 13:7]. 'If ye are prepared ye shall not fear' [D&C 38:30]" (*Ensign,* May 2003, p. 15).

How are we to prepare against the storms in our own world—in our own lives? Simply put, by coming to Christ! In referring back to that first encounter with a marriage in crisis, for instance, two things happened that still thrill me. Before describing them, however, I should state that the couple who came to see me were wonderful people, temple-worthy and totally involved in the ward, who were being driven into misery and marital discord by a host of "little" personal issues. I should also state that I had never been trained as a therapist or marriage counselor and so had absolutely no idea what to say or how to help them.

As we visited, therefore, with them revealing the difficulties that could easily have led to the termination of their eternal marriage, and with me all the while praying fervently for divine assistance, the thought came into my mind that they needed to get back to the temple—together, and regularly! As I continued to pray, the thought grew in intensity until I heard myself promising them that if they would start attending the temple together each week, ending each visit by holding hands and praying fervently for each other in silent prayer, they would be given power to restore love and harmony to their marriage.

They questioned how weekly temple attendance could possibly help end their apparently deep-seated conflict. I responded by quoting from memory (which surprised me) the scripture wherein the Lord promises power over our enemy through the temple endowment (D&C 38:31–32), and following their departure I found myself doubting and second-guessing the counsel I had given them. Even as I was questioning, however, I happened to glance at my scriptures, which had been lying open but unnoticed during the interview. Pulling them across the desk, I read the following from the open page, which I know with certainty was a message the Lord wanted me to receive:

"I, the Lord, am merciful and gracious unto those who fear me, and delight to honor those who serve me in righteousness and in truth unto the end. Great shall be their reward and eternal shall be their glory. And to them will I reveal all mysteries, yea, all the hidden mysteries of my kingdom from days of old, and for ages to come, will I make known unto them the good pleasure of my will concerning all things pertaining to my kingdom. Yea, even the wonders of eternity shall they know, and things to come will I show them, even the things of many generations. And their wisdom shall be great, and their understanding reach to heaven; and before them the wisdom of the wise shall perish, and the understanding of the prudent shall come to naught. For by my Spirit will I enlighten them, and by my power will I make known unto them the secrets of my will—yea, even those things which eye has not seen, nor ear heard, nor yet entered into the heart of man" (D&C 76:5–10).

Stunned, I read these verses again and again. This was how this couple—and the rest of us, the Spirit was whispering to me—were to obtain power through diligent temple attendance—one form of serving the Lord in righteousness and truth! By so serving, we would qualify to receive wisdom from the Lord, even His hidden secrets, which would include the secret of how to successfully navigate the rocky shoals of marriage and so turn our unions into eternal, joyful oneness with each other.

Of course there was more to these verses—much more. But at the moment, I was so focused on the issue of marriage that it was all that came to mind. In the weeks and months that followed, I gave the same counsel to other ward members, and those who diligently did as their bishop had instructed experienced marked improvement in their relationships and an increase of love and patience for each other.

SEEKING THE FACE OF THE LORD

Meanwhile, the verses from section 76 continued to play in my mind until one day the realization came that the Lord was promising us a specific sort of spiritual growth—helping us through temple and other forms of service, along with diligent efforts at righteous obedience to His commandments—to learn how to become as He is. One day, during our scripture study, my wife, Kathy, read the following: "Verily, thus saith the Lord: It shall come to pass that every soul who forsaketh his sins and cometh unto me, and calleth on my name, and obeyeth my voice, and keepeth my commandments, shall see my face and know that I am" (D&C 93:1).

Not only did this verse seem to affirm what I had been thinking, but it also added a final component I had not been considering: the promise, in addition to hidden wisdom and knowledge, of beholding the face of the Lord Jesus Christ! Galvanized, I began seeking other references and quickly discovered the following, which is obviously given by the Lord as a commandment: "And *seek the face of the Lord always*, that in patience ye may possess your souls, and ye shall have eternal life" (D&C 101:38; italics mine).

I could now see that, besides being commanded to pray diligently for charity, or the pure love of Christ, as we strive to come unto Him, we are also commanded to spend our lives seeking His face—seeking *Him!* "Therefore," the Lord continues in another reference, "sanctify yourselves that your minds become single to God, and the days will come that you shall see him; *for he will unveil his face unto you,* and it shall be in his own time, and in his own way, and according to his own will" (D&C 88:68; italics mine).

This was not new doctrine for the restored Church. In 2 Chronicles 7:14 we read, "If my people, which are called by my name, shall humble themselves, and pray, and seek my face, and turn from their wicked ways; then will I hear from heaven, and will forgive their sin, and will heal their land." And the Psalmist sang, "When thou saidst, *Seek ye my face; my heart said unto thee, Thy face, Lord, will I seek*" (Psalm 27:8; italics mine).

COMMANDMENT TO BE TAKEN LITERALLY

Elder Bruce R. McConkie writes, "There is a true doctrine on these points, a doctrine unknown to many and unbelieved by more, a doctrine that is spelled out as specifically and extensively in the revealed word as are any of the other great revealed truths. There is no need for uncertainty or misunderstanding; and surely, if the Lord reveals a doctrine, we should seek to learn its principles and strive to apply them in our lives. *This doctrine is that mortal man, while in the flesh, has it in his power to see the Lord, to stand in his presence, to feel the nail marks in his hands and feet,* and to receive from him such blessings as are reserved for those only who keep all his commandments and who are qualified for that eternal life which includes being in his presence forever" (*A New Witness for the Articles of Faith,* 492; italics mine).

LESSONS FROM THE EARLY CHURCH

Though I had never thought of it in exactly these terms, I was certainly aware that at the tender age of fourteen, Joseph Smith was privileged to behold the face of the Lord. Several years before my call, I had been commissioned to write for a film being made about Joseph Smith in Kirtland. Following my experiences as a bishop, I began pondering anew that history, and very quickly a clearer vision of what Joseph had been endeavoring to accomplish with his people formed in my mind.

Knowing from his own experience that the beholding of Christ's face was possible, it is evident that Joseph not only took the commandment to seek such a vision as literally as does Elder McConkie, but that he also applied it to all members of the Church. Several years into his ministry, in fact, he formalized the doctrine by declaring, "God hath not revealed anything to Joseph, but what he will make known unto others, and even the least Saint may know all things as fast as he is able to bear them. For the day must come when no man need say to his neighbor, *Know ye the Lord; for all shall know*

Him who remain, from the least to the greatest" (*History of the Church,* 3:380; italics mine).

Much earlier, however, in fact in the very beginning of the Church's history, Joseph was already contemplating this joyous possibility. In December 1830 he wrote in his journal, "To the joy of the little flock, which in all, from Colesville to Canandaigua, New York, numbered about seventy members, did the Lord reveal the following doings of olden times, from the prophecy of Enoch" (*History of the Church,* 1:132–33). Then followed part of the segment of the book of Enoch that is presently in chapters 6 and 7 of the book of Moses in the Pearl of Great Price. It may have been this glorious revelation that motivated Joseph to action.

THE BOOK OF ENOCH

Two aspects of Enoch's prophecy that must have seemed germane to the young prophet had now become meaningful to me. The first was that Enoch declared that he had beheld the face of the Lord. Enoch wrote, "And it came to pass that I turned and went up on the mount; and as I stood upon the mount, I beheld the heavens open, and I was clothed upon with glory; and I saw the Lord; and he stood before my face, and he talked with me, even as a man talketh one with another, face to face" (Moses 7:3–4).

At least as significant was the following: "And it came to pass that Enoch continued to call upon all the people . . . to repent; and so great was the faith of Enoch that he led the people of God, and their enemies came to battle against them; and *he spake the word of the Lord,* and the earth trembled, and the mountains fled, even according to his command; and the rivers of water were turned out of their course

. . . so great was the power of the language which God had given him. . . .

"And the Lord called [Enoch's] people Zion, because they were of one heart and one mind, and dwelt in righteousness; and there was no poor among them. . . . And Enoch and *all his people walked with God,* and he dwelt in the midst of Zion; and it came to pass that Zion was not, for God received it up into his own bosom; and from thence went forth the saying, ZION IS FLED" (Moses 7:12–13, 18, 69; italics mine).

GOD'S LANGUAGE OF POWER

Besides the obvious beholding of the Lord's face by all of Enoch's people, the language God had given Enoch, as well as the power by which such marvelous things as their being brought into the presence of God were accomplished, was the language of the Holy Priesthood. However, though Joseph now held the Melchizedek Priesthood, he did not yet know the language of power to which these scriptures referred. Soon, however, it became obvious to him that, in addition to being ordained to the priesthood, a man needed additional powers, or keys, as the Lord was soon to call them, to accomplish such divine tasks. Granted to man through sacred ordinances, it was such keys of access to God that comprised Enoch's language of power, enabling that ancient prophet to ultimately bring all his people into the Lord's presence.

A decade later Joseph spoke of this when he said, referring to Noah and other early prophets, "Thus we behold the keys of this priesthood consisted in [Noah] obtaining the voice of Jehovah, and he talked [so that He could talk] with him in a familiar and friendly manner, that he continued to him the Keys, the Covenants, the power and glory with which he blessed Adam at the beginning . . . for all the ordinances and duties that ever have been required by the priesthood under the direction and commandments of the Almighty in any of the dispensations, shall all be had in the last dispensation" (*The Words of Joseph Smith,* p. 42; hereafter referred to as *Words*).

Joseph also wrote, "Now the great and grand secret of the whole matter, and the *summum bonum* of the whole subject that is lying before us, consists in obtaining the powers of the Holy Priesthood. For him to whom these keys are given there is no difficulty in obtaining [revelation]" (D&C 128:11).

Of course, this clear understanding of priesthood power or keys to the access of God was Joseph's in the 1840s, not 1830, because the Lord had not yet made it all known to him or given him the keys he would later speak of. Joseph's task (and now mine), therefore, was to continue seeking, for clearly there was more information he needed to obtain if he was to bring his people into the presence of the Lord.

POWER FROM ON HIGH

On January 2, 1831, while still residing in New York, Joseph received from the Lord a tantalizing gem of information, given in part by way of reminder: "Wherefore, for this cause I gave unto you the commandment that ye should go to the Ohio; and there I will give unto you my law; and *there you shall be endowed with power from on high*" (D&C 38:32; italics mine. See also D&C 38:38). Although Joseph wouldn't understand this until December 27, 1832 (D&C 88:119–21), we now know that he was actually being told to go to the Ohio in order to build a temple, for it was in temples, he would learn, that ordinances of heavenly power were to be administered.

These instructions to build a temple would be followed in June 1833 with a warning: "I gave unto you a commandment that you should build a house, in the which house I design to endow those whom I have chosen with power from on high; for this is the promise of the Father unto you. . . . If you keep my commandments you shall have power to build it. If you keep not my commandments, *the love of the Father* shall not continue with you, therefore you shall walk in darkness" (D&C 95:8–9, 11–12; italics mine).

Without God's pure and perfect charity, or love, it seems, which loss would come from not keeping the commandments, particularly concerning beginning the temple's construction, Joseph and the Saints would not have the power to continue their mission.

Even without this knowledge of temples, Joseph knew of his own experiences with beholding the faces of God and Christ, he knew of the ministering of angels that he had enjoyed, and he longed for others to experience these things as he had. Joseph had indeed learned that when all conditions are met, mortals can truly stand in the presence of the eternal Gods, behold and converse with them face to face as one man speaks with another, and "not be upbraided" (James 1:5).

Nor was Joseph alone in his experiences. Not only did he have numerous scriptural examples from both the Bible and the Book of Mormon of men and women who had obtained the pure love of Christ and thereafter beheld angels and Christ in ancient times, but already in his own day a select few had enjoyed such privileges. For instance, the Three

Witnesses had beheld the angel Moroni as well as the plates from which the Book of Mormon had been translated, and Oliver Cowdery had also seen John the Baptist and Peter, James, and John.

Additionally, during a conference in June 1830, only two months after the Church was organized, Newel Knight had seen the "heaven opened, and beheld the Lord Jesus Christ, seated at the right hand of the majesty on high." Joseph, who recorded this supernal event in his journal, stated that Newel's experience inspired his heart "with joy unspeakable" and was calculated to "fill us with awe and reverence for that Almighty Being, by whose grace we had been called to be instrumental in bringing about, for the children of men, the enjoyment of such glorious blessings as were now at this time poured out upon us" (*History of the Church,* 1:85).

Newel Knight's experience in beholding the face of Jesus, while the first that we know of (other than Joseph's first vision) in this dispensation, was certainly not supposed to be the last. By the end of January, Joseph and Emma were on their way to the wilderness outpost of Kirtland, where they had been told an endowment of power would be given them, and the excited families of the Saints followed as quickly as they were able.

THE PROPHET-TEACHER

As the Saints gathered to Kirtland, Joseph labored diligently to teach them as he was being taught by the Lord. And he was being taught at an amazing rate; nearly one third of the revelations in the Doctrine and Covenants were received between August 1831 and April 1834.

As rapidly as he could, Joseph disseminated this information, though he was quickly learning that the task was formidable. Still, meetings were held several times a week, and the doctrines of the kingdom were expounded to eager people by himself and numerous others. Later Joseph said, "It is my meditation all the day and more than my meat and drink to know how I shall make the Saints of God to comprehend the visions that roll like an overflowing scourge, before my mind. O how I would delight to bring before you things which you never thought of, but poverty and the cares of the world prevent. . . . I have labored hard and sought every way to try to prepare this people to comprehend the things that God is unfolding to me" (*Words*, pp. 196, 198; spelling standardized).

The thought that some of his beloved Saints might fail must have been troubling to Joseph, for he warned, "The mystery, power and glory of the priesthood is so great and glorious that the angels desired to understand it and cannot: why, because of the tradition of them and their fathers in setting up stakes and not coming up to the mark in their probationary state" (*Words*, p. 247).

Joseph wasn't alone in wondering why so many people had a difficult time listening and accepting what he knew was divine truth. Dr. Isaac Watts, a new convert and citizen of Kirtland, wrote a hymn concerning Joseph Smith, part of which states:

Why was I made to hear thy voice,
and enter while there's room,
while thousands make a wretched choice,
and rather starve than come?

(See Godfrey, Godfrey, and Derr, *Women's Voices*, pp. 46–57).

OTHERS SEE CHRIST

Joseph's counsel seemed to be working, for gradually others reached the spiritual level where they could see and know as he had seen and known. On February 16, 1832, at the Johnson farm in Hiram, Ohio, where Joseph and others were working on the New Translation of the Bible, he and Sidney Rigdon beheld in vision not only the Father and the Son but all the holy angels and they who are sanctified before God's throne (see D&C 76:19–24). Three months later, during conference in June 1832, Lyman Wight, Harvey Whitlock, and the Prophet Joseph saw both the Father and the Son in heavenly vision (see "Levi Hancock Journal," Church Archives, pp. 91–92).

According to D&C 121:33, this was only the beginning of the visions and revelations that the Lord had promised would be poured out upon the heads of the Latter-day Saints.

FURTHER INSTRUCTIONS FROM ON HIGH

In September 1832, in response to a prayer of inquiry from Joseph and six other elders, the Lord declared, "This greater priesthood administereth the gospel and holdeth the key of the mysteries of the kingdom, even *the key of the knowledge of God. Therefore, in the ordinances thereof [of the priesthood], the power of godliness is manifest.* And without the ordinances thereof, and the authority of the priesthood, the power of godliness is not manifest unto men in the flesh; *for without this no man can see the face of God, even the Father, and live. Now this Moses plainly taught to the children of Israel in the wilderness, and sought diligently to sanctify his people that they might behold the face of God; but they hardened their hearts and could not endure his presence;* therefore, the Lord in his wrath, for his anger was kindled against them, swore that they should not enter into his rest while in the wilderness, which rest is the fulness of his glory. Therefore, he took Moses out of their midst, and the Holy Priesthood also" (D&C 84:19–25; italics mine).

Not only was I able, with this information, to see more clearly what the Spirit had guided me to tell my struggling ward members, but this understanding must also have been both exhilarating and sobering for Joseph Smith. From his study of the Old Testament, he knew that before the wrath of the Lord had been kindled against the Israelites, Moses had been able to prepare Aaron, Nadab, Abihu, and seventy of the elders of Israel so that they were able to behold the face of Jehovah (see Exodus 24). Joseph understood that Moses had done so through the use of certain priesthood keys, or powers, that were received by ordinance, which had been specifically designed by God to give the righteous access to Him—even "*the key of the knowledge of God.*"

At least as significantly, Joseph also understood that bringing the Latter-day Saints into the presence of God, so that they could feel His love and behold His face—whether in this life or the next—was far more than just a nice thing to do. Rather, it was essential for a person's exaltation. Furthermore, this crowning blessing was to be self-initiated rather than being simply waited for. However, if the people hardened their hearts against Joseph and the information from the Lord that he would yet reveal, then, as He did with the children of Israel, the Lord in his wrath would almost certainly take away these glorious privileges.

Of course, Joseph did not want that. No matter what it

took, he wanted the Latter-day Saints to be an Enoch people rather than a Moses people. And so he continued to seek further information about how this could be brought to pass.

THE SCHOOL OF THE PROPHETS

Just after Christmas in 1832, Joseph received the revelation wherein he was commanded not only to build a temple but also to organize the School of the Prophets (see D&C 88:118–41). According to the revelation, the brethren needed to attend such a school in order to prepare to better serve one another through increased knowledge and understanding.

The school began meeting in Kirtland at the end of January 1833 in a room above the Gilbert and Whitney store. These meetings, attended by twenty-one individuals who were there by special invitation or calling, provided the setting for many remarkable spiritual experiences and in-depth discussions of the principles of the gospel. To these brethren Joseph stated, "To receive revelation and the blessings of heaven it [is] necessary to have our minds on God and exercise faith and become of one heart and mind" (Kirtland Council Minute Book, Church Archives, pp. 3–4).

The school met regularly and received instructions. Zebedee Coltrin, one of those who had been called to attend, said that every time they were called together to attend to any business, they gathered in the morning about sunrise, fasting, and partook of the sacrament, and before going to school they washed themselves and put on clean linen. Then they gathered to prayer. (Minutes, Salt Lake City School of the Prophets, October 3, 1883, p. 56).

ENJOYING THE VISIONS OF HEAVEN

Brother Coltrin further stated, "About the time the school was first organized some wished to see an angel, and a number joined in the circle, and prayed. When the vision came, two of the brethren shrank and called for the vision to close or they would perish, these were Brothers Hancock and Humphries. When the Prophet came in they told him what they had done and he said the angel was no further off than the roof of the house, and a moment more he would have been in [our] midst" (Minutes, Salt Lake City School of the Prophets, October 3, 1883, p. 56).

Another of the more unusual experiences pertaining to obtaining the visions of heaven happened to Joseph Smith, Oliver Cowdery, and Zebedee Coltrin. Apparently Brother Coltrin was invited to accompany Joseph, Oliver, and Sidney Rigdon to a conference in New Portage. Zebedee recorded, "Next morning at New Portage [I] noticed that Joseph seemed to have a far off look in his eyes, or was looking at a distance, and presently he, Joseph, stepped between Brothers Cowdery and [myself] and taking [us] by the arm, said, 'Lets take a walk.' [We] went to a place where there was some beautiful grass, and grapevines and swampbeech interlaced. President Joseph Smith then said, 'Let us pray.' [We] all three prayed in turn—Joseph, Oliver and [myself]. Bro. Joseph then said, 'Now, Brethren, we will see some visions.'

"Joseph lay down on the ground on his back and stretched out his arms. . . . He told me to lie by his side with my head resting upon his arm, and Oliver in like manner upon the other side. We did so, all three looking heavenwards. As I looked I saw the blue sky open . . . and [we] saw a golden throne, on a circular foundation, something like a lighthouse, and on the throne were two aged personages . . . [whose] faces shown with youth . . . having white hair and clothed in white garments. They were the two most beautiful and perfect specimens of mankind [I] ever saw. . . . Joseph asked us if we knew who they were. We answered 'No.' Joseph said, 'That is father Adam and mother Eve.' . . . Adam was a large broadshouldered man, and Eve, as a woman, was as large in proportion" (Minutes, Salt Lake School of the Prophets, 1883, pp. 68–70; Papers of Zebedee Coltrin, Church Archives; spelling and punctuation standardized. The preceding account is a combination of information from both sources).

SEEING THE FACE OF THE LORD

On March 18, 1833, Joseph promised the members of the school that those among them who were pure in heart should see another heavenly vision. After giving all present careful instructions concerning preparing their minds as well as exactly how to kneel and pray, they all proceeded until the visions were obtained (*History of the Church,* 1:334–35).

John Murdock, one of those present, related, "About midday the visions of my mind were opened and the eyes of my understanding were enlightened, and I saw the form of a man, most lovely. The visage of his face was round and fair as the sun, His hair a bright silver gray, curled in most majestic form; his eyes a keen, penetrating blue, and the skin of his neck a most beautiful white. He was covered from the neck to the feet with a loose garment of pure white—whiter than any garment I had ever before seen. His countenance was most penetrating, and yet most lovely. When the vision was closed up, it left to my mind the impression of love, for months, and I never before felt it to that degree" ("Journal," *Utah Genealogical and Historical Magazine,* April 1937, p. 61).

Zebedee Coltrin added, "I saw a personage walk through the room, from East to West, and Joseph asked if we saw him. I saw him and suppose the others did, and Joseph answered 'That is Jesus the Son of God our elder brother.' Afterward Joseph told us to resume our former positions in prayer, which we did. Another person came through. The Prophet Joseph said this was the Father of our Lord Jesus Christ. I saw him. . . . I experienced a sensation like a consuming fire of great brightness, for He was surrounded as with a flame of fire, which was so brilliant that I could not discover anything else but His person. I saw his hands, his legs, his feet, his eyes, nose, mouth, head and body in the shape and form of a perfect man. His appearance was so grand and overwhelming that it seemed I should melt down in His presence, and the sensation was so powerful that it thrilled through my whole system and I felt it in the marrow of my bones. The Prophet Joseph said: Brethren, now you are prepared to be the apostles of Jesus Christ, for you have seen both the Father and the Son, and know that they exist and that They are two separate personages" (Minutes, Salt Lake City School of the Prophets, October 3, 1883, pp. 58–60).

WONDROUS HEAVENLY MANIFESTATIONS

Once the members of the School of the Prophets had obtained charity, or the pure love of Christ, through beholding the face of the Lord, Joseph began to focus on bringing the same blessings to all the members of the Church. To do that, of course, he needed to assist them in obtaining the endowment of power the Lord had promised. This endowment was to be a gift of knowledge derived from revelation, a gift of power emitting from God, a gift of the very language of God that Enoch had understood and used. It consisted of instructions and ordinances relating to the laws of God, including the principles of sacrifice and obedience, which were designed to give the Saints an understanding of how to ask for and receive blessings (D&C 124:95, 97).

These ordinances and instructions were first given to Adam, and they were to remain the same through all generations of time. According to the Prophet Joseph, "Commencing with Adam, who was the first man, who is spoken of in Daniel as being the 'Ancient of Days,' or in other words, the first and oldest of all, the great, grand progenitor of whom it is said in another place he is Michael, because he was the first and father of all, not only by progeny, but the first to hold the spiritual blessings, *to whom was made known the plan of ordinances for the salvation of his posterity unto the end*. . . .

"Now the purpose in [God] in the winding up scene of the last dispensation is that all things pertaining to that dispensation should be conducted precisely in accordance with the preceding dispensations. [Therefore,] God purposed in Himself that there should not be an eternal fullness until every dispensation should be fulfilled and gathered together in one, and that all things whatsoever, that should be gathered together in one in those dispensations unto the same fullness and eternal glory, should be in Christ Jesus; therefore *He set the ordinances to be the same forever and ever,* and set Adam to watch over them, to reveal them from heaven to man, or to send angels to reveal them" (*History of the Church,* 4:208; italics mine).

Joseph further declared that while many would not initially comprehend this endowment, or gift, of ordinances and instructions, bearers of the priesthood should prepare for it by purifying themselves, by cleansing their hearts and their physical bodies so that they might be prepared and able to overcome all things (see *History of the Church,* 2:309). This wondrous endowment of power was reserved for presentation to the people of God within a temple. As Joseph Smith said, "The keys are certain signs and words . . . which cannot be revealed . . . until the Temple is completed—The rich can only get them in the Temple—the poor may get them on the Mountaintop as did Moses" (*Words,* pp. 119–20).

Apparently, the Lord considered the Latter-day Saints in Kirtland sufficiently rich, for He had commanded in December 1832 that they build a temple. Five months later, on June 1, 1833, the Lord chastised the Church members for their delay in building the temple, and He admonished them to move forward quickly (see D&C 95). Repenting, the Saints began construction on June 6, 1833, following a plan that had been revealed in open vision to Joseph Smith and his two counselors, Sidney Rigdon and Frederick G. Williams (Carter, *Our Pioneer Heritage,* 10:198).

BUILDING THE TEMPLE

For three years, while they endured abject poverty, the several hundred Saints scattered throughout the United States and Canada pooled their resources and labored to construct the temple. Frequently, Joseph Smith served as foreman in the stone quarry. The brethren who were not on missions labored every spare minute; the sisters under Emma Smith's direction made stockings, pantaloons, and jackets for the workmen; and Saints living away from Kirtland sent money. Ultimately, between forty and sixty thousand dollars cash was spent on the building. It was a severe sacrifice for them all. Yet Joseph said, "A religion that does not require the sacrifice of all things never has power sufficient to produce the faith necessary unto life and salvation" (*Lectures on Faith,* p. 58). Developing within his people a "faith necessary unto life and salvation" had become Joseph's greatest goal.

Of course, this cost him, too. As the time for bringing all the Saints into the presence of the Lord approached, Joseph said, "I am weary with continual anxiety and labor, from setting the quorums in order, and striving to purify them for the solemn assembly, according to the commandment of the Lord" (*History of the Church,* 2:388).

POWER TO OPEN THE HEAVENS

Though the temple had not yet been completed and dedicated, work had progressed sufficiently by January 1836 that Joseph decided it was time to begin presenting sacred ordinances to the people, thus empowering them to feel of Christ's love and enjoy the supernal blessings thereof. As he had no doubt expected, from January 21 to May 1, 1836, as meetings in the temple were regularly held, "probably more Latter-day Saints beheld visions and witnessed other unusual spiritual manifestations than during any other era in the history of the Church" (*The Heavens Resound,* p. 285).

The first meeting was particularly significant. Oliver Cowdery said of it, "On the night of January 21, 1836, Joseph began to present the Lord's endowment to the Saints. At that time he introduced a number of ordinances designed to purify those who received them. It was during many of the meetings when these ordinances were introduced, that the heavens were opened for so many of the participants" ("1836 Diary," *BYU Studies,* 12:419).

At that meeting the First Presidency and about thirty-six others gathered together about candlelight. After spiritual anointings and blessings, the heavens were opened to Joseph and others, and Joseph beheld the celestial kingdom of God and the glory thereof. He saw the transcendent beauty of the gate through which the heirs of that kingdom will enter, which was like unto circling flames of fire. He also saw the blazing throne of God, whereon was seated the Father and the Son. He saw the beautiful streets of that kingdom, which had the appearance of being paved with gold. Many of the brethren who received the ordinances that evening also saw glorious visions. Angels ministered unto them, the power of the Highest rested upon them, the house was filled with the glory of God, and they all shouted Hosanna to God and the Lamb. Some then saw the face of the Savior, and others were ministered unto by holy angels, and the spirit of prophecy and revelation was poured out in mighty power; and loud hosannas, and glory to God in the highest saluted the heavens, for they all communed with the heavenly host (see *History of the Church,* 2:379–82).

On the day following, the apostles and presidents of the Seventy received their anointings, after which many saw heavenly beings, members were blessed with the gift of tongues, and, as Joseph said, "Angels mingled their voices with ours" (*History of the Church,* 2:383).

The spiritual manifestations continued. On Thursday, January 28, during a meeting in which the Prophet attended to the sealing of what had been administered, Zebedee

Coltrin again saw the Savior, this time nailed to the wood of the cross, "high and lifted up" (Minutes, Salt Lake School of the Prophets, October 11, 1883, pp. 68–70; Papers of Zebedee Coltrin, Church Archives). Others beheld heavenly beings, and Joseph saw a glorious vision (*History of the Church*, 2:387).

Harrison Burgess wrote of this same meeting, "I will here relate a vision which was shown to me. It was near the close of the endowments [not the full endowment as it was later administered in Nauvoo]—I was in a meeting for instruction in the upper part of the Temple, with about a hundred of the High Priests, Seventies and Elders. The Saints felt to shout 'Hosannah' and the Spirit of God rested upon me in mighty Power and I beheld the room lighted up with a peculiar light such as I had never seen before. Soft and clear and the room looked to me as though it had neither roof nor floor . . . and I beheld Joseph and Hyrum Smith and Roger Orton enveloped in the light. Joseph exclaimed aloud, 'I behold the Savior the Son of God.' Hyrum, 'I behold the angels of Heaven.' Br. Orton exclaimed, 'I behold the chariots of Israel.' All who were in the room felt the power of God to that degree that many Prophesied and the power of God was made manifest, the remembrance of which I shall never forget while I live upon the earth" (Harrison Burgess File, meeting of January 28, 1836, Church Archives).

On Saturday, February 6, the Prophet called all who had been anointed together to receive the seal of all their blessings. Many who were obedient to his instructions received unusual blessings. Some saw visions. Others were filled with the Spirit and spoke in tongues, and some prophesied. Joseph declared it to be a time of rejoicing long to be remembered (*History of the Church*, 2:391–92).

BRIGHAM YOUNG SEES ANGELS

One other incident is worthy of note. In a journal entry dated November 8, 1857, Wilford Woodruff wrote, "President Young related the circumstances of their seeing a circle of about 40 persons dressed in white robes . . . in the upper story of the Temple in Kirtland during the spring of [1836] after the Endowments. There was no person in that room at the time that was mortal, yet the room was filled with light and many personages did appear clothed in white and frequently went to the windows and looked out so that the Brethren in the street could see them plainly. Brother Young and Truman Angell stood together in the street and looked at them a long time. W. W. Phelps says he saw them for three hours. They were visible by all the Brethren present. Brother Angell said they must have stood some two feet from the floor. If they were only the size of common men they could not have been seen from the place where they stood except it should be the head, and those personages appeared nearly down to the waist as they looked out of the window with a front view" (Wilford Woodruff Journals, 1857–1861, 5:53; spelling and punctuation standardized).

THE TEMPLE DEDICATION

By the time the temple was ready for dedication on Sunday, March 27, 1836, literally hundreds of people had experienced divine manifestations. Erastus Snow wrote, "The number of all that were anointed and blessed in the house of the Lord in Kirtland was about 360. When all were anointed, the blessings were sealed by the presidency. Then we all, like as did Israel when they surrounded Jericho, with united voice gave a loud shout of 'Hosanna, Hosanna, Hosanna, to God and the Lamb; Amen, Amen and Amen.' When this was done, the Holy Ghost shed forth upon us; some spoke in tongues, some interpreted, others prophesied, some received visions of the judgements that were about to be poured out in this generation, others saw Zion in her glory, and the angels came and worshiped with us and some saw them, yea, even 12 legions of them, the chariots of Israel and the horsemen thereof" (Olsen, *Biography of Erastus Snow*, p. 19).

Following Joseph Smith's dedicatory prayer on March 27, which prayer had been given him by revelation (D&C 110), the sacred Hosanna Shout rang forth again on this earth. Again, heavenly messengers made themselves manifest to many in attendance.

According to George A. Smith, "On the first day of the dedication, President Frederick G. Williams . . . who occupied the upper pulpit, bore testimony that the Savior, dressed in his vesture without seam, came into the stand and accepted of the dedication of the house, that he saw him, and gave a description of his clothing and all things pertaining to it" (*Journal of Discourses*, 11:10).

That evening in a special meeting of 416 (or 316) priesthood holders, many of those present saw the glory of God come down upon the temple like a cloud of fire and heard the sound of a rushing wind and beheld cloven tongues of fire above the heads of many of the brethren (Oliver Cowdery, "1836 Diary," *BYU Studies*, 12:426).

George A. Smith said, "Many individuals bore testimony

that they saw angels, and David Whitmer bore testimony that he saw three angels passing up the south aisle, and there came a shock on the house like the sound of a mighty rushing wind, and almost every man in the house arose, and hundreds of them were speaking in tongues, prophesying or declaring visions, almost with one voice" (*Journal of Discourses*, 11:10).

Zebedee Coltrin added, "In the Kirtland Temple I have seen the power of God as it was in the day of Pentecost and cloven tongues of fire have rested on the brethren and they have spoken with other tongues as the Spirit gave them utterance. . . . The angels of God rested upon the temple and we heard their voices singing heavenly music. At another time while consecrating a bottle of oil, we saw visibly the finger of God enter the mouth of the bottle" (Papers of Zebedee Coltrin, Church Archives).

ANGELS ON THE TEMPLE

On Thursday following the dedication, while many of the Saints had gathered for a day of fasting, Prescindia Huntington reported that a small girl came running through her door exclaiming that the meeting was being held on top of the meetinghouse. At first Prescindia dismissed her, but the child was so insistent that at length she stepped forth to look. She says, "There I saw on the temple angels clothed in white covering the roof from end to end. They seemed to be walking to and fro; they appeared and disappeared . . . [and had done so for the second or third time] before I realized that they were not mortal men. Each time in a moment they vanished, and their reappearance was the same. This was in broad daylight, in the afternoon. A number of the children in Kirtland saw the same" (Tullidge, *Women of Mormondom,* pp. 207–8).

THE VISITS OF CHRIST, MOSES, ELIAS, AND ELIJAH

The most transcendent spiritual manifestation of all occurred a week after the dedication, for that is when many of Enoch's keys of power were again conferred upon mortals. "Following the afternoon worship service, Joseph Smith and Oliver Cowdery retired to the Melchizedek Priesthood pulpits in the west end of the lower room of the temple. The canvas partition, called a *veil,* was lowered so that they could pray in private. As they prayed, 'The veil was taken from our minds, and the eyes of our understanding were opened' (D&C 110:1). They saw a series of remarkable visions. The Lord Jesus Christ appeared, accepted the temple, and promised to manifest himself therein 'if my people will keep my commandments, and do not pollute this holy house' (D&C 110:8; see also verses 2–9).

"Moses next appeared and restored 'the keys of the gathering of Israel from the four parts of the earth, and the leading of the ten tribes from the land of the north' (v. 11). Elias then conferred 'the dispensation of the gospel of Abraham' (v. 12). Finally, in fulfillment of Malachi's prophecy (see Malachi 4:5–6) and Moroni's promise (see D&C 2) to 'turn the hearts of the fathers to the children, and the children to the fathers' (D&C 110:15), Elijah appeared to the Prophet and Oliver testifying that 'the keys of this dispensation are committed into your hands' in preparation for 'the great and dreadful day of the Lord' (v. 16). Through the sealing keys that were restored by Elijah, Latter-day Saints were prepared to perform saving priesthood ordinances in behalf of their kindred dead as well as for the living. However, these sacred ordinances . . . were not introduced to the members of the Church until the Nauvoo era.

"This great day of visions and revelation occurred on Easter Sunday, 3 April 1836. What better day in the dispensation of the fulness of times to reconfirm the reality of the Resurrection. That weekend was also the Jewish Passover. For centuries Jewish families have left an empty chair at their Passover feasts, anticipating Elijah's return. Elijah has returned—not to a Passover feast, but to the Lord's temple in Kirtland" (*Church History in the Fulness of Times,* p. 145).

NOT THE COMPLETE ENDOWMENT

Concerning the ordinances as performed in the Kirtland Temple, LDS scholars Lyndon W. Cook and Andrew F. Ehat write, "In the Kirtland Temple in 1836, after attending to the ordinance of the washing of feet, Joseph Smith said he had 'completed the organization of the church, and . . . [had given] all the necessary ceremonies' (*History of the Church,* 2:432 or *Teachings,* 110). However, four days later, he was given greater keys of authority and knowledge which he did not confer on the leaders of the Church until the Nauvoo period (see D&C 110). So while the Prophet's statement made in Kirtland refers to the finalization of all offices within the Church priesthood structure and sets the basic structure of temple ordinances, the Prophet's statement to the Relief Society . . . ('He spoke of delivering the keys of the Priesthood to the Church and said that the faithful members of the Relief Society should receive them in connection with their husbands, that the Saints whose integrity has been tried and proved faithful, might know how to ask the Lord and receive an answer' [*History of the Church,* 4:604]) portends that the same priesthood organization as finalized in Kirtland would be endowed with the greater keys and knowledge as revealed later to Joseph Smith by [Moses,] Elias and Elijah. This greater knowledge eventually effected a considerable enlarging of the scope and meaning of temple ordinances, transforming the Kirtland Temple ordinances to their Nauvoo counterparts *without* changing the order of these ordinances (see *History of the Church* 2:309 or *Teachings,* 91)" (*Words,* p. 140, footnotes).

As the spiritual manifestations experienced by several hundred Saints in Kirtland are contemplated, it is an easy matter to understand why historians refer to this period as a latter-day Pentecost, a time of rich outpourings of the Spirit as the members gave their all for their beloved Savior. For this a great many of them were rewarded with the supernal blessing of being brought into His presence, some even seeing His face.

Chapter Three

JOSEPH'S TRIUMPH AND DEFEAT

With the dedication of the Kirtland Temple, Joseph's lofty desire of establishing a Zion for this priesthood generation had begun its fulfillment. Truly had the Lord blessed His people as they struggled and sacrificed to expand their city, construct a temple to the Most High God, and become a holy people like the ancient Saints of Enoch. Like Enoch's people, these Latter-day Saints were led by a mighty prophet to whom the Lord had not only revealed His will but also given keys of priesthood powerful enough to open the heavens. These keys Joseph freely shared with the Lord's people through what the Lord termed the "endowment," thus giving all so endowed the power to bring themselves back into God's presence. And like Enoch's people, a remarkable number in this generation did so, seeing and hearing glorious heavenly manifestations during that season of rejoicing.

Surely they must have felt as did the Nephites following the appearance of the Lord: "They were in one, the children of Christ, and heirs to the kingdom of God. And how blessed were they! For the Lord did bless them in all their doings" (4 Nephi 1:17–18).

A TRAGIC APOSTASY

Sadly, those days appear to have been as troubled for the people, both individually and collectively, as they are today. Immediately after the dedication of the temple came a period of great apostasy. Most of the Saints struggled, and many of them succumbed to the enticements of Satan and the cares of the world. In August 1836 there was an armed attempt by some of the apostates to take over the temple. Though this was foiled after a few terrifying moments and the men were ultimately disfellowshipped, it was only the beginning. Warren Parish, apostle John F. Boynton, and others organized a group dedicated to overthrowing Joseph Smith, whom they were convinced had become a fallen prophet. As a result of this apostasy, fifty leading brethren were excommunicated, and they joined in the general persecution of the Saints being perpetrated in the area.

Hepzibah Richards, sister of Willard Richards, wrote, "For the last three months we as a people have been tempest tossed, and at times the waves have well nigh overwhelmed us. . . . A dreadful spirit reigns in the breasts of those who are opposed to this Church. They are above law and beneath whatever is laudable. Their leading object seems to be to get all the property of the Church for little or nothing, and drive [the Saints] out of the place" ("Hepsy Richards 1838 Letters," *Women's Voices*, pp. 76–77).

Between November 1837 and June 1838, possibly two or three hundred Saints withdrew from the Church in Kirtland, and a significant number also left the fledgling Church in Missouri. In that nine-month period, the Three Witnesses, a member of the First Presidency (Frederick G. Williams), four members of the Twelve Apostles, and several members of the First Quorum of Seventy left the Church. Because Brigham Young continually defended Joseph Smith, he was threatened with his life and forced to flee to Missouri on horseback.

Thus began a mass exodus of Latter-day Saints from Geauga County, Ohio, as more than 1,600 people abandoned their homes and property and embarked upon a new colonizing adventure in the wilderness of western America.

At the beginning of 1838, Joseph Smith wrote, "A new year dawned upon the Church in Kirtland in all the bitterness of the spirit of apostate mobocracy; which continued to rage and grow hotter and hotter, until Elder Rigdon and myself were obliged to flee from its deadly influence, as did the Apostles and Prophets of old . . . to escape mob violence, which was about to burst upon us under the color of legal process to cover the hellish designs of our enemies, and to save themselves from the just judgment of the law" (*History of the Church,* 3:1).

A SPIRIT OF WORLDLINESS WAS BEHIND THE APOSTASY

On both continents Jesus had taught, "No man can serve two masters: for either he will hate the one, and love the other; or else he will hold to the one, and despise the other. Ye cannot serve God and mammon" (Matthew 6:24; 3 Nephi

13:24). Hugh Nibley comments, "The first commandment given to the Saints in this last dispensation, delivered at Harmony, Pennsylvania, in April 1829, before the formal incorporation of the Church, was an ominous warning: 'Seek not for riches but for wisdom' (D&C 6:7)—all in one brief mandate that does not allow compromise. Why start out on such a negative note? The Lord knew well that the great obstacle to the work would be what it always had been in the past. The warning is repeated throughout the Doctrine and Covenants and the Book of Mormon again and again. The positive and negative are here side by side and back to back, making it clear, as the scriptures often do, that the two quests are mutually exclusive—you cannot go after both, you cannot serve both God and Mammon, even if you should be foolish enough to try" (*Approaching Zion*, p. 343).

It appears that a great many of the Kirtland Saints somehow lost track of the wisdom of God and shifted their allegiance from God to mammon, or the things of the world. Eliza R. Snow understood perfectly the cause of the spiritual decline, for she said that many Church members felt that "prosperity was dawning upon them . . . and many who had been humble and faithful . . . were getting haughty in their spirits, and lifted up in the pride of their hearts. As the Saints drank in the love and spirit of the world, the Spirit of the Lord withdrew from their hearts, and they were filled with pride and hatred toward those who maintained their integrity" (*History of the Church*, 2:487, footnote).

A growing spirit of speculation in Kirtland was further evidence of this. Many people had borrowed money at inflated prices in order to purchase land for resale at a substantial profit. Warren Cowdery said that these members were "guilty of wild speculations and visionary dreams of worldly grandeur, as if gold and silver were their gods, and houses, farms and merchandise their only bliss or their passport to it" (*Messenger and Advocate,* May 1837).

"Then came the crash of 1837, brought on by those same shrewd, hardheaded businessmen," Hugh Nibley writes. "'During this time,' [Heber C.] Kimball recalled, 'I had many days of sorrow and mourning, for my heart sickened to see the awful extent that things were getting to.' Many apostatized and 'also entered into combinations to obtain wealth by fraud and every means that was evil.' Later, Kimball returned to Kirtland again after a mission to England: 'The Church had suffered terribly from the ravages of apostasy.' Looking back over many years, he recalled that 'the Ohio mobbings, the Missouri persecutions, the martyrdom, the exodus, nor all that Zion's cause has suffered since, have imperiled it half so much as when mammon and the love of God strove for supremacy in the hearts of His people.' Note that they were torn between God and Mammon, and 'no man can serve both!'" (*Approaching Zion,* p. 346).

Brother Nibley continues, "Every step in the direction of increasing one's personal holdings is a step away from Zion, which is another way of saying, as the Lord has proclaimed in various ways, that one cannot serve two masters: to the degree in which he loves the one he will hate the other, and so it is with God and business, for mammon is simply the standard Hebrew word for any kind of financial dealing. . . . From the very first there were Latter-day Saints who thought to promote the cause of Zion by using the methods of Babylon. Indeed, once the Saints were told to make friends with the Mammon of unrighteousness (D&C 82:22), but that was only to save their lives in an emergency. We have the word of the Prophet Joseph that Zion is not to be built up by using the methods of Babylon. He says, 'Here are those who begin to spread out buying up all the land they are able to do, to the exclusion of the poorer ones who are not so much blessed with this world's goods, thinking to lay foundations for themselves only, looking to their own individual families and those who are to follow them. . . . Now I want to tell you that Zion cannot be built up in any such way'" (*Approaching Zion*, pp. 37, 20).

Of course, any time such worldliness takes precedence over the things of the Spirit of God, then God's Spirit departs and apostasy occurs. President Spencer W. Kimball said, "Today we worship the gods of wood and stone and metal. Not always are they in the form of a golden calf, but equally real as objects of protection and worship. They are houses, lands, bank accounts, leisure. They are boats, cars, and luxuries. They are bombs and ships and armaments. We bow down to the god of mammon, the god of luxuries, the god of dissipation" (Conference Report, October 1961, p. 33).

Once the Saints were no longer sacrificing their all for the building of the temple in Kirtland, that is exactly what happened. They began looking to themselves, and soon their personal religion was no longer a religion of spiritual power and progression. Again quoting Brother Nibley: "In ancient times, apostasy never came by renouncing the gospel but always by corrupting it. No one renounces it today, and so we have the strange paradox of people stoutly proclaiming beliefs and ideals that they have no intention of putting into practice. . . . The great apostasy in the time of the apostles was not a renouncing of the faith but its corruption and manipulation . . . [a] redirect[ion of] the gospel light . . . for convenience" (*Temple and Cosmos,* p. 395).

As time passed, and as this gospel of convenience increased its hold in the hearts and minds of Latter-day Saints, fewer and fewer of them had power to bring to pass and enjoy such spiritual experiences as had occurred in Kirtland—the coming unto Christ and feeling of His pure and perfect love—despite the fact that they had been endowed with that power from on high. Truly had their spiritual growth been slowed or in some cases even stopped altogether.

The next step, of course, was that angelic ministrations and other manifestations of the Lord's Spirit quite literally went out of fashion. Those who continued to seek and enjoy such rich spiritual blessings hesitated to discuss them or bear witness of them for fear of ridicule and outright scorn, and so their numbers grew fewer and fewer.

And the scorners? Besides the apostates and the anti-Christs, they grew to include good, well-meaning people, especially members of the Church, who had never sought such transcendent experiences, had never sacrificed the things of the world in order to experience them, and quite naturally doubted that ordinary people such as themselves could ever see, hear, feel, and know such sublime things. So they mocked and scorned and perhaps shook their heads in sorrow and pity. Could anyone be so deluded as to think that *he* or *she* had actually seen and spoken with an angel?

THE WORLD TODAY

Sadly, the situation has not improved. In our day a spirit of worldliness and faithlessness permeates not only the world but also many modern Church members. Certainly this was true in the ward over which I presided. Despite covenants to the contrary, too many of us choose to live a gospel of convenience rather than one of sacrifice, and the scorners and doubters of things spiritual reign supreme. Brother Nibley writes, "We are granted enough time on earth to serve only one master. Every day of our lives we have to make a choice, a choice that will show where our real interests and desires lie. From the very beginning of the world the choice was provided as a test for each of us during this time of probation. Satan is allowed to try and tempt us in his way, and God is allowed in his: as Moroni puts it, 'The devil . . . inviteth and enticeth to sin, and to do that which is evil continually. But behold, that which is of God inviteth and enticeth to do good continually' (Moroni 7:12–13). It is going on all the time, the ancient doctrine of the Two Ways. The point is that we cannot choose both ways. They go in opposite directions" (*Approaching Zion*, p. 125).

As a bishop I soon learned that we as a people are much like the Saints in early Kirtland, except that we have been granted even greater temple blessings and divine empowerment. Therefore we ought to enjoy the same gifts, and more. As Orson Pratt testified, "I solemnly affirm that God was there in Kirtland, his angels were there, the Holy Ghost was in the midst of the people, the visions of the Almighty were opened to the minds of the servants of the living God; the veil was taken off from the minds of many; we saw the heavens opened; we beheld the angels of God; we heard the voice of the Lord; and we were filled from the crown of our heads to the soles of our feet with the power and inspiration of the Holy Ghost. It was there that the people were blessed as they never had been blessed for generations and generations that were passed and gone" (*Journal of Discourses,* 18:132).

And if such is our desire we *can* also experience them. As the Prophet Joseph reminds us, "God hath not revealed anything to Joseph, but what he will make known unto the Twelve, and even the least Saint *may know all things as fast as he is able to bear them*" (*History of the Church,* 3:380; italics mine).

The key here is found in the words "may know . . . as fast as he is able." In other words, experiencing the things Joseph experienced, including coming unto Christ, beholding His face, and obtaining the gift of charity, or the pure love of Christ, is not automatic. If obtained at all, these things must be sought for as earnestly as Joseph and the early Saints sought them: through diligent and mighty prayer. In addition to prayer, we must be adequately prepared through ever-increasing personal righteousness. As Joseph said on another occasion, "The things of God are of deep import; and time, and experience, and careful and ponderous and solemn thoughts can only find them out. Thy mind, O man! if thou wilt lead [thy] soul unto salvation, must stretch as high as the utmost heavens, and search into and contemplate the darkest abyss, and the broad expanse of eternity—thou must commune with God" (*Teachings of the Prophet Joseph Smith,* p. 137; hereafter referred to as *Teachings*).

Consider the implications of this statement of Joseph's: "Search the revelations of God; study the prophecies, and rejoice that God grants unto the world Seers and Prophets. They are they who saw the mysteries of godliness; they saw the flood before it came; they saw angels ascending and descending upon a ladder that reached from earth to heaven; they saw the stone cut out of the mountain, which filled the whole earth; they saw the Son of God come from the regions of bliss and dwell with men on earth; they saw the deliverer come out of Zion, and turn away ungodliness from Jacob; they saw the glory of the Lord when he showed the transfiguration of the earth on the mount; they saw every mountain laid low and every valley exalted when the Lord was taking vengeance upon the wicked; they saw truth spring out of the earth, and righteousness look down from heaven in the last days, before the Lord came the second time to gather his elect; they saw the end of wickedness on earth, and the Sabbath of creation crowned with peace; they saw the end of the glorious thousand years, when Satan was loosed for a little season; they saw the day of judgment when all men received according to their works, and they saw the heaven and the earth flee away to make room for the city of God, when the righteous receive an inheritance in eternity. *And, fellow sojourners upon earth, it is your privilege to purify yourselves and come up to the same glory, and see for yourselves, and know for yourselves. Ask, and it shall be given you; seek and ye shall find; knock, and it shall be opened unto you*" (*Teachings*, pp. 12–13; italics mine).

It is the indisputable right of mortals to experience such things. Unfortunately, too many modern Latter-day Saints will not be so blessed, because the things of the world continue to mean more than the things of the Spirit. As a bishop I witnessed this firsthand, seeing some of the couples I counseled attend the temple and ultimately strengthen their marriage or overcome other problems. Those couples who ignored the counsel to attend the temple together suffered and frequently fell away.

Watching this tragic misery broke my heart, and I know that Joseph Smith took it just as personally as I did. Heber C. Kimball declared, "The greatest torment [Joseph] had and the greatest mental suffering was because this people *would not live up to their privileges*. There were many things he desired to reveal that we have not learned yet, but he could not do it. He said sometimes that he felt pressed upon and as though he were pent up in an acorn shell, and all because *the people did not and would not prepare themselves* to receive the rich treasures of wisdom and knowledge that he had to impart. He could have revealed a great many things to us if we had been ready; but he said there were many things that we could not receive because we lacked that diligence and faithfulness that were necessary to entitle us to those choice things of the kingdom" ("Extract from the Journal of Heber C. Kimball," *Times and Seasons* 2:1841; 6:1845; italics mine).

AN ENOCH OR A MOSES PEOPLE

And so I wonder, for I cannot help it. Have we, both in my dear ward and elsewhere across the earth, become an Enoch people or a Moses people? Are we *really* striving to come unto Christ? Do we seek after the face of the Lord and the gifts of His Spirit, including Christ's pure and perfect love? Or do we harden our hearts through apathy and worldliness, like the ancient Israelites, and turn away? And how does the glorified Joseph Smith feel about the course the members of the Church he restored are following now?

Chapter Four

SPIRITUAL DEATH

More than it ever has, the world with its cares and wickedness is crashing in upon us today, filling our hearts and minds with temporal nonsense and inconveniences, and leaving even the most righteous among us hard-pressed to find the time even to think of spirituality, let alone to discipline ourselves to come unto Christ as we seek His face and pray for His charity or divine love.

The question that haunts me as I consider this, and I ask it of myself far more often than I ask it concerning others, is: Knowing what I know, and having been endowed with power from on high to seek His face and also once blessed as a bishop to taste of the pure love of Christ, what is it about me that permits and even encourages, with such apparent ease, the oh-so-frequent choices that manifest a headlong diving into the very behaviors that will prevent me from coming unto Him?

PONDERINGS

A journal entry I made after three and a half years as bishop reflects this question more adequately:

> I find it amazing that being bishop is taking up so much of my time. This week alone I have been involved in half a dozen serious problems within the ward, and I have spent a significant number of hours since Tuesday morning counseling and visiting and comforting, as well as enough additional time on my knees pleading and worrying to put new blisters on my calluses. I guess it's good that I have *something* to drive me to my knees. On the other hand, I have also enjoyed some wonderful visits and interviews in the bishop's office, and I have been once to the temple, observing one of my sweet ward members as she received her endowment—the ordinances of salvation and exaltation. I cannot describe the exquisite joy I witnessed on her countenance in that holy place, or the overwhelming rush of divine love and happiness I felt in her behalf.
>
> So, being bishop is pretty much a mixed bag, thankfully comprised of more happiness than sorrow, more peace than turmoil, more joy than misery! In truth, I thoroughly enjoy working with these sweet people! Besides the amazingly wonderful core group of ward members, who have truly become righteous servants of Jesus Christ through being born of the Spirit and who have therefore become Christ's sons and daughters as well as Saviors on Mount Zion for the rest of us (and for whom I almost never have to worry or weep in sorrow and anguish), I see

wonderful evidences that the Holy Ghost is working in the hearts of scores of others, bringing them carefully and tenderly back to Christ and His fold! The temple is becoming increasingly important to them as they seek the ordinances for themselves, and many of those who are already endowed are returning with ever-increasing frequency. Surely this faithfulness is bringing added love to our ward!

I also see continued evidence of the gathering to our ward of truth-seeking people whose innermost desire is to live in righteousness and peace while loving and serving their neighbors. . . . Family after family have reported that they were led to their home and neighborhood in our ward by feelings and impressions that could not be denied. They know that the Lord has brought them here, though they have yet to determine exactly why.

Though I do not know all the whys of their coming, I do know . . . that our world is growing ever more dark, brutal, and evil, and that Satan's devilish forces are growing in power and dominion as they endeavor to entice each of us to greater and deeper sin. Even in our peaceful and secluded little ward I see evidence of Satanic success, and I am called upon as bishop (far more often than I would have imagined before my call) to try and salve the pain and misery that are *always* the devil's legacy. It seems to me, therefore, that the Lord is gathering us together for protection—for ourselves and families and for each other as a ward family—as the wicked of the world spiral downward toward their promised destruction. And how do we protect each other? Through diligent commandment-keeping, in addition to constantly declaring to one another in pure but sweet and humble testimony the good word of God, and through practicing that good word by

> ministering to each other's needs in love, with endless compassion and patience through honorable, willing service. Only in that manner can our ward be blessed and protected and each of us be led to that glorious state of spiritual strength we are all commanded to seek! Nevertheless, until Christ's return, life will remain a constant struggle for all of us. Trials and difficulties of one sort or another will beset us no matter how righteously we live, and no one of us is exempt from occasional, even serious, stumbling into sin. I have struggled to understand the deeper reasons for this tragic stumbling or choice-making (I see this in myself at least as often as I do in others, I am sad to admit), and during the past few days the Holy Ghost has been giving me a little understanding I have never before considered, at least in this context. Perhaps it is the answer.

The understanding I was speaking of began one morning during our daily scripture study. My wife, Kathy, and I were reading in section 29 of the Doctrine and Covenants, where the Lord says, "The devil tempted Adam, and he partook of the forbidden fruit and transgressed the commandment, wherein he became subject to the will of the devil, because he yielded unto temptation. Wherefore, I, the Lord God, caused that he should be cast out from the Garden of Eden, from my presence, *because of his transgression, wherein he became spiritually dead,* which is the first death, even that same death which is the last death, which is spiritual, which shall be pronounced upon the wicked when I shall say: Depart, ye cursed" (D&C 29:40–41; italics mine).

Likening the scripture to ourselves (see 1 Nephi 19:23), Kathy and I considered ourselves as if we were Adam and Eve. As we did so, it seemed suddenly obvious that this particular experience of our first parents was meant to apply to us. Like Adam and Eve, each of us becomes subject to the will of the devil by yielding to temptation and transgressing God's commandments, which every one of us who has become accountable has done! And like Adam and Eve, once subject to the will of the devil we are no longer pure and clean, no longer qualified to be in the presence of God. Therefore, we are cast out, or shut off from His presence, and so have become spiritually dead.

A UNIVERSAL SPIRITUAL DEATH

At first the starkness of this thought stunned me! *I have died spiritually!* Just like that, transgress the commandments and the consequence is applied: We are rendered spiritually dead! Dead! What a terrible sound that word has to me, made worse no doubt because of the pain and sorrow Kathy and I endured at the passing of our daughter Charity. Her death—her sweet spirit being removed from both her body and our presence—was the most difficult, painful thing I have ever been called upon to endure! And now the Lord was telling me that Kathy and I had suffered the same thing; because of willful transgression, our spirits had been removed from God's presence—a spiritual death. It seemed harsh and difficult to accept, though suddenly I found myself wondering if perhaps our Heavenly Father had suffered the same way when He observed us removing ourselves from His presence—and if our own eternal spirits felt that way when we made that spiritually fatal decision of submitting ourselves to Satan's will. Troubled by these thoughts, I began studying and praying for greater understanding.

As infants, I am now beginning to see in a slightly

different way, we came into the world pure and innocent—"little children are whole . . . even from the foundation of the world" (Moroni 8:8, 12), Jesus explained through the prophet Mormon. Yet as we grow in mortality, we begin to willfully transgress commandments, first those of our parents and then, with a little more maturity and worldly understanding, those of God. In consequence of these choices, which quickly develop into habits of disobedience, I believe the veil of forgetfulness that developed following our advent into mortality thickens and expands until it is impenetrable, at least from our side, and we are cut off or shut out from the presence of God. According to God's definition as given to Joseph Smith, like Adam and Eve we have become spiritually dead.

Righteous Abinadi agreed with this assessment, declaring that all "are carnal and devilish, and the devil has power over them; yea, even that old serpent that did beguile our first parents, which was the cause of their fall; *which was the cause of all mankind becoming carnal, sensual, devilish, knowing evil from good, subjecting themselves to the devil.* Thus all mankind were lost" (Mosiah 16:3–4; italics mine).

Unfortunately, it is we rather than the devil who bring upon ourselves this first spiritual death. How? By intentionally submitting to our own and Satan's wills rather than the will and wisdom of God, and by yearning after the things of this world rather than the things of that heaven we have so recently left behind.

A PROBLEM OF YOUTH

It seems unlikely that this spiritual death is a single major event, or even that it occurs at age eight, when the Lord says we are fully accountable before God and therefore capable of sin. Rather, I believe spiritual death is a prolonged process that begins early in our mortal lives, perhaps long before age eight. The Lord says, "Power is not given unto Satan to tempt little children, until they *begin to* become accountable before me" (D&C 29:47; italics mine). Kathy and I have watched both our children and our grandchildren, even when very young, intentionally and knowingly practice disobedience by making wrong choices in spite of parental pleadings. These choices are not yet accounted to them as sins, of course, for they are not yet wholly accountable: "Wherefore, little children are . . . not capable of committing sin" (Moroni 8:8). Nevertheless, by exercising their own will through intentional disobedience, even small children *begin* to become accountable before the Lord. In a broader sense, they, or we, have *begun* the process of submitting ourselves to temptation. And from that moment, it seems to me, we *begin* the process of separation from God that is called spiritual death.

It also seems to me, particularly after several years of laboring intensely with the youth of my ward, that this process of spiritual death is usually completed, at least in American society, by the time we are eleven, twelve, thirteen, or perhaps fourteen years old. By that age, I believe, the veil of separation, or forgetfulness, is completely in place, and we have, through hundreds and thousands of our own willful choices and decisions—submitting first to our own will and later to Satan's temptations—removed ourselves from God's presence, from the relative peace, safety, and innocence of our own personal garden of Eden. Thus each of us has become spiritually dead.

Therefore, "when they *begin* to grow up, sin conceiveth in their hearts, and they taste the bitter, that they may know to prize the good. And it is given unto them to know good from evil; wherefore they are agents unto themselves" (Moses 6:55–56; italics mine).

Put another way, and usually by the time we have reached the approximate ages I mentioned above, "Satan hath come among the children of men, and tempteth them to worship him; and men have become carnal, sensual, and devilish, and are shut out from the presence of God" (Moses 6:49).

Is it any wonder that the hallways of our junior, middle, and high schools seem such particularly wicked and unholy places? Even the thought of such newly spiritually dead children of God, who as yet have neither the experience nor the wisdom to see the damage of intentional, rampant sinning (which obviously seems to many of them both fun and innocent) is sobering.

EVEN WORSE FOR ADULTS

Far more sobering is the fact that this same thing applies to us as adult Latter-day Saints. Through intentionally submitting to Satan's temptations, which all of us have done no matter how long ago or slight our sins or transgressions, we have each become "carnal, sensual, and devilish, and . . . shut out from the presence of God" (Moses 6:49). In other words, we continue to exhibit unrighteous behavior patterns, even enhancing them through our increased knowledge and skills—usually the same ones that we so quickly decry in our youth.

And what are the effects of this often-intentional

stumbling into sin, the "carnal, sensual, and devilish" behavior that is so common to spiritually dead mankind? From the admittedly limited perspective I gained as a bishop, I would say the effects among the Latter-day Saints over whom I presided, myself included, were sorrow, pain, and misery—in spite of all the Lord has given us by way of power, understanding, and protection.

Too often we seem to make the most foolish decisions regarding our spiritual lives, decisions that jeopardize not only our present peace and happiness but also our eternal futures. More compelling, these same decisions also engender heartache and misery not only for us, the decision makers, but also for our brokenhearted families!

BEGINNING WITH BROKEN LAWS

Significantly, whenever I began digging into these painful situations, where people had finally become so unhappy and misguided that they or their loved ones had sought out the bishop, I found that the trouble had actually begun somewhere on the most basic level of intentional personal transgression, usually in one or more of the following areas:

- No or infrequent individual, couple, or family prayers.
- No or infrequent individual, couple, or family scripture study.
- No or infrequent family home evening.
- No or infrequent attendance at the temple.
- No or erratic attendance at Church.

So it has also proven in my own life! As already spiritually dead youth or adults, choosing to avoid any portion of any of these, or any other of the basic laws of the gospel, for any reason, will *always* give Satan a certain amount of power over us. Through Moses the Lord declared, "Because that Satan rebelled against me, and sought to destroy the agency of man, which I, the Lord God, had given him, and also, that I should give unto him mine own power; by the power of mine Only Begotten, I caused that he should be cast down; and he became Satan, yea, even the devil, the father of all lies, to deceive and to blind men, and *to lead them captive at his will, even as many as would not hearken unto my voice*" (Moses 4:3–4; italics mine).

Considering the devil's known penchant for misery and destruction, which all of us understand fairly clearly, I wonder why *any* of us would knowingly allow him to enter our lives. That question brings to mind an interesting answer, something the prophet Nephi foretold concerning our day. Many, Nephi declared, I believe speaking particularly of us Latter-day Saints, would the devil "pacify, and lull them away into carnal security, that they will say: All is well in Zion; yea, Zion prospereth, all is well—and thus the devil cheateth their souls, and leadeth them away carefully down to hell" (2 Nephi 28:21).

LULLED INTO CARNAL SECURITY

According to my dictionary, *pacify* means to "put at ease, to tranquilize, to neutralize"; *lull* means "to calm, sooth, or allay," as in "allay all fear"; *Carnal* means "worldly, not spiritual—of the flesh." And *hell* is a place or condition of evil, pain, disorder, and cruelty. I believe that Nephi is saying that Satan will move about among Church members of the latter days, using his well-disguised whisperings and carnal enticements. Once we have given him power, he will be able to tranquilize and thus neutralize our consciences (or the light of Christ with which we were born), thus putting us to sleep spiritually. Filled with this sleepy, yawning, eyes-closed, ho-hum attitude toward spirituality and the things of eternity, we will feel no fear as we begin to reject Christ and the power of His eternal salvation and, instead, accept the temporary security and pleasures of the flesh. Lulled by this false, carnal security (which comes from yielding to Satan's enticements to lean upon the arm of flesh rather than accepting the Holy Spirit's whispered pleadings to lean upon the arm of God), it is easy for us to feel no need for diligent prayer—or, after a time, prayer of any sort.

Reading scriptures, which are the literal voice of the Lord to His children, becomes nothing more than a boring waste of time trying to understand old-fashioned gibberish. Family home evening and temple attendance are more of the same: boring wastes. Paying tithing (a necessity for those who wish to attend the temple) becomes a foolish loss of good money. And who wants to throw away a perfectly good Sunday listening to people rag on about Church nonsense when so much "fun" is out in the world just waiting to be enjoyed? Having already suffered spiritual death as children, as adults we have now been pacified and lulled into *carnal security.*

And when our bishop or other priesthood or Relief Society leader or loved one encourages us to change those areas in our lives that he or she knows will ease our heartaches and bring peace back to our souls as well as to our families (not to mention eternal joy hereafter), far too often we look at them as if they have lost their minds. "I'm keeping the commandments as well as anyone else in this ward, Bishop," we exclaim in a huff, "so I'm a good person.

There's just no need for me to do all that praying, scripture reading, going to church, attending the temple, or holding family home evening kind of stuff!" Or, "Ignoring those stupid commandments isn't our problem, Bishop. And no, we never pray together! Never have! But so what? Our problem is that we just don't get along with each other anymore. No matter what either one of us does, we end up in a miserable fight!" Or, "I've found somebody else who is prettier, has more money, is more enticing, has a nicer house," and so forth, "and my idiot wife (or husband) just doesn't want to let me go. Can't she (or he) see that I don't love her (or him) anymore! Besides, he (or she) has *never* made me happy!" Or, "Internet chat rooms or porn sites? They're harmless, Bishop! Besides, I deserve a little pleasure in this life, and what I do in my own home is none of your blasted business!" Or, "Good grief, Bishop! I only use profanities and vulgarities because my family drives me to it. My swearing and anger are all their fault, not mine!" Or, "I'm not really hurting anyone being physically, verbally, emotionally, or sexually abusive! All I have is a #*%#@% temper problem! Besides, I have issues from my childhood, for crying out loud. So gimme a break!" Or, "These are tough times, Bishop. There's just no way we can afford to pay tithing, take time out for a Church calling, help clean our ward building each week, or make room in our lives for the Lord!" Or, "Yeah, we want the Church and the temple in our lives *someday;* we're just not ready for them yet. Besides, what's the rush? There's plenty of time for that religion stuff later." Or finally, "Are you nuts? Sunday's the only day I have to take my family snowmobiling, boating, or camping, or to go to Wendover or Las Vegas. I need that day for fishing, hunting, traveling, watching sports, shopping, sleeping, going to home shows, kicking crippled dogs, and beating up little old ladies!" And on and on we go.

Of course, the above responses are extreme and almost cartoon-like. Nevertheless, what I most often heard as I visited with my ward members, while much more polite and veiled, carried exactly the same message: "Don't bother me, Bishop! I'm perfectly happy the way I am!" Though they couldn't see it, the reality is that Satan had enticed each of these individuals, many of whom were "active" in the Church, to say, as Nephi warned, "All is well in Zion; yea, Zion prospereth, all is well." The result of this attitude for all of us, obviously, is that "the devil [is cheating our] souls, and [is leading us] away carefully down to hell"—that place or condition of evil, pain, disorder, cruelty that he has prepared for us. I wish it hadn't been so, but repeatedly I encountered various degrees of this attitude as I became involved in painful problems and situations within my ward. Far too often, even in the midst of our self-inflicted pain and misery, we really don't see the need to change!

SATANIC CHARACTERISTICS AND BEHAVIORS

Unfortunately, when we allow even small lapses in obedience to any of God's laws and do not immediately repent and come back to strict compliance, we have driven further away the Lord's Spirit and therefore given Satan even greater power—power to introduce into our souls even larger and more dangerously devilish issues (see again Moses 4:3–4). And the devil is ever so quick to take advantage of the door we are swinging ever more open. Almost instantly we find ourselves grappling with, and soon reeling from, one or more of the following Satanically inspired implants into our characters and our souls:

Impure thoughts
Self-serving motives
Lust
Anger
Fear
Stubbornness
Jealousy
Greed
Worldliness
Disdainfulness
Quickness to judge
Ingratitude
Sottishness
Disaffection
Selfishness
Confusion
Foulness of mind
Contentiousness
Self-loathing
Laziness
Reclusiveness
Frustration
Being easily offended
Promiscuity
Condescendence
Cruelty
Vulgarity
Permissiveness
Constant complaining
Lack of contrition
Loss of spiritual focus
Callousness
Diminished faith
Hatred
Seductiveness
Boredom
Profanity
Being without mercy
Self-indulgence
Slovenliness
Despair
Self-pity
Arrogance
Lechery and lewdness
Complacency
Pride
Rudeness
Discouragement
Anxiety
Narcissism
Hopelessness
Deception and dishonesty
Predatory nature
Doubt
Diminished self-esteem
Abusiveness
Crudity
Unkindness
Brutality

And so forth and so on! Old Scratch seems to have no end to his favorite tools, which are whatever happens to work best on any of us at any given moment. We must not forget to add lying as we seek to cover these things up and hide them from those who love and cherish us, our Church leaders included. Sadly, during my ministry I witnessed almost every one of these characteristics or behaviors within my ward, often several in the same person. Each of these negative traits further drives away the Lord's Spirit, leads to greater and more damaging sins of both commission and omission, and engenders and increases heartache and misery, in our own lives as well as in the lives of those who surround and care for us. Abinadi urged us to "remember that he that persists in his own carnal nature, and goes on in the ways of sin and rebellion against God, remaineth in his fallen state and the devil hath all power over him. Therefore he is as though there was no redemption made, being an enemy to God; and also is the devil an enemy to God" (Mosiah 16:5).

To put it as plainly as did Nephi and Abinadi, through these satanically originated vices or characteristics, *at our own invitation* our souls are being cheated by the devil, and we are being led carefully down to hell.

WE ARE NOT ABANDONED

Thankfully, in spite of the devilish direction we so often seem to be going, the Lord does not abandon us. Even though we have suffered our first spiritual death, or been shut out from God's presence, allowing into our lives the wickedness that, to one degree or another, always follows, and though we can no longer see and know God and Christ personally as we did in our innocent state, under certain conditions we are still entitled to the promptings of the Lord's Spirit and to spiritual experiences—even wonderful, supernal ones. To Enoch the Lord explained, "Adam and Eve, his wife, called upon the name of the Lord, and *they heard the voice of the Lord from the way toward the Garden of*

Eden, speaking unto them, [but] they saw him not; for they were shut out from his presence (Moses 5:4; italics mine).

The Lord elaborated further to Joseph Smith, saying, "I, the Lord God, gave unto Adam and unto his seed, that they should not die as to the temporal death, until I, the Lord God, should send forth angels to declare unto them repentance and redemption, through faith on the name of mine Only Begotten Son" (D&C 29:42).

It is difficult to imagine a more wonderful spiritual experience than hearing the voice of God or being ministered to by a holy angel, both of which Adam and Eve enjoyed following their spiritual deaths. So did the Saints in Kirtland. Each of us, if we as fervently desire and live for it, is entitled to the same sort of spiritual assistance and communication.

THE PLAN FOR RETURNING TO SPIRITUAL LIFE

What was it that God told Adam and Eve (or us) through their marvelous spiritual experiences? Logically, considering that their (our) problem was having submitted to temptation and its sure consequence of being eternally shut out from God's presence, the Lord was telling them (us) how to come back. For years Adam and Eve struggled and yet obediently offered up sacrifices unto the Lord, even so long that their children were marrying and rearing families of their own (Moses 5:2–3), when finally an angel appeared to Adam, asking why he offered sacrifices unto the Lord.

Adam replied, "I know not, save the Lord commanded me." Then the angel replied, "This thing is a similitude of the sacrifice of the Only Begotten of the Father, which is full of grace and truth. Wherefore, thou shalt do all that thou doest in the name of the Son, and thou shalt repent and call upon God in the name of the Son forevermore" (Moses 5:6–8).

By way of additional witness, Enoch reported, "In that day the Holy Ghost fell upon Adam, which beareth record of the Father and the Son, saying: I am the Only Begotten of the Father from the beginning, henceforth and forever, *that as thou hast fallen thou mayest be redeemed, and all mankind,* even as many as will" (Moses 5:9; italics mine).

What an amazing bit of heaven-sent information! Even though Adam and Eve (that is, my wife, myself, and everyone else who has ever had, or who ever will have, the capacity for agency or choice) had become filthy and unclean through submission to temptation and were no longer entitled to be in the presence of God, *there was a way back!* As Abinadi declared to wicked King Noah, "Thus all mankind were lost; and behold, they would have been endlessly lost were it not that God redeemed his people from their lost and fallen state" (Mosiah 16:4).

The message, then? Simply that through the miraculous suffering, death, and resurrection of Jesus Christ, or in other words His divine grace and truth, His atonement, His redemption, we are able, if we are willing to humble ourselves through sincere repentance and baptism, to receive the incredible gift of the Holy Ghost. And the Holy Ghost will instruct, enable, and empower us as we continue to repent and strive to be more obedient (Moses 5:14), to regain and thereafter retain cleanliness until we return to the presence of our Father in Heaven.

And this process, of course, is coming unto Christ, with all of its marvelous ramifications and blessings, exactly as we have been commanded to do.

Part Two

TO BE BORN AGAIN

Chapter Five

A SPIRITUAL REBIRTH

The prophet Enoch taught that God's plan of spiritual rebirth, or returning to His presence, consisted of the following: "God hath made known unto our fathers that all men must repent. And he called upon our father Adam by his own voice, saying: I am God; I made the world, and men before they were in the flesh. And he also said unto him: If thou wilt turn unto me, and hearken unto my voice, and believe, and repent of all thy transgressions, and be baptized, even in water, in the name of mine Only Begotten Son, who is full of grace and truth, which is Jesus Christ, the only name which shall be given under heaven, whereby salvation shall come unto the children of men, ye shall receive the gift of the Holy Ghost, asking all things in his namc, and whatsoever ye shall ask, it shall be given you. . . . Wherefore teach it unto your children, that all men, everywhere, must repent, or they can in nowise inherit the kingdom of God, for no unclean thing can dwell there, or dwell in his presence; for, in the language of Adam, Man of Holiness is his name, and the name of his Only Begotten is the Son of Man, even Jesus Christ, a righteous Judge, who shall come in the meridian of time (Moses 6:49–52, 57).

Summarizing, Heavenly Father's plan for all of us is that we must do the following:

1. Repent.
2. Turn to God.
3. Pay attention to His voice.
4. Believe in Him.
5. Be baptized in water in the name of His Only Begotten Son, Jesus Christ, who is the only author and provider of salvation.
6. Receive the gift of the Holy Ghost.
7. Ask (pray) and receive (express gratitude) always in Christ's name.

By doing these things wholeheartedly, we will be fulfilling the will of the Father.

The question that remains, however, is, So what? Besides earning us general and unspecified blessings, what will this accomplish? Looking at the problem logically, since we have each died spiritually, it only makes sense that God, through the power of Christ and the instrumentality of the Holy Ghost, will help and instruct us concerning how to come spiritually back to life. The Lord, whose precise use of words is stunning, calls this being born again or being reborn spiritually—a logical and joyful termination of a spiritual death. By definition, therefore, being born again, or born of the

Spirit, must mean overcoming spiritual death so that we may return to the presence of God.

BEING BORN OF WATER AND THE SPIRIT

During Jesus' mortal ministry, the beloved apostle John tells of a night when Jesus was visited by a man named Nicodemus, who was sincerely asking the same question that had been pondered some 4,000 years earlier by Adam and Eve. According to John, "There was a man of the Pharisees, named Nicodemus, a ruler of the Jews: The same came to Jesus by night, and said unto him, Rabbi, we know that thou art a teacher come from God: for no man can do these miracles that thou doest, except God be with him. Jesus answered and said unto him, Verily, verily, I say unto thee, *Except a man be born again, he cannot see the kingdom of God.* Nicodemus saith unto him, How can a man be born when he is old? can he enter the second time into his mother's womb, and be born? Jesus answered, Verily, verily, I say unto thee, Except a man be born of water and of the Spirit, he cannot enter into the kingdom of God. That which is born of the flesh is flesh; and that which is born of the Spirit is spirit. Marvel not that I said unto thee, Ye must be born again" (John 3:3–7; italics mine).

Jesus explained that once an individual has suffered spiritual death, being reborn spiritually requires two steps: being personally born of or baptized by total immersion in water, and then being born of or baptized by total immersion in the Spirit or Holy Ghost, which the Lord often likens to a cleansing fire. For instance, the prophet Nephi declares, "Wherefore . . . the gate by which ye should enter is repentance and baptism by water; and then cometh a remission of your sins by fire and by the Holy Ghost" (2 Nephi 31:17).

As Jehovah, Jesus taught Adam and Eve with greater detail the same doctrine he later presented to Nicodemus: "I give unto you a commandment, to teach these things freely unto your children, saying: That by reason of transgression cometh the fall, which fall bringeth death, and inasmuch as ye were born into the world by water, and blood, and the spirit, which I have made, and so became of dust a living soul, even so *ye must be born again* into the kingdom of heaven, of water, and of the Spirit, and be cleansed by blood, even the blood of mine Only Begotten; that ye might be sanctified from all sin, and enjoy the words of eternal life in this world, and eternal life in the world to come, even immortal glory; for by the water ye keep the commandment; by the Spirit ye are justified, and by the blood [of Christ] ye are sanctified" (Moses 6:58–60; italics mine).

ADAM AND EVE SPIRITUALLY REBORN

This process of spiritual rebirth was required of Adam and Eve—the first of the eternal ordinances Joseph Smith said Adam received. Enoch explains, "When the Lord had spoken with Adam, our father, that Adam cried unto the Lord, and he was caught away by the Spirit of the Lord, and was carried down into the water, and was laid under the water, and was brought forth out of the water. And thus he was baptized, and the Spirit of God descended upon him, and thus he was born of the Spirit, and became quickened in the inner man. And he heard a voice out of heaven, saying: Thou art baptized with fire, and with the Holy Ghost. This is the record of the Father, and the Son, from henceforth and forever. . . . Behold, thou art one in me, a son of God; and thus may all become my sons" (Moses 6:64–66, 68).

WITHIN MY WARD

A little more than six months into my ministry, I visited one evening with one of the brethren in my ward who suffered from what turned out, unfortunately, to be a fairly common problem. He was a good man, very active and serving in a leadership position. A returned missionary, he had been married in the temple to an outstanding woman. They had some great kids, and to every appearance they had it "all together," spiritually speaking. Yet he was obviously troubled as he sat down across from me, and it didn't take long to discover why.

"I don't think I believe in the Church anymore," he said abruptly, "and I guess maybe I ought to be released."

Instantly I began praying for discernment and for the wisdom to say what would be of greatest benefit to this brother's eternal future. For thirty minutes, however, I said little, merely listening as he unveiled a series of sad events and circumstances, mostly economic though also marital, that had occurred, he said bitterly, "even though I *always* pay a full tithing!"

At length I began to ask him questions pertaining to such things as his personal and family prayer habits, his temple attendance, his feelings about family home evening, and so forth. Neither did it take me long to recognize that he was one of that significant number of individuals (for a good portion of my adult life, myself included) who have relatively firm testimonies of the truthfulness of the Church and the gospel, who serve willingly and have enjoyed the blessings of the temple, but who are not yet committed enough to focus on keeping all the commandments or giving their lives wholly to the Lord.

When I pointed this out to him, however, and suggested that the source of his difficulties might be not only spiritual but related directly to his own behavior, he was not only upset but deeply hurt. "How can you say that?" he demanded. "I have always been active in the Church, and so has my family!"

"Yes, you have," I responded, "if active means merely attending meetings, doing your home teaching, and serving in your calling."

"What else could it mean?"

"Well, according to what you have told me tonight, your personal prayers are dictated by your schedule, you never pray with your wife before you go to bed or when you arise, you never study the scriptures except during Church classes, you use your temple recommend two or three times a year but find the experience boring and tedious, and you stopped holding family home evenings at least two years ago because they always turned into family brawls. Now correct me if I am wrong, but I believe each of these things has been commanded, daily or at least regularly, by the Lord. If you were sitting where I am tonight, conducting this same interview, wouldn't you be harboring serious doubts about the real activity level of the person sitting across from you?"

"So, you're saying I'm not really active?" He was stunned by my question, and his belligerence had completely evaporated.

"What do you think?"

"I . . . I . . . You know, Bishop, sometimes when we're

fighting, my wife says that same thing—that I'm not really even a Latter-day Saint. But I always thought she was saying it just to hurt me!" He smiled a little sadly. "I guess the truth does hurt, doesn't it."

I nodded. "Actually, brother, in many ways you are a wonderful member of the Lord's Church. Unfortunately, I don't believe you have ever fully come to Him. You certainly started the process years ago, but your life's patterns indicate quite plainly that you have not completed it. You died spiritually when you were a child, but you have never finished the process of being spiritually reborn."

Our discussion continued into the evening and with regular frequency for several months thereafter as he struggled to understand why what I was suggesting was important or even necessary, and then to put it into effect. Nor was he alone in this situation. During several Sunday presentations as I brought up the issue of needing to be born of the Spirit in order to overcome spiritual death, I was amazed to discover how few had any real idea what their bishop was talking about, or who saw any great need to focus on that sort of spiritual growth or direction. If we are to believe what faithful Enoch taught, however, and if we are to accept the doctrine that Jesus declared to Nicodemus, then unless we are born again—born of both the water and the Spirit, with all that such spiritual rebirth entails—then we will *never* overcome spiritual death!

FIRST PRINCIPLES AND ORDINANCES OF THE GOSPEL

In what is now known as the Wentworth Letter, Joseph Smith proclaimed to newspaper editor Charles Wentworth, of Chicago, "We believe that the first principles and ordinances of the Gospel are: first, Faith in the Lord Jesus Christ; second, Repentance; third, Baptism by immersion for the remission of sins; fourth, Laying on of hands for the gift of the Holy Ghost" (Fourth Article of Faith).

The passage we read earlier from Enoch seems to be saying that only two separate events must occur in order to be born again—baptism of water and baptism of the Spirit. What Enoch is describing, however, are the first two ordinances of the gospel as presented in the Wentworth Letter by Joseph Smith, and these can be put into effect only after the first two principles of the gospel—faith and repentance—are fully complied with. Inasmuch as baptism and the gift of the Holy Ghost follow faith and repentance, then a discussion of these first principles seems the best way to "begin at the beginning."

THE NEED FOR FAITH

When people seriously begin the process of striving to return to God's presence, they are quickly brought to the realization that they must first learn to exercise faith. Why? Because without true faith, nothing else of a spiritual nature is possible. Particularly is that true of personal revelation—our testimonies and other spiritual counsel and direction—without which we can never find our way back to God's presence. To learn the Lord's will for us personally, we must learn how to hear the whisperings of the Spirit—we must learn how to ask God and receive answers for ourselves. And that requires faith.

John Taylor related the following: "I well remember a remark that Joseph Smith made to me upwards of forty years ago. Said he, 'Elder Taylor, you have been baptized, you have had hands laid upon your head for the reception of the Holy Ghost, and you have been ordained to the holy Priesthood. Now, if you will continue to follow the leadings of that spirit, it will always lead you right. Sometimes it might be contrary to your judgment; never mind that, follow its dictates; *and if you be true to its whisperings it will in time become in you a principle of revelation, so that you will know all things*" (*Journal of Discourses,* 19:153–54; italics mine).

Joseph Smith also stated, "The Spirit of Revelation is in connection with these blessings. A person may profit by noticing the first intimation of the spirit of revelation; for instance, when you feel pure intelligence flowing into you, it may give you sudden strokes of ideas, so that by noticing it, you may find it fulfilled the same day or soon; (i.e.,) those things that were presented unto your minds by the Spirit of God, will come to pass; *and thus by learning the Spirit of God and understanding it, you may grow into the principle of revelation, until you become perfect in Christ Jesus* (*Teachings,* p. 151; italics mine).

President Gordon B. Hinckley adds, "If there is any one thing you and I need in this world it is faith, that dynamic, powerful, marvelous element by which, as Paul declared, the very worlds were framed (Hebrews 11:3). . . . Faith—the kind of faith that moves one to get on his knees and plead with the Lord and then get on his feet and go to work—is an asset beyond compare, even in the acquisition of secular knowledge. I do not minimize the need for study and labor. I would add to these faith and prayer, with the sacred promise that 'God shall give unto you knowledge by His Holy Spirit, yea, by the unspeakable gift of the Holy Ghost. . . .

"The faith to try leads to direction by the Spirit, and the fruits that flow therefrom are marvelous to behold and experience" ("God Shall Give unto You Knowledge by His Holy Spirit," *BYU Speeches of the Year,* September 25, 1973, pp. 109, 111).

Apparently we have something akin to spiritual muscles that can be strengthened only through proper "exercise." Once this "exercise," which amounts to prayerfully and in full faith seeking after God, is begun, then we can begin to "grow into the principle of revelation, until [we] become perfect in Christ Jesus."

FAITH MUST BE SPECIFICALLY DIRECTED

Concerning the importance of faith, the Prophet Joseph declared it to be "the first principle in revealed religion, and the foundation of all righteousness. . . . The author of the epistle to the Hebrews, in the eleventh chapter of that epistle and first verse, gives the following definition of the word *faith:* 'Now faith is the substance of things hoped for, the evidence of things not seen.' From this we learn that faith is the assurance which men have of the existence of things which they have not seen, and the principle of action in all intelligent beings.

"If men were duly to consider themselves, and turn their thoughts and reflections to the operations of their own minds, they would readily discover that it is faith, and faith only, which is the moving cause of all action in them; that without it both mind and body would be in a state of inactivity, and all their exertions would cease, both physical and mental. . . . And as faith is the moving cause of all action in temporal concerns, so it is in spiritual; for the Savior has said, and that truly, that 'He that *believeth* and is baptized shall be saved.' (Mark 16:16; italics added.)

"As we receive by faith all temporal blessings that we do receive, so we in like manner receive by faith all spiritual blessings that we do receive. But faith is not only the principle of action, but of power also, in all intelligent beings, whether in heaven or on earth. Thus says the author of the epistle to the Hebrews: 'Through faith we understand that the worlds were framed by the word of God, so that things which are seen were not made of things which do appear' (Heb. 11:3). . . .

"Had it not been for the principle of faith the worlds would never have been framed, neither would man have been formed of the dust. It is the principle by which Jehovah works, and through which he exercises power over all temporal as well as eternal things. Take this principle or attribute—for it is an attribute—from the Deity, and he would cease to exist. . . .

"God spake, chaos heard, and worlds came into order by reason of the faith there was in HIM. So with man also; he spake by faith in the name of God, and the sun stood still, the moon obeyed, mountains removed, prisons fell, lions' mouths were closed, the human heart lost its enmity, fire its violence, armies their power, the sword its terror, and death its dominion; and all this by reason of the faith which was in him. . . .

"Faith, then, is the first great governing principle which has power, dominion, and authority over all things; by it they exist, by it they are upheld, by it they are changed, or by it they remain, agreeable to the will of God. Without it there is no power, and without power there could be no creation nor existence!" (*Lectures on Faith,* pp. 1–8).

Next, after carefully reviewing the lifespans of the ancients from Adam to Abraham, showing that there was never a time, from the days of Adam, when any number of them were not alive on the earth to declare their witness and testimony as to the reality, character, and nature of God, Joseph continued, "The reason why we have been thus particular on this part of our subject, is [to show how] . . . God became an object of faith among men after the fall; and what it was that stirred up the faith of multitudes to feel after him—to search after a knowledge of his character, perfections and attributes, until they became extensively acquainted with him, and not only commune with him and behold his glory, but be partakers of his power and stand in his presence. . . .

"From the foregoing it is easily to be seen, not only how the knowledge of God came into the world, but upon what principle it was preserved; that from the time it was first communicated, it was retained in the minds of righteous men, who taught not only their own posterity but the world; so that there was no need of a new revelation to man, after Adam's creation to Noah, to give them the first idea or notion of the existence of a God; and not only of a God, but the true and living God. . . .

"We have now clearly set forth how it is, and how it was, that God became an object of faith for rational beings; and also, upon what foundation the testimony was based which excited the inquiry and diligent search of the ancient saints to seek after and obtain a knowledge of the glory of God; and we have seen that it was human testimony, and human testimony only, that excited this inquiry, in the first instance, in their minds. It was the credence they gave to the testimony of their fathers, this testimony having aroused their minds to inquire after the knowledge of God; the inquiry frequently terminated, indeed always terminated when rightly pursued, in the most glorious discoveries and eternal certainty" (*Lectures on Faith,* 2:56). Tying together the exhaustive pursuit of these facts (I have quoted only a fraction of all Joseph said) regarding the true source of man's belief in God, the Prophet concluded by declaring, "[We have] shown how it was that the knowledge of the existence of God came into the world, and by what means the first thoughts were suggested to the minds of men that such a Being did actually exist; and that it was by reason of the knowledge of his existence that there was a foundation laid for the exercise of faith in him, as the only Being in whom faith could center for life and salvation; for faith could not center in a Being of whose existence we have no idea, because the idea of his existence in the first instance is essential to the exercise of faith in him. 'How then shall they call on him in whom they have not believed? and how shall they believe in him of whom they have not heard? and how shall they hear without a preacher?' [or one sent to tell them?] (Romans 10:14). So, then, faith comes by hearing the word of God. (New Translation.)

"Let us here observe, that three things are necessary in order that any rational and intelligent being may exercise faith in God unto life and salvation.

"First, the idea that he actually exists.

"Secondly, a *correct* idea of his character, perfections, and attributes.

"Thirdly, an actual knowledge that the course of life which he is pursuing is according to his will. For without an acquaintance with these three important facts, the faith of every rational being must be imperfect and unproductive; but with this understanding it can become perfect and fruitful, abounding in righteousness, unto the praise and glory of God the Father, and the Lord Jesus Christ" (*Lectures on Faith,* 3:2–5).

"It follows," writes Elder Bruce R. McConkie, "that a knowledge of the true and living God is the beginning of faith unto life and salvation. . . . Faith and truth cannot be separated; if there is to be faith, saving faith, faith unto life and salvation, faith that leads to the celestial world, there must first be truth" (*Mormon Doctrine,* p. 262). Therefore did Alma declare, "Faith is not to have a perfect knowledge of things; therefore if ye have faith ye hope for things which are not seen, *which are true*" (Alma 32:21; italics mine).

FAITH IN THE FATHER AND IN THE SON IS THE SAME

In his *Lectures on Faith,* Joseph Smith did not elaborate on the difference between exercising faith in the Father and exercising faith in the Son. Why? Because it is not necessary to do so. "Faith in one is faith in the other," Elder Bruce R. McConkie declares. "Joseph Smith taught that the Father is the author of the plan of salvation and of the law of faith that is part of this great and eternal plan. This plan has become Christ's by adoption, and he has put all its terms and conditions into full operation through his infinite and eternal atonement.

"To gain salvation, men must come unto the Father,

attain the faith that he exercises, and be as he is. Christ has done so; he is both a saved being and the perfect and only illustration of what others must do to gain like inheritances and be joint-heirs with him. He is thus the way to the Father; no man cometh unto the Father but by him and by his word. He is our Mediator, Advocate, and Intercessor, all because he wrought out the perfect atonement through the shedding of his own blood. Through him, and through him only, fallen men may be reconciled to God if they repent and work righteousness" (*A New Witness for the Articles of Faith,* p. 185).

Concerning exercising faith in the Father's plan of atonement in behalf of His children, which is identified as "laying hold on every good thing" and which Christ was chosen and appointed to implement and proclaim, the prophet Mormon elaborates, "And now *I come to that faith, of which I said I would speak; and I will tell you the way whereby ye may lay hold on every good thing.* For behold, God knowing all things, being from everlasting to everlasting, behold, he sent angels to minister unto the children of men, to make manifest concerning the coming of Christ; and *in Christ there should come every good thing.* And God also declared unto prophets, by his own mouth, that Christ should come. And behold, there were divers ways that he did manifest things unto the children of men, which were good; *and all things which are good cometh of Christ; otherwise men were fallen, and there could no good thing come unto them.* Wherefore, by the ministering of angels, and by every word which proceeded forth out of the mouth of God, *men began to exercise faith in Christ; and thus by faith, they did lay hold upon every good thing;* and thus it was until the coming of Christ. And after that he came men also were saved by faith in his name; *and by faith, they become the sons of God.* And as surely as Christ liveth he spake these words unto our fathers, saying: Whatsoever thing ye shall ask the Father in my name, which is good, in faith believing that ye shall receive, behold, it shall be done unto you. Wherefore . . . Christ hath ascended into heaven, and hath sat down on the right hand of God . . . and *he claimeth all those who have faith in him; and they who have faith in him will cleave unto every good thing.* . . . For no man can be saved, according to the words of Christ, save they shall have faith in his name. . . . For if ye have not faith in him then ye are not fit to be numbered among the people of his church" (Moroni 7:21–28, 38–39; italics mine).

For a moment let us consider what constitutes such an exercise of faith in God and which must begin our quest of coming unto Christ. One day as Joseph prayed in behalf of Martin Harris, the Lord said, "Behold, I say unto him, *he exalts himself* and does not humble himself sufficiently before me; but if he will bow down before me, and *humble himself in mighty prayer and faith,* in the sincerity of his heart, then will I grant unto him a view of the things which he desires to see" (D&C 5:24; italics mine).

MIGHTY PRAYER AND FAITH

Mighty prayer and faith, then, which leads to personal revelation concerning the "actual knowledge that the course of life which [we are] pursuing is according to [God's] will" (*Lectures on Faith,* 3:2–5), must begin with complete humility. If we are exalting ourselves in any way, our prayers will not be mighty, our faith will be nonexistent, and we will obtain nothing from the Lord.

But there is more to mighty prayer than humility. As

Amulek declared to the poor of the Zoramites, "May God grant unto you, my brethren, that ye may begin to exercise your *faith unto repentance,* that ye begin to call upon his holy name, that he would have mercy upon you" (Alma 34:17; italics mine).

While we will discuss repentance more fully in the next chapter, for our prayers to be mighty in faith they must also be unto repentance, which can only be accomplished through humility. This is exemplified by Amulek's next directive: "Yea, cry unto him for mercy; for he is mighty to save. Yea, humble yourselves, and continue in prayer unto him" (Alma 34:18–19). If someone is humble enough to repent of his sins, what he is actually doing is crying out to God for mercy. In effect he is saying, "O God, I know I have chosen to sin, even when I knew better. For this I humbly apologize, and ask that in thy tender mercy thou wilt lift the burden of these sins from off my heart. Though I am unworthy, wilt thou allow the suffering of Christ, wherein He shed great drops of blood in agony caused at least in part by my willful actions, to redeem me that I might be free of sin and have peace of conscience once again."

If the repentant individual says something in this vein, continuing in prayer until divine relief is obtained, then his prayer has been mighty in faith unto repentance.

Amulek continues, "Cry unto him when ye are in your fields, yea, over all your flocks. Cry unto him in your houses, yea, over all your household, *both morning, mid-day, and evening.* Yea, cry unto him against the power of your enemies. Yea, cry unto him against the devil, who is an enemy to all righteousness. Cry unto him over the crops of your fields, that ye may prosper in them. Cry over the flocks of your fields, that they may increase. But this is not all; ye must pour out your souls in your closets, and your secret places, and in your wilderness. Yea, and when you do not cry unto the Lord, let your hearts be full, drawn out in prayer unto him continually for your welfare, and also for the welfare of those who are around you" (Alma 34:20–27; italics mine).

Praying at least morning, midday, and evening concerning our families must be added next if our prayers are to be mighty in faith (see Alma 34:21). To this must be added a willingness to pray over every aspect of our lives, just as Amulek declares. Stated another way, there is no aspect of our lives that our Heavenly Father considers unimportant or inconsequential. He is concerned about everything we think, feel, do, say, or associate with in any manner whatsoever, and He commands us to rehearse these issues before Him in our daily prayers. Then will all these aspects of our lives be consecrated to the welfare of our souls. As Nephi said, "If ye would hearken unto the Spirit which teacheth a man to pray ye would know that ye must pray; for the evil spirit teacheth not a man to pray, but teacheth him that he must not pray. But behold, I say unto you that *ye must pray always, and not faint; that ye must not perform any thing unto the Lord save in the first place ye shall pray unto the Father in the name of Christ, that he will consecrate thy performance unto thee, that thy performance may be for the welfare of thy soul*" (2 Nephi 32:8–9; italics mine).

All of these things combined—faith, repentance, humility, crying out for mercy, and praying continually over all aspects of our lives—all these together begin to constitute mighty prayer and faith. Anything less is less and will not have power sufficient to open the heavens and begin the process of learning to receive personal revelation.

According to Amulek, there is yet another aspect to mighty prayer, and it cannot be ignored. He says, "Do not suppose that this is all; for after ye have done all these things, if ye turn away the needy, and the naked, and visit not the sick and afflicted, and impart of your substance, if ye have, to those who stand in need—I say unto you, if ye do not any of these things, behold, your prayer is vain, and availeth you nothing, and ye are as hypocrites who do deny the faith" (Alma 34:28).

Manifesting for all others the gift of charity, or the pure love of Christ, is the final ingredient spoken of for a prayer to become mighty. And only after our prayers become mighty in all of these respects will we be empowered to exercise faith sufficient to "lay hold on every good thing."

FAITH MUST BE TRIED

Finally, it must be remembered that developing such faith takes time; it is a process rather than an event. Moreover, to be strong unto salvation, faith must also be tried over time in the fires of adversity, whatever they may turn out to be for each of us. Thus we read these words of Moroni: "Faith is things which are hoped for and not seen; wherefore, dispute not because ye see not, for *ye receive no witness until after the trial of your faith*" (Ether 12:6; italics mine).

Chapter Six

TRUE AND COMPLETE REPENTANCE

Having considered in some measure having faith in Christ sufficient to "lay hold on every good thing," or to "come unto Christ," let us now move on to the issue of how to do it. The second principle of the gospel of Jesus Christ is repentance, which is repentance only if it is true and complete. Anything less is not repentance at all.

This was vividly illustrated for me the night a young woman came into my office and rather boastfully announced that she had paid some money to a boy at school "to have sex with me."

Without any hesitation she then went into some explicit and very distasteful details, during which narration I finally got her to stop for a moment. "Why are you telling me all this garbage?" I demanded, for I was feeling not only irritated but also violated.

"I thought that was what I was supposed to do!"

"You are, but only if you're repenting."

"That's what I'm doing, Bishop! Haven't you heard what I've been telling you?"

"Well, I've heard your words clearly enough, but I detect no remorse, no sorrow, no regret over what you did to yourself, let alone what you did to that young man."

"Why should I regret it? He's a big boy and knew what he was doing. Besides, I wanted to know what it was like, and now I do! And it cost me some good money, too! Bishop, I have to get to another meeting, so am I through repenting, or what?"

Needless to say, little was accomplished that night in helping her understand repentance, let alone the terrible and widespread damage her selfishness had wrought. Though she and her family moved out of my ward shortly thereafter, my hope is that time and experience, along with another bishop after she has learned a little humility, will accomplish what I couldn't. Nevertheless, her lack of understanding regarding true repentance, while somewhat extreme, is far too common.

THE LAW OF REPENTANCE

First in our discussion, it would be well to define repentance, though in truth it can have numerous definitions. A simple ceasing from some act can be termed a repentance, for instance, for in that sense one has reformed or changed. For repentance to lead to salvation, however, requires more than a mere change of behavior. It must involve faith in Christ; it must involve coming to God in deep humility and sorrow; it must involve a willingness to obey the promptings of the Holy Ghost; and it must involve an acknowledgment of the role of Christ's mortal servants in the process. Elder Bruce R. McConkie writes, "In the full gospel sense, repentance is far more than reformation. The mere fact of maintaining standards of normal decency will not, of itself, qualify men for a celestial inheritance.

"In the gospel sense repentance is the system, ordained of God, whereby fallen man may be saved. It is the plan of mercy that enables sinners to be reconciled to God. It is the way whereby all men, being sinners, can escape the grasp of justice and be encircled forever in the arms of mercy. It operates in and through and because of the infinite and eternal atonement; and if there had been no atonement, the doctrine of repentance would serve no purpose and save no souls. Salvation comes because of the atonement and is reserved for those who repent.

"Thus repentance follows faith. It is born of faith; it is the child of faith; and it operates only in the lives of those who have faith—faith in the Lord Jesus Christ. Faith comes first and repentance second; one is the first principle of the gospel, the other the second.

"Thus repentance is a gift of God conferred upon those who earn the right to receive it. It comes by obedience to law. In order to repent, men must 'do works meet for repentance.' (Acts 26:20.) It is with repentance as with all the gifts of God: they are bestowed upon worthy recipients and upon none others" (*A New Witness for the Articles of Faith,* p. 217).

Since all mankind have sinned and so died spiritually, repentance is the first of several gifts given by God to those who desire it through their faith, enabling them to regain cleanliness and therefore His presence. To Adam the Lord declared, "Inasmuch as thy children are conceived in sin, even so when they begin to grow up, sin conceiveth in their hearts, and they taste the bitter, that they may know to prize the good. And it is given unto them to know good from evil; wherefore they are agents unto themselves, and I have given unto you another law and commandment. Wherefore teach it unto your children, that *all men, everywhere, must repent,* or they can in nowise inherit the kingdom of God, for *no unclean thing can dwell there, or dwell in his presence*" (Moses 6:55–57; italics mine).

What is required to be truly repentant? To obtain forgiveness from God, a person must have " a conviction of guilt, a godly sorrow for sin, and a contrite [teachable] spirit. He must desire to be relieved of the burden of sin, have a fixed determination to forsake his evil ways, be willing to confess his sins, and forgive those who have trespassed against him; he must accept the cleansing power of the blood of Christ as such is offered through the waters of baptism and the conferral of the Holy Ghost. (*Articles of Faith,* pp. 109–116.)" (*Mormon Doctrine,* p. 630).

President Hinckley concludes, "If there be any here who have . . . sinned, there is repentance and there is forgiveness, provided there is 'godly sorrow.' (See 2 Cor. 7:10). All is not lost. Each of you has a bishop, who has been ordained and set apart under the authority of the holy priesthood and who, in the exercise of his office, is entitled to the inspiration of the Lord. He is a man of experience, he is a man of understanding, he is a man who carries in his heart a love for the youth of his ward. He is a servant of God who understands his obligation of confidentiality and who will help you with your problem. Do not be afraid to talk with him" ("Be Not Deceived," *Ensign*, November 1983, p. 45).

STIRRED UP UNTO REPENTANCE

Still, reaching the point where we are willing to truly repent remains a difficult proposition. Few of us seem to have the courage to simply stand forth and do it. Because the Lord understands this weakness in our natures, He has provided an interesting form of help. To Oliver Cowdery He said, "Behold, the world is ripening in iniquity; and it must needs be that the children of men are *stirred up unto repentance,* both the Gentiles and also the house of Israel" (D&C 18:6; italics mine).

To grow spiritually beyond having faith, most of us must be "stirred up" unto true and complete repentance. And how might we be "stirred up"? In any number of ways. Some of the Zoramites were stirred up unto repentance by their poverty (Alma 32:2–3). Zeezrom was stirred up unto repentance by the testimony of Alma and Amulek, followed by a feverish illness (Alma 12:1–8; 15:3–11). Enos was stirred up unto repentance by the words of his father and because he felt no joy or peace in his life (Enos 1:1–4). Alma was stirred up unto repentance by the words of an angel (Mosiah 27:19–20; Alma 36:6–10). There seem to be almost as many ways of being stirred up unto repentance as there are people.

Though usually painful or stressful, these "stirrings up" are given by our loving Father as a means of softening and opening our hearts to the promptings of the Holy Ghost. If we are receptive rather than filled with murmuring over our misfortunes, and if we exercise mighty prayer in faith as we seek understanding and guidance through our trials, then the Holy Ghost will begin to bear witness of our sins and iniquities so that we can know what we need to repent of and feel godly sorrow for it.

This, too, is according to divine design. Apparently, because of bad memory, faulty judgment, and so forth, we do not have the capacity to remember or see clearly our own sins and weaknesses. Therefore, the Lord has agreed to make them known to us by the power of the Holy Ghost, who as the Spirit of Truth communicates the truthfulness of all things directly to our spirits (Romans 8:16; 1 John 5:6; Moroni 10:5).

To William E. McLellin the Lord said, "You are clean, but not all; repent, therefore, of those things which are not pleasing in my sight, saith the Lord, *for the Lord will show them unto you*" (D&C 66:3; italics mine). To His apostles Christ taught, "It is expedient for you that I go away: for if I go not away, *the Comforter* will not come unto you; but if I depart, I will send him unto you. And when he is come, *he will reprove the world of sin*" (John 16:7–8; italics mine).

For us to obtain this oftentimes painful but significant revelation through the power of the Holy Ghost, we must part the heavens, with complete humility and sincerity, in mighty prayer and ask the Lord to reveal our sins to us. "And if men come unto me I will show unto them their weakness" (Ether 12:27).

So that we can obtain this revelation, we are also instructed to pray for the companionship of the Holy Ghost, not just once but as often as it takes until we feel his presence. Christ declares, "Ask the Father in my name, in faith believing that you shall receive, and you shall have the Holy

Ghost, which manifesteth all things which are expedient unto the children of men" (D&C 18:18).

Once this is done, the Lord will make known to us every sin for which we have never repented. We will then have an accurate picture of our position before the Lord, and we will no doubt begin to feel remorseful about how we have lived.

GODLY SORROW

Once we have been sufficiently stirred up unto repentance and are pleading constantly with the Lord for relief from our sins, then through the marvelous power of His Spirit our heretofore selfish guilt and remorse will be turned to godly sorrow. As Paul taught, "I rejoice, not that ye were made sorry, but that ye sorrowed to repentance; for ye were made sorry after a godly manner. . . . For godly sorrow worketh repentance to salvation . . . but the sorrow of the world worketh death" (JST 2 Corinthians 7:9–10).

President Ezra Taft Benson explains, "Godly sorrow is a gift of the Spirit. It is a deep realization that our actions have offended our Father and our God. It is the sharp and keen awareness that our behavior caused the Savior, He who knew no sin, even the greatest of all, to endure agony and suffering. Our sins caused Him to bleed at every pore. This very real mental and spiritual anguish is what the scriptures refer to as having a 'broken heart and a contrite spirit' (3 Nephi 9:20; Moroni 6:2; D&C 20:37; 59:8; Psalms 34:18; 51:17; Isaiah 57:15). Such a spirit is the absolute prerequisite for true repentance" (*Ensign,* October 1989, p. 4).

How is godly sorrow made manifest in our lives? As President Benson reminds us, through having a broken heart and a contrite spirit. To the Nephites the Lord explained that this was actually a sacrifice that we are all required to make if we desire to come unto Him (3 Nephi 9:20). In confirmation that this doctrine remains true for our day, the Lord declared through Joseph Smith, "Thou shalt offer a sacrifice unto the Lord thy God in righteousness, even that of a broken heart and a contrite spirit" (D&C 59:8).

Having a broken heart means that we have reached the point where we are so heartbroken over the fact that we have sinned, and therefore taken part in wounding Christ, that we are willing and anxious to repent and obtain forgiveness. And having a contrite spirit means that we are humble enough to be teachable in all things, either by those who preside over us or by the Lord through the witnessing of the Holy Ghost. It is these two qualities that indicate that we are truly repentant.

If our godly sorrow is manifested by a broken heart and a contrite spirit, then we will be absolutely willing to repent of whatsoever the Lord reveals to us concerning our sins, no matter how embarrassing or painful the process might be. This is true and complete repentance. If we do not completely repent once the Lord has revealed our sins to us, we will be in a position of knowing but doing nothing, and we will then be under condemnation. The great King Benjamin, in teaching his people the doctrines given him by an angel, said, "*Wo, wo unto him who knoweth that he rebelleth* against God! For salvation cometh to none such except it be through repentance and faith on the Lord Jesus Christ" (Mosiah 3:12; italics mine).

Alma adds, "And now, my brethren, I wish from the inmost part of my heart, yea, with great anxiety even unto pain, that ye would hearken unto my words, and cast off your sins, *and not procrastinate* the day of your repentance" (Alma 13:27; italics mine).

Therefore, to know must be to do. If our hearts are adequately broken through godly sorrow, and our spirits are sufficiently contrite, then through the power of the Holy Ghost we will be enabled to truly and completely repent of all our sins. This is the beginning of "laying hold on every good thing" and coming to Christ. President Joseph F. Smith stated, "God has not and will not suffer the gift of the Holy Ghost to be bestowed upon any man or woman, *except through compliance with the laws of God.* Therefore, no man can obtain a remission of sins; no man can obtain the gift of the Holy Ghost; no man can obtain the revelations of God; no man can obtain the Priesthood, and the rights, powers and privileges thereof; no man can become an heir of God and a joint heir with Jesus Christ, except through compliance with the requirements of heaven" (*Gospel Doctrine,* p. 49; italics mine).

BLESSINGS AND CURSINGS

Perhaps if we clearly understood the nature of sin, we would be more anxious to have it purged from our souls and left in the wake of our increasing spirituality. To do that, however, we must also understand the nature of blessings and curses, and the relationship between the two.

Brigham Young declared, "There is one principle I would like to have the Latter-day Saints perfectly understand—that is, of blessings and cursings" (*Journal of Discourses,* 18:262).

THE LAW OF BLESSINGS

With this principle in mind—that both blessings and cursings exist—we must remember that any blessing we obtain is based on our obedience to a specific law of God. As the Lord explained to Joseph Smith, "There is a law, irrevocably decreed in heaven before the foundations of this world, upon which all blessings are predicated—and when we obtain any blessing from God, it is by obedience to that law upon which it is predicated" (D&C 130:20–21).

For example, those who pay their tithing will not be burned at the Lord's coming (D&C 64:23), and those who keep the Word of Wisdom are promised that they will have "health in their navel and marrow to their bones; and shall find wisdom and great treasures of knowledge, even hidden treasures; and shall run and not be weary, and shall walk and not faint. And . . . the destroying angel shall pass by them, as the children of Israel, and not slay them" (D&C 89:18–21).

As these examples show, *all* God's laws have specific blessings attached to them, and these blessings come to those who obey. This is the law of blessings.

THE LAW OF CURSES

Frequently the Lord has spoken to His prophets concerning curses, which are judgments, or consequences, that follow disobedience (Moses 7:9, 16; Joshua 8:34; Proverbs 3:33; Jeremiah 11:3). Through Joseph Smith the Lord declared to us, "Hearken and hear, O ye my people, saith the Lord and your God, ye whom I delight to bless with the greatest of all blessings, ye that hear me; and *ye that hear me not will I curse,* that have professed my name, with the heaviest of all cursings" (D&C 41:1; italics mine).

Brigham Young taught, "We read that war, pestilence, plagues, famine, etc., will be visited upon the inhabitants of the earth; but if distress through the judgements of God comes upon this people, it will be because the majority have turned away from the Lord. Let the majority of the people turn away from the Holy Commandments which the Lord has delivered to us, and cease to hold the balance of power in the Church, and we may expect the judgements of God to come upon us; but while six-tenths or three-fourths of this people will keep the commandments of God, *the curse* and judgements of the Almighty will never come upon them, though we will have trials of various kinds, and the elements to contend with—natural and spiritual elements" (*Journal of Discourses,* 18:262; italics mine).

Besides blessings, God's laws also have curses attached to them, which arbitrarily fall upon those who choose to disobey. Mormon declares that "repentance is unto them that are under condemnation and *under the curse of a broken law*" (Moroni 8:24; italics mine), and Malachi proclaims, "Even from the days of your fathers ye are gone away from mine ordinances, and have not kept them. Return unto me, and I will return unto you, saith the Lord of hosts. But ye said, Wherein shall we return? Will a man rob God? Yet ye have robbed me. But ye say, Wherein have we robbed thee? In tithes and offerings. *Ye are cursed with a curse:* for ye have robbed me, even this whole nation. Bring ye all the tithes into the storehouse, that there may be meat in mine house, and prove me now herewith, saith the Lord of hosts, if I will not open you the windows of heaven, and pour you out a blessing, that there shall not be room enough to receive it. And I will rebuke the devourer for your sakes, and he shall not destroy the fruits of your ground; neither shall your vine cast her fruit before the time in the field, saith the Lord of hosts" (Malachi 3:7–11; italics mine).

According to Malachi, three things bring this particular curse upon a member of the house of Israel: (1) going away from, or not living, God's ordinances, which would include baptismal and temple covenants; (2) robbing God by not paying an honest tithe; and (3) not offering up a broken heart and a contrite spirit (3 Nephi 9:20; D&C 59:8). If we are guilty of *any one* of these three categories of sin (and it is interesting that all of them have to do with sincere temple worship), then we will be cursed by something called "the devourer," which according to Malachi has power to destabilize and even destroy our economic lives.

How is the curse removed? By returning to the Lord in all three areas—by repenting. Then the Lord (and *only* He) will rebuke the devourer, and the curse will be ended or removed so that God can pour out blessings upon us. Otherwise the curse must apparently run its course to a full end, whatever that means, and until then the blessings are withheld.

This is especially significant in light of the Lord's word to Joseph Smith concerning those who have been endowed in His holy temples: "If you build a house unto my name, and do not do the things that I say, I will not perform the oath which I make unto you, neither fulfil the promises which ye expect at my hands, saith the Lord. For *instead of blessings, ye, by your own works, bring cursings*, wrath, indignation, and judgments upon your own heads, by your follies, and by all your abominations, which you practice before me, saith the Lord" (D&C 124:47–48; italics mine).

Since both of these scriptures regarding curses pertain to

integrity in temple worship, the conclusion is inescapable that whenever the Lord's people have had access to the blessings of the priesthood as administered within the holy temples, and have not lived up to all they have covenanted to do therein, then with their sins they have brought upon themselves cursings rather than blessings, which curses bring upon them wrath, indignation, and the judgments of God.

Thus, curses are placed upon people by their own actions as a consequence of their sins and can be removed only by their enduring the curse until it has fully ended, or through the redemptive power of the Savior, which comes through total and sincere repentance (Galatians 3:13).

SINS ARE BONDS OF INIQUITY

Scripturally, the Lord also uses other terms to describe sins and their curses, or consequences, terms that are even more graphic. Alma the Elder says, "And now as ye have been *delivered by the power of God . . . from the bonds of iniquity* . . . even so I desire that ye should *stand fast in this liberty* wherewith ye have been made free" (Mosiah 23:13; italics mine). He also stated that his people were "*bound with the bands of iniquity*" (Mosiah 23:12; italics mine), which evokes images of rope-bound captives of the devil.

And Alma the Younger declared, following his complete repentance, "My soul hath been redeemed from the gall of bitterness and *bonds of iniquity*" (Mosiah 27:29; italics mine). Years later when speaking to his own son, he stated, "All men that are in a state of nature, or I would say, in a carnal state, are in the gall of bitterness and in the *bonds of iniquity*; they are without God in the world, and they have gone contrary to the nature of God; therefore, they are in a state contrary to the nature of happiness" (Alma 41:11; italics mine). Thus, the curse placed upon all sin is a loss of happiness and a removal—spiritual death or separation—from God.

Nor is this wickedness all ancient. Moroni writes of conditions in our day: "Yea, it shall come in a day when there shall be great pollutions upon the face of the earth; there shall be murders, and robbing, and lying, and deceivings, and whoredoms, and all manner of abominations; when there shall be many who will say, Do this, or do that, and it mattereth not, for the Lord will uphold such at the last day. But *wo unto such, for they are in the gall of bitterness and in the bonds of iniquity*" (Mormon 8:31; italics mine).

CURSES ARE YOKES OF BONDAGE

On the other hand, Paul, writing to those who had received a remission of their sins through Christ, encouraged them to "stand fast therefore in the liberty wherewith Christ hath made [them] free, and be not entangled again with *the yoke of bondage*" (Galatians 5:1; italics mine).

This is slightly different imagery, and it pertains to the consequences of sins—their attached curses—rather than to the sins themselves. This is what the Lord means when He tells us that "the yoke of bondage may begin to be broken off from the house of David" (D&C 109:63). Jeremiah declared that anciently the Lord had "broken thy yoke, and burst thy bands" from Israel, but they had turned again to their wickedness, bringing back upon themselves the yoke of bondage He had suffered to remove (Jeremiah 2:20).

And Nephi wrote that the ultimate design of the great and abominable church was to "*yoketh [the people] with a yoke of iron, and bringeth them down into captivity*" (1 Nephi 13:5;

italics mine). The captivity spoken of here is the captivity of the devil, "a yoke of iron," which, as Isaiah proclaims repeatedly, can be removed only by the Savior: "And it shall come to pass in that day, that his burden shall be taken away from off thy shoulder, *and his yoke* from off thy neck, and *the yoke shall be destroyed because of the anointing*" (Isaiah 10:27; italics mine). "Is not this the fast that I have chosen?" Christ asks, "to loose the bands of wickedness, to undo the heavy burdens, and to let the oppressed go free, and that ye *break every yoke?*" (Isaiah 58:6; italics mine). And Paul wrote, "Christ hath redeemed us from the curse of [a broken] law" (Galatians 3:13).

The bonds of iniquity refer to sins, and yokes of bondage refer to the curses thereof. Bonds of iniquity, when repented of, are removed or forgiven quickly by the Savior. But yokes of bondage, which are the curses or consequences of sin, can be removed before their time only through the laws and ordinances of the priesthood, that is, being born of the water and the Spirit, which brings a remission of sins.

THE PURPOSE OF THE PRIESTHOOD

This is the great and grand purpose of the priesthood, which is without beginning of days or end of years, for from eternity to all eternity it is designed to provide the sacred ordinances through which Christ redeems the souls of the repentant from their sins, and also the curses thereof, and restores them to the Father. As Mormon explained to his son Moroni, "Repentance is unto them that are under condemnation and under *the curse of a broken law.* And the *first fruits of repentance is baptism;* and baptism cometh by faith unto the fulfilling the commandments; and the *fulfilling the commandments bringeth remission of sins*" (Moroni 8:24–25; italics mine).

Therefore, "every one that hearkeneth to the voice of the Spirit cometh unto God, even the Father. And the Father teacheth him of the covenant [of the priesthood] which he has renewed and confirmed upon you, which is confirmed upon you for your sakes, and not your sakes only, but for the sake of the whole world. And the whole world lieth in sin, and groaneth under darkness and under *the bondage of sin.* And by this you may know they are under the bondage of sin, because they come not unto me. *For whoso cometh not unto me is under the bondage of sin*" (D&C 84:47–51; italics mine).

This means that the whole world, meaning the inhabitants of the earth and not the earth itself (*Words*, p. 25, footnote 9) is cursed, especially those who know the will of God and do not do it. Such people are bound by strong bonds of iniquity and groan under heavy yokes of bondage, insomuch that the devil has great power over them. Neither can the Lord stretch forth His hand to lift them up in their carnal state, for He is a God of law and must abide by all the precepts of the law that He has established. Therefore, those who are cursed are left unto themselves insofar as they are cursed, and they can prosper and progress only as their own mortal limitations allow.

FORGIVENESS NOT ALWAYS A REMISSION OF SINS

Let me state again what was written above. Bonds of iniquity, when repented of, are removed or forgiven quickly through the mercy of the Savior. But yokes of bondage, the curses that are the consequences of sin, will be removed by Christ before their time only through the laws and ordinances of the priesthood, that is, being born of both the water and the Spirit, including complete and total repentance, which is the only way a person may obtain a remission of sins. In other words, there can be a difference between being forgiven of a sin and obtaining a remission of sins.

If a person commits a particular sin and then feels bad enough about it to confess it in humility and ask forgiveness of the Lord, he or she is freely forgiven of that sin (or the bond of iniquity is removed). As the Psalmist exclaimed, "Thou, Lord, art good, and ready to forgive; and plenteous in mercy unto all them that call upon thee" (Psalm 86:5). John the Beloved wrote, "If we confess our sins, he is faithful and just to forgive us our sins" (1 John 1:9). Through Alma the Lord stated that as often as His people repented he would forgive them (Mosiah 26:30), and Moroni added that as often as we repent and seek forgiveness, with real intent, we are forgiven (Moroni 6:8). In our day the Lord has said, "I, the Lord, forgive sins unto those who confess their sins before me and ask forgiveness" (D&C 64:7).

Interestingly, this forgiveness seems to be granted even though the person may be committing other sins at the time. Thus, one who enjoys lusting may at the same time repent of and obtain forgiveness for stealing or lying. Or one who gossips may repent of and obtain forgiveness for immorality.

Unfortunately, such a person, while blessed with forgiveness for all the sins he chooses to repent of, nevertheless "persists in his own carnal nature" because he is intentionally going "on in the ways of sin and rebellion against God." Because he has not repented of *all* his sins, he "remaineth in his fallen state and the devil hath all power over him" (Mosiah 16:5). In other words, he remains "entangled . . . with *the yoke of bondage*" (Galatians 5:1; italics mine), which means that even though he has been forgiven of some things, he continues to suffer the effects of the curses his iniquitous ways have incurred. "Therefore, he is as though there was no redemption made, being an enemy to God; and also is the devil an enemy to God" (Mosiah 16:5). As Enoch declared, "Behold Satan hath come among the children of men, and tempteth them to worship him; and men have become carnal, sensual, and devilish, *and are shut out from the presence of God*" (Moses 6:49; italics mine).

That is why forgiveness of some or even most of our sins is not, never has been, and never will be sufficient to bring us to Christ. Even though we are blessed for having repented of some things, we are *not* granted peace and joy through a complete remission of our sins! We are *not* redeemed and brought back into the presence of God! That is why the Psalmist pleaded, "Look upon mine affliction and my pain; and forgive *all* my sins" (Psalm 25:18; italics mine). It is also why Samuel the Lamanite could declare, "If ye believe on his name ye will repent of *all* your sins, that thereby ye may have a remission of them through his merits" (Helaman 14:13; italics mine).

POCKETS FULL OF MARBLES

As a boy I played hundreds of games of marbles. I had my favorite "taw," a couple of "steelies," and some "clayies," and a huge "cat's eye" glass marble that wouldn't budge if hit by an opponent's "taw." These were my favorites, and I carried them hidden in my back pocket, separate from the other marbles I used in normal situations. I did this because I didn't want others to know I had them, I didn't want to risk giving them away or losing them, and I truly enjoyed owning them.

It seems that many of us treat sins in the same manner that I treated my marbles. Our repentance is sufficient to rid ourselves of most of our sins, those we like to consider the "big" ones. Yet because we enjoy them so, and because they are not what we think of as "big," and besides cannot possibly hurt anyone but ourselves, we take our half-dozen or so favorite "little" sins and place them, carefully hidden, in our back pockets or our handbags. There we keep them safe and secure, ready to be pulled out and indulged in at a moment's notice, with no one but ourselves the wiser, and no one but ourselves hurt by them.

Put this way, such a practice sounds silly. Yet what else can be said about the active priesthood holder who, whenever he thinks he is alone, exposes his mind to pornography or lustful fantasies or crude stories? Or the temple-attending sister who indulges in romantic or even lustful fantasizing because she is bored or her life is not all she had dreamed it would be? Or the practicing Latter-day Saint who lies or gossips because it is politically or socially correct? As a matter of fact, Nephi was speaking of such people when he said that "there shall also be many which shall say: Eat, drink, and be merry; nevertheless, fear God—he will justify in committing *a little sin;* yea, lie a little, take the advantage of one because of his words, dig a pit for thy neighbor; there is no harm in this; and do all these things, for tomorrow we die; and if it so be that we are guilty, God will beat us with a few stripes, and at last we shall be saved in the kingdom of God. Yea, and there shall be many which shall teach after this manner, false and vain and foolish doctrines, and shall be puffed up in their hearts, and shall seek deep to hide their counsels from the Lord; and their works shall be in the dark" (2 Nephi 28:8–9; italics mine).

Such people, no matter how "active" they are in the Church, are not repentant. Therefore, they cannot possibly be enjoying the blessings of the Spirit or of coming to Christ. They cannot possibly exercise mighty prayer unto the "laying hold on every good thing," including charity, or the pure love of Christ. In fact, because they ignore or disdain true spirituality and deny the spirit of prophecy and revelation that therefore must lie dormant within themselves, then like the Nephite members of the Church described below, they are left to muddle their way through mortality on their own strength.

As Mormon wrote, "It was because of the pride of their hearts, because of their exceeding riches, yea, it was because of their oppression to the poor, withholding their food from the hungry, withholding their clothing from the naked, and smiting their humble brethren upon the cheek, *making a mock of that which was sacred, denying the spirit of prophecy and of revelation,* murdering, plundering, lying, stealing, committing adultery, rising up in great contentions, and deserting away [from the Church]—And because of this their great wickedness, and their boastings in their own strength, *they were left in their own strength; therefore they did not prosper, but were afflicted and smitten*" (Helaman 4:12–13; italics mine).

When life finally got difficult enough, the Nephites began to examine themselves, to see where the fault of their troubles might lie, and they were startled to discover "that they had been a stiffnecked people, and that they had set at naught the commandments of God. And that they had altered and trampled under their feet the laws of [God]; . . . and they saw that their laws had become corrupted, and that they had become a wicked people, insomuch that they were wicked even like unto the Lamanites. *And because of their iniquity the church had begun to dwindle; and they began to disbelieve in the spirit of prophecy and in the spirit of revelation;* and the judgments of God did stare them in the face" (Helaman 4:21–23; italics mine). Abinadi wrote, "And then shall the wicked . . . have cause to howl, and weep, and wail, and gnash their teeth, and this because they would not hearken to the voice of the Lord; therefore the Lord redeemeth them not. For they are carnal and devilish, and the devil has power over them" (Mosiah 16:2–3).

Even such sins as the ones we think of as little and completely private, and maybe especially such sins as these, must be utterly given up and abandoned if we are to come to Christ, obtain charity, and behold His face. Otherwise we are left unto ourselves and our own miserable destination. The resurrected Christ proclaimed, "No unclean thing can enter into his kingdom; therefore nothing entereth into his rest save it be those who have washed their garments in my blood, because of their faith, and *the repentance of all their sins,* and their faithfulness unto the end" (3 Nephi 27:19; italics mine).

GIVING AWAY ALL OUR SINS

If we want to enjoy a complete remission of our sins by having our garments washed in the blood of Christ, we must give them *all* up! This can be accomplished only if we are willing, as was Lamanite king Lamoni's startled father, to "give away" not just part of, and not even most of, but *all* of our sins. After Aaron, one of the four missionary sons of King Mosiah, had expounded the fall of Adam and the atonement of Jesus Christ to Lamoni's father, this heretofore wicked but very powerful king, stunned by the knowledge of his own satanically inspired condition of filthiness and sin, pleaded of the missionary, "What shall I do that I may have this eternal life of which thou hast spoken? Yea, what shall I do that I may be born of God, having this wicked spirit rooted out of my breast, and receive his Spirit, that I may be filled with joy, that I may not be cast off at the last day? Behold, said he, I will give up all that I possess, yea, I will forsake my kingdom, that I may receive this great joy. But Aaron said unto him: If thou desirest this thing, if thou wilt bow down before God, yea, if thou wilt repent of all thy sins, and will bow down before God, and call on his name in faith, believing that ye shall receive, then shalt thou receive the hope which thou desirest. And it came to pass that when Aaron had said these words, the king did bow down before the Lord, upon his knees; yea, even he did prostrate himself upon the earth, and cried mightily, saying: O God, Aaron hath told me that there is a God; and if there is a God, and if thou art God, wilt thou make thyself known unto me, and *I will give away all my sins to know thee,* and that I may be raised from the dead, and be saved at the last day" (Alma 22:15–18; italics mine).

The humble, childlike attitude of this ancient Lamanite king brings to mind a doctrine which another great king and prophet, a Nephite whose name was Benjamin, was taught by a holy angel—that "the natural [spiritually dead] man is an enemy to God, and has been from the fall of Adam, and will be forever and ever, unless he yields to the enticings of the Holy Spirit; and putteth off the natural man and becometh a saint through the atonement of Christ the Lord, *and becometh as a child, submissive, meek, humble, patient, full of love, willing to submit to all things which the Lord seeth fit to inflict upon him, even as a child doth submit to his father*" (Mosiah 3:19; italics mine).

Another helpful aspect of being childlike was illustrated for my wife and me when our eldest daughter was about two. She loved music, but with her limited vocabulary she referred to it all—from the doorbell to radio to the Tabernacle Choir—as "the ding-dong." One morning we realized that she was jumping up and down with excitement at our front window, calling for us as she gazed out into our snowy yard. As we drew near we realized that she was seeing something that she wished to share with us. "See the ding-dong!" she repeated as she pointed with her tiny finger. "See the ding-dong! See Jesus! Jesus happy! See the ding-dong!"

Of course, we saw nothing but the snow, but neither of us doubted that, in her purity and innocence, she was "seeing" a great deal more. Through giving up all our sins so that we "becometh as a child," it is reasonable to expect that the resultant child-like purity will enable each of us to better "see" things as they really are—as they really should be.

Putting off the natural man or exhibiting a humble, submissive, childlike purity and willingness to give up all our sins, then, means giving up even our favorite "little" ones, those personally enjoyable sins (my own "favorite marbles") that we have somehow deluded ourselves into thinking don't really matter, or perhaps won't be noticed.

They do! And they are!

SEEKING CHARITY, OR THE PURE LOVE OF CHRIST

If we are willing to utterly forsake our sins, we will finally be in compliance with the gospel's first two principles of faith and repentance. It is at this point, filled with godly sorrow and earnestly endeavoring to become true followers of Christ so that we may receive a full remission of our sins, that praying for charity, or the pure love of Christ, must become our main focus. As Mormon explained, "If a man be meek and lowly in heart, and confesses by the power of the Holy Ghost that Jesus is the Christ, he must needs have charity; for if he have not charity he is nothing; wherefore he must needs have charity. And charity suffereth long, and is kind, and envieth not, and is not puffed up, seeketh not her own, is not easily provoked, thinketh no evil, and rejoiceth not in iniquity but rejoiceth in the truth, beareth all things, believeth all things, hopeth all things, endureth all things. Wherefore, my beloved brethren, if ye have not charity, ye are nothing, for charity never faileth. Wherefore, cleave unto charity, which is the greatest of all, for all things must fail—But charity is the pure love of Christ, and it endureth forever; and whoso is found possessed of it at the last day, it shall be well with him. Wherefore, my beloved brethren, *pray unto the Father with all the energy of heart, that ye may be filled with this love, which he hath bestowed upon all who are true followers of his Son, Jesus Christ*" (Moroni 7:44–48; italics mine).

COMING TO CHRIST

In this spiritual state, we will also begin to feel after these words of the great prophet Moroni, who wrote, "And now, I would commend you to *seek this Jesus* of whom the prophets and apostles have written, that the grace of God the Father, and also the Lord Jesus Christ, and the Holy Ghost, which beareth record of them, may be and abide in you forever" (Ether 12:41; italics mine). "Yea, *come unto Christ,* and be perfected in him, and deny yourselves of all ungodliness; and if ye shall deny yourselves of all ungodliness and love God with all your might, mind and strength, then is his grace sufficient for you, that by his grace ye may be perfect in Christ; and if by the grace of God ye are perfect in Christ, ye can in nowise deny the power of God. And again, if ye by the grace of God are perfect in Christ, and deny not his power, then are ye sanctified in Christ by the grace of God, through the shedding of the blood of Christ, which is in the covenant of the Father unto the remission of your sins, that ye become holy, without spot" (Moroni 10:32–33; italics mine).

That is why, with Nephi, we "talk of Christ, we rejoice in Christ, we preach of Christ, we prophesy of Christ, and we write according to our prophecies, that our children may know to what source they may look for a remission of their sins" (2 Nephi 25:26).

Chapter Seven

BEING BORN AGAIN

For those men and women who have offered up mighty prayer in faith and who are willing to give up all their sins through complete repentance, receiving a full remission of their sins is the next step in their spiritual rebirth, or return to the presence of the Father. For this to be experienced, however, a mighty change of heart is required; they must be born of both the water and the Spirit and so become new creatures.

This is confirmed by the Prophet Joseph, who said, "You might as well baptize a bag of sand as a man, if not done in view of the remission of sins and getting of the Holy Ghost. Baptism by water is but half a baptism, and is good for nothing without the other half—that is, the baptism of the Holy Ghost" (*Teachings*, p. 314).

Some wonder if this actually happens, but I testify that it

does, and that such a spiritual rebirth literally changes people for the better. It took little time for me to realize, as a bishop, that out of approximately one hundred families in my ward, a little more than twenty were headed by men or women who had been fully born of the Spirit. I was soon referring to them—without ever specifically naming them, of course—as my "core" families. These were men and women who could absolutely be counted on, under any and all conditions, to carry forward the work of Christ within my ward. Though none of them was perfect, I never had to worry about their worthiness or their support, either of myself or of the Church and its programs. They were always first to volunteer themselves and their families for service or welfare projects; they were continually reaching out in love and kindness to those around them, never waiting to be asked or assigned; they quickly and freely acknowledged mistakes, weaknesses, and even sins; I never heard one of them complain or malign anyone else in the ward; they refused to be part of cliques or to look down on those who were less fortunate; none of them ever murmured that a particular calling was "beneath" them or their abilities; none that I was ever aware of aspired to callings "greater" than what they held; they dealt positively and humbly with whatever adversity they might have been afflicted with, being patient and "faithful in tribulation" (D&C 58:2); and whenever I was near them or, at times, even thought of them, I felt the Lord's Spirit radiating from them or bearing witness to me of their righteousness before Him. How I leaned upon them during the years of my ministry! And how I also leaned upon the numerous other ward members whom the Spirit testified were moving steadily in that same divinely appointed direction—redemption through the baptism of fire and the Holy Ghost.

BAPTIZED BY WATER

According to Joseph Smith, the first step to being born again is being baptized by water, which is for the remission of sins unto all who have answered the ends of the law by repenting and coming unto Christ. Because we in the Church today baptize children who have arrived at the age of accountability as well as adults, let us consider each of these separately.

In these the last days of wickedness and sin before the Second Coming, God has made it clear that the age for baptism and reception of the gift of the Holy Ghost is while we are yet fairly young—eight years of age. To Joseph Smith the Lord commanded, "Inasmuch as parents have children in Zion, or in any of her stakes which are organized, that teach them not to understand the doctrine of repentance, faith in Christ the Son of the living God, and of baptism and the gift of the Holy Ghost by the laying on of the hands, when eight years old, the sin be upon the heads of the parents. For this shall be a law unto the inhabitants of Zion, or in any of her stakes which are organized. And their children shall be baptized for the remission of their sins when eight years old, and receive the laying on of the hands" (D&C 68:25–27).

As was pointed out earlier, inasmuch as little children are alive in Christ (Moroni 8:12) and cannot sin (meaning that they are not held accountable by God for the things they do) until they have reached the age of accountability (D&C 29:47), which is eight years of age (D&C 68:27), then simply by humbling themselves enough to be baptized, all that they have done wrong as they have learned accountability is remitted through baptism, and they stand clean before the Lord, fully worthy of receiving the gift of the Holy Ghost.

As an aside, I wonder if age eight was chosen because, while we are mature enough to be fully accountable, at age eight we have not yet submitted ourselves sufficiently to Satan's temptations to have died spiritually. Therefore, we are still sufficiently responsive both to our parents and to the Lord's guiding Spirit to allow these ordinances to be performed.

PARENTAL RESPONSIBILITY

In the verses quoted above, we as parents are commanded by the Lord to teach our children; He also gives us specific things to teach them and then explains why. The first step is to teach them, when they are young, that all misdeeds require repentance; that Jesus Christ knows, loves, and understands us individually, at least in part because He has already suffered for those very sins; that baptism is for the remission of our sins only if we sincerely believe in Christ; and that the laying on of the hands is to present another of Heavenly Father's gifts to us because of our repentance and obedience—the gift of the Holy Ghost. Thus, when these ordinances are performed at age eight, our children will understand and be prepared to take part in them and to use them in their lives. Moreover, they will have begun the process through which they can ultimately overcome spiritual death by being born again.

PARENTS SENT FORTH AS "MESSENGERS"

I am also impressed that in our day it is the parents who are divinely commissioned and "sent forth" by the Lord, as were angels in the days of Adam, to declare to our beloved children these first or most basic principles and ordinances of the gospel. He doesn't talk about Primary teachers, priesthood and Young Women advisors, or bishops. Only parents! Even Adam and Eve, once they had been properly instructed, were sent forth as divinely commissioned messengers when the Lord commanded them, "Teach these things freely unto your children" (Moses 6:58). It is obvious from these instructions that the Lord wants our children to be taught His gospel in our homes. He does not want our children's separation from Him to be permanent!

In the revelation quoted above, the Lord continues his instructions to parents, saying, "They shall also teach their children to pray, and to walk uprightly before the Lord. And the inhabitants of Zion shall also observe the Sabbath day to keep it holy. And the inhabitants of Zion also shall remember their labors, inasmuch as they are appointed to labor, in all faithfulness; for the idler shall be had in remembrance before the Lord. Now, I, the Lord, am not well pleased with the inhabitants of Zion, for there are idlers among them; and their children are also growing up in wickedness; they also seek not earnestly the riches of eternity, but their eyes are full of greediness. These things ought not to be, and must be done away from among them" (D&C 68:28–32).

By being commanded to teach our children "to pray, and to walk uprightly before the Lord," we are brought back not only to the example of Adam and Eve "call[ing] upon the name of the Lord" (Moses 5:4) but also to those basic laws of the modern gospel that, when ignored or done halfheartedly, open the door for Satan to begin his ugly work of destruction. Personal, companion, and family prayer;

personal, companion, and family scripture study; family home evening; regular temple attendance; weekly attendance at Church meetings—it is obvious that all these are essential to our fulfilling this commandment regarding teaching prayer and upright living to our children, especially in this complex, chaotic, wicked world where messages to do otherwise are constantly being pounded into them.

In addition, we are also to teach our children by our own personal examples—the Lord points out two areas of concern. First, He says that we should "observe the Sabbath day to keep it holy." It is imperative that our children see us making the Sabbath a holy day instead of a holiday or a day of play and recreation—or simply another day of labor at our job or in the yard. Only in that way can they learn to honor, respect, and therefore sincerely worship and accept the Lord Jesus Christ, who, they will eventually come to understand, is their only source of true happiness and joy. Second, we are commanded to "remember [our] labors, inasmuch as [we] are appointed to labor, in all faithfulness; for the idler shall be had in remembrance before the Lord." As I see it, the labors of which the Lord is speaking, in which we are to set an example of faithfulness before our children, are not so much our daily employment but rather our Church callings and assignments, our appointments—home and visiting teaching, Church callings and attendance, and regular temple worship being of primary importance. Such an example is the surest way of teaching our children to look outward rather than inward, to look up rather than down, to joyfully serve others instead of forever indulging themselves—which service, in fact, is serving the Lord their God (see Mosiah 2:17).

Interestingly, the Lord elaborates on this issue by pointing out His displeasure with Church members who will not accept—or who will accept but then do not fulfill—either in whole or in part, their callings, assignments, appointments, and responsibilities. Calling them "idlers," Christ then points out the significant impact of such unrighteous, lazy behavior on their posterity: "Their children are also growing up in wickedness; they also seek not earnestly the riches of eternity, but their eyes are full of greediness." They are selfish, worldly children, He is saying, who have no idea they are in the midst of an eternal, spiritual life with God that they are in grave danger of losing forever. In thundering finality, the Lord then commands, "These things ought not to be, and must be done away from among them!"

But if our children are not so instructed? I find it more than troubling that God takes this mission of parents teaching their children righteousness so seriously that He warns that if we do not do so, whether intentionally or unintentionally, it is we parents who will be under condemnation—"the sin be upon the heads of the parents." That ought to give any of us significant pause!

A FORM OF ABUSE

Consider the following from Ph.Ds R. Wayne and Leslee S. Boss:

> In an effort to help their children become responsible adults, parents sometimes make decisions based on what their children want to do rather than what the children ought to do. They argue that the best way to keep their children active in the Church is to never insist that they do anything they don't want to do. After all, they don't

want to do anything to offend their children. Operationally, that means if the children don't want to attend church on Sunday, they simply don't have to do so.

An attitude such as this is an invitation to disaster. For parents to allow their children to determine how the family is to be run makes about as much sense as allowing passengers on an airplane to decide how the plane should be flown. Neither group knows enough to make those kinds of decisions. Two year olds are not in a position to identify appropriate behavior for sacrament meeting. Teenagers also don't know enough about nutrition to insure that they get the proper vitamins and minerals. Remember, the Lord commanded parents to bring up their children in light and truth, not the other way around. Parents should never give their children control of their family. A bishop described what happened to a family he knew who did not understand this important concept:

"Recently a man in my ward came to me for advice. He and his wife had separated, and their only child, a 14-year-old boy, was in jail. He asked, 'What went wrong in our family? How did this happen?'

"I responded, 'I don't know. But somewhere along the way, the power in your family shifted from the parents to the child.'"

Parents who abdicate their parental responsibilities are asking for trouble. A frustrated stepmother, who had been married less than six weeks, expressed her concerns about what was taking place in her family:

"Rick will not establish any limits or rules for Julie (age 13), because he is afraid that she will get mad at him, stop going to church, and maybe even go live with her mother [full-time]. So he lets her get away with murder.

Julie determines what our family will do, how we function, and how we, as parents, conduct our lives. We don't have family prayer. We don't read the scriptures. We don't hold Family Home Evening. Why? Because Julie doesn't want to!"

That happened five years ago. Today Julie has left the Church and is living with her boyfriend.

Parents need to understand this common parenting myth: "My child should always like and love me." The logic of this myth is as follows:

"Emerging from the economic prosperity of the late nineteen fifties and the 'If it feels good, do it' philosophy of the nineteen sixties, came a pervasive societal belief that parents were placed on earth to make sure their kids were always happy and always have what they want. As a result of this societal conditioning, many parents are now very afraid of damaging their children by upsetting them. As a result, they really do damage them by 'stealing' any opportunities for the child to learn about real world struggles and consequences. Please don't steal from your child.

"Wise parents know that *not* getting one's way from time to time is actually good practice for life! Children who are always protected from being upset become always-upset adults.

"Deep down in their souls, kids are really most happy when they have to earn what they want and are not allowed to run the house. Nevertheless, if a child is anywhere close to being normal, he or she will occasionally experiment with 'You hate me' to see if a parent crumbles with guilt. If the parent stands firm in a loving way, the child learns a healthy lesson about life: 'You don't always get what you want—and that's just the way it is. Nothing personal.' In contrast, if the parent gives in, the child learns something very unhealthy: 'When you don't get what you want, it's unfair and mean. But if you cry, whine or argue, people might just give in'" (Jim and Charles Fay, *Love and Logic Magic: When Kids Leave You Speechless* [Golden, Colo.: Love and Logic Press, 2000], p. 194).

Parental responsibility is the Lord's system. The Lord has ordained it. He has placed within children a natural affection and trust for their parents, which means that parents have a greater capacity to teach and shape minds than anyone else. To abuse that trust is to forfeit eternal blessings. . . .

Parents sometimes allow their children to bully them. As a result, they permit their kids to do anything they want in order to get them to stay active in the Church. They do this because they are afraid of their children. They reason that, "If I insist that we read the scriptures, or go to church, they won't love me, . . . they won't go to church, they won't live the gospel, they won't keep the commandments, . . . or they will run away from home." A stake president reminded us of the consequences of such behavior:

"Letting your child bully you is a form of child abuse. Solomon reminds us to 'Train up a child in the way he should go' (Proverbs 22:6). To fail to educate a child spiritually is to abuse the child. To fail to teach integrity, faith and a love for truth is to warp the spirit of the child. Jesus said, 'But whoso shall offend one of these little ones which believe in me, it were better for him that a millstone were hanged around his neck, and that he were drowned in the depths of the sea' (Matthew 18:6). Parents who fail to teach their children gospel truths abuse the sacred trust given them by God. They also abuse their children by not providing them with the doctrinal foundation they need to withstand the influence of Satan. When parents teach children, either by precept or example, to ridicule truth or prophetic testimony, they place a millstone around [not only their own but] their child's neck that will drag them down to hell. There are eternal implications for this kind of a mistake.

"The world never judges people on divine criteria. The world judges people by wealth, prominence, position, business accomplishment. The Lord judges people on character. His criteria are faith, obedience, and humility, and the characteristics of Godliness. That means that the great parents are the ones who have the courage to pull the handcart across the plains, and they produce a legacy out of which apostles and prophets grow. The great parents are the ones who refuse to give up when hit with overwhelming obstacles. They put their faith in God. The great parents are the ones who recognize that mortality is a test. The question is, 'How do you handle obstacles?' [And the answer?] By magnifying their calling as parents and fulfilling the Lord's admonition to 'teach their children to pray, and to walk uprightly before the Lord.'" ("Single Parents," in an untitled, unpaginated manuscript in process of publication).

A WARNING FROM OUR PROPHET

In all of our teaching and training of our children, however, we must exercise great care lest we sin against them by being too overbearing and dictatorial. President Gordon B. Hinckley declares, "There is need for discipline with families. But discipline with severity, discipline with cruelty, inevitably leads not to correction, but rather to resentment and bitterness. It cures nothing and only aggravates the problem. It is self-defeating. The Lord, in setting forth the spirit of governance in his church has also set forth the spirit of governance in the home in these great words of revelation: 'No power or influence can or ought to be maintained, . . . only by persuasion, by long-suffering, by gentleness and meekness, and by love unfeigned; . . . reproving betimes with sharpness, when moved upon by the Holy Ghost; and then showing forth afterwards an increase of love toward him whom thou hast reproved, lest he esteem thee to be his enemy; that he may know that thy faithfulness is stronger than the cords of death' (D&C 121:41, 43–44).

"Behold your little ones and teach them. I need not remind you that your example will do more than anything else in impressing upon their minds a pattern of life. It is always interesting to meet the children of old friends and to find in another generation the ways of their fathers and mothers. . . .

"How much more beautiful would be the world and the society in which we live if every father looked upon his children as the most precious of his assets, if he led them by the power of his example in kindness and love, and if in times of stress he blessed them by the authority of the holy priesthood; and if every mother regarded her children as the jewels of her life, as gifts from the God of heaven who is their Eternal Father, and brought them up with true affection in the wisdom and admonition of the Lord" ("Behold Your Little Ones," *Ensign,* November 1978, pp. 19, 20).

And for both parents President Hinckley continues: "How beautiful is that home where lives a man of godly manner, who loves those for whose nurture he is responsible, who stands before them as an example of integrity and goodness, who teaches industry and loyalty, not spoiling his children by indulging their every wish, but rather setting before them a pattern of work and service which will underpin their lives forever. How fortunate is the man whose wife radiates a spirit of love, of compassion, of order, of quiet beneficence, whose children show appreciation one for another, who honor and respect their parents, who counsel with them and take counsel from them. Such home life is within the reach of all who have cultivated in their hearts a resolution to do that which will please their Father in Heaven ("To Please Our Heavenly Father," *Ensign,* May 1985, p. 50).

"Never forget that these little ones are the sons and daughters of God and that yours is a custodial relationship to them, that He was a parent before you were parents and that He has not relinquished His parental rights or interest in these His little ones. Now, love them, take care of them. Fathers, control your tempers, now and in all the years to come. Mothers, control your voices, keep them down. Rear your children in love, in the nurture and admonition of the Lord. Take care of your little ones, welcome them into your homes, and nurture and love them with all of your hearts. They may do, in the years that come, some things you would not want them to do, but be patient, be patient. You have not failed as long as you have tried. Never forget that" (Salt Lake University Third Stake Conference, November 3, 1996).

BAPTISM FOR ADULTS

For adults, who because of mature accountability are able to repent, which "repentance is unto them that are under condemnation and under the curse of a broken law" (Moroni 8:24), being baptized for a remission of sins is slightly more arduous. The Lord has declared "by way of commandment to the church concerning the manner of baptism—All those who humble themselves before God, and desire to be baptized, and come forth with broken hearts and contrite spirits, and witness before the church that they have truly repented of all their sins, and are willing to take upon them the name of Jesus Christ, having a determination to serve him to the end, and truly manifest by their works that they have received of the Spirit of Christ unto the remission of their sins, shall be received by baptism into his church" (D&C 20:37). Put another way, baptismal candidates must exercise faith in Christ sufficient to repent and desire baptism, which "cometh by faith unto the fulfilling the commandments; and the fulfilling the commandments bringeth remission of sins" (Moroni 8:25) through receiving "of the Spirit of Christ unto the remission of their sins" (D&C 20:37). These, then, are worthy to have the gift of the Holy Ghost confirmed upon them by the laying on of hands. As Mormon writes, "The remission of sins bringeth meekness, and lowliness of heart; and because of meekness and lowliness of heart cometh the visitation of the Holy Ghost" (Moroni 8:26).

Joseph Smith taught, "Baptism is a sign to God, to angels, and to heaven that we do the will of God, and there is no other way beneath the heavens whereby God hath ordained for man to come to Him to be saved, and enter into the Kingdom of God, except faith in Jesus Christ, repentance, and baptism for the remission of sins, and any other course is in vain; then you have the promise of the gift of the Holy Ghost" (*Teachings,* p. 198).

THE GIFT OF THE HOLY GHOST

All who are official members of the Church have been baptized in water and have received the gift of the Holy Ghost by the laying on of hands; they have thus taken the first step of this spiritual rebirthing process. Nevertheless, it should be clearly understood that receiving the gift of the Holy Ghost is usually only the promise of the second step, being born of the Spirit, and rarely the actual event. That is because most of us have been baptized when we are still mostly innocent and immature.

Elder Bruce R. McConkie writes, "Mere compliance with the formality of the ordinance of baptism does not mean that a person has been born again. No one can be born again without baptism, but the immersion in water and the laying on of hands to confer the Holy Ghost do not of themselves guarantee that a person has been or will be born again. The new birth takes place only for those who actually enjoy the gift or companionship of the Holy Ghost, only for those who are fully converted, who have given themselves without restraint to the Lord. Thus Alma addressed himself to his 'brethren of the church,' and pointedly asked them if they had 'spiritually been born of God,' received the Lord's image in their countenances, and had the 'mighty change' in their hearts which always attends the birth of the Spirit. (Alma 5:14–31.)" (*Mormon Doctrine,* p. 101).

A SPIRITUAL REBIRTH

Being born of the Spirit—quickened in the inner man, redeemed of God, or changed from a carnal state to a state of righteousness, undergoing a mighty change of heart—means that, after we have lost the innocence we had as children, we gain a mature understanding of ourselves, our sins and the pain they have brought ourselves and others, our weakness and tendency to sin, and our anguish and sorrow that we have willingly submitted to Satan rather than God. Only this mature understanding, granted through harsh experience stirring us up unto repentance, as well as the guidance of the Holy Ghost coupled with determined desire to put aside the world through repentance so that we can be restored through Christ to our original purity and so return to the presence of God—only these can bring to pass the supernal event of complete spiritual rebirth that Enoch says was experienced by Adam.

Yet experience it we must—at least if we want, as did Adam and Eve, to return to the presence of our Heavenly Father! As the prophet Lehi explained, "Behold, [Christ] offereth himself a sacrifice for sin, to answer the ends of the law, unto all those who have a broken heart and a contrite spirit; and unto none else can the ends of the law be answered" (2 Nephi 2:7). In elaboration he taught that all men and women are lost and fallen and will remain so forever, unless and until they rely upon the redeeming power of Jesus Christ to allow them spiritual rebirth (1 Nephi 10:4–6; 2 Nephi 2:21).

To further emphasize this critical need for a spiritual rebirth that follows baptism and confirmation, as well as its universal necessity for both men and women, the Lord declared to a humbly repentant Alma the Younger, "Marvel not that *all mankind, yea, men and women, all nations, kindreds, tongues and people, must be born again; yea, born of God, changed from their carnal and fallen state, to a state of righteousness, being redeemed of God, becoming his sons and daughters; and thus they become new creatures;* and unless they do this, they can in nowise inherit the kingdom of God" (Mosiah:27:25–26; italics mine).

Later Alma added, "Ye must repent, and be born again; for the Spirit saith *if ye are not born again ye cannot inherit the kingdom of heaven*" (Alma 7:14; italics mine).

The Prophet Joseph said, "Except a man be born again, he cannot see the kingdom of God. This eternal truth settles the question of all men's religion. A man may be saved, after the judgment, in the terrestrial kingdom, or in the telestial kingdom, but he can never see the celestial kingdom of God, without being born of water and the Spirit" (*Teachings*, p. 12).

In emphasis of this doctrine, which declares it to be the entire point of the gospel, the Savior said to Joseph Smith, "This is my gospel—repentance and baptism by water, and *then cometh the baptism of fire and the Holy Ghost,* even the Comforter, which showeth all things, and teacheth the peaceable things of the kingdom" (D&C 39:6; italics mine).

THE TWO BAPTISMS MAY OCCUR AT THE SAME TIME

But what happens if a person, no matter his age, presents himself for baptism having been fully converted and having fulfilled all the requirements necessary to be born again? The answer is that such a person, manifesting godly sorrow for his sins through a broken heart and a contrite spirit, and expressing a complete willingness to obey God's commandments and serve Him to the end, is visited immediately with fire and the Holy Ghost unto a complete remission of his sins. Therefore, when he receives the Holy Ghost through the laying on of hands, he is also born again and made free of the curses of his sins. Thus, Elder Bruce R. McConkie writes, "When converted persons are baptized for the remission of sins, the sacred baptismal ordinance is designed to free them from past and future sins. Those sins committed after baptism are forgiven whenever members of the Church, by full compliance with the law of forgiveness, again get themselves in the same state of righteousness and purity previously attained in connection with their baptisms" (*Mormon Doctrine,* p. 296).

While this is not often considered, all of the adult Saints in Kirtland were converts. It stands to reason that most of them had manifested godly sorrow for their sins through a broken heart and a contrite spirit. Expressing a complete willingness to obey God's commandments and serve Him to the end, they were visited with fire and the Holy Ghost unto a complete remission of their sins. Therefore, when they received the Holy Ghost through the laying on of hands, they were also born again and made ready to come unto Christ as their history reveals that they did.

FEELINGS AS ONE APPROACHES BEING BORN OF THE SPIRIT

For those of us who desire a closer walk with God with such intensity that we seek this new birth with all the energy of our souls, the scriptures inform us that we will feel:

- A Godly sorrow for all sin (2 Corinthians 7:10).
- An unending desire to repent and be made clean (Alma 29:4).
- An understanding that this cleanliness cannot be self-induced (1 Corinthians 15:3; Alma 5:27).

- A fixed determination to purify ourselves until such cleanliness has been granted (Alma 5:21; D&C 121:45).
- A profound willingness to live so that such pain and sorrow as is being experienced will never again come upon us (Acts 17:30; 2 Nephi 9:23; 3 Nephi 11:32; D&C 133:16).
- An understanding that all sins, even favorite little ones, are a source of great pain to the Savior (Matthew 5:19; Alma 45:16).
- A recognition that it was we ourselves, by our own bad choices, who drove the nails that day on Golgotha (Hebrews 6:6).
- A willingness to apologize to Christ for choosing to wound Him (Mosiah 26:29–30).
- An unending anxiety to plead that Christ, through the spilling of His precious blood, will remove the burden of pain from us, allowing us to be finally and forever free of our guilt (Mosiah 27:24–26; Alma 36:13–21; Alma 38:8).
- A fervent anxiousness to obtain charity, Christ's pure and supernal love (Moroni 7:48).
- A burning desire to sing the song of redeeming love (Alma 5:26).

If we have not yet felt all of these, but if we will nevertheless be willing to persist in this quest for peace and a knowledge that we have been made clean every whit through the blood of Christ, and do so for as many days, weeks, months, or years as the Lord chooses to require of us, then the promise is that He will finally grant our petitions.

THE BAPTISM OF FIRE

Once we truly have a God-given broken heart and a contrite spirit because of our own past life and have given our entire future without restraint to the Lord, then in the Lord's time we will experience the second half of being born again—the baptism of fire. The Lord says, "Yea, repent and be baptized, every one of you, for a remission of your sins; yea, be baptized even by water, *and then cometh the baptism of fire and of the Holy Ghost*" (D&C 33:11; italics mine). "And . . . thou shalt declare repentance and faith on the Savior, and remission of sins by baptism, and by fire, yea, even the Holy Ghost" (D&C 19:31).

This experience is also called the mighty change (Alma 5:14), being born of the Spirit (Mosiah 27:24), becoming newborn babes in Christ (1 Peter 2:2), being spiritually begotten of Christ (Mosiah 5:7, Ether 3:14), and being born of God and overcoming the world (1 John 5:4).

A WITNESS FROM THE FATHER

After John the Baptist had baptized Jesus, he saw that "the heavens were opened, and the Holy Ghost descended upon [Jesus] in the form of a dove, and sat upon him, and there came a voice out of heaven saying: This is my beloved Son" (D&C 93:15). The Father bore this same testimony to Peter, James, and John on the Mount of Transfiguration (Matthew 17:5) and to Joseph Smith in the Sacred Grove (Joseph Smith–History 1:17).

For most of us, however, the Father bears testimony of the Son in a different way. The resurrected Christ said to the Nephites that "whoso believeth in me believeth in the Father also; and unto him will the Father bear record of me, for *he will visit him with fire and with the Holy Ghost. And thus will the Father bear record of me*" (3 Nephi 11:35–36; italics mine).

Therefore, all who are born of the Spirit are being witnessed to by the Father, who is bearing record of the divinity of the life and atonement of His Beloved Son, the Lord Jesus Christ.

BEING BORN AGAIN BRINGS A COMPLETE REMISSION OF SINS

Nephi taught, "Wherefore, do the things which I have told you I have seen that your Lord and your Redeemer should do; for, for this cause have they been shown unto me, that ye might know the gate by which ye should enter. For the gate by which ye should enter is repentance and baptism by water; and *then cometh a remission of your sins by fire and by the Holy Ghost*" (2 Nephi 31:17; italics mine).

While my dictionary's first definition of *remission* is a forgiveness or pardon, as of sins or crimes, the second definition is a cancellation or release from a debt. This is interesting in light of the fact that the Lord has referred to His atonement as the act of buying us (Isaiah 43:24; 52:3; 1 Corinthians 6:20). In other words, he has paid our debt. Peter declared, "Ye were not redeemed with corruptible things, as silver and gold. . . . But with the precious blood of Christ, as of a lamb without blemish and without spot" (1 Peter 1:18–19).

Acknowledging the purchase and therefore ownership by our Lord Jesus Christ, and willingly accepting all the conditions of that ownership, allows us to repent of all our sins and thus obtain their remission through the baptism of fire and the Holy Ghost (see 2 Nephi 31:17), which means we will be miraculously relieved of *all* the burden of our indebtedness to Christ. All guilt will be swept away in an incredibly sweet experience with the Holy Ghost (Mosiah 27:24–26; Alma 36:12–21). We will then be born of the Spirit (John 3:7). We will have experienced the baptism of fire (Matthew 3:11; 2 Nephi 31:13–14). We will have experienced the mighty change (Mosiah 5:2; Alma 5:12–14). Finally, we will then be privileged to enjoy the companionship of the Holy Ghost more and more frequently until this companionship becomes constant in our lives (D&C 121:46).

THE PURE LOVE OF CHRIST

As our sins are completely remitted through the precious blood of Christ, we will experience, for hours or occasionally even days, an amazing and overwhelming sense of love. This is a divine manifestation of charity, or the pure love of Christ, and it is the Father's witness to us, through the power of the Holy Ghost, not only that we are loved of God but also that this love has been made manifest in our personal lives through the atonement of Christ. Thus we are redeemed of God and made clean.

PEACE IN A TROUBLED WORLD

Once we have felt the pure love of Christ, even if only for a short time, we begin to experience a deep and abiding sense of inner peace. This spiritual peace comes to us no matter what is transpiring in the world around us. Called "the peace of God, which passeth all understanding" (Philippians 4:7), this peace is a gift of God to the obedient (Psalm 37:37). "Great peace have they which love the law, and nothing shall offend them" (Psalm 119:165; Isaiah 26:3).

As long as men and women continue to press forward in righteousness, both praying and repenting always as they seek the face of Christ, this peace will continue "as a river, and [their] righteousness as the waves of the sea," though "there is no peace, saith the Lord, unto the wicked" (Isaiah 48:18, 22; 57:21).

Should their spirituality start to decline and their enthusiasm for coming unto Christ begin to wane, however, it would be well to remember that to "be carnally minded is death; but to be spiritually minded is life and peace" (Romans 8:6). In other words, their precious inner peace will begin to dissipate. Why? Because Christ's gospel, which such people are beginning to neglect in favor of the things of the world, is a "gospel of peace" (Romans 10:15; Ephesians 6:15), and only in His gospel can peace be found. "For the kingdom of God is not meat and drink; but righteousness, and peace, and joy in the Holy Ghost. For he that in these things serveth Christ is acceptable to God, and approved of men. Let us therefore follow after the things which make for peace" (Romans 14:17–19). "God is not the author of confusion, but of peace" (1 Corinthians 14:33).

No matter how traumatic, chaotic, and troubled the world around us grows, no matter how much turbulence and tribulation afflicts us in our own lives, those who continue seeking after the face of Christ with all diligence have this divine promise: "Peace I leave with you, my peace I give unto you: not as the world giveth, give I unto you. Let not your heart be troubled, neither let it be afraid" (John 14:27; 16:33).

OWNED BY CHRIST

Those who have been "bought" by Christ through the offering of His precious blood are now "owned" by Him. Therefore, we who are "owned" are under strict obligation to do all that He says, that is, to keep all His commandments. Each time we keep His commandments, however, He rewards, or blesses, us commensurate with what we have done, keeping the ledger balanced always in His favor. Thus King Benjamin taught that "he doth require that ye should do as he hath commanded you; for which if ye do, he doth immediately bless you; and therefore he hath paid you. And ye are still indebted unto him, and are, and will be, forever and ever" (Mosiah 2:24).

"Perhaps," Elder Neal A. Maxwell writes, "our . . . mistake is to think that we own ourselves. . . . Of course, we have our agency and an inner sovereignty, but disciples are to sacrifice themselves to do Jesus' bidding with enough faith in God . . . to say, in effect, 'Thy [will] be done'" (*The Promise of Discipleship,* p. 87–88).

Each time we do not keep His commandments, each time we sin, we incur a debt that, since we are not our own, we cannot pay. Only our owner, the Lord Jesus Christ, can pay this debt for us. And He will, but only on condition of repentance. Otherwise, because of our unsatisfied debt, we must be delivered over for judgment, which will be far worse than we can imagine. As Jesus said, "Therefore I command you to repent—repent, lest I smite you by the rod of my mouth, and by my wrath, and by my anger, and your sufferings be sore—how sore you know not, how exquisite you know not, yea, how hard to bear you know not. For behold, I, God, have suffered these things for all, that they might not suffer if they would repent; but if they would not repent they must suffer even as I; which suffering caused myself, even God, the greatest of all, to tremble because of pain, and to bleed at every pore, and to suffer both body and spirit—and would that I might not drink the bitter cup, and shrink—nevertheless, glory be to the Father, and I partook and finished my preparations unto the children of men" (D&C 19:15–19).

A COMPLETE AND MIGHTY CHANGE

But returning to our former wickedness does not need to happen. In fact, God gives divine assistance through the Holy Spirit so that it won't. Thus, those who have paid the price to obtain the baptism of fire and remission of sins will also experience a fundamental change of heart, which leaves them disinclined toward their former wicked ways. In scripture this is called *the mighty change* (see Mosiah 5:2; Alma 5:14).

To illustrate the magnitude of this change, consider the words of Samuel the Lamanite: "Ye do know of yourselves, for ye have witnessed it, that as many of [the Lamanites] as are brought to the knowledge of the truth, and to know of the wicked and abominable traditions of their fathers, and are led to believe the holy scriptures, yea, the prophecies of the holy prophets, which are written, which leadeth them to faith on the Lord, and unto repentance, *which faith and repentance bringeth a change of heart unto them*" (Helaman 15:7; italics mine).

If the Lamanites could make such a change, then surely the Holy Ghost can also bring about a mighty change within us. President Benson has said, "When you choose to follow

Christ, you choose to be changed. 'No man,' said President David O. McKay, 'can sincerely resolve to apply to his daily life the teachings of Jesus of Nazareth without sensing a change in his own nature. The phrase *born again* has a deeper significance than many people attach to it. This *changed feeling* may be indescribable, *but it is real.*' . . . Our Lord told Nicodemus that 'except a man be born again, he cannot see the kingdom of God' (John 3:3). Of these words President Spencer W. Kimball said, 'This is the simple total answer to the weightiest of all questions. . . . To gain eternal life there must be a rebirth, a transformation.' . . . Christ called for an entire revolution of Nicodemus's 'inner man.' His manner of thinking, feeling and acting with reference to spiritual things would have to undergo a fundamental and permanent change" (*The Teachings of Ezra Taft Benson,* pp. 77–78).

Such people have "no more disposition to do evil, but to do good continually" (Mosiah 5:2). "They, after being sanctified by the Holy Ghost, having their garments made white, being pure and spotless before God, [can]not look upon sin save it [is] with abhorrence" (Alma 13:12). And "their hearts [have] been changed; that they [have] no more desire to do evil" (Alma 19:33).

How is such a change brought to pass? Only through the power of God, who sheds forth his Spirit upon the completely repentant through the blessings of the Atonement. Thus the resurrected Christ could declare to the Nephites, "The Father having raised me up unto you first, *and sent me to bless you in turning away every one of you from his iniquities;* and this because ye are the children of the covenant" (3 Nephi 20:26; italics mine).

Throughout the entire history of Adam's family, righteous men and women have borne testimony to the truthfulness of the Savior's words. Through His matchless power, they have been literally turned from their sins and so have become new creatures. As the scripture says concerning King Benjamin's people, "They all cried with one voice, saying: Yea, we believe all the words which thou hast spoken unto us; and also, we know of their surety and truth, because of *the Spirit of the Lord Omnipotent, which has wrought a mighty change in us, or in our hearts*" (Mosiah 5:2; italics mine). And John the Beloved adds, "Whosoever is born of God doth not continue in sin; for the spirit of God remaineth in him; and *he cannot continue to sin,* because he is born of God, having received that holy Spirit of promise" (JST 1 John 3:9; italics mine).

The issue, as always, comes back to us. As Alma frankly asked, "Have ye spiritually been born of God? Have ye received his image in your countenances? Have ye experienced this mighty change in your hearts?" (Alma 5:14).

President Benson pleads with all of us: "May we be convinced that Jesus is the Christ, choose to follow Him, be changed for Him, captained by Him, consumed in Him, and born again" (*The Teachings of Ezra Taft Benson,* p. 13).

CLEARING UP A MISUNDERSTANDING

It is assumed by many that phrases such as "no more disposition to do evil, but to do good continually" (Mosiah 5:2) and "could not look upon sin save it were with abhorrence" (Alma 13:12) mean that those who are born again must thereafter remain perfect and without sin forever afterward. This is not so. When one has no more disposition to do evil, it means simply that he or she has no more *desire* to sin. The same is true when sin has become abhorrent. Because their hearts have undergone a mighty change through the power of God, and because they fully understand the suffering of Jesus Christ in their behalf, those who have been born of the water and of the Spirit do their best to remain steadfast in avoiding intentional sin.

However, this does not mean that they never sin. As long as men and women remain in mortality, even though they have been born again, they are subject to the vicissitudes of the flesh, which means they will make mistakes and struggle with the weaknesses common to mortality.

They are also deeply ingrained with old habits and genetically induced tendencies or weaknesses, all of which must ultimately be faced, dealt with, and laid upon the altar of Christ before they can be overcome. But this honest facing of self is a process, not an event, and it occurs, usually with thankfully diminishing relapses, over an extended period of time. In other words, weaknesses are being turned, through the grace of Christ, into strengths. And this is all part of God's plan—His way of helping us develop spiritual strength sufficient to return to Him. To Moroni he explained, "If men come unto me I will show unto them their weakness. *I give unto men weakness that they may be humble;* and my grace is sufficient for all men that humble themselves before me; for if they humble themselves before me, and have faith in me, then will I make weak things become strong unto them" (Ether 12:27; italics mine).

I personally find it helpful to substitute the word *allow* for "give." Thus, God "allows" us to be willful and sinful; He "allows" the devil to tempt us; He "allows" us to have mortal weakness. Why? Because exercising our agency or freedom to choose is such a vital part of our spiritual growth, and His work and glory is to bring to pass our spiritual triumph. Therefore, because of our mortal weakness which God allows, mistakes and even intentional sinning are going to occur. So what is to be done? The same as at first. We must choose again to repent! Daily, constantly, sincerely, humbling ourselves before the Lord by imploring both God and man for forgiveness of all new mistakes and transgressions. And by making a fervently renewed effort, each time we stumble, through the remainder of our lives, to live more righteously. Then will Christ continue to strengthen us in the Spirit and ultimately restore us to His perfect purity and cleanliness.

As King Benjamin so beautifully tells us, "If ye have come to a knowledge of the goodness of God, and his matchless power, and his wisdom, and his patience, and his long-suffering towards the children of men; and also, the atonement which has been prepared from the foundation of the world, that thereby salvation might come to him that should put his trust in the Lord *and should be diligent in keeping his commandments, and continue in the faith even unto the end of his life, I mean the life of the mortal body—I say, that this is the man who receiveth salvation,* through the atonement which was prepared from the foundation of the world for all mankind, which ever were since the fall of Adam, or who are, or who ever shall be, even unto the end of the world" (Mosiah 4:6–7; italics mine).

THE DESIRES OF OUR HEARTS

Through this diligent effort to repent, we are manifesting both good works and a true and earnest desire for obedience to Christ, which good works and desire for righteousness—rather than perfection—seem to be sufficient to the Lord for the duration of this life. Thus, many years after his own mighty change of heart, a still-repentant Alma the Younger taught his sons, "It is requisite with the justice of God that men should be judged according to their works; and *if their works were good in this life, and the desires of their hearts were good,* that they should also, at the last day, be restored unto that which is good. And if their works are evil they shall be restored unto them for evil . . . the one raised to happiness according to his desires of happiness, or good according to his desires of good; and the other to evil according to his desires of evil; for as he has desired to do evil all the day long even so shall he have his reward of evil when the night cometh. And so it is on the other hand. *If he hath repented of his sins, and desired righteousness until the end of his days,* even so he shall be rewarded unto righteousness. These are they that are redeemed of the Lord" (Alma 41:3–7; italics mine).

SANCTIFIED AND JUSTIFIED

How is this mighty change of heart best noted? From my own observance of ward members whom the Spirit testified had experienced it, once such redeemed people discover that they have sinned, then unlike the rest of the world, they repent immediately. They also begin an instant campaign within their own hearts to see that such sins do not occur again. In addition, they begin a diligent process of mighty prayer wherein they plead before the Lord for that particular weakness or sin to be taken from them or made a strength unto them. It is because of this righteous approach to their own spiritual progression that those who have been born again are sanctified and justified.

JUSTIFICATION

There are two parts to this aspect of our coming to Christ—His part and our part. According to the scriptures, the Savior's part has to do with what is called justification. On the day the Church was organized, Joseph Smith declared "that justification through the grace of our Lord and Savior Jesus Christ is just and true" (D&C 20:30). To Moses the Lord said, "By the water ye keep the commandment; *by the Spirit ye are justified,* and by the blood ye are sanctified" (Moses 6:60; italics mine). To Joseph Smith the Lord said, "All kingdoms have a law given. . . . And unto every kingdom is given a law; and unto every law there are certain bounds also and conditions. All beings who abide not those conditions are not justified" (D&C 88:36, 38–39). Justification and its necessity are also spoken of at great length by the Apostle Paul and other New Testament writers, all of whom declare that it is a gift from Christ reserved only for the righteous (Luke 18:14; Acts 13:39; Romans 2:13, 4:16, 5:1, 9; 8:30; Galatians 2:16–17, 3:24–29).

Justification is part of the law of justice. In that law the Lord says that for every obedience to law there is a blessing, while for every disobedience there is a punishment (D&C 130:20–21). In other words, we receive joy from obedience and misery from disobedience. So, we should always be obedient to all God's laws, for then the law of justice would demand that we have pure joy. However, none of us keeps all the laws of God perfectly. That is why Lehi taught that "by the law no flesh is justified" (2 Nephi 2:5). In other words, because of the law of justice we will never make it on our own merits, will never know true joy. Why? Because we have experienced our own personal fall from premortal purity—our own spiritual death!

But this does not mean that we should all give up in despair. Lehi says, "Redemption [from our personal sins] cometh in and through the Holy Messiah." Thus, we are condemned by the law but redeemed by the Messiah, Jesus Christ, "who is full of grace and truth" (2 Nephi 2:6). These, grace and truth, are the ingredients that give Christ the enabling power to become our Redeemer. And who enjoys this great redemption brought about by Christ's enabling power? Only those "who have a broken heart and a contrite spirit; and unto none else can the ends of the law be answered" (2 Nephi 2:7). In other words, this blessing comes only to those who have brought forth true repentance through faith and godly sorrow until they have experienced the mighty change of heart and been born of water and of the Spirit. These will be justified by Christ's sacrifice and atonement.

Jesus says, "Listen to him who is the advocate with the Father, who is pleading your cause before him—saying: Father, behold the sufferings and death of him who did no sin, in whom thou wast well pleased; behold the blood of thy Son which was shed, the blood of him whom thou gavest that thyself might be glorified; wherefore, Father, spare these my brethren that believe on my name, that they may come unto me and have everlasting life" (D&C 45:3–5).

As a modern example of this process, consider the words of the Lord concerning Joseph Smith: "*After* it was truly manifested unto this first elder that *he had received a remission of his sins, he was entangled again in the vanities of the world;* but after repenting, and humbling himself sincerely, through faith, God ministered unto him by an holy angel, whose countenance was as lightning, and whose garments were pure and white above all other whiteness; and gave unto him commandments which inspired him; and gave him power from on high" (D&C 20:5–8; italics mine).

Clearly, no matter our spiritual status or ecclesiastical calling, we are all mortal and all under the obligation of constant, sincere repentance as we continue the process of overcoming the world and coming to Christ. "Wherefore, how great the importance to make these things known unto the inhabitants of the earth, that they may know that there is no flesh that can dwell in the presence of God, save it be through the merits, and mercy, and grace of the Holy Messiah, who layeth down his life according to the flesh, and taketh it again by the power of the Spirit, that he may bring to pass the resurrection of the dead, being the first that should rise. Wherefore, he is the firstfruits unto God, inasmuch as he shall make intercession for all the children of men; and they that believe in him shall be saved" (2 Nephi 2:8–9).

The law of justification is simply that after we have gone through repentance and godly sorrow until our sins have been forgiven and fully remitted, we are acquitted of our sinful natures. Those who are justified are prone to mortal weaknesses, but they rarely sin intentionally, and God allows them almost instant forgiveness. Of course, such people ask for forgiveness instantly, and they do all within their power to avoid making the same mistakes again. Thus they are justified, and they are allowed to progress onward toward sanctification and, ultimately, the pure love of Christ with its supernal blessings (D&C 129:3, 6).

SANCTIFICATION

Becoming sanctified is the first great personal reward granted to those who have become justified and who have then gone to work for the Lord. Where justification comes strictly through Christ's great efforts rather than our own (2 Nephi 25:23), sanctification is granted us through the Holy Ghost based upon *our own* efforts. Elder Bruce R. McConkie writes, "To the saints the continual cry of the gospel is: *Sanctify yourselves.* (D&C 39:18; 43:9, 11, 16; 133:4; Lev. 11:14; 1 Peter 1:15.) This is accomplished by obedience to the 'law of Christ' (D&C 88:21, 34–35), and is possible because of His atoning sacrifice. (D&C 76:41.)" (*Mormon Doctrine*, p. 675).

According to Brigham Young, "Sanctification . . . consists in overcoming every sin and bringing all into subjection to the law of Christ. God has placed in us a pure spirit; when this reigns predominant . . . and triumphs over the flesh and rules and governs and controls as the Lord controls the heavens and the earth, this I call the blessing of sanctification" (*Journal of Discourses,* 10:173). Such Saints have become "pure and spotless before God," being unable to "look upon sin save it were with abhorrence" (Alma 13:12).

President Spencer W. Kimball stated that the attitude basic to sanctification "is that the former transgressor must have reached a 'point of no return' to sin wherein there is not merely a renunciation but also a deep abhorrence of the sin—where the sin becomes most distasteful to him and where the desire or urge to sin is cleared out of his life" (*The Miracle of Forgiveness*, pp. 354–55).

Sanctification, then, is the process of becoming pure and spotless before God through the power of the sanctifier, who is the Holy Ghost, through true and constant repentance and a love of that which is good.

EVEN THE REDEEMED CAN BACKSLIDE

Can those who have been so reborn and redeemed slide backward, losing what they have gained? Absolutely! That is why Alma, addressing the members of the Church on another day, pointedly questioned them: "Have ye spiritually been born of God? Have ye received his image in your countenances? Have ye experienced this mighty change in your hearts? . . . I say unto you, can ye look up to God . . . with a pure heart and clean hands? I say unto you, can you look up, having the image of God engraven upon your countenances? . . . Behold, I say unto you, my brethren, if ye have experienced a change of heart, and if ye have felt to sing the song of redeeming love, *I would ask, can ye feel so now?*" (Alma 5:14, 19, 26; italics mine).

A third definition of the word *remission* is a relatively prolonged lessening or disappearance of a thing. Thus, when cancer is in remission, its growth is slowed or stopped, though it has not necessarily gone away. If remission of sins is thought of in this way, then we realize why King Benjamin spoke so forcefully concerning *retaining* a remission of our sins (Mosiah 4:11–30), explaining to his people that Christ's name, once obtained, could and would be blotted out of our hearts through unrepented transgression. He then pleaded, "I would that ye should remember to retain the name written always in your hearts, that ye are not found on the left hand of God, but that ye hear and know the voice by which ye shall be called, and also, the name by which he shall call you. For how knoweth a man the master whom he has not served, and who is a stranger unto him, and is far from the thoughts and intents of his heart? . . . Therefore, I would that ye should be steadfast and immovable, always abounding in good works, that Christ, the Lord God Omnipotent, may seal you his, that you may be brought to heaven, that ye may have everlasting salvation and eternal life, through the wisdom, and power, and justice, and mercy of him who created all things, in heaven and in earth, who is God above all" (Mosiah 5:12–13, 15).

If those who have had their sins fully remitted intentionally return to their former wickedness, then their remission of sins is canceled, and they are burdened again with their bonds of iniquity as well as Satan's iron yoke of bondage. It is to such people that the Lord declares, "Go your ways and sin no more; but unto that soul who sinneth shall the former sins return, saith the Lord your God" (D&C 82:7).

THE BLESSING OF THE SACRAMENT

In addition to other things, it is for the purpose of helping us to retain a remission of our sins and our commensurate spiritual growth toward Christ that the Lord instituted the ordinance of the sacrament of the Lord's Supper. As President Gordon B. Hinckley explains, "The mighty Jehovah made a great and solemn promise to Abraham. He said that his seed should become as the sand upon the seashore, that all nations would be blessed through him. He made this covenant with him, that he would be their God and they would be His people. We hear those words but we do not think of them very seriously. There was established then a relationship that was of eternal consequence in the eternal lives of all who would enter into it. Marvelous are its implications: if we will act as the children of God should act, He will be our God to bless us, to love us, to direct us, to help us.

"Now, in this dispensation, that everlasting covenant has been reaffirmed. We, in effect, made that covenant when we were baptized. We became a part of His divine family, as it were. All of God's children are of his family, but in a particular and wonderful way there is a special relationship between God and the children of His covenant. And *when we came into the Church, whether by lineage or whether by adoption, we became a part of a covenant people; and each time we partake of the sacrament, not only do we do it in remembrance of the sacrifice of the Son of God, who gave His life for each of us, but there is the added element that we take upon ourselves the name of Jesus Christ and pledge ourselves to keep His commandments and He pledges with us that He will bless us with His Holy Spirit [because] we are a covenant people, and great are the obligations which go with that covenant.* We cannot be ordinary people. We must rise above the crowd. We must stand a little taller. We must be a little better, a little kinder, a little more generous, a little more courteous, a little more thoughtful, a little more outreaching to others" (*Teachings of Gordon B. Hinckley*, pp. 148–49; italics mine).

Elder Bruce R. McConkie tells us, "Precisely and identically this same covenant [of baptism] is made by persons who partake of the sacrament. In other words, if they have been baptized (thus making the covenant of baptism), and if they then partake of the sacrament, they are renewing or making again the very covenant which brought remission of sins to them. Each time baptized members of the Church partake of the bread and water of the Lord's Supper, they most solemnly promise: 1. To remember the body of the Son of God which was crucified for them; 2. To take upon them the name of the Son; and 3. To 'always remember him and keep his commandments which he has given them.' In return, as his part of the covenant, the Lord promises: 1. That the saints shall 'have his Spirit to be with them'; and 2. That they shall have 'eternal life at the last day.' (D. & C. 20:75–79; John 6:54.)" (*Mormon Doctrine,* p. 297).

Knowing these things, is it any wonder that the resurrected Lord, each time He appeared among the Nephites, administered the sacrament to them? (3 Nephi 26:13).

Chapter Eight

CALLED AS SONS AND DAUGHTERS OF CHRIST

During one of the youth firesides I presided over as bishop, I mentioned the fact that dutiful compliance with the laws and ordinances of the gospel, which included for the young men the preparing for and then serving of an honorable mission, would entitle them to be called the sons of God. Immediately one of my young men raised his hand. "Bishop," he queried, "I've heard that before, and it makes no sense to me. I mean, we're all the sons and daughters of God, and that can't change no matter how we live. He is our Heavenly Father, isn't He? So what's all this about becoming again the sons of God?"

The question was indeed a fair one, and I did my best to answer it "on the spot," so to speak, by explaining that while we are all children of God the Father, it is to God the Son that we refer when we speak of our adopted son or daughter status. Whether or not he understood, I still find myself wishing that I had anticipated his question and made available, for myself as well as for him, the material that follows.

BECOMING ADOPTED CHILDREN OF GOD—OF CHRIST

Those who have been born again and so redeemed from their sins are adopted as sons and daughters of God, meaning Jesus Christ. To the Nephites following His resurrection, Christ said, "Behold, I am Jesus Christ the Son of God . . . *as many as have received me, to them have I given to become the sons of God;* and even so will I to as many as shall believe on my name" (3 Nephi 9:15, 17; italics mine).

"Those who are born again," writes Elder Bruce R. McConkie, "not only live a new life, but they also have a new father. Their new life is one of righteousness, and their new father is God. They become the sons of God; or, more particularly, they become the sons and daughters of Jesus Christ. They bear, ever after, the name of their new parent. . . . They become by adoption the seed or offspring of Christ, the children in his family, the members of his household, which is the perfect household of perfect faith" (*A New Witness for the Articles of Faith,* p. 284).

One man who became one of God's sons was the Lamanite king known only as Lamoni's father. He was joined in his adoption into Christ's family by many thousands of his people. Also similarly blessed were the repentant people under the righteous rule of King Benjamin. Once they had learned of and accepted the marvelous doctrines of Christ from their king, these mature men and women, whom we assume were members of the Lord's church, "all cried with one voice, saying: Yea, we believe all the words which thou hast spoken unto us; and also, we know of their surety and truth, because of the Spirit of the Lord Omnipotent, *which has wrought a mighty change in us, or in our hearts,* that we have no more disposition to do evil, but to do good continually. . . . And it is the faith which we have had on the things which our king has spoken unto us that has brought us to this great knowledge, whereby we do rejoice with such exceedingly great joy. And we are willing to enter into a covenant with our God to do his will, and to be obedient to his commandments in all things that he shall command us, all the remainder of our days, that we may not bring upon ourselves a never-ending torment, as has been spoken by the angel, that we may not drink out of the cup of the wrath of God" (Mosiah 5:2, 4–5; italics mine).

These good people were wholeheartedly covenanting, or promising, as have we, to give away, or hand back, to the Lord Jesus Christ *all* their sins, not just that day but for the rest of their lives. Continuing, the scripture states that these words of his people, no doubt carried into the heart of their king by the witnessing power of the Holy Ghost, pleased him immensely. Therefore, he declared to his beloved Saints, "The covenant which ye have made is a righteous covenant. And now, *because of the covenant which ye have made ye shall be called the children of Christ, his sons, and his daughters; for behold, this day he hath spiritually begotten you;* for ye say that your hearts are changed through faith on his name; therefore, ye are born of him and have become his sons and his daughters. . . . And it shall come to pass that whosoever doeth this shall be found at the right hand of God, for he shall know the name by which he is called; for he shall be called by the name of Christ" (Mosiah 5:6–7, 9; italics mine).

The premortal Christ taught this same marvelous doctrine, including the fact that all men and women who thoroughly repent and experience a spiritual rebirth are thereby adopted into His own eternal family and so are called thereafter by His family name. To a man known scripturally only as the brother of Jared, the Lord announced, "Behold, I am he who was prepared from the foundation of the world to redeem my people. Behold, I am Jesus Christ. I am the Father and the Son. In me shall all mankind have life, and that eternally, even they who shall believe on my name; *and they shall become my sons and my daughters*" (Ether 3:14; italics mine).

To nineteen-year-old Orson Pratt, the Lord Jesus Christ declared that He "so loved the world that he gave his own life, that as many as would believe might become the sons of God. Wherefore [Orson] you are my son" (D&C 34:3).

This doctrine of being called as children of Christ through a personal covenant and mighty works is expounded upon elsewhere. Elder James E. Talmage wrote, "By the new birth—that of water and the Spirit—mankind may become children of Jesus Christ, being through the means by Him provided 'begotten sons and daughters unto God' (D&C 76:24). This solemn truth is further emphasized in the words of the Lord Jesus Christ given through Joseph Smith in 1833: 'And now, verily I say unto you, I was in the beginning with the Father, and am the Firstborn; and all those who are begotten through me are partakers of the glory of the same, and are the church of the Firstborn' (D&C 93:21, 22). . . . An analogous instance of sonship attained by righteous service is found in the revelation relating to the order and functions of Priesthood, given in 1832: 'For whoso is faithful unto the obtaining of these two priesthoods of which I have spoken, and the magnifying their calling, are sanctified by the Spirit unto the renewing of their bodies. They become the sons of Moses and of Aaron and the seed of Abraham, and the church and kingdom, and the elect of God' (D&C 84:33, 34)" (*The Articles of Faith,* p. 470, footnotes).

Moses says, "[Adam] heard a voice out of heaven, saying: Thou art baptized with fire, and with the Holy Ghost. This is the record of the Father, and the Son, from henceforth and forever; and thou art after the order of him who was without beginning of days or end of years, from all eternity to all eternity. *Behold, thou art one in me, a son of God; and thus may all become my sons*" (Moses 6:66–68; italics mine).

Moroni pleads, "I beseech of you, brethren, that ye should search diligently in the light of Christ that ye may know good from evil; and if ye will lay hold upon every good thing, and condemn it not, ye certainly will be *a child of Christ*" (Moroni 7:19; italics mine).

To the wicked King Noah, Abinadi declared that through obedience to the words of the prophets, men and women would become Christ's seed or posterity. "When his [Christ's] soul has been made an offering for sin he shall see his seed. And now what say ye? And who shall be his seed? Behold I say unto you, that whosoever has heard the words of the prophets, yea, all the holy prophets who have prophesied concerning the coming of the Lord—I say unto you, that all those who have hearkened unto their words, and believed that the Lord would redeem his people, and have looked forward to that day for a remission of their sins, I say unto you, that these are his seed, or they are heirs of the kingdom of God. For these are they whose sins he has borne; these are they for whom he has died, to redeem them from their transgressions. And now, *are they not his seed?*" (Mosiah 15:10–12; italics mine).[1]

Finally, Mormon, as he spoke of "the meek and lowly in heart" who had confessed "by the power of the Holy Ghost that Jesus is the Christ" and so had obtained "charity [which] is the pure love of Christ," stated that this spiritual gift would endure with them forever. Then he added significantly, "Wherefore, my beloved brethren, pray unto the Father with all the energy of heart, that ye may be filled with this love, which he hath bestowed upon all who are true followers of his Son, Jesus Christ; *that ye may become the sons of God;* that when he shall appear we shall be like him, for we shall see him as he is; that we may have this hope; that we may be purified even as he is pure" (Moroni 7:48; italics mine).

In other words, those who have been born again, by the purity granted them through the power of the Holy Ghost, are worthy to be made members of Jesus Christ's personal eternal family.

BLESSINGS OF BEING A MEMBER OF THE FAMILY OF CHRIST

As members of this royal family, those who are being justified by the Holy Spirit, and who set up no stakes or limitations for themselves by choosing to sin and remain in sin by not repenting, will be given permission and the power to go on toward obtaining all the blessings mentioned by Joseph Smith when he said, "After a person has faith in Christ, repents of his sins, and is baptized for the remission of his sins and receives the Holy Ghost, (by the laying on of hands), which is the first Comforter, then let him continue to humble himself before God, hungering and thirsting after righteousness, and living by every word of God, and the Lord will soon say unto him, Son, thou shalt be exalted" (*Teachings,* p. 150).

Some of the blessings that sons and daughters of Christ are blessed to pursue and even enjoy, at least provisionally, as they continue to seek Christ's face and His absolute promise of exaltation when their calling and election is made sure, include being the Savior's friend (John 15:14–15; D&C 93:45–46); enjoying membership in the Church of the Firstborn, Christ's heavenly church (D&C 76:50–70, 94–96); having their ordinances sealed upon them by the Holy Spirit of Promise (D&C 76:53, 132:7–8); being chosen as part of the elect of God (D&C 84:33–34); and finally becoming joint heirs with Christ, to inherit with Him all that the Father has promised throughout all eternity. As Elder McConkie explained, "The elect of God comprise a very select group, an inner circle of faithful members of The Church of Jesus Christ of Latter-day Saints. They are the portion of church members who are striving with all their hearts to keep the fulness of the gospel law in this life so that they can become inheritors of the fulness of gospel rewards in the life to come.

"To gain this elect status they must be endowed in the temple of the Lord (D&C 95:8), enter into that 'order of the priesthood' named 'the new and everlasting covenant of marriage' (D&C 131:1–4), and overcome by faith until, as the sons [and daughters] of God, they merit membership in the Church of the Firstborn. (D&C 76:50–70, 94–96). The elect of God are the chosen of God; and he has said: 'There are many who have been ordained among you, whom I have called but few of them are chosen' (D&C 95:5; 121:34–40)" (*Mormon Doctrine*, pp. 217–18).

Elder McConkie later wrote, "'The Spirit itself beareth witness with our spirit, that we are the children of God; and if children, then heirs; heirs of God, and joint-heirs with Christ; if it so be that we suffer with him, that we may be also glorified together.' That is, because we have been adopted into the family of Christ, because we have taken his name upon us, and because he has accepted us in full, we are also accepted by his Father. We become joint-heirs with the Son. We are adopted into a state of sonship by the Father. Christ is his natural heir, and as adopted sons [and daughters], we become joint-heirs, receiving, inheriting, and possessing as does the Natural Heir. Because we conform 'to the image of his Son,' we are also 'glorified' with him. (Romans 8:4–30.)" (*A New Witness for the Articles of Faith*, p. 287).

FURTHER BLESSINGS

As worthy members of the family of Christ, we find that Satan is losing his power over us as we draw ever nearer to our Redeemer. Why? Because we are beginning to take upon ourselves His attributes, with all their attendant blessings. As Mormon joyfully declares, "The remission of sins bringeth meekness, and lowliness of heart; and because of meekness and lowliness of heart cometh the visitation of the Holy Ghost, which Comforter filleth with hope and perfect love [charity or the pure love of Christ], which love endureth by diligence unto prayer, until the end shall come, when all the saints shall dwell with God" (Moroni 8:26).

We who bring ourselves through continued prayer and repentance to this spiritual level of redemption from sin and divine rebirth into Christ's eternal family and then remain there, as did Adam and Eve, the brother of Jared, the father of King Lamoni, and, presumably, Alma's and King Benjamin's humble people, will thereafter find ourselves constantly engaged in teaching our children "to pray, and to walk uprightly before the Lord. And . . . also [to] observe the Sabbath day to keep it holy. And . . . also . . . [to] remember [our] labors, inasmuch as [we] are appointed to labor, in all faithfulness" (D&C 68:28–30). Additionally, we who repent "and hardeneth not [our] heart[s] . . . shall have claim on mercy through [the] Only Begotten Son, unto a remission of [our] sins; and [we] shall enter into [the Lord's] rest" (Alma 12:34), "which rest is the fulness of his glory" (D&C 84:24). Put another way, we will have been spiritually reborn and so have regained the right to enjoy the presence of God, and we will thereafter behold His face and bask in his pure love. In that spiritual state, we will be "given . . . to know the mysteries of God. . . . Therefore, . . . he that will not harden his heart, to him is given the greater portion of the word, until it is given unto him to know the mysteries of God until he know them in full" (Alma 12:9–10).

In this glorious but still-mortal state, we will also receive an additional and marvelous promise of divine power: "It is given to abide in you; the record of heaven; the Comforter; the peaceable things of immortal glory; the truth of all things; that which quickeneth all things, which maketh alive all things; that which knoweth all things, and hath all power according to wisdom, mercy, truth, justice, and judgment" (Moses 6:61; Alma 5:12–14).

NOTE

1. In an interesting sequel to this thought of seeds, the resurrected Lord declared to the Nephites that only the humble and righteous (the seed of Christ) would be allowed to sprout and have eternal roots and branches, which obviously has reference to dwelling with eternal families (see 3 Nephi 25:1–2), which is called a "continuation of the seeds forever and ever" (D&C 132:19).

Chapter Nine

CONCLUSIONS ABOUT BEING BORN OF THE SPIRIT

Throughout the scriptures there are accounts of individuals and groups who have been born of the Spirit and have undergone the "mighty change" (Mosiah 5:2). Some of these are Enos (Enos 1), Alma the Younger (Mosiah 27; Alma 36), Paul (Acts 9), King Benjamin's people (Mosiah 1–5), and a specific group of Lamanites that the Savior referred to (3 Nephi 9:20; Helaman 5). In considering these scriptural accounts, as well as what we have previously discussed, several aspects of this change become apparent. Among these are some that seem very significant to me personally, and some that seem less so.

SIGNIFICANT ASPECTS

1. The birth of the Spirit, being born again, most often occurs after we have been stirred up to complete repentance

of all our sins, usually through uncomfortable circumstances of some sort. There was some sort of stirring up in all the accounts listed above.

2. We must have been taught of Christ's atonement prior to the experience and have a sincere desire to believe in it.

3. We must show forth godly sorrow for our sins, manifested as a broken heart and a contrite spirit.

4. The birth of the Spirit occurs only after crying out to God for mercy in mighty prayer, which is exercising faith in Christ unto repentance.

5. As the experience concludes, we will feel our guilt swept away as we receive a remission of sins through the power of the Holy Ghost. This is the baptism of fire and the Holy Spirit, which some in modern times have described as a sensation of incredible warmth that sweeps over their body in a cleansing action that is otherwise indescribable. Others describe it as being filled with an overwhelming feeling of love, which lingers for an indeterminate period of time and is absolutely indescribable. This is certainly a manifestation of charity or Christ's pure love.

6. Knowing that our sins have been remitted, we feel complete peace of conscience for all our past sins. This feeling is so wonderful that all sin becomes abhorrent to us, we have no more disposition to do evil, and we resolve never to sin intentionally again. However, this does not mean that we will never sin again—only that we will do everything in our power to avoid sinning intentionally. Nor does it mean that we forget our sins; it seems that memory is left until the resurrection so that learning will occur. Witness Alma's detailed memory of his own wickedness that he shared with his son Helaman (Alma 36:6–27), and Benjamin's commandment

to his people to remember what they had been through. However, with guilt being swept away through the atonement of Christ, the memory of our sins is no longer painful, and it will ever after be useful for instruction of self and others. That is why Benjamin said to "remember, and perish not" (Mosiah 4:30).

7. Once the experience is over, we are filled with an amazingly heightened sense of love for our fellow beings, which is a further manifestation of charity, or the pure love of Christ. This love will be manifested by long-suffering, kindness, lack of envy, loss of pride, selflessness, being not easily provoked to anger, thinking only good rather than evil, rejoicing not in iniquity but only in the truth, and being perfectly willing to bear all things, believe all things, hope all things, and endure all things (Moroni 7:45).

8. Consumed with this love, we are also filled with the burning desire to acquaint all others with what we have discovered concerning Christ and His power to deliver from sin—this that they might enjoy the same peace and happiness we have found.

9. From this time forward, we will strive for a closer relationship with God and His Son. We will do this through intensive study, humble living, constant repentance, earnest keeping of the commandments, and diligent service to those around us. With the light of heaven resting upon us, the course we are to pursue is now lighted plainly. In exactly following this course, we will be manifesting the image of Christ in our countenances.

10. Through this process, we have received a witness from the Father that Christ's suffering and dying have been the gifts of God and that those gifts have wrought an at-one-ment

in our lives, making us one with, or bringing us into the family of, the Lord Jesus Christ.

LESS SIGNIFICANT ASPECTS

1. Though a time period of indeterminate length may be involved in the spiritual rebirth while we continue to be harrowed up by the realization and comprehension of our sins, such as Paul's and Alma's three days, the experience might also occur very quickly, as it did with King Benjamin's people. It might also continue over a much longer period.

2. During this time of total repentance, we may or may not suffer some sort of physical malady, again like Paul and Alma. Perhaps this and the length of time mentioned above might be related to the degree of wickedness we exhibited prior to our repentance.

3. During the experience we may or may not hear the voice of the Lord in our minds, as did Enos, and we may or may not have the eyes of our spirits opened to visions, as did Paul and Alma.

4. We may or may not know what is happening to us when this experience occurs. Either way, we are entitled to all the blessings enjoyed by those who have been born again and are diligently laboring to retain a remission of their sins, including continued spiritual growth unto Christ.

This last point brings up an interesting question: Are all people conscious of or aware that the mighty change has occurred, that they have been born again? The answer is: Not necessarily. To the righteous Nephites in the land Bountiful, the resurrected Lord declared, "Ye shall offer for a sacrifice unto me a broken heart and a contrite spirit. And whoso cometh unto me with a broken heart and a contrite spirit, him will I baptize with fire and with the Holy Ghost, even as the Lamanites, because of their faith in me at the time of their conversion, were baptized with fire and with the Holy Ghost, *and they knew it not*" (3 Nephi 9:20; italics mine).

Hence, there are surely many among us today who do not know that they have been baptized by fire and received a remission of their sins. Yet their righteous works follow them, they are frequently identified by the Spirit to bishops and other priesthood leaders, Saints and others everywhere are blessed by and because of them, and in the Lord's own time they will be informed of their significant spiritual growth. Meanwhile, they are fully entitled to all the blessings of inner joy and peace that come to those who have been called as sons and daughters of Jesus Christ.

AN ADDITIONAL BLESSING

Though not previously discussed, it seems that those who have been born again and are filled with the Holy Ghost will have the scriptures opened to their understanding to a degree that would have been unimaginable prior to their experience.

Joseph Smith wrote, "Immediately on our coming up out of the water after we had been baptized, we experienced great and glorious blessings from our Heavenly Father. No sooner had I baptized Oliver Cowdery, than the Holy Ghost fell upon him, and he stood up and prophesied many things which should shortly come to pass. And again, so soon as I had been baptized by him, I also had the spirit of prophecy, when standing up, I prophesied concerning the rise of this church, and many other things connected with the Church, and this generation of the children of men. We were filled with the Holy Ghost, and rejoiced in the God of our salvation.

"*Our minds being now enlightened, we began to have the Scriptures laid open to our understandings, and the true meaning and intention of their more mysterious passages revealed unto us in a manner which we never could attain to previously, nor ever before had thought of*" (*History of the Church,* 1:42–43; italics mine).

HOW THE HOLY GHOST IS MANIFESTED IN US

As a final thought on being born again, consider the words of President Brigham Young, who asked the question, "How shall I know [if the mighty change has occurred]?" He then answered his own question: "By the Spirit that shall come unto you through obedience, which will make you feel like little children, and cause you to delight in doing good, to love your Father in Heaven and the society of the righteous. Have you malice and wrath then? No, it is taken from you, and you feel like the child in its mother's lap. You will feel kind to your children, to your brothers and sisters, to your parents and neighbors, and to all around you; you will feel a glow, as of fire, burning within you; and if you open your mouths to talk you will declare ideas which you did not formerly think of; they will flow into your mind, even such as you have not thought of for years. The Scriptures will be opened to you, and you will see how clear and reasonable everything is which this or that Elder teaches you. Your hearts will be comforted, you can lie down and sleep in peace, and wake up with feelings as pleasant as the breezes of summer. This is a witness to you" (*Discourses of Brigham Young,* p. 331).

President Ezra Taft Benson adds in more contemporary terms, "Yes, Christ changes men, and changed men can change the world. Men changed for Christ will be captained by Christ. Like Paul they will be asking, 'Lord, what wilt thou have me do?' (Acts 9:6). Peter stated they will 'follow his steps.' (1 Peter 2:21) John said they will 'walk, even as he walked.' (1 John 2:6).

"Finally men captained by Christ will be consumed in Christ. To paraphrase President Harold B. Lee, they set fire in others because they are on fire. (Harold B. Lee, *Stand Ye In Holy Places,* Salt Lake City, Deseret Book Co., 1974, p. 192).

"Their will is swallowed up in his will. (John 5:30) They do always those things that please the Lord. (John 8:29) Not only would they die for the Lord, but, more important, they want to live for him.

"Enter their homes, and the pictures on their walls, the books on their shelves, the music in the air, their words and acts reveal them as Christians. They stand as witnesses of God at all times, and in all things, and in all places. (Mosiah 18:9) They have Christ on their minds, as they look unto Him in every thought. (D&C 6:36) They have Christ in their hearts as their affections are placed on Him forever. (Alma 37:36).

"Almost every week they partake of the sacrament and witness anew to their Eternal Father that they are willing to take upon them the name of His Son, always remember Him, and keep His commandments. (Moroni 4:3)

"In Book of Mormon language, they 'feast upon the

words of Christ' (2 Nephi 32:3), 'talk of Christ' (2 Nephi 25:26), 'rejoice in Christ' (2 Nephi 25:26), 'are made alive in Christ' (2 Nephi 25:25), and 'glory in [their] Jesus' (2 Nephi 33:6). In short, they lose themselves in the Lord and find eternal life (Luke 17:33)" ("Born of God," *Ensign*, July 1989, pp. 4–5).

Finally, according to Elder Bruce R. McConkie, "The spiritual birth . . . is to die as pertaining to worldliness and carnality and to become a new creature by the power of the Spirit. It is to begin a new life, a life in which we bridle our passions and control our appetites, a life of righteousness, a spiritual life. Whereas we were in a deep abyss of darkness, now we are alive in Christ and bask in the shining rays of his everlasting light. Such is the new birth, the second birth, the birth into the household of Christ" (*A New Witness for the Articles of Faith*, p. 282).

If we find that such descriptions are of us, or of how we are sincerely and constantly striving to be, then we may be assured that we have been born again.

Chapter Ten

A SIMPLE BUT ETERNAL CHOICE

So we continue, if that is our deepest desire, drawing ever closer to Christ until finally we find ourselves perfected through Him and, either before or after having died a temporal death, are brought back into the glorious, literal presence of our Heavenly Father. There, as did our Savior, we will receive a fullness of joy, and with our righteous loved ones we will bask in perfect happiness ever after.

What do we suppose this whole process of God's loving interaction with us, from spiritual death to spiritual rebirth and on to God's infinitely loving presence, might be called? According to Enoch, the Lord has declared, "*This is the plan of salvation unto all men,* through the blood of mine Only Begotten, who shall come in the meridian of time" (Moses 6:62; italics mine).

Isn't that interesting! The plan of our own individual,

personal salvation, given through the love and mercy of God the Father through His Beloved Son, the Lord Jesus Christ—a glorious, simple, easy-to-follow plan. The plan is not given to everyone willy-nilly, however, but only to those who will seek it with all their heart, might, mind, and strength. By doing what? Again, by being baptized, receiving confirmation and the gift of the Holy Ghost, and thereafter wholeheartedly following its promptings by repenting of all our sins and then fervently calling upon God in the name of Christ as we are born of the Spirit, and then on again through the balance of our mortal lives, diligently practicing righteousness and constant repentance while serving each other, and teaching our children to do the same. Thus we will be striving, as did Adam and Eve, to reestablish communication with the heavens, to the happy end that we and our loved ones may be brought back into God's presence and Christ's eternal family.

Not only is this the best way of coming unto Christ and regaining the presence of the Father; *it is the only way!* Thus, the holy angel declared to King Benjamin that "this is the means whereby salvation cometh. And *there is none other salvation save this which hath been spoken of;* neither are there any conditions whereby man can be saved except the conditions which I have told you" (Mosiah 4:8; italics mine).

But, what happens if we do not desire such divine closeness? What happens if we don't believe in Christ, or we do believe but can't see the importance of all this religious intensity? In other words, what if we can't be bothered? What happens if we're too busy to have daily personal, companionship, or family prayer or scripture study? What happens if we would rather not hold family home evening to instruct our tender children in the ways of Christ, or attend and worship God in His holy temple, or be an active part of the diligent followers of Christ who dwell within our individual wards?

"SETTING UP STAKES"

Joseph Smith taught that we all have agency to go as far as we want toward the celestial kingdom, but that most, including the angels, would "set up stakes" or personal limitations and say, "I cannot or will not go any further." Nor would we, because we have so decided (*Words,* pp. 244–47, 256).

The great Book of Mormon prophet Abinadi, speaking of those unfortunates who would be delivered over to the devil after the resurrection, declared their damnation: "*Having gone according to their own carnal wills and desires;* having never called upon the Lord while the arms of mercy were extended towards them; for the arms of mercy were extended towards them, and they would not; they being warned of their iniquities and yet they would not depart from them; and they were commanded to repent *and yet they would not repent*" (Mosiah 16:12; italics mine).

These people, singly and individually, for any number of reasons that must have seemed to them perfectly logical at the time, refused to repent. Alma the Younger, who had not so refused, and filled with a burning desire to proclaim the word of God to all the earth, continues this theme: "*I know that he granteth unto men according to their desire,* whether it be unto death or unto life; yea, I know that he allotteth unto men, yea, decreeth unto them decrees which are unalterable, *according to their wills,* whether they be unto salvation or unto destruction" (Alma 29:4; italics mine).

Each of us will be given that which we want the most—

according to our desires. If our wants are worldly rather than spiritually or Christ-centered, then of course those things will be our reward, and we will never in mortality know the thrill and eternal joy of spiritual growth and rebirth.

While all who are granted the wondrous blessing of Church membership thereafter receive from the Lord every opportunity for spiritual growth and rebirth, sadly, the Latter-day Saints who have set up stakes are choosing to ignore these blessings. Even many who partake of the sealing ordinances in the temple, thus setting the stage for far greater blessings for themselves and their families, choose by the way they live to remain spiritually dormant or immature, never partaking of the divine power of the endowment. They have obtained the gift of the Holy Ghost but only occasionally do they exercise that gift or enjoy the fruits thereof. They choose never to pray for charity or to offer up mighty prayer unto complete repentance and the obtaining a remission of their sins, all of which are required for spiritual rebirth.

Thus, like the good brother who came to me as his bishop in utter frustration and discouragement because he felt so spiritually stagnant, they cannot open the heavens and are never quite certain of their status or position before the Lord. Though they might serve diligently all their lives and receive blessings for such service, in terms of spiritual growth they have stopped in the progression that God has ordained should be accomplished here in mortality.

NOT NECESSARILY WICKED BUT VERY DANGEROUS

A legitimate question might be: Are such people being bad or wicked? After all, many good people have lived and died without seeing angels or having superlative spiritual experiences. In fact, numerous good Latter-day Saints have probably passed through mortality without ever fully being born again. Is that such a bad thing?

The answer would be: It depends on who we want to be. President Ezra Taft Benson states, "In the usual sense of the term, *Church membership* means that a person has his or her name officially recorded on the membership records of the Church. By that definition, we have more than [eleven] million members of the Church.

"But the Lord defines a member of His Kingdom in quite a different way. In 1829, through the Prophet Joseph Smith, He said, 'Behold, this is my doctrine—whosoever repenteth and cometh unto me, *the same is my church*' (D&C 10:67; italics added). To Him whose Church this is, membership involves far more than simply being a member of record" ("A Mighty Change of Heart," *Ensign,* October 1989, p. 2).

If spiritual rebirth and membership in the Lord's spiritual kingdom is wanted, rather than simply mortal Church membership, then setting up stakes is not only wrong but also incredibly foolish. To understand this, it must be kept in mind that Jesus Christ lived, suffered, and died so that each of us might have the capacity, through faith, to repent of our sins, obtain their remission through baptisms of water and fire, and begin our return to God's presence. This is the gospel of Jesus Christ, which in His kindness and mercy He has restored to the earth through modern prophets (3 Nephi 27:20–21; D&C 39:6). He has given us scriptures, both ancient and modern, so that we might know *how* to return to His presence. And finally He has restored the highest, or Melchizedek, priesthood with its ordinances and keys so that we might *have the power,* as members of an eternally sealed family unit, to open the heavens and thus return to His presence (D&C 84:19–22).

In all of this, Christ's whole aim is to see that we obtain not only salvation but also exaltation—the privilege of becoming as He is, where He is, for the rest of eternity. Nowhere has He given us encouraging instructions on how to become telestial beings, terrestrial beings, or even celestial beings who are ministering servants for those who are worthy of exaltation.

Rather, every doctrine we are taught, every scriptural verse or passage we read, every ordinance performed in our behalf is designed expressly to lead us to spiritual rebirth and exaltation in the presence of God, and that in as direct and rapid a manner as possible.

That is why putting off repenting and obtaining a remission of sins and the other aspects of spiritual rebirth, for whatever reason, is the same as choosing to remain *in* our sins. Thereby we are ignoring the will of Christ and placing our eternal futures in jeopardy. Paul urged the Hebrew Saints, "Let us go on unto perfection; not laying *again* the foundation of repentance . . . and . . . faith" (Hebrews 6:1; italics mine).

In other words, today—this *very* day—is the time to get off the fence! It is time to stop our constantly repeated halfhearted repenting. Instead of wandering around the mountain for forty years like the frightened and recalcitrant children of Israel, we need to climb the slopes ourselves and discover the very thing that Moses discovered—that we, too, can stand in the presence of God. As Paul put it, having "tasted of the heavenly gift, . . . the good word of God, and the powers of the world to come" (Hebrews 6:4–5), they could no longer delay their own spiritual growth lest they lose the promise. Paul warns, "Be not slothful, but followers of them who through faith and patience inherit [are inheriting] the promises" (Hebrews 6:12).

These "promises" referred to by Paul were explained to Joseph Smith when the Lord declared, "Sanctify yourselves that your minds become single to God, and the days will come that you shall see him; for he will unveil his face unto you, and it shall be in his own time, and in his own way, and according to his own will. *Remember the great and last promise which I have made unto you*" (D&C 88:68–69; italics mine).

By setting up stakes or being slothful about our spiritual growth and rebirth, we not only prolong and make much more difficult what we must one day accomplish if we truly want exaltation, but by not having obtained the promise in this life, we may well end up not accomplishing it at all.

TRAGIC RESULTS OF "SETTING UP STAKES"

If we do choose to disdain God's wonderful plan of salvation in this life, then by so doing we end up condoning, accepting, and then wholeheartedly embracing into our very natures many of the items on that lengthy litany of satanically inspired characteristics listed earlier. Quite literally, we assist Satan in increasing the strength and power of our own natural man—our own spiritual death (Mosiah 16:1–5). Furthermore, as the strength of our natural man increases, we find ourselves no longer being simply lazy or indifferent but actively working not only against God but also against ourselves, against our own happiness and well-being. As Alma warned his own wayward son, natural men and women are "without God in the world, and they have gone contrary to the nature of God; therefore, *they are in a state contrary to the nature of happiness*" (Alma 41:11). Why? "Because . . . *wickedness never was happiness*" (Alma 41:10; italics mine).

Rather than choosing Christ's plan of inner joy, happiness, peace, spiritual enlightenment, and tranquillity as we traverse the already rocky path of mortality toward Christ, we end up choosing instead the devil's plan—the increased misery, sorrow, pain, suffering, spiritual darkness, and inner turmoil that actually brings satanic laughter and rejoicing to Satan and his angels because we are moving steadily toward him. As Enoch saw in glorious but terrible vision, the devil "had a great chain in his hand, and it veiled the whole face of the earth with darkness; *and he looked up and laughed, and his angels rejoiced*" (Moses 7:26; italics mine).

Father Lehi, no doubt fearful that some of his own beloved sons would choose badly and therefore hear that horrid laughter being directed at them, pleaded with practically his dying breath, "My sons, I would that ye should look to the great Mediator, and hearken unto his great commandments; and be faithful unto his words, and choose eternal life, according to the will of his Holy Spirit; and not choose eternal death, according to the will of the flesh and the evil which is therein, *which giveth the spirit of the devil power to captivate, to bring you down to hell,* that he may reign over you in his own kingdom" (2 Nephi 2:28–29; italics mine).

TWO CHURCHES ONLY

As Nephi stood upon the top of the exceedingly high mountain, wrapped in heavenly vision, his angelic instructor taught him what some today might consider to be hard doctrine: "If the Gentiles shall hearken unto the Lamb of God in that day . . . and harden not their hearts against the Lamb of God, they shall be numbered among . . . the house of Israel; and they shall be a blessed people upon the promised land forever; they shall be no more brought down into captivity; and the house of Israel shall no more be confounded. And that great pit, which hath been digged for them by that great and abominable church, which was founded by the devil and his children, that he might lead away the souls of men down to hell—yea, that great pit which hath been digged for the destruction of men shall be filled by those who digged it, unto their utter destruction, saith the Lamb of God; not the destruction of the soul, save it be the casting of it into that hell which hath no end. For behold, this is according to the captivity of the devil, and also according to the justice of God, upon all those who will work wickedness and abomination before him.

"And it came to pass that the angel spake unto me, Nephi, saying: Thou hast beheld that if the Gentiles repent it shall be well with them; and thou also knowest concerning the covenants of the Lord unto the house of Israel; and thou also hast heard that *whoso repenteth not must perish.* Therefore, wo be unto the Gentiles if it so be that they harden their hearts against the Lamb of God.

"For the time cometh, saith the Lamb of God, that I will work a great and a marvelous work among the children of men; a work which shall be everlasting, *either on the one hand or on the other—either to the convincing of them unto peace and life eternal, or unto the deliverance of them to the hardness of their hearts and the blindness of their minds unto their being brought down into captivity, and also into destruction, both temporally and spiritually, according to the captivity of the devil,* of which I have spoken. And it came to pass that when the angel had spoken these words, he said unto me: Rememberest thou the covenants of the Father unto the house of Israel? I said unto him, Yea. And it came to pass that he said unto me: Look, and behold that great and abominable church, which is the mother of abominations, whose founder is the devil. And he said unto me: Behold *there are save two churches only; the one is the church of the Lamb of God, and the other is the church of the devil;* wherefore, *whoso belongeth not to the church of the Lamb of God belongeth to that great church, which is the mother of abominations;* and she is the whore of all the earth" (1 Nephi 14:1–10; italics mine).

SATAN OUR ETERNAL HEAD

As he thereafter became with Lehi's rebellious sons, if through our own indifference or laziness we remain members of the church of the devil, thus giving him power to lead us into outright rebellion against God and his plan of salvation through Christ, then through these same foolish and unrighteous choices we will have determined that Satan rather than Christ will become *our* eternal head; *our* eternal father! (John 8:44). What a terrifying thought—to be ruled over, as we struggle through all the vicissitudes of mortality and then immortal life hereafter, by a being who is so eternally miserable, self-serving, and unhappy!

And why is Satan so horribly distressed? Because "he ha[s] fallen from heaven, and ha[s] become miserable forever" (2 Nephi 2:18). And what does he intend to do about his misery? Get rid of it by repenting and thereafter following Christ? Oh, no! Instead, he would rather pull all the rest of us down to his demented level; therefore, "he [seeks] also the misery of all mankind. Wherefore . . . he seeketh that all men might be miserable like unto himself" (2 Nephi 2:18, 27).

It is hard for me to imagine why any of us would submit to such a plan of darkness, destruction, and misery, either here or hereafter. Yet both intentional and unwitting submission is what far too many of us are in the midst of doing. Lehi's righteous son Jacob elaborated concerning the terrible consequence of this unfortunate decision when he explained that "our spirits must . . . become like unto him, *and we become devils, angels to a devil,* to be shut out from the presence of our God, and to remain with the father of lies, in misery, like unto himself" (2 Nephi 9:9; italics mine).

Angels to the devil! What a tragically miserable consequence! After putting off our complete repentance and thus allowing ourselves to be miserable through this life, we die in our sins and enter the eternal world, where our misery immediately grows infinitely worse! Why? Because we have now become devils—literally Satan's angels—the unclean spirits that are occasionally mentioned in the scriptures (1 Nephi 11:31). Therefore, we "who are filthy shall be filthy still; wherefore, they who are filthy are the devil and his angels; and they shall go away into everlasting fire, prepared for them; and their torment is as a lake of fire and brimstone, whose flame ascendeth up forever and ever and has no end" (2 Nephi 9:16).

Put another way, "The spirit of the devil did enter into them . . . and these shall be cast out into outer darkness;

there shall be weeping, and wailing, and gnashing of teeth, and this because of their own iniquity, being led captive by the will of the devil. Now this is the state of the souls of the wicked, yea, in darkness, and a state of awful, fearful looking for the fiery indignation of the wrath of God upon them; thus they remain in this state, as well as the righteous in paradise, until the time of their resurrection. . . . And then . . . an awful death cometh upon the wicked; for they die as to things pertaining to things of righteousness; *for they are unclean*" (Alma 40:13–14, 25–26; italics mine; see also 1 Nephi 11:31).

What absolute horror! What terrible tragedy! I'm certain none of us is capable of imagining the depth of anguish these people will experience. Yet Enoch, having been given a sense of it by revelation, concludes his account of Adam's and Eve's experience by saying, "Our father Adam taught these things, and many have believed and become the sons of God, and many have believed not, and have perished in their sins, *and are looking forth with fear, in torment,* for the fiery indignation of the wrath of God to be poured out upon them" (Moses 7:1; italics mine).

A SUMMARY

To summarize this issue of spiritual rebirth, each of us who has reached accountability and accepted baptism and confirmation has first died spiritually because of submission to temptation. Yet through the teachings of the prophets as well as the marvelous gift of the Holy Ghost, we have also been given God's plan of salvation—the understanding of how to be reborn, and the power through Christ's atonement to do so. Whether or not we will pursue such rebirth through continued repentance and faith on the Lord Jesus Christ, however, is left entirely up to us. But a choice must be made, for God has so ordered His plan that we can neither stand still nor go in both directions!

Part Three

GO YE OUT FROM BABYLON

Chapter Eleven

THE LORD'S SCHOOL

Once we have been born again and have experienced the mighty change of heart, and if we choose to continue in all diligence to seek the face of Christ and to pray for His pure love, we will find that we are actually at the beginning of a remarkable spiritual journey—a journey toward exaltation. As was quoted earlier, the Prophet Joseph taught, "After a person has faith in Christ, repents of his sins, and is baptized for the remission of sins and receives the Holy Ghost, (by the laying on of the hands), which is the first Comforter, then let him continue to humble himself before God, hungering and thirsting after righteousness, and living by every word of God, and the Lord will soon say unto him, Son, thou shalt be exalted" (*Teachings*, p. 150).

GOING OUT OF SPIRITUAL BABYLON

This very specific journey toward exaltation was required of the fledgling Church in Kirtland. "Go ye out from Babylon," the Lord commanded. "Be ye clean that bear the vessels of the Lord. . . . Go ye out of Babylon . . . from the four winds, from one end of heaven to the other. . . . Go ye out from among the nations, even from Babylon, *from the midst of wickedness, which is spiritual Babylon*" (D&C 133:5, 7, 14; italics mine).

The Lord is not necessarily referring to departure from a physical place, such as the supernally wicked city whose inhabitants built the tower of Babel (the city that became King Nebuchadnezzar's Babylon and the fearful bane of ancient Israel and today is an empty ruin approximately fifty-five miles south of Baghdad, Iraq.) Where or what, therefore, is this spiritual Babylon that we are commanded to leave? Two days before giving the above revelation, now known as section 133, the Lord had given another revelation (section 1) wherein He answered our question: "The anger of the Lord is kindled, and his sword is bathed in heaven, and it shall fall upon the inhabitants of the earth. And the arm of the Lord shall be revealed; and the day cometh that they who will not hear the voice of the Lord, neither the voice of his servants, neither give heed to the words of the prophets and apostles, shall be cut off from among the people; for they have strayed from mine ordinances, and have broken mine everlasting covenant; they seek not the Lord to establish his righteousness, but every man walketh in his own way, and after the image of his own god, *whose image is in the likeness of the world,* and whose substance is that of an idol, which waxeth old and shall perish in Babylon, even Babylon the great, which shall fall" (D&C 1:13–16; italics mine).

SPIRITUAL BABYLON DEFINED

Babylon, therefore, refers to the world, or worldliness, or the forbidden things of the world (*Mormon Doctrine,* p. 69). "What is Babylon?" Brigham Young asked. "It is the confused world: come out of her then, and cease to partake of her sins, for if you do not you will be partakers of her plagues" (*Journal of Discourses,* 12:282). Hugh Nibley writes, "I could quote a hundred scriptures to show that Babylon is nothing but the inverse image of Zion. Babylon is a state of mind, as Zion is, with its appropriate environment. Just like Zion, Babylon is a city. 'Babylon the great is fallen, is fallen' (Revelation 18:2). The great world center of commerce and business, 'the kings of the earth have committed fornication with her, and the merchants of the earth are waxed rich through the abundance of her delicacies' (Revelation 18:3). Indeed, 'thy merchants were the great men of the earth; for by thy sorceries were all nations deceived' (Revelation 18:23). Babylon's economy is built on deceptions. Babylon is described fully in Revelation 18: She is rich, luxurious, immoral, full of fornications, merchants, riches, delicacies, sins, merchandise, gold, silver, precious stones, pearls, fine linens, purples, silks, scarlets, thyme wood, all manner of vessels, ivory, precious wood, brass, iron, marble, and so on. She is a giant delicatessen, full of wine, oil, fine flour, wheat; a perfume counter with cinnamon, odors, ointments, and frankincense; a market with beasts and sheep. It reads like a savings stamp catalog or a guide to a modern supermarket or department store. Horses and chariots and all manner of services are available; slaves in the souls of men. These are 'the fruits thy soul lusted after . . . and all things which were dainty and goodly' (Revelation 18:14). And it is all for sale. 'O virgin daughter of Babylon, . . . thou hast labored . . . [with] thy merchants, from thy youth' (Isaiah 47:1, 15). In her power and affluence she is unchallenged. 'For thou hast trusted in thy wickedness: thou hast said, None seeth me. Thy wisdom and thy knowledge, it hath perverted thee; and thou hast said in thine heart, I am, and none else beside me' (Isaiah 47:10). Babylon is number one. She dominates the world. Her king is equated to Lucifer, who says, 'I will be like the most High' (Isaiah 14:14). And all the nations are weakened at her expense. He was the man that 'made the earth to tremble, that did shake kingdoms; that made the world as a wilderness' (Isaiah 14:16–17). The 'lady of kingdoms' who rules over polluted lands and says, 'I shall be a lady forever' (Isaiah 47:5, 7)—she leads the world. 'The nations have drunken of her wine; therefore the nations are mad' (Jeremiah 51:7). 'Babylon the great, all nations have drunk of the wine of the wrath of her fornication' (Revelation 18:3). And when Babylon falls, all the world is involved: 'At the noise of the taking of Babylon the earth is moved, and the cry is heard among the nations' (Jeremiah 50:46). And 'at Babylon shall fall the slain of all the earth' (Jeremiah 51:49). Her clever, experienced, and unscrupulous men will be helpless. She thinks she can get away with anything, and says, 'None seeth me.' But 'thy wisdom and thy knowledge, it hath perverted thee' (Isaiah 47:10). 'And I will make drunk her men; and they shall sleep a perpetual sleep' (Jeremiah 51:57). Her military might is helpless: 'A sound of battle is in the land, and of great destruction. How is the hammer of the whole earth cut asunder and broken!' (Jeremiah 50:22–23)" (*Approaching Zion*, p. 14).

These worldly things, then—issues, practices, habits, policies, pleasures, fixtures, possessions, entertainments, conversations, trappings, attitudes, and so forth—are described as unclean and having the substance of an idol, and they divert the children of God from hearing the apostles and prophets, seeking the Lord's ordinances, and keeping His everlasting covenant. It doesn't matter where we find these Babylonian "things" or even what they are; in subtle and not so subtle ways they distract or divert us from diligently coming unto Christ and seeking His face, or of praying for charity, or His pure love. That is why, just four months after the Church was organized, the Lord declared, "Thou shalt lay aside the things of this world and seek for the things of a better" (D&C 25:10). Why? Because worldly things are not Godly things, and so we are commanded to leave them behind!

LEAVING WORLDLINESS BEHIND

We must remember, however, that leaving worldliness behind is a serious business—an absolute commandment. "I, the Lord, who was crucified for the sins of the world, *give unto you a commandment* that you shall forsake the world" (D&C 53:2; italics mine). We have many scriptural examples of this doctrine. In ancient times, both Jesus and Moses forsook the world by going into the wilderness, fasting, with literally nothing of the world in their pockets or backpacks. Elijah was allowed to eat only what was brought him by ravens (see 1 Kings 17:4–6). Of Lehi it is written that he left his house, and the land of his inheritance, and "his gold, and his silver, and his precious things, and took nothing with him, save it were his family, and provisions, and tents, and departed into the wilderness" (1 Nephi 2:4). All else was left behind, according to the commandment of the Lord.

While our own worldly possessions and attitudes may not, because of our righteousness and humility, be a hindrance to our coming to Christ and beholding His face, the chances are great that they are. Why? Because a vast number of us are part of an exceptionally selfish, hedonistic society, totally caught up in the business of getting gain and following Satan's first two articles of faith, which are that we can buy anything in this world with money, and that we can buy it now and pay for it later on. To even imagine that there are among us a significant number who have somehow escaped this unholy influence and bondage is tragically ludicrous.

Brigham Young saw this clearly even in his day, praying fervently as he dedicated the Manti Temple, "We ask Thee that Thou would hide up the treasures of the earth, . . . preserve thy people from the inducements which these perishable things offer, which are liable to decoy the minds of Thy saints. . . . And cause that these things may not come in their path to tempt them" (*Approaching Zion,* p. 333). And in one of the last public addresses he ever gave, President Young declared, "Many professing to be saints seem to have no knowledge, no light to see anything beyond a dollar or a pleasant time, or a comfortable house, or a fine farm. . . . O fools, and slow of heart to understand the purposes of God and his handiwork among his people" (*Journal of Discourses,* 8:63). "Go to the child," he continued on another occasion, "and what does its joy consist in? Toys, we may call them, . . .

and so it is with our youth, our young boys and girls; they are thinking too much of this world; and the middle-aged are striving and struggling to obtain the good things of this life, and their hearts are too much upon them. So it is with the aged. Is not this the condition of the Latter-day Saints? It is. What is the general expression through out our community? It is that the Latter-day Saints are drifting as fast as they can into idolatry . . . drifting into the spirit of the world and into pride and vanity" (*Journal of Discourses,* 18:237, 239).

"We wish the wealth or things of the world; we think about them morning, noon and night; they are first in our minds when we awake in the morning, and the last thing before we go to sleep at night; and we dream about how we shall do this, and how we shall obtain that, and our minds are continually lusting after the things of the world. Is not this too much the case with the Latter-day Saints?" (*Journal of Discourses,* 18:238–39).

"One man has his eye on a gold mine, another is for a silver mine, another is for marketing his flour or his wheat, another for selling his cattle, another to raise cattle, another to get a farm, or building here and there, and trading and trafficking with each other, just like Babylon, taking advantage wherever we can. . . . Babylon is here, and we are following in the footsteps of the inhabitants of the earth, who are in a perfect sea of confusion. Do you know this? You ought to, for there are none of you but what see it daily; it is a daily spectacle . . . to see the Latter-day Saints trying to take advantage of their brethren. There are Elders in this Church who would take the widow's last cow, for five dollars, and then kneel down and thank God for the fine bargain they had made" (*Journal of Discourses,* 17:41).

As Brother Nibley writes, “This is the great voice of the economy of Babylon. It does not renounce its religious pretensions for a minute. Many in it think they are identical with a pious life” (*Approaching Zion,* p. 334). Too many of us are guilty of such piety even today, good elders and high priests such as Brigham Young was dealing with in the nineteenth century: “If you ask them if they are ready to build up the kingdom of God, their answer is prompt—‘Why, to be sure we are, with our whole souls; but we want first to get so much gold, speculate and get rich, and then we can help the Church considerably. We will go to California and get gold, go and buy goods and get rich, trade with the emigrants, build a mill, make a farm, get a large herd of cattle, and *then* we can do a great deal for Israel.’ When will you be ready to do it? ‘In a few years, brother Brigham, if you do not disturb us. We do not believe in the necessity of doing military duty, in giving over our surplus property for tithing; we never could see into it; but we want to go and get rich, to accumulate and amass wealth, by securing all the land adjoining us, and all we have a knowledge of.’ If that is not the spirit of this people, then I do not know what the truth is concerning the matter” (*Journal of Discourses,* 15:4).

“If we had all the gold in these mountains run into ingots and piled up in one huge heap, what good would it do us? None, and we cannot form any calculation as to the amount of harm it would do us” (*Journal of Discourses,* 10:271).

A more recent prophet, President Spencer W. Kimball, sounded a dire warning on the occasion of the nation’s 200th anniversary. In discussing this address, Brother Nibley writes that it “gives us a picture of the Church, the nation, and indeed the world that is a miracle of clarity and condensation, placing the physician's finger with unerring accuracy on the really important issues. First, by way of introduction, a general observation: 'When I review the performance of this people in comparison with what is expected, I am appalled and frightened.' Not a particularly cheerful or even optimistic message. What is it that so frightens and appalls [President Kimball]? Three things in particular:

"1. *The abuse of the environment:* 'When I . . . fly over the vast and beautiful expanses of our globe, . . . I have the feeling that the good earth can hardly bear our presence upon it. . . . The Brethren constantly cry out against . . . pollution of mind, body, and our surroundings. . . . That such a cry should be necessary among a people so blessed is amazing to me.'

"2. *The pursuit of personal affluence:* 'Carnal man has tended to transfer his trust in God to material things. . . . When men have fallen under the power of Satan and lost the faith, they have put in its place a hope in the 'arm of flesh' and in 'gods of silver, and gold, of brass,' . . . that is, in idols. . . . Many people spend most of their time working in the service of a self-image that includes sufficient money, stocks, bonds, investment portfolios, property, credit cards, furnishing, automobiles and the like to *guarantee* carnal security throughout, it is hoped, a long and happy life.'

"3. *Trust in military security:* 'We commit vast resources to the fabrication of gods of stone and steel—ships, planes, missiles, fortifications—and depend on them for protection and deliverance. When threatened, we become anti-enemy instead of pro-kingdom of God; we train a man in the art of war and call him a patriot, thus, in the manner of Satan's counterfeit of true patriotism, perverting the Savior's teaching. . . . What are we to fear when the Lord is with us? Can we not take the Lord at his word and exercise a particle of faith in him? . . . We must leave off the worship of modern-day idols and a reliance on the 'arm of flesh,' for the Lord has said to all the world in our day, 'I will not spare any that remain in Babylon' (D&C 64:24)' ("The False Gods We Worship," *Ensign*, June 1976, 3–4).

"And how did the Saints," Brother Nibley continues, "who never tire of saying, 'The Prophet! The Prophet! We have a prophet!' receive his words? As might be expected, reaction has ranged from careful indifference to embarrassed silence and instant deep freeze. As to the three things against which they were warned, it can be shown with cruel documentation that Utah leads the nation, at least through its representatives, in outspoken contempt for the environment, unabashed reverence for wealth, and ardent advocacy of military expansion. . . .

"'Israel, Israel, God is calling,' we often sing, 'Babylon the great is falling.' But we have taken our stand between them; Brigham Young speaks of Latter-day Saints who want to take Babylon by one hand and Zion by the other—it won't work. Since World War II, it seems that we have been steadily converging with Babylon while diverging from some of the old teachings. Latter-day Saint children of the rising generation have never heard of their Guardian Angel, or of the recording of our every deed in a book in heaven; they were never told as we were as children that 'it is a sin to kill a fly,' and have never heard that satirical little verse which General Authorities used to quote in stake conference: 'Money, O Money, thy praises I'll sing! Thou art my Savior, my God and my King!' That would be quite unthinkable today, a kind of sacrilege. Because some of the old teachings are still preserved in the temple, certain anomalies appear to the younger generation. A bishop told me this month that people coming to renew their recommends when they are asked whether they keep all their covenants frequently answer no, explaining that they do not keep the law of consecration. A General Authority recently told me that the important thing is to observe the law of consecration 'spiritually.' Yes indeed, say I, and the law of tithing also—how much better to observe *it* spiritually than in a gross, material way—a great comfort to the rich. And yet the express purpose of both those laws is to test the degree of our attachment to material things, not to provide an exercise in 'spiritual' semantics" (*Approaching Zion*, pp. 366, 279–80).

Again quoting President Kimball: "It is hard to satisfy us. The more we have, the more we want. Why another farm, another herd of sheep, another bunch of cattle, another ranch? Why another hotel, another cafe, another store, another shop? Why another plant, another office, another service, another business? Why another of anything if one has that already which provides the necessities and reasonable luxuries? Why continue to expand and increase holdings, especially when those increased responsibilities draw one's interests away from proper family and spiritual commitments, and from those things to which the Lord would have us give precedence in our lives? Why must we always be expanding to the point where our interests are divided and our attentions and thoughts are upon the things of the world? Certainly when one's temporal possessions become great, it is very difficult for one to give proper attention to the spiritual things. . . .

"Zion can be built up only among those who are the pure in heart, not a people torn by covetousness or greed, but a pure and selfless people. Not a people who are pure in appearance, rather a people who are pure in heart. Zion is to be in the world and not of the world—not dulled by a sense of carnal security, nor paralyzed by materialism. No, Zion is not things of the lower, but of the higher order, things that exalt the mind and sanctify the heart.

"Zion is 'every man seeking the interest of his neighbor, and doing all things with an eye single to the glory of God.' (D&C 82:19.) As I understand these matters, Zion can be established only by those who are pure in heart, and who labor for Zion, for 'the laborer in Zion shall labor for Zion; *for if they labor for money they shall perish.*' (2 Nephi 26:31.)" (*Teachings of Spencer W. Kimball,* pp. 354–55, 363; italics mine).

STIRRED UP UNTO HUMILITY

Having now noted, perhaps with some chagrin, that to one degree or another we have all been part of these Babylonian descriptions, this next thought should make great sense. Whether we think we need to give them up or not, it seems that the Lord is frequently willing to help us in the giving up of worldly things. He might do this by allowing financial reversals to occur, bringing loss of homes, cars, boats, and incomes; personal or corporate bankruptcy; and so forth. We might also experience a severe loss of health or death of a loved one, which can do the same thing by making worldly things unattractive or meaningless. As was pointed out in a previous chapter, scripturally this is called being stirred up unto repentance. In this case, however, I will substitute the word *humility*, which always strikes at the heart of pride, vanity, and worldliness! "Behold, the world is ripening in iniquity; and it must needs be that the children of men are stirred up unto *humility*, both the Gentiles and also the house of Israel" (D&C 18:6); and, "The kingdom of the devil must shake, and they which belong to it must needs be stirred up unto *humility*, or the devil will grasp them with his everlasting chains, and they . . . perish" (2 Nephi 28:19).

When we experience this divine assistance in leaving behind the things of the world—and to some degree we all will experience it—then above all else we ought to be filled with joy and rejoicing in the Lord's goodness and mercy (D&C 52:43).

THE LORD'S PROSPERITY

We must also remember that once worldliness has been left behind, we are not to return to it. That does not mean we will never again prosper, for the Lord always prospers the righteous. However, with the Lord guiding our journey, prosperity may be other than economic. And whether prosperity is economic or not, our hearts and spirits must under all conditions remain pure and without greed and avarice. This was a difficult lesson for the Nephites, who seemed to plummet into destruction as often as the Lord financially prospered them. On the rare occasions that they succeeded, however, it was because "they did not send away any who were naked, or that were hungry, or that were athirst, or that were sick, or that had not been nourished; and they did not set their hearts upon riches; therefore they were liberal to all, both old and young, both bond and free, both male and female, whether out of the church or in the church, having no respect to persons as to those who stood in need" (Alma 1:30).

While many in Kirtland maintained this same Christlike attitude, Eliza R. Snow wrote that "prosperity was dawning upon them . . . and many who had been humble and faithful . . . were getting haughty in their spirits, and lifted up in the pride of their hearts. As the Saints drank in the love and spirit of the world, the Spirit of the Lord withdrew from their hearts, and they were filled with pride and hatred toward those who maintained their integrity" (*History of the Church,* 2:487, footnotes).

Valuable lessons to consider!

DELIVERANCE FROM EVIL

Every time the Lord's people have been commanded to leave Babylon, they have also been delivered by Him from some great evil or danger. Of the Jaredites we are told that they and their friends were delivered from having their language confounded at Babel's tower (Ether 1:35–43). Moses and the children of Israel were delivered from the Egyptians (Exodus 13–14). And Nephi and his family were delivered not only from the hands of the people of Jerusalem (1 Nephi 2:1) but also from the destruction of Jerusalem at the hands of King Nebuchadnezzar's worldly Babylonians (1 Nephi 1:18). Later, Nephi had his own deliverance, which occurred after he and his father's family had arrived in the promised land. Nephi records that "the Lord did warn me, that I, Nephi, should depart from [my brothers] and flee into the wilderness, and all those who would go with me" (2 Nephi 5:5).

Other deliverees included Alma, who, "having been

warned of the Lord that the armies of king Noah would come upon them, and having made it known to his people, therefore they gathered together their flocks, and took of their grain, and departed into the wilderness before the armies of king Noah" (Mosiah 23:1); and even the little-known Mulekites, or people of Zarahemla, who "came out from Jerusalem at the time that Zedekiah, king of Judah, was carried away captive into Babylon. And they journeyed in the wilderness, and were brought by the hand of the Lord across the great waters, into the land where Mosiah discovered them; and they had dwelt there from that time forth" (Omni 1:15–16).

Father Abraham records, "I, Abraham, saw that it was needful for me to obtain another place of residence" (Abraham 1:1) "[because] the priests laid violence upon me, that they might slay me" (Abraham 1:12). Therefore, "as they lifted up their hands upon me, that they might offer me up and take away my life, behold, I lifted up my voice unto the Lord my God, and the Lord hearkened and heard, and he filled me with the vision of the Almighty, and the angel of his presence stood by me, and immediately unloosed my bands; and his voice was unto me: Abraham, Abraham, behold, my name is Jehovah, and I have heard thee, and have come down to deliver thee, and to take thee away from thy father's house, and from all thy kinsfolk, into a strange land which thou knowest not of" (Abraham 1:15–16).

For the Kirtland Saints, the wilderness of frontier Ohio was a land of poverty and privation. Not only had they given up most of their worldly goods just to get there, but once they arrived they had to sacrifice even further as they struggled to build their magnificent temple. Yet through their very poverty they were delivered out of danger—the deadly danger of worldliness that had been consuming them prior to their conversion to the Lord. It is to be the same for us. As the Lord says, "After today cometh the burning—this is speaking after the manner of the Lord—for verily I say, tomorrow all the proud and they that do wickedly shall be as stubble; and I will burn them up, for I am–the Lord of Hosts; and I will not spare any that remain in Babylon" (D&C 64:24).

DESTINATION—SPIRITUAL ZION

Where would the Lord have us go after we have left that horrid place, that Babylon? According to Joseph Smith, if we travel exactly as the Lord has directed, exercising faith in God, repenting of all our sins, partaking of God's sacred ordinances, and seeking Christ with all our hearts every day for the remainder of our lives, then ultimately we will "come unto Mount Zion, and unto the city of the living God, the heavenly Jerusalem, and to an innumerable company of angels; to the general assembly and church of the Firstborn, which are written in heaven, and to God the judge of all, and to the spirits of just men made perfect, and to Jesus the Mediator of the new covenant" (*Teachings*, p. 12; see also Hebrews 12:22–24).

And where or what is Mount Zion? Elder Bruce R. McConkie writes, "Paul uses the term *Mount Zion* to refer to the abode of exalted beings, those who overcome all things and inherit the fulness of the Father's kingdom. . . . (Hebrews 12:22–24)" (*Mormon Doctrine*, p. 855). Joseph Smith is telling us that our goal, as we seek the face of Christ and His pure love, is to join those who have already achieved it, both mortal and immortal. This is coming unto Mount Zion.

But an examination of Zion itself is instructive. Elder McConkie continues, "Zion is the name given by the Lord to his saints; it is the name by which the Lord's people are always identified. Of the saints in Enoch's day the record says, 'And the Lord called his people ZION, because they were of one heart and one mind, and dwelt in righteousness; and there was no poor among them' (Moses 7:18). 'This is Zion—THE PURE IN HEART,' he said in this day (D&C 97:21)" (*Mormon Doctrine,* p. 855).

The pure in heart! Who can even imagine being absolutely pure in heart? For us who have determined to come out of Babylon, forsaking the world as we strive to come unto Christ, Zion is not so much about "being" as it is "becoming." Zion is our destination, and we have only to follow carefully and diligently the Lord's road map to one day arrive.

TRAVELING CAREFULLY

How are we to travel? Carefully, thoughtfully, and with a determination that is fixed and resolute. "But verily, thus saith the Lord, let not your flight be in haste, but let all things be prepared before you; and he that goeth, let him not look back lest sudden destruction shall come upon him" (D&C 133:15).

THE JOURNEY

Nephi explains that repentance and a remission of our sins "by fire and by the Holy Ghost" take us through the gate, placing us *at the beginning* of the "straight and narrow path which leads to eternal life" (2 Nephi 31:17–18; italics mine). He says, "And now, my beloved brethren, after ye have gotten into this strait and narrow path, *I would ask if all is done? Behold, I say unto you, Nay*; for ye have not come thus far save it were by the word of Christ with unshaken faith in him, relying wholly upon the merits of him who is mighty to save. Wherefore, *ye must press forward with a steadfastness in Christ, having a perfect brightness of hope, and a love of God and of all men.* Wherefore, if ye shall press forward, feasting upon the word of Christ, and endure to the end, behold, thus saith the Father: Ye shall have eternal life. And now, behold, my beloved brethren, this is the way; and there is none other way nor name given under heaven whereby man can be saved in the kingdom of God. And now, behold, *this is the doctrine of Christ, and the only and true doctrine of the Father, and of the Son, and of the Holy Ghost,* which is one God, without end. . . . And now, behold . . . I suppose that ye ponder somewhat in your hearts concerning that which ye should do after ye have entered in by the way. . . . Wherefore, I said unto you, *feast upon the words of Christ; for behold, the words of Christ will tell you all things what ye should do.* . . . Behold, this is the doctrine of Christ" (2 Nephi 31:19–21, 32:1, 3, 6; italics mine).

King Benjamin went to similar lengths to teach his followers what was expected of them once they had experienced the mighty change or entered in by the way. "As ye have come to the knowledge of the glory of God, or if ye have known of his goodness and have tasted of his love, and have received a remission of your sins, which causeth such exceedingly great joy in your souls, even so I would that ye should remember, and always retain in remembrance, the greatness of God, and your own nothingness, and his goodness and long-suffering towards you, unworthy creatures, and humble yourselves even in the depths of humility, calling on the name of the Lord daily, and standing steadfastly in the faith of that which is to come, which was spoken by the mouth of the angel. And behold, I say unto you that if ye do this ye shall always rejoice, and be filled with the love of God, and always retain a remission of your sins; and ye shall grow in the knowledge of the glory of him that created you, or in the knowledge of that which is just and true" (Mosiah 4:11–12).

Benjamin then instructed his people to adopt into their personal lives the Christlike attributes of charity, or pure love: to (1) live peaceably and kindly with each other; (2) give diligent attention to the spiritual and temporal needs of their children; (3) teach their children the peaceable way of Christ; (4) impart freely of their substance to any who stood in need of it, "every man according to that which he hath, such as feeding the hungry, clothing the naked, visiting the sick and administering to their relief, both spiritually and temporally, according to their wants" (Mosiah 4:26); (5) never take advantage of another by borrowing and not returning; (6) always watch their thoughts, words, and deeds, observing the commandments of God and continuing "in the faith of what [they had] heard concerning . . . [the] Lord, even unto the end of [their] lives" (Mosiah 4:30).

These, and Nephi's *"feasting upon the word of Christ,"* are things that we must do if we are to retain a remission of our sins—if we are to prosper in our journey from Babylon to Zion. If we are willing to do them, following with exactness the counsel of Nephi, King Benjamin, and Joseph Smith, then truly we are ready to embark on the most exciting and glorious journey of discovery any of us have ever imagined—a heavenly directed course of study, granted with the intent of bringing to pass, in this life as well as the next, absolute trust and purity.

SPIRITUAL TRAINING IN THE WAYS OF THE LORD

Concerning the need for such divine instruction, Joseph Smith stated, "We consider that God has created man with a mind capable of instruction, and a faculty which may be enlarged in proportion to the heed and diligence given to the light communicated from heaven to the intellect; and that the nearer man approaches perfection, the clearer are his views, and the greater his enjoyments, till he has overcome the evils of his life and lost every desire for sin; and like the ancients, arrives at that point of faith where he is wrapped in the power and glory of his Maker and is caught up to dwell with Him. But we consider that this is a station to which no man ever arrived in a moment: he must have been instructed in the government and laws of that kingdom by proper degrees, until his mind is capable in some measure of comprehending the propriety, justice, equality, and consistency of the same. For further instruction we refer you to Deut. 32, where the Lord says, that Jacob is the lot of His inheritance. *He found him in a desert land, and in the waste[d], howling wilderness; He led him about, He instructed him, He kept him as the apple of His eye*, etc.; which will show the force of the last item advanced, that it is necessary for men to receive an understanding concerning the laws of the heavenly kingdom, before they are permitted to enter it: we mean the celestial glory" (*Teachings*, p. 51; italics mine).

THE WILDERNESS

Considering all the above, there is ample evidence to suggest that an appropriate name or description for our own journey of divine tutelage, after we have gone out of Babylon, might be a "traveling through the wilderness," which might indeed seem, as Joseph put it, "wasted" and "howling." Jesus went fasting into the wilderness for forty days (Mark 1:14); Moses did the same (Exodus 24:18). It was in "the wilderness" that Joseph of old was stripped of his many-colored coat by his brethren, thus beginning his Egyptian sojourn of learning and growth (Genesis 37). Of Adam's experience we are told that he was driven from the garden into what Lehi called a dark and dreary waste (1 Nephi 8:7), which Lehi also called his own "tribulation in the wilderness" (2 Nephi 2:1). Both Ether and Moroni were well acquainted with wilderness schooling (Ether 13:13; Mormon 8:5), and John the Baptist received his preparation there, living on locusts and wild honey (Mark 1:3–6).

Concerning ancient Israel's forty-year wilderness experience, Hugh Nibley writes, "The Israelites always looked back upon the days of the wandering in the wilderness as the true schooling of the Chosen People and the time when they were most nearly fulfilling the measure of their existence. The concept of man as a wanderer and an outcast in a dark and dreary world is as old as the records of the human race. The desert has always had two aspects, that of refuge and asylum on the one hand, and of trial and tribulation on the other; in both respects it is a place where God segregates and tests his people. Throughout the history of Israel zealous minorities among the people have gone out into the wilderness from time to time in an attempt to get back to the ways of the patriarchs and to live the old Law in its purity, fleeing from Idumea, or the wicked world" (*An Approach to the Book of Mormon,* p. 145).

It appears that the Lord has always required of those who desire to be His people, to be Zion, a complete withdrawal from the world and its unholy ways. Thus, we are commanded to depart from Babylon and head out into the uncertain wilderness of specific, individualistic tutelage in the Lord's highly specialized school, our ultimate destination Zion, or complete purity of heart.

THE LORD'S SCHOOL

Among the definitions of the word *school* in my dictionary, we read: "2. an institution for instruction in a particular skill or field; 6. the activity or process of learning under instruction; 12. any place, situation, etc., tending to teach anything; 13. the body of pupils or followers of a master system, method, etc., 15. any group of persons having common attitudes or beliefs" (*Webster's Encyclopedic Unabridged Dictionary of the English Language,* [New York, Gramercy Books, 1996], p. 1715). These definitions adequately describe the Lord's wilderness school, though the particular "skill or field" mentioned in definition number two merits further consideration.

Before considering the precise nature of this heavenly directed course of study, it would be well to reconsider two statements made by the Prophet Joseph, which were quoted in chapter five. To John Taylor, Joseph said: "Now, if you will continue to follow the leadings of that spirit [the Holy Ghost or Spirit of God], it will always lead you right. Sometimes it might be contrary to your judgment; never mind that, follow its dictates; *and if you be true to its whisperings it will in time become in you a principle of revelation, so that you will know all things*" (*Journal of Discourses,* 19, pp. 153–54, italics mine).

Joseph Smith also stated: "A person may profit by noticing the first intimation of the spirit of revelation; for instance, when you feel pure intelligence flowing into you, it may give you sudden strokes of ideas, so that by noticing it, you may find it fulfilled the same day or soon; (i.e.,) those things that were presented unto your minds by the Spirit of God, will come to pass; *and thus by learning the Spirit of God and understanding it, you may grow into the principle of revelation, until you become perfect in Christ Jesus* (*Teachings,* pp. 151, italics mine).

As I see it, then, the course of study we enroll in once we have been admitted to the Lord's wilderness school, might well be titled "Learning to Listen to and Always Obey the Spirit of God," or "Growing into the Principle of Revelation." But to what end? Why is the Lord so desirous that we each learn to hear Him? What, exactly, does He wish to tell us?

For an answer, let us consider once again another of Joseph's statements: "Let us here observe, that three things are necessary in order that any rational and intelligent being may exercise faith in God unto life and salvation.

"First, the idea that he actually exists.

"Secondly, a *correct* idea of his character, perfections, and attributes.

"Thirdly, an actual knowledge that the course of life which he is pursuing is according to his will. For without an acquaintance with these three important facts, the faith of every rational being must be imperfect and unproductive; but with this understanding it can become perfect and fruitful, abounding in righteousness, unto the praise and glory of God the Father, and the Lord Jesus Christ" (*Lectures in Faith, Lecture Third,* p. 3).

The course of study we have entered into, then, is designed by God to assist us in growing into the principle of revelation, this in order that Christ can communicate to us a correct and ultimately perfect understanding of who He is, His "character, perfections, and attributes," as well as an understandable witness that our own life is moving in appropriate ways toward our being like Him. In short, his school teaches us how to ultimately become, gods and goddesses.

NOT A RETREAT FROM SOCIETY

For those in our day who desire to continue their spiritual growth to a fullness of coming unto Christ , however, wilderness schooling will likely be spiritual rather than physical. Elder William J. Critchlow Jr., said, "We live in a wicked world like unto Babylon of old. Our latter-day prophets, like the prophets of old, have cried, 'Come out, come out of Babylon.' To come out physically presents a problem, but spiritually it is possible, and spiritually we must come out if we are to prosper in the land" (Conference Report, October 1961, p. 56).

President Gordon B. Hinckley has taught, "It is not always easy to live in the world and not be a part of it. We cannot live entirely with our own or unto ourselves, nor would we wish to. We must mingle with others. In so doing, we can be gracious. We can be inoffensive. We can avoid any spirit or attitude of self-righteousness. But we can maintain our standards. The natural tendency will be otherwise, and many have succumbed to it.

"In 1856, when we were largely alone in these valleys, some thought we were safe from the ways of the world. To such talk, President Heber C. Kimball responded: 'I want to say to you, my brethren, the time is coming when we will be mixed up in these now peaceful valleys to that extent that it will be difficult to tell the face of a Saint from the face of an enemy to the people of God. Then, brethren,' he went on, 'look out for the great sieve, for there will be a great sifting time, and many will fall; for I say unto you there is a test, a *Test,* a TEST coming, and who will be able to stand?' (Whitney, *Life of Heber C. Kimball,* p. 446.)

"I do not know the precise nature of that test. But I am inclined to think the time is here and that the test lies in our capacity to live the gospel rather than adopt the ways of the world.

"*I do not advocate a retreat from society.* On the contrary, we have a responsibility and a challenge to take our places in the world of business, science, government, medicine, education, and every other worthwhile and constructive vocation. We have an obligation to train our hands and minds to excel in the work of the world for the blessing of all mankind. In so doing we must work with others. But this does not require a surrender of standards" (*Be Thou an Example,* p. 27; italics mine).

In other words, while we are all compelled to work in this world, we are under obligation to make certain we are working toward the blessing and uplifting of others, no matter the nature of our work. To that same end, the blessing and uplifting of others, we are also to excel in our work to the best of our abilities. Furthermore, that same end must *always* be the focus of our labors and *never* the procurement of money. Remember Nephi's declaration: "The laborer in Zion shall labor for Zion; for if they labor for money they shall perish" (2 Nephi 26:31). Surely this admonition applies to us today!

The Lord said to the Prophet Joseph, "Behold, that which you hear is as the voice of one crying in the wilderness—in the wilderness, because you cannot see him—my voice, because my voice is Spirit; my Spirit is truth; truth abideth and hath no end; and if it be in you it shall abound. And if your eye be single to my glory, your whole bodies shall be filled with light, and there shall be no darkness in you; and that body which is filled with light comprehendeth all things. Therefore, sanctify yourselves that your minds become single to God, and the days will come that you shall see him; for he will unveil his face unto you, and it shall be in his own time, and in his own way, and according to his own will" (D&C 88:66–68).

Clearly the Lord is saying that as we give up the world (having eyes single to God's glory rather than departing into some desert hideout), we learn to hear the voice of God crying out of the wilderness (meaning He cannot be seen). And by hearing His voice, we are preparing ourselves for the day when we will behold His face.

OUR OWN DELIVERANCE

Having been delivered at last from our sins, if we also desire with all our hearts to be delivered from our enemies (including the worldliness that often seems to engulf us and swallow up our peace), then we have but to ask in faith and it will be done. We will be admitted into the wilderness of the Lord, where we will be forged, refined, and purified by the Lord Jesus Christ, who is "like a refiner's fire, and like fullers' soap," and who will "purify the [wilderness sojourners], and purge them as gold and silver, that they may offer unto the Lord an offering in righteousness" (Malachi 3:2–3).

This refining is the entire point of the wilderness journey upon which those who have begun to come unto Christ are invited to embark.

Chapter Twelve

COMPANIONSHIP OF THE HOLY GHOST

Those who have come out of Babylon and entered the Lord's wilderness, where they might obtain His love and behold His face, are in fact seeking for the heavenly light and knowledge necessary to enable them, personally and individually, to do so. As the Prophet Joseph said of such heavenly or spiritual knowledge, "Knowledge is power, and the man who has the most knowledge has the greatest power" (*Words,* p. 202). He also said, "Without knowledge we cannot be saved. . . . A man is saved no faster than he gets knowledge" (*Words,* p. 113–14).

As I ministered as a bishop, I was surprised by how literally this is to be taken. Again and again I spoke to the adults of my ward, fasting and praying that I would be led in what I was to say, and doing all in my power to be worthy of speaking by the power of the Holy Ghost. Thus prepared as well as I was able, I periodically spoke to them on fifth Sundays, occasionally during sacrament meetings, and constantly during private interviews. While the agendas of these interviews were always set by the members, in all cases and in all meetings I used the scriptures and personal testimony—as directed or constrained by the Spirit—to direct their thinking toward exercising faith, repenting of even the "smallest" of sins, serving and worshiping with family and others in a more diligent way, and refocusing their lives toward the temple and its attendant blessings.

In every case the ward members listened dutifully to their bishop, but in so many cases they departed having heard little or nothing, their hearts for whatever reasons being closed to, or out of tune with, the words I was speaking. I do not fault them for this; the problem in many cases may have been mine. Nevertheless, some of these good Saints departed having gained no knowledge whatsoever of what the Spirit had directed me to teach; neither did their lives noticeably change.

Those who heard me, however, those whose hearts were open to the message the Spirit was conveying from their bishop to them, increased steadily in knowledge and understanding, in light and truth. Armed with this divine power, they grew in faith, changes occurred in their lives, and in all cases they progressed steadily toward a closer walk with Christ. In some cases they completed the process of being born of the Spirit. In others they developed a greater capacity to hear the whisperings of the Spirit and thus to commune with God. And in all cases they grew closer to their wives, husbands, and children, many resolving difficulties that had threatened them or their loved ones with some form of destruction.

ALL TO SEEK SPIRITUAL KNOWLEDGE

Though such spiritual knowledge, which all of us should be seeking, is sacred and carefully guarded, our expectation to receive it is nevertheless proper. As the Lord declared to us through the Prophet Joseph, "*God shall give unto you knowledge by his Holy Spirit, yea, by the unspeakable gift of the Holy Ghost,* that has not been revealed since the world was until now. . . . A time to come in the which nothing shall be withheld . . . [when all things] shall be revealed and set forth upon all who have endured valiantly for the gospel of Jesus Christ" (D&C 121:26, 28–29; italics mine).

The knowledge we are seeking, therefore, must be the kind that comes from Christ through the Holy Ghost—it must be revealed knowledge! Lest we doubt that we ordinary Saints are the ones who should receive such revelation, the Lord continues, "How long can rolling waters remain impure? What power shall stay the heavens? As well might man stretch forth his puny arm to stop the Missouri river in its decreed course, or to turn it up stream, as to hinder the Almighty from *pouring down knowledge from heaven upon the heads of the Latter-day Saints*" (D&C 121:33; italics mine).

BRIGHAM YOUNG'S DREAM

At noon on February 17, 1847, as Brigham Young lay ill at Winter Quarters, he dreamed that he went to see Joseph Smith. After pleading to be reunited with the Prophet and being told that the time was not right, President Young asked if Joseph at least had a word of counsel for the Saints.

President Young continued, "Joseph stepped toward me and looking very earnestly, yet pleasantly, said, 'Tell the people to be humble and faithful, and be sure to keep the Spirit of the Lord and it will lead them right. Be careful and do not turn away the still small voice; it will teach them what to do and where to go; it will yield the fruits of the kingdom. Tell the brethren to keep their hearts open to conviction, so that when the Holy Ghost comes to them, their hearts will be ready to receive it. They can tell the Spirit of the Lord from all other spirits; it will whisper peace and joy to their souls; it will take malice, strife and all evil from their hearts, and their whole desire will be to do good, bring forth righteousness and build up the Kingdom of God. Tell the brethren if they will follow the Spirit of the Lord they will go right. Be sure and tell the people to keep the Spirit of the Lord, and if they will, they will find themselves just as they were organized by our Father in Heaven, before they came into the world. Our Father in Heaven organized the human family, but they are all disorganized and in great confusion.'

"Joseph then showed me the pattern, how they were in the beginning. This I cannot describe, but I saw it, and saw where the priesthood had been taken from the earth [and then restored] and how it must be joined together, so that there would be a perfect chain, from Father Adam to his latest posterity. Joseph again said, 'Tell the people to be sure and keep the Spirit of the Lord and to follow it, and it will lead them just right'" (Nibley, *Exodus to Greatness,* pp. 328–29).

Six times in Brigham Young's dream, Joseph Smith counseled all Church members to get and keep the Spirit of the Lord. Can any of us imagine that he did not mean us? Or that we can have the Spirit and not also enjoy the blessings of inspiration and revelation? Elder Bruce R. McConkie explains, "Every devoted, obedient, and righteous person on earth has and does receive revelation from God. Revelation is the natural inheritance of all the faithful. 'No man can receive the Holy Ghost,' the Prophet said, 'without receiving revelations. The Holy Ghost is a revelator.' (*Teachings*, p. 328.) God is no respecter of persons, meaning that the gift of the Holy Ghost, always and invariably, will be poured out upon all those who abide the law entitling them to that divine companionship. (Acts 10:1). That Being 'with whom is no variableness, neither shadow of turning' (James 1:17) always bestows the same reward for obedience to the same law.

"To the faithful the Lord promises: 'Assuredly as the Lord liveth, who is your God and your Redeemer, even so surely shall you receive a knowledge of whatsoever things you shall ask in faith, with an honest heart, believing that you shall receive. . . . Yea, behold, I will tell you in your mind and in your heart, by the Holy Ghost, which shall come upon you and which shall dwell in your heart. Now, behold, this is the spirit of revelation.' (D&C 8:1–3; D&C 46:7; Matt. 7:7–8; James 1:5)" (*Mormon Doctrine*, p. 644).

ALL WILL NOT RECEIVE REVEALED KNOWLEDGE

The fact having been established that God will indeed give knowledge by revelation to His people, individually as well as collectively, He immediately does so by revealing why so many of us won't receive the knowledge He is offering. And though this revelation is directed toward holders of the priesthood, there is no doubt that it is applicable to us all. "Behold," He points out, "there are many called, but few are chosen. And why are they not chosen?" (D&C 121:34). This is He who is asking the question—the Lord God Jehovah! Since He obviously knows the answer, He must therefore be endeavoring to get us to think, to consider, to ponder. And the question? Why are we who have been *called* of God—not just to priesthood or Church callings but also to enter the waters of baptism and thereafter be called His sons and daughters through the baptism of the Holy Spirit—why are we *not chosen* to receive the further light and knowledge He has promised?

The answer He then gives is both straightforward and stunning: "Because their hearts are set so much upon the things of this world, and aspire to the honors of men," meaning that we have not yet *really* come out of Babylon, "that they do not learn this one lesson—That the rights of the priesthood are inseparably connected with the powers of heaven, and that the powers of heaven cannot be controlled nor handled only upon the principles of righteousness" (D&C 121:35–36).

There it is. To obtain the priesthood power and knowledge sufficient to open the heavens for ourselves, halfhearted attempts at righteousness will not do! Babylon, with all its alluring trappings and earthly treasures, must be completely abandoned, and we must thereafter seek with all the energy of our souls to please God and live by His precepts and commandments.

But, we say, we've done all that—mostly. Look how far we have come, how much enlightenment from heaven we have obtained! Besides, our remaining sins have become so few and so small, our worldly appetites so thin and anemic. Surely the Lord will cut us a little slack!

If our desires are sincere and pure, He will—just as He did with the children of Israel, prolonging our wilderness experience as we labor to gain control of those sins, lusts, and appetites that still plague our hearts. Yet this divine patience is combined with a stark warning: "That [our callings, either in the priesthood, the Church, or as God's sons and daughters] may be conferred upon us, it is true; but when we undertake to cover our sins, or to gratify our pride, our vain ambition, or to exercise control or dominion or compulsion upon the souls of the children of men, in any degree of unrighteousness, behold, the heavens withdraw themselves; the Spirit of the Lord is grieved; and when it is withdrawn, Amen to the priesthood or the authority of that man. Behold, ere he is aware, he is left unto himself, to kick against the pricks, to persecute the saints, and to fight against God. We have learned by sad experience that it is the nature and disposition of almost all men, as soon as they get a little authority, as they suppose, they will immediately begin to exercise unrighteous dominion. Hence many are called, but few are chosen" (D&C 121:37–40).

Put another way, "There are many . . . whom I have called but few of them are chosen. They who are not chosen have sinned a very grievous sin, in that they are walking in darkness at noon-day." And what does this mean? "If you keep not my commandments, the love of the Father shall not continue with you, therefore [in spite of the true light that surrounds you] you shall walk in darkness" (D&C 95:5–6, 12).

SPECIFICS ON HOW TO GAIN REVEALED KNOWLEDGE

In His loving way, the Lord then explains exactly *how* we should proceed if we wish to obtain the knowledge and power He has promised: "No power or influence can or ought to be maintained by virtue of the priesthood, only by persuasion, by long-suffering, by gentleness and meekness, and by love unfeigned; by kindness, and pure knowledge, which shall greatly enlarge the soul without hypocrisy, and without guile—reproving betimes with sharpness, when moved upon by the Holy Ghost; and then showing forth afterwards an increase of love toward him whom thou hast reproved, lest he esteem thee both to be his enemy; that he may know that thy faithfulness is stronger than the cords of death" (D&C 121:41–44).

"Let thy bowels also be full of charity towards all men, and to the household of faith," He then instructs us. "Let virtue garnish thy thoughts unceasingly." (D&C 121:45). Since we are seeking charity, or pure and unconditional love, we see that the Lord desires us to have the same, from the core of our beings, for *all* our neighbors on this earth, both in the Church and out. This becomes even more dramatic when we understand that He also wishes us to constantly cover our thoughts with a mantle of virtue or purity. Such an amazing impact these things would have on interpersonal relationships! Lust and each of its attended sexual vices would be done away; so would hatred and anger, cheating in big and little ways, lying, and every other imaginable crime or ill. If everyone would live this way, the whole world would be filled with love—the earth would be heaven, the home of Christ and His Father!

Of course, we immediately think of how far-fetched that sounds, until we realize that it is exactly what Christ's heavenly home is like. And since we are trying, through our wilderness experience, to come into His presence, behold His face, and be filled eternally with His pure and holy love, now as well as hereafter, we then realize that He is specifically instructing us—personally and individually—how to achieve that incredible goal. He even phrases it as a promise, one that for each of us is an ironclad guarantee. If we do all He has instructed, this *will* follow: "Then shall thy confidence wax strong *in the presence of God;* and the doctrine of the priesthood shall distill upon thy soul as the dews from heaven. *The Holy Ghost shall be thy constant companion,* and thy scepter an unchanging scepter of righteousness and truth; and thy dominion shall be an everlasting dominion, and without compulsory means it shall flow unto thee forever and ever" (D&C 121:45–46; italics mine).

Of course, what is being promised here, by God to us, is the same godhood that He possesses, an eternal association with Him in His glorious presence, with the Holy Ghost constantly empowering us to do, say, think, feel, know, and understand all things. As Christ tells us, "They who dwell in his presence are the church of the Firstborn; and they see as they are seen, and know as they are known, having received of his fulness and of his grace; and he makes them equal in power, and in might, and in dominion" (D&C 76:94–95).

But it begins here, in this life, as we come out of Babylon and make our way forward through the Lord's wilderness, seeking earnestly through the power of the Holy Ghost to remain out of Babylon while we grow toward Zion as sons and daughters—men and women—of Christ. How vital, therefore, is the association of the Holy Spirit! It is no wonder that Joseph was so insistent that we all obtain, and then retain, the Spirit. Neither is it any wonder that Elder Bruce R. McConkie has declared, “Men ought—above all things in this world—to seek for the guidance of the Holy Spirit. There is nothing as important as having the companionship of the Holy Ghost. Those who first receive this endowment and who then remain in tune with this member of the Eternal Godhead will receive a peace and a comfort that passeth all understanding; they will be guided and preserved in ways that are miraculous; they will be instructed until they receive all truth; they will sanctify their souls so as to dwell spotless before the Sinless One in his everlasting kingdom.

“There is no price too high, no labor too onerous, no struggle too severe, no sacrifice too great, if out of it all we receive and enjoy the gift of the Holy Ghost” (*A New Witness for the Articles of Faith,* p. 253).

Chapter Thirteen

TRAVELING ONLY AS THE LORD DIRECTS

All who travel in the Lord's wilderness are required to go precisely where He directs. Any deviation, however minor, simply adds time and additional trials to the wilderness experience, while major deviations may bring it to a halt altogether. Abraham was told, "I will lead thee by my hand, and I will take thee . . . unto a land that I will show thee" (Abraham 1:18, 2:3). Of the Jaredites, Mormon records, "They did travel in the wilderness, and did build barges, in which they did cross many waters, being directed continually by the hand of the Lord" (Ether 2:6). Lehi's obedience was chronicled as follows: "The Lord commanded my father, even in a dream, that he should take his family and depart into the wilderness. And . . . he was obedient unto the word of the Lord, wherefore he did as the Lord commanded him . . . and . . . departed into the wilderness" (1 Nephi 2:2–4).

Moses, who led the recalcitrant children of Israel into their major wilderness experience, said, "Then we turned, and took our journey into the wilderness by the way of the Red sea, as the Lord spake unto me" (Deuteronomy 2:1; Exodus 13:17–18). Later the Lord directed that they circle a certain mountain again and again until a particular lesson had been learned. Only then would He allow them to proceed along their very specific course (Deuteronomy 2:1–7).

TRUST IN THE LORD

For those who would travel in the Lord's wilderness, this lesson seems to be one of the most difficult to grasp. For some reason it is in our nature to want to stand independent above all other creatures, God included, as we forge our way through life, learning for ourselves what is right and what is wrong. At least a dozen times, I heard some variation of the following: "I'll be happy to accept this calling (or assignment), Bishop, but only on the condition that you allow me to do it my own way" (making up or changing lessons from what is in the manuals; skipping certain topics, weeks, or even months while other activities are pursued; keeping all the commandments "but this one," whatever that might be; and so on). However it might have played out in my (or any other) ward, this sort of prideful attitude is *not* to be part of the Lord's wilderness. He alone is in charge of the school of spiritual growth, and He will provide for our needs and instructions in His own time and manner. As Moses declared to Israel, "The Lord thy God . . . knoweth thy walking through this great wilderness: these forty years the Lord thy God hath been with thee; thou hast lacked nothing" (Deuteronomy 2:7).

President Spencer W. Kimball warned, "You probably think you have found a new freedom: to think wholly for yourself, to make wholly your own determinations, to criticize and decide for yourself what is right and wrong. That was decided eternities ago. Right and wrong are not to be determined by you or me. Those elements were decided for us before our birth. We have the free agency to do the right or do the wrong, but who are we to alter those changeless things? We can scoff at sacred things, express our own little opinions, but remember that millions of men and women with keener minds than ours, with more erudite training than yours and mine, have said things and done things more startling, more ugly, more skeptical than you or I could think of. . . . They have all come to grief or will ultimately. Shall the violin say to Tony Stradivarius, 'You did not make me'? Shall the created thing question the creator?" (*The Teachings of Spencer W. Kimball*, p. 160).

OBEDIENCE LEADS TO UNDERSTANDING OR KNOWLEDGE OF GOD

What the Lord is asking from wilderness wanderers is nothing less than absolute trust, absolute faith, absolute obedience. And why is that? Because in this way only can we gain godly, godlike knowledge. "There is a law, irrevocably decreed in heaven before the foundations of this world, upon which all blessings are predicated—And when we obtain any blessing from God, it is by obedience to that law upon which it is predicated" (D&C 130:20–21).

Concerning obtaining the blessing of knowledge, Joseph Smith taught, "A man is saved no faster than he gets knowledge, for if he does not get knowledge, he will be brought into captivity by some evil power in the other world, as evil spirits will have more knowledge, and consequently more power than many men who are on the earth. Hence [we] need revelation to assist us, and give us knowledge of the things of God" (*Teachings*, p. 217).

It is only with this righteous knowledge that we can come fully to Christ. Elder Neal A. Maxwell puts it this way: "Jesus' divinity is not only a reality; it is a very directing and drawing reality. We are to 'feast upon the words of Christ; for behold, the words of Christ will tell [us] all'—all, not some—of the things we should do. And, so often, 'what' we are to do is to be learned from the 'what' of the Lord we worship. So the truly Christ-centered life is one in which—without being incantational—'we talk of Christ, we rejoice in Christ, we preach of Christ, we prophesy of Christ.'

"Yet *He cannot fully receive us until we fully follow Him.* His love for us is unconditional and perfect, but ours for Him is clearly not. Being just, He cannot deviate from His standards by giving us blessings without our obedience to the laws upon which such blessings are predicated. His devotion to truth is such that even in His mercy, He cannot lie, including to Himself, about our readiness. He knows our weaknesses, but, mercifully, He also knows how to succor us as we seek to cope with them. And whatever weaknesses remain in us, He will tutor us and train us to exculpate these, if we will but let Him" (*Even As I Am*, p. 33; italics mine).

UNDERSTANDING GOD'S THOUGHTS AND WAYS

Lest we forget the goal here, the purpose of the Lord's wilderness school is to train us to think as He does and to be as He is, in all things, at all times, and in all places—in other words, to utterly purify our hearts. The Lord says, "My thoughts are not your thoughts, neither are your ways my ways. . . . For as the heavens are higher than the earth, so are my ways higher than your ways, and my thoughts than your thoughts" (Isaiah 55:8–9).

Still, the only way we can successfully graduate from the Lord's school into Zion is by manifesting through our own behavior the Lord's thoughts and ways. It is this knowledge Joseph the Prophet was speaking of earlier, when he declared that "a man is saved no faster than he gets knowledge." That is why, as was revealed through the Prophet Joseph, "the Lord requireth the heart and a willing mind" (D&C 64:34) as we become "as a child, submissive, meek, humble, patient, full of love, willing to submit to all things which the Lord seeth fit to inflict upon [us], even as a child doth submit to his father" (Mosiah 3:19). Only by developing such attributes do we learn of God. And such saving knowledge can come in no other way.

A WILLING MIND

This willing mind is made manifest first by our not complaining or wavering no matter the circumstances, and second by our never making a decision or pursuing some goal without first obtaining the mind and will of the Lord concerning it. In other words, we exercise our agency by choosing to obey. As Brigham Young said, "Does it follow that a man is deprived of his rights, because he lists [desires] in his heart to do the will of God? Must a man swear to prove that he has an agency? I contend there is no necessity for that, nor for stealing nor for doing any wrong. I can manifest to the heavens and to the inhabitants of the earth that I am free-born, and have my liberty before God, angels and men, when I kneel down to pray, certainly as much as if I were to go out and swear. I have the right to call my family together at certain hours for prayer, and I believe that this course proves that I am a free agent, as much as if I were to steal, swear, lie, and get drunk" (*Journal of Discourses,* 10:323).

FOLLOWING THE LORD

Once the Lord's mind and will is obtained, of course, there should be no deviation from strict obedience to what He has directed. And how do we know what He has directed? By following His prophets, and by following His Spirit, which are absolutely interrelated acts of obedience. Let us, however, first consider following the Spirit.

Elder Bruce R. McConkie declares, "Personal revelation is not limited to gaining a testimony and knowing thereby that Jesus, through whom the gospel came, is Lord of all, nor is it limited to receiving guidance in our personal and family affairs—although these are the most common examples of revelation among the Lord's people. In truth and in verity, there is no limit to the revelations each member of the Church may receive. It is within the power of every person who has received the gift of the Holy Ghost to see visions, entertain angels, learn the deep and hidden mysteries of the kingdom, and even see the face of God.

"If all things operate by law, and they do; if God is no respecter of persons, and certainly he is perfectly impartial; if his course is one eternal round, never varying from age to age, and such truly is the case—then all of the gifts and graces and revelations ever given to any prophet, seer, or revelator in any age will be given again to any soul who obeys the law entitling him so to receive. While discoursing about the Second Comforter and in setting forth that those whose callings and elections have been made sure have the privilege of seeing the face of the Lord while they yet dwell in the flesh, the Prophet Joseph Smith said: 'God hath not revealed anything to Joseph, but what He will make known unto the Twelve, and even the least Saint may know all things as fast as he is able to bear them' (*Teachings of the Prophet Joseph Smith,* p. 149.)" (*A New Witness for the Articles of Faith,* pp. 489–90).

It is not only our right but also our responsibility to learn to hear the Lord—to hear the whisperings of His Spirit as they come into our minds and hearts. Through Joseph Smith the Lord said, "Assuredly as the Lord liveth, who is your God and your Redeemer, even so surely shall you receive a knowledge of whatsoever things you shall ask in faith, with an honest heart, believing that you shall receive. . . . Yea, behold, *I will tell you in your mind and in your heart, by the Holy Ghost,* which shall come upon you and which shall dwell in your heart. Now, behold, this is the spirit of revelation" (D&C 8:1–3; italics mine).

Moreover, we are commanded not only to seek this revelation but also to follow with exactness that which we receive. "But ye are commanded in all things to ask of God, who giveth liberally; and *that which the Spirit testifies unto you even so I would that ye should do in all holiness of heart,* walking uprightly before me, considering the end of your salvation, doing all things with prayer and thanksgiving, that ye may not be seduced by evil spirits, or doctrines of devils, or the commandments of men; for some are of men, and others of devils. Wherefore, beware lest ye are deceived" (D&C 46:7–8; italics mine).

Is there to be any limitation to revelatory experience, any end to it? With the exception of praying about things over which we have no stewardship or over which others do, apparently not. The Lord declares, "If thou shalt ask, thou shalt receive revelation upon revelation, knowledge upon knowledge, that thou mayest know the mysteries and peaceable things—that which bringeth joy, that which bringeth life eternal" (D&C 42:61). "For thus saith the Lord—I, the Lord, am merciful and gracious unto those who fear me, and delight to honor those who serve me in righteousness and in truth unto the end. Great shall be their reward and eternal shall be their glory. And to them will I reveal *all mysteries, yea, all the hidden mysteries of my kingdom from days of old, and for ages to come, will I make known unto them the good pleasure of my will concerning all things pertaining to my kingdom.* Yea, even the wonders of eternity shall they know, and things to come will I show them, even the things of many generations. And their wisdom shall be great, and their understanding reach to heaven; and before them the wisdom of the wise shall perish, and the understanding of the prudent shall come to naught. *For by my Spirit will I enlighten them, and by my power will I make known unto them the secrets of my will—yea, even those things which eye has not seen, nor ear heard, nor yet entered into the heart of man*" (D&C 76:5–10; italics mine).

FOLLOWING THE PROPHETS

On Tuesday, April 6, 1830, during the meeting in the home of Peter Whitmer wherein was organized The Church of Jesus Christ of Latter-day Saints—"the only true and living church upon the face of the whole earth, with which I, the Lord, am well pleased" (D&C 1:30)—the Lord explained through Joseph Smith the divinely appointed role of His mortal prophet, as well as the marvelous blessings due to those who give heed to his inspired pronouncements:

"Wherefore, meaning the church, thou shalt *give heed unto all his words and commandments* which he shall give unto you as he receiveth them, walking in all holiness before me; *For his word ye shall receive, as if from mine own mouth, in all patience and faith.* For by doing these things *the gates of hell shall not prevail against you; yea, and the Lord God will disperse the powers of darkness from before you, and cause the heavens to shake for your good,* and his name's glory" (D&C 21:4–6, italics mine).

Following the prophet, then, is a commandment—a law the Lord has given us, which by living it or allowing it to govern us, blesses us to be "preserved by law and perfected and sanctified by the same" (D&C 88:34). Put another way, following the Prophet protects us from all sorts of temporal and spiritual difficulties and satanic traps while we are growing in purity and holiness—drawing ever nearer to the Lord Jesus Christ.

However, when we refuse to hearken to or obey the Prophet's counsel (or any other God-given law), "and abideth not by law, but seeketh to become a law unto [ourselves], and willeth to abide in sin, and altogether abideth in sin, [we] cannot be sanctified by law, neither by mercy, justice, nor judgment. Therefore, [we] must remain filthy still" (D&C 88:35).

By way of further explanation, Elder Maxwell writes: "Among the requirements that God has laid upon us is to pay heed to His living prophets. In our dispensation this has been described as 'following the Brethren.' It is a dimension of obedience that has been difficult for some in every dispensation. It will be particularly hard in ours, the final dispensation. Secularly, every form of control, except self-control, seems to be increasing, and yet obedience rests on self-control. . . .

"Elder Marvin J. Ashton warned of another consequence of not heeding: 'Any Church member not obedient to the leaders of this Church will not have the opportunity to be obedient to the promptings of the Lord' (Munich Area Conference Report, August 1973, p. 24). A lack of obedience to the leaders will, therefore, mean that we will not have the precious promptings of the Spirit, which we need personally—so much and so often. This potential loss would be reason enough for us to be obedient to the prophets, for apparently we cannot have one without the other. Vital as the words of the prophets are, these come to us only periodically. We need the directions of the Spirit daily, even hourly" (*All These Things Shall Give Thee Experience*, pp. 101, 104).

Concerning the benefits of following the Brethren, President Gordon B. Hinckley adds, "I give you my witness that the leaders of this church will never ask us to do anything that we cannot perform with the help of the Lord. We may feel inadequate. That which we are asked to do may not be to our liking or fit in with our ideas. But if we will try with faith and prayer and resolution, we can accomplish it.

"I give you my testimony that the happiness of the Latter-day Saints, the peace of the Latter-day Saints, the progress of the Latter-day Saints, the prosperity of the Latter-day Saints, and the eternal salvation and exaltation of this people lie in walking in obedience to the counsels of the priesthood of God" ("If Ye Be Willing and Obedient," *Ensign*, December 1971, p. 125).

Traveling through the wilderness only as the Lord directs is nothing more nor less than an exercise in obedience and humility. For most of us it will be a difficult exercise, "unless," as Elder Maxwell says, "through humility and obedience, we can transform feeling owned into a grand sense of belonging, and being purchased into gratitude for being rescued, and dependency into appreciation for being tutored by an omniscient God, which He does in order that we might become more dependable and have more independence and scope for service in the future" (*All These Things Shall Give Thee Experience*, p. 24).

HOW TO RECOGNIZE THE SPIRIT

A recognition of the whisperings of the Spirit, as well as an understanding of exactly what is being whispered, is absolutely essential if we are to come unto Christ in the fullest sense of the word. Few of us are so adept, but fortunately this can be learned by practice—by trial and error as we seek diligently to come unto Christ. Remember Joseph's statement: "By learning the Spirit of God and understanding it, you may grow into the principle of revelation, until you become perfect in Christ Jesus" (*Teachings*, p. 151).

If our hearts are right before the Lord and our desires are to follow Him at all hazards, then He will lead and guide us with patience as infinite as He, constantly guiding, encouraging, forgiving, and lifting, leading us tenderly until "the principle of revelation" has grown within us unto peace and perfection.

Chapter Fourteen

A SEPARATION FROM WORLDLY PEOPLE

Ancient wilderness travelers frequently found it necessary to separate themselves spiritually from friends and associates and even beloved family members who chose to remain worldly or attached to the wickedness of the world. This was because the Lord required the wilderness traveler's heart and soul to plumb new depths of spiritual understanding, which others, including loved ones, were frequently unwilling to consider.

As a bishop I frequently found myself giving this exact counsel, particularly to young people who, in association with certain "friends," had chosen paths of behavior that were sinful and had produced heartache and misery, not only for themselves but also for their loved ones. And in all but one of the disciplinary councils held by my bishopric, separation from unrighteous associates was a major requirement of the individual's repentance.

This concept is particularly important for those who desire to seek the face of the Lord and bring themselves into His presence. Jesus "said unto another, Follow me. But he said, Lord, suffer me first to go and bury my father. Jesus said unto him, Let the dead bury their dead: but go thou and preach the kingdom of God. And another also said, Lord, I will follow thee; but let me first go bid them farewell, which are at home at my house. And Jesus said unto him, No man, having put his hand to the plough, and looking back, is fit for the kingdom of God" (Luke 9:59–62).

Elder Bruce R. McConkie explained what Jesus meant: "I have called you; forsake the things of this world and seek for those of a better. What is the life or death of family or friends to those who are taking life and salvation to a dying world? Let those who are spiritually dead bury those in whose bodies the breath of life no longer dwells. Go thou: preach the gospel of the kingdom; proclaim faith, repentance, baptism, and the gift of the Holy Ghost. Bring souls unto me, and you shall have rest with them in the kingdom of my Father" (*The Mortal Messiah,* 2:274).

As Abraham found, leaving behind loved ones can be a difficult but necessary experience. He wrote, "My fathers, having turned from their righteousness, and from the holy commandments which the Lord their God had given unto them, unto the worshiping of the gods of the heathen, utterly refused to hearken to my voice" (Abraham 1:5).

"Accordingly a famine prevailed throughout all the land of Chaldea, and my father was sorely tormented because of the famine, and he repented of the evil which he had determined against me, to take away my life" (Abraham 1:30).

"Now the Lord had said unto me: Abraham, get thee out of thy country, and from thy kindred, and from thy father's house, unto a land that I will show thee. Therefore I left the land of Ur, of the Chaldees, to go into the land of Canaan; and I took Lot, my brother's son, and his wife, and Sarai my wife; and also my father followed after me, unto the land which we denominated Haran. And the famine abated; and my father tarried in Haran and dwelt there, as there were many flocks in Haran; and my father turned again unto his idolatry, therefore he continued in Haran. But I, Abraham, and Lot, my brother's son, prayed unto the Lord, and the Lord appeared unto me, and said unto me: Arise, and take Lot with thee; for I have purposed to take thee away out of Haran, and to make of thee a minister to bear my name in a strange land which I will give unto thy seed after thee for an everlasting possession, when they hearken to my voice" (Abraham 2:3–6).

Nephi's experience was similar. "As we journeyed in the wilderness, behold Laman and Lemuel, and two of the daughters of Ishmael, and the two sons of Ishmael and their families, did rebel against us; yea, against me, Nephi, and Sam, and their father, Ishmael, and his wife, and his three other daughters. And it came to pass in the which rebellion, they were desirous to return unto the land of Jerusalem" (1 Nephi 7:6–7).

These people wanted nothing to do with wilderness deliverance or schooling. In their rebelliousness they had never repented and been born again, and so to them what they were going through was nothing more than extreme pain and difficulty. Despite all the evidence of the hand of God in their affairs, they were blind to it, and they murmured and schemed constantly how to get out of it.

"And now I, Nephi, being grieved for the hardness of their hearts, therefore I spake unto them, saying, yea, even unto Laman and unto Lemuel: Behold ye are mine elder brethren, and how is it that ye are so hard in your hearts, and so blind in your minds, that ye have need that I, your younger brother, should speak unto you, yea, and set an example for you? How is it that ye have not hearkened unto the word of the Lord? How is it that ye have forgotten that ye have seen an angel of the Lord? Yea, and how is it that ye have forgotten what great things the Lord hath done for us, in delivering us out of the hands of Laban, and also that we should obtain the record? Yea, and how is it that ye have forgotten that the Lord is able to do all things according to his will, for the children of men, if it so be that they exercise faith in him? Wherefore, let us be faithful to him. And if it so be that we are faithful to him, we shall obtain the land of promise" (1 Nephi 7:8–13).

As Nephi points out, one who desires to live the law of the wilderness must learn not to murmur when things become painful—even if death appears to be imminent or in fact occurs. Thus, "We were about to be swallowed up in the depths of the sea. And after we had been driven back upon the waters for the space of four days, my brethren began to see that the judgments of God were upon them, and that they must perish save that they should repent of their iniquities; wherefore, they came unto me, and loosed the bands which were upon my wrists, and behold they had swollen exceedingly; and also mine ankles were much swollen, and great was the soreness thereof. Nevertheless, I did look unto my God, and I did praise him all the day long; and I did not murmur against the Lord because of mine afflictions" (1 Nephi 18:15–16).

Righteous parents suffer excruciatingly when their children choose worldliness and the ways of Satan because of hardened hearts. Of his own parents' experience, Nephi wrote, "My father, Lehi, had said many things unto them, and also unto the sons of Ishmael; but, behold, they did breathe out much threatenings against anyone that should speak for me; and my parents being stricken in years, and having suffered much grief because of their children, they were brought down, yea, even upon their sick-beds. Because of their grief and much sorrow, and the iniquity of my brethren, they were brought near even to be carried out of this time to meet their God; yea, their grey hairs were about to be brought down to lie low in the dust; yea, even they were near to be cast with sorrow into a watery grave" (1 Nephi 18:17–18).

In spite of their parents' suffering, Nephi's brothers continued to harden their hearts against Nephi and the other righteous members of his family. Therefore, the Lord directed that Nephi separate himself from his brothers. "The Lord did warn me, that I, Nephi, should depart from them and flee into the wilderness, and all those who would go with me. Wherefore, it came to pass that I, Nephi, did take my family, and also Zoram and his family, and Sam, mine elder brother and his family, and Jacob and Joseph, my younger brethren, and also my sisters, and all those who would go with me. And all those who would go with me were those who believed in the warnings and the revelations of God;

wherefore, they did hearken unto my words. And we did take our tents and whatsoever things were possible for us, and did journey in the wilderness for the space of many days. And after we had journeyed for the space of many days we did pitch our tents" (2 Nephi 5:5–7).

A SIMILAR SEPARATION

For those of us who would enter the wilderness of the Lord, a separation of sorts must also occur as we leave behind those who do not wish to travel where we are going. In our day this separation will usually be more spiritual and emotional than physical, but it will be every whit as real and as difficult as a physical separation might be. It will mean, therefore, that world-oriented loved ones will have less and less in common with us, conversations concerning things of the Spirit will decrease as our knowledge concerning the things of God increases, and our growing sense of responsibility for the spiritual welfare of our loved ones will be increasingly disdained by them. For these and numerous other reasons, separations—usually temporary—do and will occur. In this context, however, it is good to look again at the counsel of President Gordon B. Hinckley: "It is not always easy to live in the world and not be a part of it. We cannot live entirely with our own or unto ourselves, nor would we wish to. We must mingle with others. In so doing, we can be gracious. We can be inoffensive. We can avoid any spirit or attitude of self-righteousness" (*Be Thou an Example,* p. 27).

In spite of the need for courtesy to everyone, we seekers after the face of Christ must look forward to a certain amount of loneliness. If we talk of our spiritual experiences with others who are not fellow travelers, we will either be misunderstood or maligned, mocked, and perhaps even persecuted. After one or two such encounters, we learn to keep our mouths closed and lean wholly upon the strength of the Lord for our companionship. Thus does our journey become private, and even, like Nephi's and Lehi's, a guarded secret.

Hugh Nibley writes, "'He leadeth away the righteous into precious lands, and the wicked he destroyeth, and curseth the land unto them' (1 Nephi 17:38). Such was always the Lord's way. When he brought Lehi out of Jerusalem, 'no one knew about it save it were himself and those whom he brought out of the land.' Exactly so did the Lord bring Moses and the people in secret out of the wicked land of Egypt, and Abraham fled by night and secretly from Ur of the Chaldees as Lot did from Sodom and Gomorrah, and so was the city of Enoch removed suddenly to an inaccessible place. And in every case, the wicked world thus left behind is soon to be destroyed, so that those who leave the flesh-pots and the 'precious things' behind and lose all for a life of hardship are actually losing their lives to save them. It would be hard to say whether this pattern is more clearly set forth in the Old Testament or the New, but certainly it is most fully exemplified in the Book of Mormon" (*An Approach to the Book of Mormon,* p. 139).

WE WILL RETURN

It has been noted that the separation we have been speaking of, whether physical or not, must also be considered as temporary. This is because the Lord invariably expects His successfully graduated wilderness students to carry the things they have learned back to the people who have previously disdained them. That is as it should be, for the closer the seeker after Zion draws to the Lord, the more filled with charity, Christ's pure love, he becomes, and the more anxious he is to share his joyous knowledge. Of the repentant sons of Mosiah (whose wilderness school was among the Lamanites), the record states, "They were desirous that salvation should be declared to every creature, for they could not bear that any human soul should perish; yea, even the very thoughts that any soul should endure endless torment did cause them to quake and tremble. And thus did the Spirit of the Lord work upon them" (Mosiah 28:3–4).

Both Jesus Christ and Moses willingly returned to teach the very people they were originally led away from, and Enos and Alma each left vivid descriptions of their lifelong efforts to bring the message of Christ to the people they called enemies—those they loved who had chosen the things of Babylon over the things of God. In these labors they were doing nothing more than the prophets have asked of us as we reach senior citizen status—to give the remainder of our lives over to declaring the good word of God in whatever manner we are capable of doing so. As I served as bishop, I interviewed many older couples concerning various sorts of missions they might consider. (In these days we are frequently given a choice concerning how we might serve, including service missions where we never even leave our homes.) Some declined for obvious health reasons, but others declined simply because they wished to retire, relax with their grandchildren, or play away their "golden years." But for those who have been born of the Spirit and therefore desired to serve the Lord, no matter the sacrifices and inconvenience, their rewards will always be as sweet and glorious as those experienced by Enos and Alma.

Enos records, "I, Enos, went about among the people of Nephi, prophesying of things to come, and testifying of the things which I had heard and seen. And I bear record that the people of Nephi did seek diligently to restore the Lamanites unto the true faith in God. But our labors were vain . . . and they were continually seeking to destroy us. . . .

"And the people [of Nephi] were [also] a stiffnecked people, hard to understand. And there was nothing save it was exceeding harshness, preaching and prophesying of wars, and contentions, and destructions, and continually reminding them of death, and the duration of eternity, and the judgments and the power of God, and all these things—stirring them up continually to keep them in the fear of the Lord. I say there was nothing short of these things, and exceedingly great plainness of speech, would keep them from going down speedily to destruction. . . .

"And it came to pass that I began to be old. . . . And I saw that I must soon go down to my grave, having been wrought upon by the power of God that I must preach and prophesy unto this people, and declare the word according to the truth which is in Christ. And I have declared it in all my days, and have rejoiced in it above that of the world. And I soon go to the place of my rest, which is with my Redeemer; for I know that in him I shall rest. And I rejoice in the day when my mortal shall put on immortality, and shall stand before him; then shall I see his face with pleasure, and he will say unto me: Come unto me, ye blessed, there is a place prepared for you in the mansions of my Father. Amen" (Enos 1:19–20, 22–23, 25–27).

Alma also declared concerning the success of his life's work, "The Lord doth give me exceedingly great joy in the fruit of my labors; for because of the word which he has imparted unto me, behold, many have been born of God, and have tasted as I have tasted, and have seen eye to eye as I have seen; therefore they do know of these things of which I have spoken, as I do know; and the knowledge which I have is of God. And I have been supported under trials and troubles of every kind, yea, and in all manner of afflictions; yea, God has delivered me from prison, and from bonds, and from death; yea, and I do put my trust in him, and he will still deliver me. And I know that he will raise me up at the last day, to dwell with him in glory; yea, and I will praise him forever" (Alma 36:25–28).

So must it be with us.

Chapter Fifteen

THE WILDERNESS EXPERIENCE

As they passed through the wilderness, all of the Lord's highly favored experienced great trials and tribulations. Lehi wasn't just being trite when he called his own experience "the wilderness of mine afflictions" (2 Nephi 3:1) and spoke of "the days of my tribulation in the wilderness" (2 Nephi 2:1). Rather than simply handing them everything as they needed it, the Lord required the Nephites to work, to think, to use their own creativity as a means of solving their difficult problems. Yet always the Lord was near, neither taking away agency nor denying opportunities for needed lessons, but ready nevertheless to help in whatever manner He saw fit.

Yet Hugh Nibley writes, "God has more to offer those who break with the world than 'wearying in a land of sands and thorns.' The wilderness is only a transition, a difficult exercise of disengaging from the fashion of the world: 'He did straiten them in the wilderness with his rod' (1 Nephi 17:41). Besides the 'mysteries of God,' there was more awaiting the faithful: 'Ye shall prosper, and be led to a land of promise . . . which I have prepared for you; yea, even a land which is choice above all other lands' (1 Nephi 2:20). 'He leadeth away the righteous into precious lands, and the wicked he destroyeth, and curseth the land unto them for their sakes' (1 Nephi 17:38)." (*The Prophetic Book of Mormon,* p. 504). Thus, with hard work under difficult circumstances, the Lord prepares His people for the blessings He desires to impart.

THE WILDERNESS IS A SCHOOL OF WORK

Moroni wrote concerning the work the Jaredites were required to perform, "And the Lord said: Go to work and build, after the manner of barges which ye have hitherto built. And it came to pass that the brother of Jared did go to work, and also his brethren. . . . And it came to pass that the brother of Jared cried unto the Lord, saying: O Lord, I have performed the work which thou hast commanded me, and I have made the barges according as thou hast directed me" (Ether 2:16, 18).

All this was well and good. But suddenly the Jaredites perceived a problem. This voyage was going to last many days (344, as it turned out), and would therefore require more air than the vessels could possibly hold. Additionally, when the barges were closed up, they were completely dark inside, and it was discomforting to think of traveling so long in total darkness. Wishing to be obedient, and yet not knowing how to solve this problem, the brother of Jared again approached the Lord.

Interestingly, the Lord gave a solution for the problem of air, instructing them to make a hole in the top and bottom of each barge so that air could be replenished when they were above water (Ether 2:19–21). On the other hand, He left the problem of light for the brother of Jared to solve, though He did more thoroughly explain the parameters. "And the Lord said unto the brother of Jared: What will ye that I should do that ye may have light in your vessels? For behold, ye cannot have windows, for they will be dashed in pieces; neither shall ye take fire with you, for ye shall not go by the light of fire. For behold, ye shall be as a whale in the midst of the sea; for the mountain waves shall dash upon you. Nevertheless, I will bring you up again out of the depths of the sea; for the winds have gone forth out of my mouth, and also the rains and the floods have I sent forth. And behold, I prepare you against these things; for ye cannot cross this great deep save I prepare you against the waves of the sea, and the winds which have gone forth, and the floods which shall come. Therefore what will ye that I should prepare for you that ye may have light when ye are swallowed up in the depths of the sea?" (Ether 2:23–25).

Rather than answering the Lord immediately, the brother of Jared apparently withdrew and gave the matter some careful thought. An inspired plan formed in his mind, and he set out immediately to put that plan into action.

"And it came to pass that the brother of Jared, (now the number of the vessels which had been prepared was eight) went forth unto the mount, which they called the mount Shelem, because of its exceeding height, and did molten out of a rock sixteen small stones; and they were white and clear, even as transparent glass; and he did carry them in his hands upon the top of the mount, and cried again unto the Lord" (Ether 3:1).

Mahonri Moriancumer's prayer, recorded in the scriptures, is beautiful. But the beauty lies more in the incredible faith and confidence it manifests than in the poetic nature of the words themselves. As a result of that faith and confidence in the Lord, the brother of Jared received the blessing he was seeking. "And it came to pass that when the brother of Jared had said these words, behold, the Lord stretched forth his hand and touched the stones one by one with his finger" (Ether 3:6).

The Nephites had a similar experience as they were required to build a ship (1 Nephi 17:8), which was to be constructed after the manner of the Lord rather than the manner of man. Adding to the difficulty of this undertaking was the necessity of smelting ore with which to manufacture tools. Yes, the Lord revealed the location of the ore, but the labor was left up to Nephi, who had no choice but to go to work and get it done (1 Nephi 17:10–11, 16).

For Nephi the difficulties did not end there, for he had to endure the scorn and wrath of his rebellious brothers, who would not step forth to help. After he attempted to teach them, they wanted to murder him. Yet at this juncture the Lord stepped in, as he had done by touching the stones of the brother of Jared, and filled Nephi with His Spirit to such a degree that Laman and Lemuel could not stand before him but were shocked by the force of the Lord's power (1 Nephi 17:17–55). Therefore they agreed to help with the ship, and the labor was accomplished.

MURMURING IS UNRIGHTEOUS

There was also another difficulty that affected many wilderness travelers. It was the difficulty of emotional trauma and turmoil—the despair of believing that all was hopeless and that there could be no positive end to the experience.

Both Lehi and Sariah found some of the trials of the wilderness to be almost more than they could bear. They each murmured, repented, and then bore powerful testimony of the goodness of God in allowing them to enter their wilderness experience (1 Nephi 5:1–3, 16:20). And of course we are all familiar with the murmuring of the children of Israel.

DEVELOPING FAITH

For those who would pass through the Lord's wilderness school as we seek the face of Christ today, it is vital to realize that the process is helping us develop the faith and confidence in God necessary to go forth with full equanimity of spirit, no matter how difficult we find our labors. Why? Because the Lord will not do for us what we can do for ourselves, neither will He always protect us from pain, sorrow, suffering, or even death. Nevertheless, He will not depart from us. Elder Boyd K. Packer says that even when our gospel roots are firm, "some things won't seem to change a great deal. You will still have to work for what you get. You won't be immune to illness or death. You will still have problems to solve, but you will have great strength, and you will be prompted by the Spirit of the Lord in the solution of these problems" (Conference Report, October 1962, p. 49).

As Elder Robert D. Hales taught, "There is meaning and purpose in our earthly challenges. Consider the Prophet

Joseph Smith: throughout his life he faced daunting opposition—illness, accident, poverty, misunderstanding, false accusation, and even persecution. One might be tempted to ask, 'Why didn't the Lord protect His prophet from such obstacles, provide him with unlimited resources, and stop up the mouths of his accusers?' The answer is, Each of us must go through certain experiences to become more like our Savior. In the school of mortality, the tutor is often pain and tribulation, but the lessons are meant to refine and bless us and strengthen us, not to destroy us. Said the Lord to faithful Joseph: 'My son, peace be unto thy soul; thine adversity and thine afflictions shall be but a small moment. . . . If thou be cast into the deep; if the billowing surge conspire against thee; if fierce winds become thine enemy; if the heavens gather blackness, and all the elements combine to hedge up the way; . . . know thou, my son, that all these things shall give thee experience, and shall be for thy good' (D&C 121:7; 122:7).

"Despite many tribulations in the Prophet Joseph's life, great things were brought to pass for the Restoration of the gospel in these latter days. Joseph came to understand and has taught us that when he was struggling with a challenge, the Lord did not let him perish. Similarly, tests of our faith are priceless opportunities to discover how deeply the Master cares about the welfare of our souls [and helps] us endure to the end" (*Ensign*, May 2003, p. 17).

President Gordon B. Hinckley adds to our understanding: "We may know much of loneliness. We may know discouragement and frustration. We may know adversity and trouble and pain. I would hope not. But you know, and I know, that suffering comes to many. Sometimes it is mental. Sometimes it is physical. Sometimes it may even be spiritual. . . .

"One of my favorite newspaper columnists is Jenkin Lloyd Jones. In a recent article . . . he commented: 'Anyone who imagines that bliss is normal is going to waste a lot of time running around shouting that he's been robbed. The fact is that most putts don't drop. Most beef is tough. Most children grow up to be just ordinary people. Most successful marriages require a high degree of mutual toleration. Most jobs are more often dull than otherwise. . . .

"'Life is like an old-time rail journey—delays, sidetracks, smoke, dust, cinders, and jolts, interspersed only occasionally by beautiful vistas and thrilling bursts of speed. The trick is to thank the Lord for letting you have the ride.' (*BYU Speeches*, 1973, pp. 106–107). . . .

"Ours is the duty," President Hinckley continues, "to walk by faith. Ours is the duty to walk in faith, rising above the evils of the world. We are sons and daughters of God. Ours is a divine birthright. Ours is a divine destiny. We must not, we cannot sink to the evils of the world—to selfishness and sin, to hate and envy and backbiting, to the 'mean and beggarly' elements of life.

"You and I must walk on a higher plane. It may not be easy, but we can do it. Our great example is the Son of God whom we wish to follow" (*Teachings of Gordon B. Hinckley*, p. 7).

Thus, in the labor and other trials required of us, the Lord will always inspire us, instruct us, grant us the necessary strength and raw materials to accomplish what He has asked, and even step forward with miraculous solutions when we have reached the limits of our abilities.

THE LAW OF SACRIFICE

Frequently our progression requires the giving up of much (or even all) that is cherished in order to accomplish without murmuring or complaint the labor God has asked of us. This is the essence of the law of sacrifice, and only by living this law to the fullest extent possible will our wilderness experience produce the hoped-for results.

Joseph Smith taught the law of sacrifice in these words: "For a man to lay down his all, his character and reputation, his honor, and applause, his good name among men, his houses, his lands, his brothers and sisters, his wife and children, and even his own life also—counting all things but filth and dross for the excellency of the knowledge of Jesus Christ—requires more than mere belief or supposition that he is doing the will of God; but actual knowledge, realizing that, when these sufferings are ended, he will enter into eternal rest, and be a partaker of the glory of God. . . .

"A religion that does not require the sacrifice of all things never has power sufficient to produce the faith necessary [to lead] unto life and salvation; for, from the first existence of man, the faith necessary unto the enjoyment of life and salvation never could be obtained without the sacrifice of all earthly things. It was through this sacrifice, and this only, that God has ordained that men should enjoy eternal life; and it is through the medium of the sacrifice of all earthly things that men do actually know that they are doing the things that are well pleasing in the sight of God. When a man has offered in sacrifice all that he has for the truth's sake, not even withholding his life, and believing before God that he has been called to make this sacrifice because he seeks to do his will, he does know, most assuredly, that God does and will accept his sacrifice and offering, and that he has not, nor will not seek his face in vain. Under these circumstances, then, he can obtain the faith necessary for him to lay hold on eternal life.

"It is vain for persons to fancy to themselves that they are heirs with those, or can be heirs with them, who have offered their all in sacrifice, and by this means obtained faith in God and favor with him so as to obtain eternal life, unless they, in like manner, offer unto him the same sacrifice, and through that offering obtain the knowledge that they are accepted of him. . . . From the days of righteous Abel to the present time, the knowledge that men have that they are accepted in the sight of God is obtained by offering sacrifice. . . .

"Those, then, who make the sacrifice, will have the testimony that their course is pleasing in the sight of God; and those who have this testimony will have faith to lay hold on eternal life; and will be enabled, through faith, to endure unto the end, and receive the crown that is laid up for them that love the appearing of our Lord Jesus Christ. But those who do not make the sacrifice cannot enjoy this faith, because men are dependent upon this sacrifice in order to obtain this faith: therefore, they cannot lay hold upon eternal life, because the revelations of God do not guarantee unto them the authority so to do, and without this guarantee faith could not exist" (*Lectures on Faith,* pp. 58–60).

A MODERN EXAMPLE

There lived in my ward a couple of about fifty years of age whom I considered to be wonderful people. The woman was very active, serving in various callings, attending the temple, and constantly blessing the rest of us through acts of service and kindness. Yet in her heart she grieved continually, for her husband, inactive since youth, would have nothing to do with the Church. More troublesome, their only son had followed the father's example into adulthood, and so as parents they were regularly dealing with the consequences of his poor choices. Yet the woman and her grown daughters, both active in the Church, continued to live as they had been commanded, praying that the promises made in priesthood blessings—that one day both the father and the son would somehow be touched in their hearts—might come to pass.

Then came terrible trouble—the son and his young wife split apart. The court determined that neither of them could care for their children—who ranged in age from five years down to less than a year—and so the grandparent couple in my ward were made their legal guardians.

Staggered by the magnitude of "starting over again" as parents, the couple nevertheless assumed the massive responsibility and brought the children into their home. It was not easy. In fact, in many ways it was excruciatingly difficult, with sufficient terrible days to make the good ones days to cherish. I am not exaggerating when I say that our entire ward stood in awe of the willingness these people showed in "sacrificing" their "golden" years to rear a second family.

Nevertheless, out of this sweet and selfless sacrifice grew an unusual but certainly hoped-for blessing. One evening the husband appeared in my office. "Bishop," he said quietly, "I need your help. I made a mess of fatherhood the first time around! Whatever it takes for these sweet little grandkids, this time I intend to do it right! I know that's got to include being in the Church, for me as well as them, so tell me what I have to do."

There followed several searching interviews, always interspersed with the sorrow and anguish of a broken heart as this dear brother "[brought] forth fruit meet for repentance" (Alma 12:15; 13:13). At home under his direction (and to his wife's utter amazement), the principles and practices of the gospel began to be lived, including daily (and frequently intense) scripture study, personal and family prayer, family home evening, and regular and diligent church attendance. This brother also received several blessings from his bishop and others, and a change in his countenance was soon noticeable. It wasn't long before the Melchizedek Priesthood was conferred upon him, and shortly he was also giving blessings—to his thrilled wife and beloved grandchildren. Within a few additional months the couple were in the temple, first for his endowment and then for their sealing, after which their daughters were sealed to them. More, they have absolute faith that the son—the father of their little ones—will one day follow.

Can there be any doubt that the Lord is both accepting, and honoring with His love and blessings, the sacrifice of this dear couple? As they continue forward and endure to the end in their own unique circumstances, they will be perfectly entitled through these same sacrifices to the eternal blessings promised by the Lord through the Prophet Joseph Smith.

THE LAW OF THE FAST

One of the ways a sacrifice can be offered up by anyone, when the wilderness traveler feels the need for a particular blessing, is through fasting. This was taught most forcefully by the Savior, whose entire life was proclaimed as a fast. "Is not this the fast that I have chosen? to loose the bands of wickedness, to undo the heavy burdens, and to let the oppressed go free, and that ye break every yoke?" (Isaiah 58:6).

Scripturally we learn that righteous fasts are offered up to express joy in the Lord (Alma 45:1), to obtain humility and faith (Helaman 3:35), to do missionary work (Alma 6:6), to obtain the spirit of prophecy and revelation (Alma 17:3), and to teach with the power and authority of God (Alma 17:3).

As Elder Bruce R. McConkie put it, "Fasting, with prayer as its companion, is designed to increase spirituality; to foster a spirit of devotion and love of God; to increase faith in the hearts of men, thus assuring divine favor; to encourage humility and contrition of soul; to aid in the acquirement of righteousness; to teach man his nothingness and dependence upon God; and to hasten those who properly comply with the law of fasting along the path to salvation" (*Mormon Doctrine*, p. 275).

The most common way of fasting is by abstaining from both food and water for a particular period of time—usually twenty-four hours. This is an effective way of offering up sacrifice, especially when the cautionary instructions of Christ are remembered: "When ye fast, be not, as the hypocrites, of a sad countenance: for they disfigure their faces, that they may appear unto men to fast. Verily I say unto you, They have their reward. . . . That thou appear not unto men to fast, but unto thy Father which is in secret: and thy Father, which seeth in secret, shall reward thee openly" (Matthew 6:16, 18). We should also remember that in fasting our joy should be full, for "this is fasting and prayer, or in other words, rejoicing and prayer" (D&C 59:14).

OTHER FORMS OF FASTING

Not always does fasting mean going without food and water for a specific period of time. As a teenage boy I worked frequently with my father in communities distant from our own. Our lunches were eaten in restaurants, and it soon became painfully obvious that for one week each month, Dad changed our menu. During that week we drank water instead of soda, I got no chocolate shakes, and there were no other "treats" for either of us. When I complainingly grilled him about this, he explained that it was his way of fasting, and that he hoped I would be willing to fast with him.

Of course, I was, mostly, and I learned over time that fasting from food and water made him so ill with migraines that, after much desperate prayer, he had at last felt inspired to fast in this manner (which fast was made easier if I was doing it with him). This sort of fast is consistent with the counsel of our modern prophets. President Joseph F. Smith explained, "The Lord has instituted the fast on a reasonable and intelligent basis, and none of his works are vain or unwise. His law is perfect in this as in other things. Hence, those who can are required to comply thereto; it is a duty from which they cannot escape; but let it be remembered that the observance of the fast day by abstaining 24 hours from food and drink is not an absolute rule, it is no iron-clad law to us, but it is left with the people as a matter of conscience, to exercise wisdom and discretion. Many are subject to weakness, others are delicate in health, and others have nursing babies; of such it should not be required to fast" (*Gospel Doctrine,* p. 244).

In the scriptures I have read of at least two alternatives to the typical fast used by most of us today. One I will mention is what I call the Daniel fast. "In those days I Daniel was [fasting] *three full weeks.* I ate no pleasant bread, neither came flesh nor wine in my mouth, neither did I anoint myself at all, till three whole weeks were fulfilled" (Daniel 10:2–3; italics mine). Daniel offered up this fast in order to obtain specific information from the Lord. God responded by sending Daniel a heavenly messenger—Gabriel—with even more than the sought-after revelation.

To determine when and how we should fast or offer up other sacrifice, we who seek purity of heart must obtain the mind and will of God. If through that source we are given directions that seem difficult, and yet if we are certain about the source of our instructions and inspiration, then obedience to the whisperings of the Spirit—the only true option—will bring us great blessings, drawing us ever nearer to the veil behind which we will one day see the face of the Lord, Jesus Christ.

THE LORD TAKES CARE OF ALL WORLDLY NEEDS

Ancient wilderness travelers universally discovered that if they sincerely did their best to be obedient, the Lord took care of their worldly needs. As Abraham declared, "[We] dwelt in tents as we came on our way; *therefore, eternity was our covering and our rock and our salvation,* as we journeyed from Haran by the way of Jershon, to come to the land of Canaan" (Abraham 2:15–16; italics mine).

To the children of Israel, who were in a barren desert, the Lord revealed His power in a miraculous manner, giving them meat in the form of quail and then a daily portion of what they called manna. This miracle continued, week in and week out, for forty long years, until they could finally provide for themselves (Exodus 16:11–26).

The Nephites were treated differently than the children of Israel, being allowed to gather provisions from the land and to hunt for their food. "We did take our bows and our arrows, and go forth into the wilderness to slay food for our families. . . . And it came to pass that we did travel for the space of many days, slaying food by the way, with our bows and our arrows and our stones and our slings" (1 Nephi 16:14–15).

Then Nephi broke his bow, which must have seemed a horrible setback to the people. Thus the Nephites learned that even in the Lord's wilderness there will be setbacks and opposition. But through faith and diligence even these will be made into blessings—simply aiding us in the true wilderness experience.

"And it came to pass that we did return without food to our families, and being much fatigued, because of their journeying, they did suffer much for the want of food. . . . And it came to pass that I, Nephi, did make out of wood a bow, and out of a straight stick, an arrow; wherefore, I did arm myself with a bow and an arrow, with a sling and with stones. And I said unto my father: Whither shall I go to obtain food? And it came to pass that he did inquire of the Lord, for they had humbled themselves because of my words; for I did say many things unto them in the energy of my soul. And it came to pass that the voice of the Lord came unto my father; and he was truly chastened because of his murmuring against the Lord, insomuch that he was brought down into the depths of sorrow. . . .

"And it came to pass that I, Nephi, did go forth up into

the top of the mountain, according to the directions which were given upon the ball. And it came to pass that I did slay wild beasts, insomuch that I did obtain food for our families" (1 Nephi 16:19, 23–25, 30–31).

As with the children of Israel, miracles were also performed for the Nephites. Among the more unusual were that the people were made stronger than normal, and their meat was sweetened so that it could be eaten raw, without being cooked. "And thus we see," Nephi summarizes, "that . . . if it so be that the children of men keep the commandments of God he doth nourish them, and strengthen them, and provide means whereby they can accomplish the thing which he has commanded them; wherefore, he did provide means for us while we did sojourn in the wilderness" (1 Nephi 17:3).

TRUST IN THE LORD WITH ALL THINE HEART

So, we come again to learning to trust the Lord. The proverb says, "Trust in the Lord with all thine heart; and lean not unto thine own understanding. In all thy ways acknowledge him, and he shall direct thy paths" (Proverbs 3:5–6). As seekers after the face of Christ, if instead of trusting the Lord to provide for us, we allow our minds to be preoccupied with worry and vain and frantic maneuvering concerning our temporal needs, then we only prolong the trials and difficulties of our wilderness journey. As the above scriptural examples amply testify, God is not only capable but also willing and anxious to assist in providing us with exactly what we need in order to survive His wilderness. But in the Lord's wilderness school the key is sufficiency, not excess. While Elijah was in the wilderness the Lord commanded him,

"Thou shalt drink of the brook; and I have commanded the ravens to feed thee there. So [Elijah] went and did according unto the word of the Lord: for he went and dwelt by the brook Cherith, that is before Jordan. And the ravens brought him bread and flesh in the morning, and bread and flesh in the evening; and he drank of the brook" (1 Kings 17:4–6).

These were not the kinds of meals Elijah might have chosen, yet they seem to have been sufficient, and they were granted in a miraculous manner. After the brook dried up, the Lord commanded Elijah to depart: "Get thee to Zarephath, which belongeth to Zidon, and dwell there: behold, I have commanded a widow woman there to sustain thee." In other words, the Lord was now ready to take the widow woman into her own wilderness. "So [Elijah] arose and went to Zarephath. And when he came to the gate of the city, behold, the widow woman was there gathering of sticks: and he called to her, and said, Fetch me, I pray thee, a little water in a vessel, that I may drink. And as she was going to fetch it, he called to her, and said, Bring me, I pray thee, a morsel of bread in thine hand. And she said, As the Lord thy God liveth, I have not a cake, but an handful of meal in a barrel, and a little oil in a cruse: and, behold, I am gathering two sticks, that I may go in and dress it for me and my son, that we may eat it, and die. And Elijah said unto her, Fear not; go and do as thou hast said: but make me thereof a little cake first, and bring it unto me, and after make for thee and for thy son. For thus saith the Lord God of Israel, The barrel of meal shall not waste, neither shall the cruse of oil fail, until the day that the Lord sendeth rain upon the earth. And she went and did according to the saying of Elijah: and she, and he, and her house, did eat many days. And the barrel of meal wasted not, neither did the cruse of oil fail, according to the word of the Lord, which he spake by Elijah" (1 Kings 17:9–16).

As both Elijah and the widow learned, while in the wilderness we will always have sufficient but usually not much more.

THE LAW OF THE TRUE LAST MINUTE

Additionally, often that sufficient amount will not come until the last possible moment, which might be called "the law of the true last minute." Why? Because the Lord is not in the business of feeding us and making us wealthy. Rather, He is in the business of teaching us, stretching us beyond our individual self-perceived limitations, sanctifying and purifying us, and bringing us to the point where, when no earthly solution can possibly help, He stretches forth His hand and lifts our burdens. After enough of this infinitely designed stretching, which may occur repeatedly for years, our trust and confidence in Him will finally become absolute. Only in that state can we hope to come to Mount Zion with its blessings of exaltation.

Thus, in the wilderness, our temporal needs are strictly incidental to our spiritual needs. Like the widow who fed Elijah, our temporal needs will be met only when our faith has been tried sufficiently for spiritual growth to have occurred. And that seems to occur best when circumstances come down to the last possible minute—not *our* last minute but the Lord's—when there is no possible way any meal can be left in the barrel.

Hence I call it the law of the *true* last minute.

Chapter Sixteen

DISCOVERING OUR NATURAL MAN

When the children of Israel first left Egypt, the Lord led them into what the scripture calls the Wilderness of Sin (Exodus 16:1). There, immediately following their miraculous deliverance from Pharaoh, they turned against Moses and the Lord and began murmuring (Exodus 16:2). In other words, they came face to face with their own carnal natures.

After their miraculous deliverance from the wicked at the tower of Babel, and the Lord's leading them through the wilderness, the Jaredites camped in a lovely valley they called Moriancumer, where they rested for a time—four years, in fact. And there the brother of Jared, after he had been chastised for three hours by the Lord for not remembering to call upon His name during the entire time of their encampment, came face to face with his natural man (Ether 2:14–15).

All of these wilderness travelers discovered—to their

sorrow—that despite their desires to remain free from sin, they were continually beset by it. Thus, they seemed to need an inordinate amount of time on their knees repenting, and even more time on their feet as they went about their daily tasks castigating themselves and feeling godly sorrow that they were such weak servants of the Lord. The guilt of the brother of Jared, particularly, was made worse by the knowledge he had of the incredible blessings the Lord had been pouring out upon him, blessings of knowledge and understanding, of spiritual communication, of priesthood power. All these he had probably always assumed were reserved for the totally righteous, not for the spiritual flunky he now felt himself to be.

Interestingly, this is exactly the place the great Nephi had reached in his own wilderness of afflictions when he exclaimed, "Notwithstanding the great goodness of the Lord, in showing me his great and marvelous works, my heart exclaimeth: O wretched man that I am! Yea, my heart sorroweth because of my flesh; my soul grieveth because of mine iniquities. I am encompassed about, because of the temptations and the sins which do so easily beset me. And when I desire to rejoice, my heart groaneth because of my sins; nevertheless, I know in whom I have trusted. My God hath been my support; he hath led me through mine afflictions in the wilderness; and he hath preserved me upon the waters of the great deep. He hath filled me with his love, even unto the consuming of my flesh [Nephi's obtaining charity as well as the baptism of fire]. He hath confounded mine enemies, unto the causing of them to quake before me. Behold, he hath heard my cry by day, and he hath given me knowledge by visions in the nighttime. And by day have I waxed bold in mighty prayer before him; yea, my voice have I sent up on high; and angels came down and ministered unto me. And upon the wings of his Spirit hath my body been carried away upon exceedingly high mountains. And mine eyes have beheld great things, yea, even too great for man; therefore I was bidden that I should not write them.

"O then, if I have seen so great things, if the Lord in his condescension unto the children of men hath visited men in so much mercy, why should my heart weep and my soul linger in the valley of sorrow, and my flesh waste away, and my strength slacken, because of mine afflictions? And why should I yield to sin, because of my flesh? Yea, why should I give way to temptations, that the evil one have place in my heart to destroy my peace and afflict my soul? Why am I angry because of mine enemy?" (2 Nephi 4:17–27).

These are powerful questions Nephi was asking, most certainly paralleling the questions other wilderness sojourners have been plagued with. Why do we continue to sin, even when we know better? Thankfully, there are answers that should allow hope to replace the despair we frequently feel.

DISCOVERING OUR OWN MORTAL WEAKNESS

To Moroni the Lord declared, "If men come unto me I will show unto them their weakness. I give unto men weakness that they may be humble" (Ether 12:27). As should be evident, the word "weakness" is not plural and so cannot in its strictest sense be referring to the multitude of sins and inclinations to sin that we all struggle with. Being singular, it must refer to that aspect of our mortality that is also called the "natural man" (1 Corinthians 2:14; Mosiah 3:19; Alma 26:21; D&C 67:12) or "carnal nature" (D&C 67:12; Mosiah 16:5; Alma 42:10). It is what we obtained or became following our spiritual death through submission to the will of the devil.

Because of this mortal weakness, each of us has an inherent tendency to commit sin. This tendency, according to what the Lord told Moroni (and which we discussed earlier in this volume), was intentionally given or allowed us by God. How was it allowed? Through inherited genetic traits, conditions under which we are raised, the tormentings of Satan and his evil horde, circumstances we are forced to live through, consequences of sins we have committed, and so forth. And why was it allowed? To help keep us humble, penitent, and filled with faith (Ether 12:27).

Elder Bruce R. McConkie writes, "Mortal man is by nature carnal, sensual, and devilish (Alma 42:10), meaning that he has an inherent and earthly inclination to succumb to the lusts and passions of the flesh. This life is the appointed probationary estate in which it is being determined whether he will fall captive to temptations or rise above the allurement of worldly things so as to merit the riches of eternity. . . .

"Temptation—though its existence is essential to God's plan—is not of God, but is of the Devil. (Alma 34:39; 3 Nephi 6:17.) 'Blessed is the man that endureth temptation: for when he is tried, he shall receive the crown of life, which the Lord hath promised to them that love him. Let no man say when he is tempted, I am tempted of God: for God cannot be tempted with evil, neither tempteth he any man: But every man is tempted, when he is drawn away of his own lust, and enticed. Then when lust hath conceived, it bringeth forth sin: and sin, when it is finished, bringeth forth death.' (James 1:12–15)" (*Mormon Doctrine,* pp. 781–82).

TENDENCIES TO PERSONAL SIN ARE LIMITED

But there is more we can learn about our God-allowed weakness called the natural man, or the temptations, lusts, passions, and appetites that seem to be a part of it. First, no part of it will ever be so overpowering that it cannot be overcome. As Paul taught, "There hath no temptation taken you but such as is common to man: but God is faithful, who will not suffer you to be tempted above that ye are able; but will with the temptation also make a way to escape, that ye may be able to bear it" (1 Corinthians 10:13).

Second, and this became absolutely clear to me as I served as bishop, if we will examine our own behavior closely and prayerfully, we will discover that this carnal or natural man is composed of tendencies, inclinations, or appetites toward certain specific types of sin. More, these tendencies do not entice us to wickedness in every area of sin available. Rather they seem to be more limited, so that the temptations we experience, as well as the sins we commit, will generally fall into two or three areas rather than the hundreds that might be possible. In other words, God may have given us weakness, but He certainly didn't give all of them to each of us!

While one of us may struggle with alcohol or tobacco problems, another, who is not troubled with those temptations at all, will do battle daily with being honest and meanwhile not lusting. Another of us may struggle with terrible feelings of self-doubt and a lack of faith in God's ability to love such a one as us. A fourth may be required to fight constantly against anger, violence, and other abusive activities. And a fifth may labor diligently to overcome homosexual desires.

Having such tendencies or inclinations, no matter their exact nature, does not mean we are evil. Rather, wickedness occurs as we submit to them and go "contrary to the nature of God" (Alma 41:11) by committing sin (Mosiah 3:19). Remember, God has allowed us these carnal or natural tendencies as we submitted to the will of the devil. Why? So that by striving to rise above them according to "the enticings of the Holy Spirit," we can become humble, penitent, and filled with faith in the Lord Jesus Christ. And since these latter are attributes the wilderness traveler needs to develop, and since he or she is seeking to overcome his or her own "natural man," it follows that we must come to a thorough understanding of the nature of our own personal weakness before we can overcome it. And by understanding our own natural weakness, we will be better armed to completely overcome not only it but also those particular sins our natural man begets that we battle against so constantly.

THE GRACE OF CHRIST

So, how do we come to understand our natural man and put it behind us? In the same way that we learned of all our sins before we were born of the Spirit: by going before God and asking for it to be made known—in all of its ramifications and details. That is why the Lord said, "If men come unto me I will show unto them their weakness." He will! A step at a time and over time, He will! And there is eternal hope in this, for the Lord continues, "My *grace is sufficient for all men that humble themselves before me;* for if they humble themselves before me, and have faith in me, *then will I make weak things become strong unto them.* Behold, I will show unto the Gentiles their weakness and I will show unto them that *faith, hope and charity bringeth unto me*—the fountain of all righteousness" (Ether 12:27–28; italics mine).

In other words, we must continue our quest to come unto Christ with all the glorious ramifications we have discussed. Having this same knowledge, Nephi concluded his lament by exclaiming, as should we, "Awake, my soul! No longer droop in sin. Rejoice, O my heart, and give place no more for the enemy of my soul. Do not anger again because of mine enemies. Do not slacken my strength because of mine afflictions. Rejoice, O my heart, and cry unto the Lord, and say: O Lord, I will praise thee forever; yea, my soul will rejoice in thee, my God, and the rock of my salvation. O Lord, wilt thou redeem my soul? Wilt thou deliver me out of the hands of mine enemies? Wilt thou make me that I may shake at the appearance of sin? May the gates of hell be shut continually before me, because that my heart is broken and my spirit is contrite! O Lord, wilt thou not shut the gates of thy righteousness before me, that I may walk in the path of the low valley, that I may be strict in the plain road! O Lord, wilt thou encircle me around in the robe of thy righteousness! O Lord, wilt thou make a way for mine escape before mine enemies! Wilt thou make my path straight before me! Wilt thou not place a stumbling block in my way—but that thou wouldst clear my way before me, and hedge not up my way, but the ways of mine enemy.

"O Lord, I have trusted in thee, and I will trust in thee

forever. I will not put my trust in the arm of flesh; for I know that cursed is he that putteth his trust in the arm of flesh. Yea, cursed is he that putteth his trust in man or maketh flesh his arm. Yea, I know that God will give liberally to him that asketh. Yea, my God will give me, if I ask not amiss; therefore I will lift up my voice unto thee; yea, I will cry unto thee, my God, the rock of my righteousness. Behold, my voice shall forever ascend up unto thee, my rock and mine everlasting God. Amen" (2 Nephi 4:28–35).

Chapter Seventeen

COMING TO THE LAND BOUNTIFUL

After Lehi and his family had been journeying in the wilderness for a period of eight years, the Lord gave them a temporary reprieve from their daily toil and struggles. This reprieve they called the Land Bountiful "because of its much fruit and also wild honey." Nephi wrote, "All these things were prepared of the Lord that we might not perish. And we beheld the sea, which we called Irreantum, which, being interpreted, is many waters. And it came to pass that we did pitch our tents by the seashore; and notwithstanding we had suffered many afflictions and much difficulty, yea, even so much that we cannot write them all, we were exceedingly rejoiced when we came to the seashore; and we called the place Bountiful, because of its much fruit" (1 Nephi 17:5–6).

Abraham was also granted reprieves—two, in fact—from the terrible famine that pervaded his wilderness experience.

He first went to Haran, where "the famine abated" (Abraham 2:4–5). Later he left Haran and made his way toward the land of Egypt, for though the famine was everywhere else, in Egypt there was plenty, and Abraham prospered there (Abraham 2:21).

The Jaredites were also led to a "land Bountiful," which they called Moriancumer, after the name of Jared's brother, where they tarried and rested for four years, recouping their strength and preparing to continue their journey (Ether 2:13).

THE LORD ALLOWS OCCASIONAL REST FROM OUR LABORS

Modern wilderness travelers will also be granted occasional periods of rest—lands of Bountiful or Moriancumer where the intensity of the wilderness schooling will be eased. During these periods of "rest," it is expected that we will prepare for further wilderness experiences by taking advantage of all the Lord gives us. It is further expected that, as both Nephi and the brother of Jared were commanded, we use the time of respite to draw ever nearer to the Lord through rejoicing with gratitude, as well as fasting and mighty prayer.

Chapter Eighteen

THE MINISTRY OF ANGELS

One day as I was sitting in a Gospel Doctrine class, a brother made an interesting comment. "In our Church we believe in the ministry of angels," he declared rather sarcastically, "but if you don't want to get kicked out of the Church, you hadn't better ever see one!"

Feeling troubled, I pondered his comment for some time, and finally I called him in to visit with me. "Do you really believe that?" I asked after repeating his earlier remark.

"Pretty much, yes," he responded. "What would you do, Bishop, if I stood up in testimony meeting and announced that an angel had appeared to me and had given me a message from the Lord?"

"I suppose I'd listen to see what the message was."

"What difference would that make?"

"All the difference in the world. You see, the issue is

stewardship. If you described receiving a message that was clearly for yourself or your family, and the experience had strengthened your testimony, I would rejoice in your spiritual growth and encourage you to cherish the experience.

"If, on the other hand, you began announcing a message that was for the entire ward, or worse yet, for the Church or for all mankind, I would arise and ask you to take your seat and come visit with me after the meeting."

"Because I don't have the stewardship for such a revelation or visitation," he mused. "That makes sense, and I think you'd be doing the right thing. But you really wouldn't question me if I claimed to have actually seen an angel? One who came only to help me or my family?"

"Why should I?" I asked. "Don't you think I believe in them?"

"Well, yeah, I guess so. But . . . I mean, have *you* ever known anyone who saw an angel?"

"Yes. Me."

"You?" He was absolutely incredulous, and in that instant the Spirit whispered to me that the man's real problem was a lack of faith—he didn't really believe in angels at all.

"That's right," I went on. "My daughter Charity was an angel, and I saw her every day for nearly eight years."

"That's not what I meant, and you know it!"

"Actually, brother, I think it is. After all, who, really, are angels? Children of God, just as we are, who are in a different stage of their eternal progression. Charity's patriarchal blessing indicated that she was sent to us, by the Lord, as a mighty blessing to and for our family. Isn't that a good description of the mission of an angel?"

He nodded. "I guess so. Yeah."

"Moreover, as the Lord sent messengers to teach Adam and Eve, so He then sent Adam and Eve to teach those same things to their children. Doesn't that place them in the same position as angels? And since he has commanded each of us in the latter-day Church to teach those same things to *our* children, might we not also be regarded as angelic messengers, on an errand from the Lord? In addition to which, how do you know what roles you, personally, played during the eternities you spent in the premortal world? Might not any or even all of us have served as angels or messengers to those who were already in mortality—whether they saw us and recorded our visits or not?"

Clearly he had never considered such things, and he left the bishop's office with a new attitude toward the ministry of angels, not only believing in them but for the first time actually considering their real identity.

SEEKING MESSENGERS

Adam's quest to obtain messengers, once he had entered the lone and dreary world of his wilderness experience, is no idle tale. Beginning with him, all who sought the face of the Lord anciently also sought for such visitations. And if they remained faithful in gospel study, strict obedience, mighty prayer, and the proper attitude during both the hard times and the Bountifuls, they grew stronger and stronger in the Spirit, and closer and closer to the Lord, until they were blessed with what the Lord calls the ministering of angels. Thus, after profound personal anguish and diligent prayer, an angel finally appeared to Adam (can his relief even be imagined?) and instructed him in the law of sacrifice and obedience (Moses 5:6–7). More, an angel delivered Abraham from the sacrificial altar in Ur of the Chaldees (Abraham 1:15), and Jacob obtained his endowment and new name (Israel) from an angel (Genesis 32:24–30).

One of the most singular aspects of the Book of Mormon is its consistent testimony of the ministry of angels to mortal men and women. In 1 Nephi we learn that an angel visited Nephi and his brothers while they hid in the cavity of a rock (1 Nephi 3:29–30). More, an angel as well as the premortal Christ conducted Nephi through his great vision of the history of the world (1 Nephi 11:14). King Benjamin was given the words of his final address to his people by an angel of God (Mosiah 3:2–27), Amulek saw an angel who told him of Alma's coming (Alma 10:7), Nephi the son of Helaman had angels minister unto him daily (3 Nephi 7:18), and many of King Lamoni's people saw angels (Alma 19:34).

Alma, Ammon, Aaron, Omner, and Himni were warned of their own impending destruction by an angel (Mosiah 27:11–16). Later the same angel appeared to Alma, complimented him on the righteousness of his repentance, and gave him further instructions concerning his missionary work (Alma 8:15). No doubt because of his own experiences, Alma spoke frequently of angels and their missions, saying, "The voice of the Lord, by the mouth of angels, doth declare [the Savior's coming] unto all nations; yea, doth declare it, that they may have glad tidings of great joy; yea, and he doth sound these glad tidings among all his people, yea, even to them that are scattered abroad upon the face of the earth; wherefore [angels] have come unto us. . . . For behold, angels are declaring it unto many at this time in our land; and this is for the purpose of preparing the hearts of the children of men to receive his word at the time of his coming in his glory. And now we only wait to hear the joyful news declared unto us by the mouth of angels, of his coming; . . . and it shall be made known unto just and holy men, by the mouth of angels, at the time of his coming, that the words of our fathers may be fulfilled" (Alma 13:22, 24–26).

"And now, he imparteth his word by angels unto men, yea, not only men but women also. Now this is not all; little children do have words given unto them many times, which confound the wise and the learned" (Alma 32:23).

"Is it not as easy at this time for the Lord to send his angel to declare these glad tidings unto us as unto our children, or as after the time of his coming?" (Alma 39:19).

And "by the ministering of angels," Mormon wrote, "and by every word which proceeded forth out of the mouth of God, men began to exercise faith in Christ; and thus by faith, they did lay hold upon every good thing" (Moroni 7:25).

In fact, the words *angel* and *angels* appear 138 times in the Book of Mormon, attesting to the importance the Nephite prophets placed upon angelic ministrations.

THE IDENTITY OF ANGELS

But who exactly are these angels, and is there a particular order to them and their ministry? While wrapped in vision with Sidney Rigdon, Joseph Smith declared, "We saw the glory of the celestial [kingdom], which excels in all things—where God, even the Father, reigns upon his throne forever and ever. . . . They who dwell in his presence are the church of the Firstborn; and they see as they are seen, and know as they are known, having received of his fulness and of his grace; and he makes them equal in power, and in might, and in dominion" (D&C 76:92, 94–95).

The Apostle Paul declared to those Hebrews who had come unto Christ, "Ye are come unto mount Sion, and unto the city of the living God, the heavenly Jerusalem, and to an innumerable company of angels, to the general assembly and church of the firstborn, which are written in heaven, and to God the Judge of all, and to the spirits of just men made perfect, And to Jesus the mediator of the new covenant" (Hebrews 12:22–24). In other words, the righteous Hebrew Saints had attained the right to the ministry and association of the angelic members of Christ's heavenly Church—the general assembly and Church of the Firstborn.

SPIRITUAL ORGANIZATION IN THE HEREAFTER

Joseph Smith declared, "The organization of the spiritual and heavenly worlds, and of spiritual and heavenly beings, was agreeable to the most perfect order and harmony: their limits and bounds were fixed irrevocably, and voluntarily subscribed to in their heavenly estate by themselves, and were by our first parents subscribed to upon the earth. Hence the importance of embracing and subscribing to principles of eternal truth by all men upon the earth that expect eternal life" (*History of the Church,* 6:51).

This perfect organization of heavenly beings associated with this world, according to President John Taylor, refers to the different grades or levels of angels. He wrote, "The angels are our watchmen, for Satan said to Jesus: 'He shall give his angels charge concerning thee: and in their hands they shall bear thee up, lest at any time thou dash thy foot against a stone' (Matthew 4:6). It would seem from a careful perusal of the scriptures, that the angels, while God has saints upon the earth, stay in this lower world to ward off evil: for the prophet Isaiah has left this testimony on the subject (Isaiah 63:7–9).

"The angels that have gone forth at sundry times to execute the decrees of God, fully substantiate this fact: Abraham, Hagar, Jacob, Balaam, Joshua, Gideon, together with the enemies of the Lord, are the witnesses who knew the power and offices of angels on earth.

"But lest we take up too much time on the resurrected bodies, who go and come at the bidding of him who was, and is, and is to come, we will change the theme to the thoughts and witnesses of the heart. The action of the angels, or messengers of God, upon our minds, so that the heart can conceive things past, present, and to come, and revelations from the eternal world, is, among a majority of mankind, a greater mystery than all the secrets of philosophy, literature, superstition, and bigotry, put together. Though some men try to deny it, and some try to explain away the meaning, still there is so much testimony in the Bible, and among a respectable portion of the world, that one might as well undertake to throw the water out of this world into the moon with a teaspoon, as to do away with the supervision of angels upon the human mind. . . . *But, without going into a particular detail of the offices and duties of the different grades of angels,* let us close by saying that the angels gather the elect, and pluck out all that offends. They are the police of heaven and report whatever transpires on earth, and carry the petitions and supplications of men, women, and children to the mansions of remembrance, where they are kept as tokens of obedience by the sanctified, in 'golden vials' labelled 'the prayers of the saints'" (*The Gospel Kingdom,* p. 31; italics mine).

These different grades of angels would include resurrected beings (D&C 129:1), the spirits of just individuals made perfect (D&C 129:3), and translated beings (D&C 7:6). A fourth class of spirit beings might be departed members of the Church who are still "coming unto Christ" and yet are called, from time to time, to minister to their mortal loved ones. It is possible that these people are also part of what is referred to as the "general assembly and church of Enoch, and of the Firstborn" (D&C 76:67, Hebrews 12:22–23).

In a nontechnical sense, all these beings can be referred to as angels, for all are allowed to interact with mortals and to have communion with members of the mortal church—according to their respective stewardships. Therefore, under the direction of Christ and by the power of the Holy Ghost, they speak the words of Christ (Moroni 7:31; 2 Nephi 32:3), thereby encouraging and giving power and direction to members of the mortal Church.

RESURRECTED BEINGS

Resurrected beings are the highest order of beings who make up the heavenly general assembly and Church of the Firstborn. The Lord has said that these are true angels, resurrected personages who have taken back their formerly mortal bodies of flesh and bone, just as Jesus did in His resurrection (D&C 129:1).

As an example, Joseph Smith declared, "We read in Genesis, 4th chap., 4th verse, that Abel brought of the firstlings of the flock and the fat thereof, and the Lord had respect to Abel and to his offering. And, again, "By faith Abel offered unto God a more excellent sacrifice than Cain, by which he obtained witness that he was righteous, God testifying of his gifts; and by it he being dead, yet speaketh." (Heb. 11:4). How doth he yet speak? Why he magnified the Priesthood which was conferred upon him, and died a righteous man, and therefore *has become an angel of God by receiving his body from the dead,* holding still the keys of his dispensation; and was sent down from heaven unto Paul to minister consoling words, and to commit unto him a knowledge of the mysteries of godliness" (*History of the Church,* 4:208).

SPIRITS OF JUST INDIVIDUALS MADE PERFECT

The second order or level of beings in the heavenly Church are the spirits of just individuals made perfect, they who are not yet resurrected but inherit the same glory (D&C 129:1, 3). While resurrected beings can appear as glorious beings *or* as normal individuals, the spirits of just individuals made perfect can appear only in their glory (D&C 129:6).

During his funeral address for Brother James Adams, the Prophet Joseph revealed some insight into these spirits of the just. He declared, "I assure the Saints that truth, in reference to these matters, can and may be known through the revelations of God in the way of His ordinances, and in answer to prayer. The Hebrew Church 'came unto the spirits of just men made perfect, and unto an innumerable company of angels, unto God the Father of all, and to Jesus Christ, the Mediator of the new covenant.' What did they learn by [the] coming of the spirits of just men made perfect? Is it written?

No. What they learned has not been and could not have been written. What object was gained by this communication with the spirits of the just? It was the established order of the kingdom of God: the keys of power and knowledge were with them to communicate to the Saints. Hence the importance of understanding the distinction between the spirits of the just and angels.

"*Spirits can only be revealed in flaming fire or glory. Angels have advanced further, their light and glory being tabernacled; and hence they appear in bodily shape.* The spirits of just men are made ministering servants to those who are sealed unto life eternal, and it is through them that the sealing power comes down.

"Patriarch Adams is now one of the spirits of the just men made perfect; and, if revealed now, must be revealed in fire; and the glory could not be endured. Jesus [a resurrected being] showed Himself to His disciples, and they thought it was His spirit, and they were afraid to approach His spirit. Angels have advanced higher in knowledge and power than spirits. . . .

"The spirits of the just are exalted to a greater and more glorious work [than are mortals]; hence they are blessed in their departure to the world of spirits. Enveloped in flaming fire, they are not far from us, and know and understand our thoughts, feelings, and motions, and are often pained therewith" (*History of the Church,* 6:51–52; italics mine).

TRANSLATED BEINGS

The third group of beings who are part of the heavenly Church are known as translated beings. As the Lord declared to the Prophet Joseph, "[John the Revelator] has undertaken a greater work; *therefore I will make him as flaming fire and a ministering angel;* he shall minister for those who shall be heirs of salvation who dwell on the earth" (D&C 7:6; italics mine).

The Prophet Joseph also gave an example of a translated being, saying, "Now this Enoch God reserved unto Himself, that he should not die at that time, and appointed unto him a ministry unto terrestrial bodies, of whom there has been but little revealed. He is reserved also unto the Presidency of a dispensation, and more shall he said of him and terrestrial bodies in another treatise. He is a ministering angel, to minister to those who shall be heirs of salvation and appeared unto Jude as Abel did unto Paul; therefore Jude spoke of him (Jude, 14, 15 verses). And Enoch, the seventh from Adam, revealed these sayings: 'Behold, the Lord cometh with ten thousands of His Saints.'

"Paul was also acquainted with this character, and received instructions from him. 'By faith Enoch was translated, that he should not see death, and was not found, because God had translated him; for before his translation he had this testimony, that he pleased God; but without faith, it is impossible to please Him, for he that cometh to God must believe that He is, and that he is a revealer to those who diligently seek him.' (Heb. 11:5).

"Now the doctrine of translation is a power which belongs to this Priesthood. There are many things which belong to the powers of the Priesthood and the keys thereof, that have been kept hid from before the foundation of the world; they are hid from the wise and prudent to be revealed in the last times" (*History of the Church,* 4:209–10).

SPIRITS OF RIGHTEOUS MEN AND WOMEN

Finally, there is a fourth group of spirit beings who have lived good and honorable lives and then passed on but have not yet made their callings and elections sure. Nevertheless, they have obtained paradise, where they are allowed to rest from the temptations of Satan and the cares of the world while continuing their eternal progression. As far as we know, these people minister, as they are able or allowed, to their own mortal loved ones.

These, as well as the ministrations of resurrected beings, translated beings, and the spirits of just individuals who have been made perfect, all of them working through the power of the Holy Ghost, are what comprise the ministering of angels.

MESSENGERS

Primarily, according to the scriptures, heavenly beings act as messengers to mortals—delivering priesthood ordinances and keys (D&C 13; 128:20–21), teaching the doctrines of salvation (Mosiah 3), calling to repentance (Moroni 7:31; Mosiah 27:11–17), instructing in the performance of callings (Genesis 24:7), and performing every needful thing relative to God's work (Moroni 7:29–33). As D&C 129:4 says, "When a messenger comes saying he has a message from God . . ." They are bearers of information.

Always these messages will be delivered through the power of the Holy Ghost, and they will be the words of Christ. As the prophet Nephi declared, "Angels speak by the power of the Holy Ghost; wherefore, they speak the words of Christ" (2 Nephi 32:3).

MODERN MINISTRATIONS

All who enter the Lord's wilderness school are given access by the Lord to the ministering of angels—this that each of us might successfully accomplish God's work of bringing us unto Christ. As earnest seekers after Christ and His pure love, we now begin a rapid education in the doctrines of the priesthood through the ministrations of our heavenly fellow Saints—the angels of God.

Concerning this, Joseph Smith said on August 13, 1843, "You have come to an innumerable company of angels [and] to the general assembly and church of the First Born. And for what were [you] brought thus far? I answer, [you] came to these personages to learn of the things of God and to hear revealed through them the order and glory of the kingdoms of God" (*Words*, p. 240).

The Lord states, "The power and authority of the higher, or Melchizedek Priesthood, is to hold the keys of all the spiritual blessings of the church—to have the privilege of receiving the mysteries of the kingdom of heaven, to have the heavens opened unto [you], to commune with the general assembly and church of the Firstborn, and to enjoy the communion and presence of God the Father, and Jesus the mediator of the new covenant. The power and authority of the lesser, or Aaronic Priesthood, is to hold the keys of the ministering of angels" (D&C 107:18–20).

Brigham Young declared, "What is the sum of the whole teachings of him who has created [the universe]? Simply this—Son, daughter, live before me, so that I can come and visit you; order your lives with that propriety, that I will not be disgraced to come and abide with you for a season; or, when I send my angels or my minister the Holy Ghost to reveal my mind and will to you, or to bless you with abiding comfort, that they may not be disgraced in your society.

"I say, all the revelations of God teach simply this—Son, daughter, you are the workmanship of mine hands: walk and live before me in righteousness; let your conversation be chaste; let your daily deportment be according to my law; let your dealings one with another be in justice and equity; let my character be sacred in your mouth, and do not profane my holy name and trample upon mine authority; do not despise any of my sayings, for I will not be disgraced. *I wish to send one of my servants to visit you.* What for? That you may see and know as others have—that you may see as you are seen—that you may understand those principles pertaining more particularly to the kingdom you are in. You have descended below all things. I have, in my wisdom, reduced you; I have caused that you should drink of the dregs of the bitter cup. I have placed you in the depths of ignorance, and have surrounded you with weakness, to prove you. I have subjected you to all misery, and darkness, and every species of unbelief and wickedness reign, to prove you, that you may understand and know the good from the evil, and be capable of judging between these with a righteous judgment.

"I have caused all this to be done; and now, son and daughter, the inhabitants of the whole earth that have lived from the days of Adam until now, the first and the last,—the grand aim of all that I, the Lord have revealed is to instruct you to live so that I can come and visit you, *or send my angels, that they can enter into your habitations, walk and converse with you, and they not be disgraced.* By so doing, you shall be made partakers of all knowledge and wisdom, power and glory that the sanctified, or glorified beings enjoy. And this is, first of all, what the Lord wishes of the people" (*Journal of Discourses,* 6:284–85; italics mine).

AN ORDER IN ALL THINGS

Because the ministering of angels requires a lesser amount of power, or spiritual preparation, than does communing with God and Christ, it follows that angels will come first in the spiritual growth of the wilderness traveler. Thus the Lord has stated, "Ye are not able to abide the presence of God now, neither the ministering of angels; wherefore, continue in patience until ye are perfected" (D&C 67:13). He has also said, "Marvel not at these things, for ye are not yet pure; ye can not yet bear my glory; but ye shall behold it if ye are faithful in keeping all my words that I have given you, from the days of Adam to Abraham, from Abraham to Moses, from Moses to Jesus and his apostles, and from Jesus and his apostles to Joseph Smith, whom I did call upon by mine angels, my ministering servants, and by mine own voice out of the heavens, to bring forth my work" (D&C 136:37).

THE SPIRITS OF ELIAS AND ELIJAH

On Sunday, March 10, 1844, Joseph Smith stood in the Nauvoo Temple and gave an address in which he stated, "The Spirit of Elias is first, Elijah second, and Messiah last. Elias is a forerunner to prepare the way, and the spirit and power of Elijah is to come after, holding the keys of power, building the temple to the capstone, placing the seals of the Melchizedek Priesthood upon the house of Israel and making all things ready. Then Messiah . . . which is all power in Heaven and in Earth . . . comes to his temple, which is last of all" (*Words,* pp. 331–32, 336).

While this had obvious reference to the coming of the Savior, Moses, Elias, and Elijah to Joseph Smith and Oliver Cowdery in the Kirtland Temple on April 3, 1836, it is just as apparent that Joseph wished the Saints to understand the way or order in which these visitations applied to them. Besides the blessings that flow to all of us through the restoration of their keys and powers, worthy individuals who have been born of the Spirit would progress into and through the wilderness, learning divine knowledge through the administrations of selected angelic messengers—each acting as an Elias or forerunner—until they are prepared to receive for themselves, through the sealing powers of Elijah as conferred upon the prophets, the highest ordinances available to mortals. And all this, of course, is preparatory to seeing the face of Christ by receiving the Messiah as Second Comforter and being ministered to by Him.

A clear recognition of the labor of angels, as well as a deepening understanding of the mysteries of godliness as granted through personal revelation, makes the ministering of angels while in the wilderness much easier to comprehend and accept.

Chapter Nineteen

THE SCRIPTURES AND MIGHTY PRAYER

In His mercy the Lord provided His ancient wilderness travelers with miraculous means of direct communication with Him, which gave them necessary day-to-day information about how to survive His schooling. "The Lord commanded [the Jaredites] that they should go forth into the wilderness, yea, into that quarter where there never had man been. And it came to pass that the Lord did go before them, and did talk with them as he stood in a cloud, and gave directions whither they should travel" (Ether 2:5). For Abraham, the Lord provided revelatory instruments whose names have become quite famous in the generations since. "I, Abraham, had the Urim and Thummim, which the Lord my God had given unto me, in Ur of the Chaldees" (Abraham 3:1).

At first Lehi received personal revelation through dreams

and open visions. But as his wilderness experience progressed, the Lord gave him and his family a tool with which they could obtain daily revelation about how they were to survive as they journeyed forward: "The voice of the Lord spake unto my father by night, and commanded him that on the morrow he should take his journey into the wilderness. And it came to pass that as my father arose in the morning, and went forth to the tent door, to his great astonishment he beheld upon the ground a round ball of curious workmanship; and it was of fine brass. And within the ball were two spindles; and the one pointed the way whither we should go into the wilderness" (1 Nephi 16:9–10).

"And it came to pass that the voice of the Lord said unto him: Look upon the ball, and behold the things which are written. And it came to pass that when my father beheld the things which were written upon the ball, he did fear and tremble exceedingly, and also my brethren and the sons of Ishmael and our wives. And it came to pass that I, Nephi, beheld the pointers which were in the ball, that they did work according to the faith and diligence and heed which we did give unto them. And there was also written upon them a new writing, which was plain to be read, which did give us understanding concerning the ways of the Lord; and it was written and changed from time to time, according to the faith and diligence which we gave unto it. And thus we see that by small means the Lord can bring about great things" (1 Nephi 16:26–29).

These examples indicate that the Lord had no single way of helping his ancient people receive revelation. Whatever would bring the best all-around results for each group, both temporally and spiritually, was the method He apparently chose to use.

THE SCRIPTURES—THE VOICE OF THE LORD

We have already discussed the importance of obtaining the companionship of the Holy Ghost so that we might receive revelation through His power. In our day, however, He has given us an added means of obtaining His voice and His will. Today He has given us the scriptures—the word of the Lord, which is His voice (D&C 84:60) as it has been revealed to and recorded by His designated and authorized servants—made clear in our minds and hearts by the power of the Holy Ghost. Therefore, to successfully come unto Christ and behold His face as we attain Mount Zion, we must make a constant, careful, and prayerful study of His word. If this is neglected, the wilderness experience will be prolonged, perhaps forever.

Nephi records concerning their scriptures, the plates of brass, "I and my father had kept the commandments wherewith the Lord had commanded us. And we had obtained the records which the Lord had commanded us, and searched them and found that they were desirable; yea, even of great worth unto us, insomuch that we could preserve the commandments of the Lord unto our children. Wherefore, it was wisdom in the Lord that we should carry them with us, as we journeyed in the wilderness towards the land of promise" (1 Nephi 5:20–22).

Abraham was also given the scriptures prior to his journeying into the wilderness, so that he, too, might become familiar with them. By diligent study, therefore, he was enabled to more easily recognize the voice of the Lord: "The records of the fathers, even the patriarchs, concerning the right of Priesthood, the Lord my God preserved in mine own hands; therefore a knowledge of the beginning of the creation, and also of the planets, and of the stars, as they were made known unto the fathers, have I kept even unto this day, and I shall endeavor to write some of these things upon this record, for the benefit of my posterity that shall come after me" (Abraham 1:31).

BRIGHAM REMEMBERS JOSEPH

For the Lord's modern wilderness travelers, an occasional cursory examination of the scriptures is not sufficient. After all, the scriptures are His voice, which we have been commanded to hearken to and obey. How can we do either if we are not totally familiar with what He has said? Besides which, after we have been born again, the Holy Ghost enlightens our minds about the meaning of the scriptures in our own lives. Earlier Joseph Smith was quoted describing how the Holy Ghost enlightened his mind so that the scriptures, including their most mysterious passages, were made plain and simple (Joseph Smith–History 1:74).

Adding to our information about how this opening of scriptural knowledge was used by Joseph Smith, Brigham Young said, "What is the nature and beauty of Joseph's mission? You know that I am one of his Apostles. When I first heard him preach, he brought heaven and earth together; and all the priests of the day could not tell me anything correct about heaven, hell, God, angels, or devils; they were as blind as Egyptian darkness. When I saw Joseph Smith, he took heaven, figuratively speaking, and brought it down to earth; and he took the earth, brought it up, and opened up, in plainness and simplicity, the things of God; and that is the beauty of his mission. . . . Did not Joseph do the same to your understandings? Would he not take the Scriptures and make them so plain and simple that everybody could understand? Every person says, 'Yes'" (*Journal of Discourses,* 5:332).

Truly the things of God are known only by the power of the Spirit of God (1 Corinthians 2). Therefore, the scriptures must become a daily source of inspiration and instruction. In fact, earnest seekers ought to go before the Lord at least daily, seeking direction on where and what to study in the scriptures in order to obtain His mind and will concerning them for that particular day.

UNDER CONDEMNATION

One unsettling facet of scripture study is what happens if it is neglected. This is particularly serious for wilderness travelers, for as the Lord says, "Your minds in times past have been darkened because of unbelief, and *because you have treated lightly the things you have received*—which vanity and unbelief have brought the whole church under condemnation. And this condemnation resteth upon the children of Zion, even all. And they shall remain under this condemnation until they repent and remember the new covenant, even *the Book of Mormon and the former commandments which I have given them, not only to say, but to do according to that which I have written*—that they may bring forth fruit meet for their Father's kingdom; otherwise there remaineth a scourge and judgment to be poured out upon the children of Zion" (D&C 84:54–58; italics mine).

BUT THERE IS MORE

As we travel in the Lord's wilderness, the Lord is anxious to communicate directly with us—to grant us direct, personal revelation according to our faith and preparation. And this, too, brings us back to scripture study. Elder Bruce R. McConkie has written, "Each pronouncement in the holy scriptures . . . is so written as to reveal little or much, depending on the spiritual capacity of the student. To a carnal person, a passage of scripture may mean nothing; to an honest though uninformed truth seeker, it may shed forth only a few rays of heavenly light; but to one who has the mind of Christ, the same passage may blaze forth an effulgence of celestial light. That which is a mystery to one is plain and simple to another. The things of the Spirit can be understood only by the power of the Spirit" (*A New Witness for the Articles of Faith*, pp. 71–72).

To those who have been born of the Spirit and are diligently seeking the face of Christ, scriptural understanding becomes expansive, meaning that it concerns more than the written words themselves. Elder McConkie continues, "I sometimes think that one of the best-kept secrets of the kingdom is that *the scriptures open the door to the receipt of revelation*" (*Doctrines of the Restoration*, 243; italics mine). Elder Dallin H. Oaks explains this by saying, "Just as continuing revelation enlarges and illuminates the scriptures, so also a study of the scriptures enables men and women to receive revelations. . . . This happens because scripture reading puts us in tune with the Spirit of the Lord.

"The idea that scripture reading can lead to inspiration and revelation opens the door to the truth that a scripture is not limited to what it meant when it was written but may also include what the scripture means to a reader today. Even more, scripture reading may also lead to current revelation on whatever else the Lord wishes to communicate to the reader at that time. *We do not overstate the point when we say that the scriptures can be a Urim and Thummim to assist each of us to receive personal revelation*" ("Scripture Reading and Revelation," *Ensign,* January 1995, p. 7; italics mine).

PRAYING FOR ANSWERS

Of course, to receive personal revelation through scripture study or otherwise, heartfelt personal prayer—mighty prayer—must also be a part of our constant devotionals. In this manner we open a two-way line of communication with heaven through which we may not only ask but also receive. To survive the wilderness, therefore, we must be able to pray, ask direct questions, and obtain specific, often immediate, answers. According to President Harold B. Lee, "The fundamental and soul-satisfying step in our eternal quest is to come in a day when each does know, for himself, that God answers his prayers. This will come only after 'our soul hungers,' and after *mighty prayer and supplication*" (Conference Report, April 1969, p. 133; italics mine). As Joseph Smith said, "The only way to obtain truth and wisdom, is not to ask it from books, but to go to God in prayer and obtain divine teaching" (*Words,* p. 77). This comprises receiving personal revelation.

REVELATION FOR ALL—THE ORDER IN HEAVEN

Again according to Joseph Smith, "All men are liars who say they are of the true Church without the revelations of

Jesus Christ and the priesthood of Melchizedek, which is after the order of the Son of God. It is in the order of heavenly things that God should always send [revelations] into the world" (*Discourses of the Prophet Joseph Smith,* p. 52). At another time Joseph declared, "Now if any man has the testimony of Jesus has he not the spirit of prophecy? And if he has the spirit of prophecy I ask is he not a prophet? And if a prophet he can receive revelation. Any man that does not receive revelation for himself must be damned, for the testimony of Jesus is the spirit of prophecy. For Christ says, ask and you shall receive. And if he happens to receive anything, I ask, will it not be a revelation?" (*Words,* p. 230, spelling and punctuation standardized).

Because there is such order in all heavenly things (D&C 129:7; D&C 132:8) there must also be order in the process of praying and of obtaining answers to prayer. In heaven there are laws, rules, regulations, order! Upon these is Father's heavenly society based. He abides totally by order, and as we come to learn and follow that same order, we draw closer and closer to the society of God, until finally we are one with Him. As He so eloquently declared to Joseph Smith more than a hundred and fifty years ago, "All who will have a blessing at my hands shall abide the law which was appointed for that blessing, and the conditions thereof, as were instituted from before the foundation of the world" (D&C 132:5).

Thus it will be seen that if we truly want to communicate with God through prayer, we have only to abide the eternal laws appointed to prayer, and the conditions thereof, and through the power of the Holy Ghost we will be allowed to receive personal revelation (D&C 121:46).

Joseph Smith said, "The Lord cannot always be known by the thunder of his voice, by the display of his glory, or by the manifestations of his power, and those that are the most anxious to see these things, are the least prepared to meet them. . . . We would say to the brethren, seek to know God in your closets, call upon him in the fields. Follow the directions of the Book of Mormon, and pray over, and for your families, your cattle, your flocks, your herds, your corn, and all things that you possess; ask the blessing of God upon all your labors, and everything that you engage in. Be virtuous and pure; be men of integrity and truth; keep the commandments of God; and then you will be able more perfectly to understand the difference between right and wrong—between the things of God and the things of men; and your path will be like that of the just, which shineth brighter and brighter unto the perfect day" (*Teachings,* p. 247).

Elder Bruce R. McConkie adds, "There is more to the doctrine of revelation than the calling of apostles and prophets and the sending of them forth to proclaim the gospel to the world. The very gospel plan itself requires that *every believing soul attune himself to the Infinite and get personal revelation in order to be saved.* Personal revelation to the weak and the simple and the lowly is as essential to salvation as is the general revelation that comes to the spiritual giants who proclaim light to the world. . . .

"If all things operate by law, and they do; if God is no respecter of persons, and certainly he is perfectly impartial; if his course is one eternal round, never varying from age to age, and such truly is the case—then all of the gifts and graces and revelations ever given to any prophet, seer, or revelator in any age will be given again to any soul who obeys the law entitling him so to receive. While discoursing about the Second Comforter and in setting forth that those whose callings and elections have been made sure have the privilege of seeing the face of the Lord while they yet dwell in the flesh, the Prophet Joseph Smith said: 'God hath not revealed anything to Joseph, but what He will make known unto the Twelve, and *even the least Saint may know all things* as fast as he is able to bear them.' (*Teachings of the Prophet Joseph Smith,* p. 149.) . . .

"Be it noted that the Lord desires and seeks to give revelations and visions to his servants; nothing pleases him more than to have them attain that state of spiritual perfection in which they can be enlightened from on high. Of those so attaining, he continues: 'Great shall be their reward and eternal shall be their glory. And to them will I reveal all mysteries, yea, all the hidden mysteries of my kingdom from days of old, and for ages to come, will I make known unto them the good pleasure of my will concerning all things pertaining to my kingdom. Yea, even the wonders of eternity shall they know, and things to come will I show them, even the things of many generations. And their wisdom shall be great, and their understanding reach to heaven; and before them the wisdom of the wise shall perish, and the understanding of the prudent shall come to naught. For by my Spirit will I enlighten them, and by my power will I make known unto them the secrets of my will—yea, even those things which eye has not seen, nor ear heard, nor yet entered into the heart of man.' (D&C 76:5–10)" (*A New Witness for the Articles of Faith,* pp. 487, 490–91).

"LAWS" CONCERNING PRAYER

From my own limited scripture study I have identified eight reasons why we who are seeking the Lord's face should practice constant, mighty prayer. I call these eight reasons the laws of prayer, readily acknowledging that I am using the word *law* loosely and also that there are likely many more such laws or points that I have not identified. Nevertheless, these eight seem particularly applicable for those who seek the face of Christ.

1. Constant praying invokes "the law of asking." Simply by asking for divine assistance and guidance, we invoke the heavenly and eternal law which allows God to respond openly to our needs (3 Nephi 14:7–8). Jesus said, "Ask, and it shall be given unto you; seek, and ye shall find; knock, and it shall be opened unto you. For every one that asketh, receiveth; and he that seeketh, findeth; and to him that knocketh, it shall be opened" (3 Nephi 14:7–8). To obtain any specific blessing from God, we must initiate the process. We ask—He gives. We seek—He helps us find. We knock—He opens unto us. Once we exercise faith sufficient to initiate the action (pray—ask), then by eternal law God is free to respond to our request (answer). Simple and obvious, but true.

2. Constant praying invokes "the law of consecrated performances." Simply by humbling ourselves enough to address our Heavenly Father before we do something, we invoke the heavenly law that allows God to consecrate (or count) the thing we are doing for our eternal well-being (2 Nephi 32:9). Otherwise, God must apparently count it as a good deed worthy of mortal blessings, but no more.

3. Constant praying establishes clearly whose side we are

on in the eternal struggle between right and wrong, light and darkness, Christ and Lucifer (2 Nephi 32:8). I call this the "law of Christ's cause." Only those who are willing to humble themselves in mighty prayer—"with real intent" of heart (Moroni 6:8)—can be enlisted in the cause of Christ. Truthfully, this is where all wilderness travelers wish to be.

4. Constant praying allows us to learn of and then understand the mysteries of Godliness (1 Timothy 3:16; Alma 26:22). Hence, this is "the law of God's mysteries." These, "the peaceable things of the kingdom" (D&C 36:2; 39:6), are what give us power to return to God's celestial realms on high (D&C 42:61) and not to be taken captive by the devil (Alma 12:9–11).

5. Constant praying gives us power to be lifted up at the last day (Alma 37:35–37); that is "the law of being lifted up." This means that we will have come off conqueror in the war against evil, and we will be made clean so that we can be lifted up to behold the face of Christ and come with Him in His glory, to rule and reign with Him through all eternity.

6. Constant praying gives us power to become mighty missionaries, capable of bringing thousands of God's children to a knowledge of the truth (Alma 26:22): "the law of missionary service." Declaring the gospel to others is one way we have of serving righteously and so retaining a remission of our sins (Mosiah 4:11–12).

7. Constant praying gives us power to become teachers of deep and eternal truths, "reveal[ing] things which never have been revealed" (Alma 26:22; D&C 121:26). This, "the law of teaching truth," enables us, as the angels, to "speak by the power of the Holy Ghost; wherefore, [we will be speaking] the words of Christ" (2 Nephi 32:3).

8. Constant praying allows us to continue to recognize, confess, and then obtain forgiveness for our personal sins (1 Nephi 7:21; Ether 12:27). This, "the law of obtaining forgiveness," is expressed by the Lord as follows: "I, the Lord, forgive sins unto those who confess their sins before me and ask forgiveness" (D&C 64:7).

RECOGNIZING ANSWERS

Having obtained the wilderness of the Lord through complete repentance and a remission of sins, we are worthy in all respects to enjoy the companionship and presence of the Holy Ghost. However, while it is His responsibility to be with us when we are worthy, it is our responsibility to learn to recognize the manifestations of His presence within us. If we feel nothing, then it is appropriate to ask God each time we pray, in the name of Christ, to allow the Holy Ghost to fill our hearts and minds until we can feel Him (3 Nephi 19:9, 13; D&C 130:22). Then, if all else is in order, we will. And it is these manifestations of the Holy Ghost, or His workings within us, that will first indicate the Lord's answers to our prayers (Moroni 10:4–5).

But remember, we cannot receive such answers unless we listen—in other words, stay on our knees, asking, waiting, asking, listening or feeling, remaining patiently until we feel something. Being in a hurry, or not waiting for an answer, is surely one of the major reasons why more people don't receive answers to their prayers.

PHYSICAL REACTIONS TO THE HOLY SPIRIT

Because our spirits are housed in physical bodies, the effect of the Holy Ghost's influence on our spirits and minds is almost always accompanied by at least some physical reaction; our bodies feel the workings of the Spirit. When Lehi saw a vision, "he did quake and tremble exceedingly" (1 Nephi 1:6). Joseph Smith said on one occasion that his "bones [did] quake" (D&C 85:6) when the Spirit was working within him. Also, many accounts exist of Joseph's glowing as though a light were within him when the Holy Ghost came upon him. Philo Dibble, in describing Joseph Smith and Sidney Rigdon experience receiving what became the 76th section of the Doctrine and Covenants, said that Joseph glowed and looked serene because he was used to such things, but Sidney Rigdon, who was not so accustomed to the physical rigors of spiritual experiences, was left weak and limp as a wet rag (*Juvenile Instructor*, May 15, 1892, pp. 303–4).

The scriptures point out several ways that the Holy Ghost affects feelings, emotions and physical bodies. Let us itemize some of them here, with a little elaboration:

1. A burning in the bosom (D&C 9:8). This is a warm, almost-choking or difficulty-in-breathing sort of feeling in the area of the chest. It might also be a feeling of warmth all over one's body.

2. A quaking frame (D&C 85:6; 1 Nephi 1:6). This would be a slight trembling of the body, like a chill or a shiver, except that it isn't cold. This might increase with intensity the more powerful the manifestation of the Spirit.

3. A still, small voice. Our mind "hears" a new thought or idea that gives us knowledge or direction. The voice also "whispereth through and pierceth all things" (D&C 85:6). On occasion this voice may become audible to our mind (Enos 1:10) or even our natural ears.

4. Crying, or weeping. People shouldn't be ashamed of

this joyful response to the Spirit or judge others harshly when it occurs, for this is truly one of the most common effects of the Spirit upon a physical body.

5. Enlightened minds or sudden strokes of ideas (D&C 6:15; D&C 11:13). As we know, the Holy Ghost is a spirit and so will communicate directly with our own spirit as we receive answers to our prayers. The overall effect of this Spirit-to-spirit communication is to enlighten our minds. The Lord says, "Blessed art thou for what thou hast done; for thou hast inquired of me, . . . and as often as thou hast inquired thou hast received instruction of my Spirit. If it had not been so, thou wouldst not have come to the place where thou art at this time. Behold, thou knowest that thou hast inquired of me and I did *enlighten thy mind;* and now I tell thee these things that thou mayest know that thou hast been enlightened by the Spirit of truth; yea, I tell thee, that thou mayest know that there is none else save God that knowest thy thoughts and the intents of thy heart" (D&C 6:14–16).

6. Peace in the mind and heart (D&C 6:23)—no earthly serenity feels like this does. It can come in the midst of great turmoil and will remove fear.

7. A constraining or impression not to say or do a specific thing (4 Nephi 1:48). This is where we would be literally prevented from or prompted to avoid doing something that the Lord does not want done or said. This can be a physical constraint, a verbal constraint, or even a mental constraint. Almost always, however, it comes in response to prayers of faith, offered by ourselves or others, for divine direction, protection, or preservation.

8. A stupor of thought (D&C 9:9). This is an understanding that a decision we have made is not in harmony

with God's will. The sensation is best described as a sense of darkness or confusion, a feeling of anxiety that something is not working out no matter how hard we might be trying to bring it to pass. A simple prayer of acceptance of God's will brings this awful feeling to an abrupt halt, and we know it has been a communication from God.

9. Comfort from distress or sorrow (Alma 17:9–10). If we will only humble ourselves and ask, the Lord says, "blessed are all they that mourn, for they shall be comforted" (3 Nephi 12:4).

There are no doubt other feelings or physical responses to the presence of the Spirit, for we will not all react in exactly the same way or degree. But we *will* be affected, and that is how we begin receiving personal revelation. Thus Joseph Smith declared, "The first Comforter or Holy Ghost has no other effect than pure intelligence. It is more powerful in expanding the mind, enlightening the understanding, and storing the intellect with present knowledge, of a man who is of the literal seed of Abraham, than one that is a Gentile, *though it may not have half as much visible effect upon the body;* for as the Holy Ghost falls upon one of the literal seed of Abraham, it is calm and serene; and his whole soul and body are only exercised by the pure spirit of intelligence; while the effect of the Holy Ghost upon a Gentile, is to purge out the old blood, and make him actually of the seed of Abraham. . . . In such a case, there may be more of a powerful effect upon the body, and visible to the eye, than upon an Israelite, while the Israelite might be far before the Gentile in pure intelligence" (*Teachings*, p. 150; italics mine).

ASKING SPECIFIC QUESTIONS

Unfortunately, most prayers are offered without any questions being asked—no specific questions at all! It is vital that we become specific in our requests of the Lord. Just imagine what would have been the result had the light-seeking brother of Jared gone upon the mount Shelem and prayed only in general terms for health, protection, and so forth. The ocean-going Jaredites would have certainly experienced a long, dark passage. Or suppose that Nephi, who wanted to see the vision that his father Lehi had seen, had knelt and simply asked in general terms for a good day. He would most certainly have been blessed with a good day, but had he not been specific, millions of us would have missed not only the interpretation of Lehi's vision but also the marvelous additional views the Lord granted him. So yes, it is important to be specific in our praises to the Lord and in our requests of Him as we seek to have our needs fulfilled.

KEEPING QUESTIONS SIMPLE

As we grow into the principle of revelation, which is something like starting in kindergarten and graduating upward as our spiritual understanding increases, it is a good idea to learn to keep our questions simple enough that they can be answered with either a "yes" or a "no." That way, when the physical effects of the Spirit are felt in response to a question (and each of us will feel the Spirit in our own way), we can assume that the answer to at least some portion of our question is yes. If we feel nothing or experience a withdrawal, then the answer would be either no or an invitation to rephrase the question.

Later, as growth into the principle of revelation continues, pure knowledge or information will begin to flow into the mind as the Lord elaborates on His "yes" or "no" answers.

CALLING UPON THE NAME OF THE LORD

There is one other aspect of mighty prayer that ought to be discussed, and that is the necessity of calling upon the name of the Lord (D&C 133:6). Interestingly, this appears to be a requirement of those who have been born again. King Benjamin said, "As ye have come to the knowledge of the glory of God, or if ye have known of his goodness and have tasted of his love, and have received a remission of your sins, which causeth such exceedingly great joy in your souls, even so I would that ye should remember, and always retain in remembrance, the greatness of God, and your own nothingness, and his goodness and long-suffering towards you, unworthy creatures, and humble yourselves even in the depths of humility, *calling on the name of the Lord daily,* and standing steadfastly in the faith of that which is to come, which was spoken by the mouth of the angel" (Mosiah 4:11; italics mine). And Alma added, "[God] sent angels to converse with them, who caused men to behold of his glory. *And they began from that time forth to call on his name;* therefore God conversed with men, and made known unto them the plan of redemption, which had been prepared from the foundation of the world; and this he made known unto them according to their faith and repentance and their holy works" (Alma 12:29–30; italics mine).

BLESSINGS ARE PROMISED

Scripturally, we are informed that diligent "calling on the name of the Lord" brings certain blessings. For instance,

Adam and his posterity were taught by angels to call upon the name of God, after which mortals *had the plan of salvation revealed to them* (Moses 5:4–9, 58–59; italics mine). The righteous among Adam's sons and daughters, including Seth, "call[ed] upon the name of the Lord, and *the Lord blessed them*" (Moses 6:4; italics mine). So did Moses, who said, "I will not cease to call upon [the name of] God, *I have other things to inquire of him*" (Moses 1:18; italics mine).

Elsewhere we are promised mercy—"for the Lord will be merciful unto all who call on his name" (Alma 9:17). We are told that it is a part of repenting and casting off sins (Alma 13:27), that calling on the name of the Lord will protect us from being tempted above that which we can bear, and calling upon the name of God is essential to being led by "the Holy Spirit, becoming humble, meek, submissive, patient, full of love and all long-suffering" (Alma 13:28).

Those who call on the name of God are also promised divine protection—"They did rejoice and cry again with one voice, saying: May the God of Abraham, and the God of Isaac, and the God of Jacob, protect this people in righteousness, so long as they shall call on the name of their God for protection" (3 Nephi 4:30). This protection includes, interestingly enough, having the power to recognize and then cast out Satan (Moses 1:18).

Also, calling upon the holy name of the Lord is essential for those who would "make known his wonderful works among the people" (D&C 65:4), or in other words, serve as teachers and missionaries within the kingdom.

From these passages we see that righteous individuals are being commanded to call on the name of the Lord, have been so commanded since the days of Adam, and have been blessed by God for doing so. One who got into trouble for *not* doing it was mentioned earlier in this volume. Moroni recorded, "At the end of four years . . . the Lord came again unto the brother of Jared, and stood in a cloud and talked with him. And for the space of three hours did the Lord talk with the brother of Jared, *and chastened him because he remembered not to call upon the name of the Lord*" (Ether 2:14; italics mine).

It does not make sense to me that the brother of Jared had simply stopped praying during those four long years. That does not seem like him. Rather, I believe he had stopped praying in a particular manner or using particular words, and this was what brought forth the Lord's chastisement.

NAMES OF GOD

In an effort to substantiate this and perhaps discover the specific words, I began to examine the various names of the Lord, wondering if—or how often—they were used today. Some that I found are "God," "God the Lord" and "Lord God" (Moses 3:4), "Eternal" (Moses 7:35), "Lord God Almighty" and "Endless" (Moses 1:3; 7:35; D&C 19:10). "Ahman" is one of the names by which God was known to Adam (D&C 78:20). God is also called "Everlasting" (Moses 1:3; 7:35; D&C 19:10); "The everlasting Father" (Isaiah 9:6); "God of Israel" (1 Nephi 19:7–17; 3 Nephi 11:7–17); the "God of Jacob" (Psalm 146:5; Isaiah 2:3; D&C 136:21); "the Lord God, the Mighty One of Israel" (D&C 36:1); "the Lord God of the Hebrews" (Exodus 3:18); "Holy" (Isaiah 57:15); "Jehovah" (D&C 110:1–10); "Man of Holiness" and

"Man of Counsel" (Moses 6:57; 7:35); and "Messiah," "the King of Zion," and "the Rock of Heaven" (Moses 7:53).

NORMAL PRAYER

But what about how most of us pray every day—to our Heavenly Father or Father in Heaven? Is such prayer wrong or ineffective? Of course not, for unless we are in Christ's literal presence and He has commanded us to pray directly to Him (3 Nephi 19:18, 22, 25, 30), all our prayers must be addressed to our eternal Father in the name of His Beloved Son! As Jesus commanded the Nephites, "Therefore ye must always pray unto the Father in my name" (3 Nephi 18:19). And, if *all* else is in order in our lives, including praying "always" (3 Nephi 18:15–20), this may also be termed "mighty prayer."

USAGE TODAY

Nevertheless, do we ever in our prayers use the particular names of God listed above, the words and phrases that have been so important to praying men and women from Adam through Joseph Smith and to our day? Yes, frequently. For instance, if we listen each Sunday as the sacrament prayers are offered, we will discover that each of them begins with the words "O God, the Eternal Father" (Moroni 4:3; 5:2). Are we not weekly participants in these "priesthood ordinance" prayers?

Such words are also used in temple ordinances, where they help give prayer greater power to penetrate the heavens than can be invoked in any other way. In a direct reference to ancient temple worship, Moses recorded in Genesis, "[Isaac] builded an altar there, and called upon the name of the Lord. . . . And the Lord appeared unto him the same night" (Genesis 26:25, 24). In our day the Prophet Joseph declared, "The Great God has a name by which He will be called which is Ahman" (*Words,* p. 64).[1] Then, referring to temple ordinances, Joseph continued, "Also in asking have reference to a personage like Adam. . . . Now this is a key for you to know how to ask and obtain" (*Words,* p. 64). And finally, Bathsheba W. Smith, wife of apostle George A. Smith, declared, "When speaking in one of our general fast meetings, [Joseph Smith] said that we did not know how to pray to have our prayers answered. But when I and my husband had our endowments . . . Joseph Smith presiding, he taught us the order of prayer" (*Juvenile Instructor,* June 1, 1892, p. 345; also *Words,* p. 54, footnote 19).

Thus it will be seen that the most powerful way of calling upon the name of the Lord that we are aware of is found in temple worship—attending the temple for and in behalf of those who have died and at the same time involving ourselves in what President Thorpe B. Isaacson called "the true order of prayer" (Conference Report, October 1959, p. 96). In those holy places wherein we are commanded to stand (D&C 87:8), more than anywhere else on earth, we are given power to approach the Lord and obtain further light and knowledge concerning whatever it might be that we righteously desire.

NOTE

1. This name, a word from the Adamic language, means Highest or Most Holy Man (see *Mormon Doctrine,* p. 29).

Chapter Twenty

CONFRONTING SATAN

Part of the reality of this life is Satan, or the devil, who, before he was cast out of heaven was known as "Lucifer, a son of the morning" (D&C 76:26). Looking back, I am amazed at how many encounters I had with him or his "angels" within my ward, as well as the devastation and misery that always followed in their wake. How grateful I became for the power, as a disciple of Jesus Christ, to rebuke and cast out in Christ's holy name, and to witness the peace and tranquillity that immediately followed the devil's departure.

Since the days of Adam, Satan has claimed to rule the world, and he has done all in his power to stop righteous men and women from growing spiritually and coming unto Christ. In doing this he presents himself as some sort of awesome and all-powerful being who is to be both feared and obeyed. Yet in speaking of him, Isaiah declared, "How art thou fallen from heaven, O Lucifer, son of the morning! how art thou cut down to the ground, which didst weaken the nations! For thou hast said in thine heart, I will ascend into heaven, I will exalt my throne above the stars of God: I will sit also upon the mount of the congregation, in the sides of the north: I will ascend above the heights of the clouds; I will be like the most High. Yet thou shalt be brought down to hell, to the sides of the pit. *They that see thee shall narrowly look upon thee, and consider thee, saying, Is this the man that made the earth to tremble, that did shake kingdoms; that made the world as a wilderness,* and destroyed the cities thereof; that opened not the house of his prisoners?" (Isaiah 14:12–17; italics mine).

As the accounts that follow relate, Satan uses not only temptation but also deception, intimidation, fear, and anything else that will work in his cunning efforts to usurp the power and authority of God and Christ, and at the same time to make each of us as miserable as he is.

LEHI IN THE PROMISED LAND

Lehi taught his sons about Satan, saying, "I, Lehi, according to the things which I have read, must needs suppose that an angel of God, according to that which is written, had fallen from heaven; wherefore, he became a devil, having sought that which was evil before God. And because he had fallen from heaven, and had become miserable forever, he sought also the misery of all mankind. . . . Wherefore, men are free according to the flesh; and all things are given them which are expedient unto man. And they are free to choose liberty and eternal life, through the great Mediator of all men, or to choose captivity and death, according to the captivity and power of the devil; for he seeketh that all men might be miserable like unto himself" (2 Nephi 2:17–18, 27).

And Jacob, Lehi's son, added, "O that cunning plan of the evil one! O the vainness, and the frailties, and the foolishness of men! When they are learned they think they are wise, and they hearken not unto the counsel of God, for they set it aside, supposing they know of themselves, wherefore, their wisdom is foolishness and it profiteth them not. And they shall perish" (2 Nephi 9:28).

JESUS IN THE WILDERNESS

After Jesus was baptized by both the water and the Spirit, he was led into the wilderness by the Holy Ghost to be with God. Combining all the scriptural references on the Savior's wilderness experience, we read, "And he was there in the wilderness forty days, *Satan seeking to tempt him;* and was with the wild beasts; and the angels ministered unto him" (JST Mark 1:11; italics mine).

"And when he had fasted forty days and forty nights, and had communed with God, he was afterwards an hungered, and *was left to be tempted of the devil*" (JST Matthew 4:2; italics mine).

"And when the tempter came to him, he said, If thou be the Son of God, command that these stones be made bread. But [Jesus] answered and said, It is written, Man shall not live by bread alone, but by every word that proceedeth out of the mouth of God" (Matthew 4:3–4).

"And the Spirit brought him to Jerusalem, and set him

on the pinnacle of the temple. Then the devil came unto him and said, . . ." (JST Luke 4:9)

"If thou be the Son of God, cast thyself down: for it is written, He shall give his angels charge concerning thee: and in their hands they shall bear thee up, lest at any time thou dash thy foot against a stone. Jesus said unto him, It is written again, Thou shalt not tempt the Lord thy God" (Matthew 4:6–7).

"And again, Jesus was in the Spirit, and it taketh him up into an exceeding high mountain, and sheweth him all the kingdoms of the world, and the glory of them. And the devil came unto him again, and said, All these things will I give unto thee, if thou wilt fall down and worship me. Then saith Jesus unto him, Get thee hence, Satan: for it is written, Thou shalt worship the Lord thy God, and him only shalt thou serve. Then the devil leaveth him, and, behold, angels came and ministered unto him" (JST Matthew 4:8–10).

As can be seen, Jesus not only accepted the reality of Satan but also allowed himself to be subjected to the evil one's temptations. Attacking human appetites (food and pride), as Satan did with Christ, are common temptations to all mankind, and it is the devil's right to torment us with them (Moses 4:4, 21). However, when Satan reached the point where he was demanding that he be worshiped rather than God, Jesus drew the line. He knew who was to be worshiped in righteousness in this world, and it was not Lucifer. Neither could Jesus countenance the usurper's vain efforts to overthrow God (see Moses 4:3). That war had already been fought and won. Therefore he commanded him, "Get thee hence," and Satan was gone.

MOSES ON THE MOUNTAIN

Of Moses' experience with the devil we read, "The words of God, which he spake unto Moses at a time when Moses was caught up into an exceedingly high mountain, and he saw God face to face, and he talked with him, and the glory of God was upon Moses; therefore Moses could endure his presence. . . . And the presence of God withdrew from Moses, that his glory was not upon Moses; and Moses was left unto himself. . . . And it came to pass that . . . Satan came tempting him, saying: Moses, son of man, worship me. And it came to pass that Moses looked upon Satan and said: Who art thou? For behold, I am a son of God, in the similitude of his Only Begotten; and where is thy glory, that I should worship thee? For behold, I could not look upon God, except his glory should come upon me, and I were transfigured before him. But I can look upon thee in the natural man. Is it not so, surely? Blessed be the name of my God, for his Spirit hath not altogether withdrawn from me, or else where is thy glory, for it is darkness unto me? And I can judge between thee and God; for God said unto me: Worship God, for him only shalt thou serve. Get thee hence, Satan; deceive me not; for God said unto me: Thou art after the similitude of mine Only Begotten. And he also gave me commandments when he called unto me out of the burning bush, saying: Call upon God in the name of mine Only Begotten, and worship me. And again Moses said: I will not cease to call upon God, I have other things to inquire of him: for his glory has been upon me, wherefore I can judge between him and thee. Depart hence, Satan. And now, when Moses had said these words, Satan cried with a loud voice, and ranted upon the earth, and commanded, saying:

I am the Only Begotten, worship me. And it came to pass that Moses began to fear exceedingly; and as he began to fear, he saw the bitterness of hell. Nevertheless, calling upon God, he received strength, and he commanded, saying: Depart from me, Satan, for this one God only will I worship, which is the God of glory. And now Satan began to tremble, and the earth shook; and Moses received strength, and called upon God, saying: In the name of the Only Begotten, depart hence, Satan. And it came to pass that Satan cried with a loud voice, with weeping, and wailing, and gnashing of teeth; and he departed hence, even from the presence of Moses, that he beheld him not. And now of this thing Moses bore record; but because of wickedness it is not had among the children of men" (Moses 1:1–2, 9–23).

In Moses' experience Satan does not seem to have wasted much time with temptations of the flesh. Either that or they were simply not discussed scripturally. Instead he demanded immediate worship, which Moses just as immediately rejected, bearing testimony to Satan of his devotion to God as he did so. Then Moses commanded him to depart.

Interestingly, Satan went nowhere but only grew angry and threw a temper tantrum. Moses began to feel fear at this devilish display, and as he feared, he saw the bitterness of hell—an interesting commentary on the fate of those who fear the devil. But calling on God, Moses received strength to calm his fear, and finally he rebuked Satan in the name of the Only Begotten, who is Jesus Christ. At that point Satan left.

The scripture continues, "When Satan had departed from the presence of Moses, . . . Moses lifted up his eyes unto heaven, being filled with the Holy Ghost, which beareth record of the Father and the Son; and calling upon the name of God, he beheld his glory again, for it was upon him; and he heard a voice, saying: Blessed art thou, Moses, for I, the Almighty, have chosen thee, and thou shalt be made stronger than many waters; for they shall obey thy command as if thou wert God. And lo, I am with thee, even unto the end of thy days; for thou shalt deliver my people from bondage, even Israel my chosen" (Moses 1:24–26).

Then the Lord took time to instruct Moses regarding the reality of the devil's life and mission. "I, the Lord God, spake unto Moses, saying: That Satan, whom thou hast commanded in the name of mine Only Begotten, is the same which was from the beginning, and he came before me, saying—Behold, here am I, send me, I will be thy son, and I will redeem all mankind, that one soul shall not be lost, and surely I will do it; wherefore give me thine honor. But, behold, my Beloved Son, which was my Beloved and Chosen from the beginning, said unto me—Father, thy will be done, and the glory be thine forever. Wherefore, because that Satan rebelled against me, and sought to destroy the agency of man, which I, the Lord God, had given him, and also, that I should give unto him mine own power; by the power of mine Only Begotten, I caused that he should be cast down; and he became Satan, yea, even the devil, the father of all lies, to deceive and to blind men, and to lead them captive at his will, even as many as would not hearken unto my voice. . . . Wherefore he sought to destroy the world" (Moses 4:1–4, 6).

FROM JOSEPH SMITH

Though Joseph Smith had a great deal to say about the devil and his host of evil spirits, much of which we will discuss a little later, these two statements seem appropriate at this time: "The policy of the wicked spirit is to separate what God has joined together [marriages, families, etc.], and unite what He has separated [homosexuality, etc.], which the devil has succeeded in doing to admiration in the present society" (*Teachings*, p. 103). He also taught, "All the religious world is boasting of righteousness; it is the doctrine of the devil to retard the human mind, and hinder our progress, by filling us with self-righteousness. The nearer we get to our heavenly Father, the more we are disposed to look with compassion on perishing souls; we feel that we want to take them upon our shoulders, and cast their sins behind our backs. My talk is intended for all this society; if you would have God have mercy on you, have mercy on one another" (*Teachings*, p. 241).

ASPECTS OF THE DEVIL

The above accounts illustrate several important aspects of the devil. First, he is miserable forever, and so he seeks a similar misery for all mankind (2 Nephi 2:18, 27). Second, his deceptions and false revelations are a "cunning plan," one that is particularly effective against those who struggle with vanity and pride (2 Nephi 9:28). Third, we have the absolute freedom to follow him or to ignore him and follow Christ (2 Nephi 2:27). Fourth, he is a liar from the beginning (D&C 93:25) and is called the "father of lies" (2 Nephi 9:9) and the "father of all lies" (Moses 4:4). Fifth, his goal is to destroy the world (Moses 4:6). Sixth, he seeks to separate what God has joined together and unite what God has separated (*Teachings*, p. 103). Seventh, he encourages self-righteousness (*Teachings*, p. 241). Eighth and finally, he is constantly seeking to usurp or take upon himself the power, glory, and missions of both Christ and the Father (Moses 4:3; Isaiah 14:12–17). It is this last and perhaps most serious aspect upon which we will now focus our attention.

TRUE KNOWLEDGE TO COME ONLY FROM CHRIST THROUGH THE HOLY GHOST

"The devil was before Adam," the Lord said to Joseph Smith, "for he rebelled against me, saying, Give me thine honor, which is my power" (D&C 29:36). "By the word of my power, have I created . . . worlds without number . . . which [word of power] is mine Only Begotten" (Moses 1:32–33). And of course Christ's honor or word of power was not only to create worlds without number but also to implement the Father's plan of salvation through His atonement to all the inhabitants thereof; to proclaim by His own voice the Father's message (thus Christ is the Word [John 1:1]), which is carried into the hearts and minds of man through the power of the Holy Ghost, telling us "all things what [we] should do" to obtain salvation (2 Nephi 32:3; D&C 8:1–3; 46:7; Matthew 7:7–8; James 1:5). To Joseph Smith the Lord proclaimed, "God shall give unto you knowledge by his Holy Spirit, yea, by the unspeakable gift of the Holy Ghost, that has not been revealed since the world was until now" (D&C 121:26). Brigham Young declared, "By the revelations of the Lord Jesus we understand things as they were, that have been made known unto us; things that are in the life which we now enjoy, and things as they will be . . . in order to give us the experience necessary in this life to prepare us to enjoy eternal life hereafter" (*Journal of Discourses*, 12:112). Thus did the Prophet Joseph teach that "knowledge through our

Lord and Savior Jesus Christ is the grand key that unlocks the glories and mysteries of the kingdom of heaven" (*Teachings*, p. 298).

EVE IN THE GARDEN

With these things in mind, consider what happened in the Garden of Eden to Eve, whom Satan sought to tempt (D&C 29:36, 40) or beguile (Moses 4:6; Mosiah 16:3) in order that he might destroy the world (Moses 4:6). Approaching Eve after Adam had utterly rejected him, the devil handed her the fruit of the tree of knowledge of good and evil, trying to persuade her to eat of it (Moses 4:7–12). At first Eve resisted, replying that God had warned that by eating or even touching that fruit, she and Adam would surely die (JST Genesis 3:9; Abraham 5:12–13).

Instantly calling God a liar by proclaiming that she "would *not* surely die" (JST Genesis 3:10)—a lie of his own—the devil then proclaimed a truth: "God doth know, that in the day ye eat thereof [partake of knowledge], then your eyes shall be opened, and ye shall be as gods, knowing good and evil" (JST Genesis 3:10). Quickly Satan then switched back to his own tactics by appealing to Eve's appetites, pointing out that besides the value of knowledge the "tree was good for food, and that it was pleasant to the eyes, and a tree to be desired to make one wise" (Genesis 3:6).

Apparently understanding that knowledge was important to her mortal mission, and being sorely tempted by the fruit's taste and desirability but sensing that *something* about the devil's presentation was not quite right, Eve very innocently (for she still didn't know with whom she was dealing) asked if there was not some other way for her to receive this knowledge. Satan replied that there was no other way—again a lie masked behind a truth. Eve most certainly needed knowledge in order to overcome her innocence and have posterity (the truth); but from the foundation of the world, as was pointed out above, it has been Christ's right, rather than Lucifer's, to reveal such knowledge—in other words, to reveal light and truth (Alma 38:9; Ether 4:12; D&C 84:45; 88:5–7; 93:9–10).

By taking from the tree the fruit (knowledge that was Christ's to give by revelation) which had been temporarily forbidden Adam and Eve by the Lord (D&C 29:40), and then pressing it upon Eve, the devil not only lied about there being no other way for her to obtain this knowledge—than from him, immediately, he was implying—but in that same instant he usurped Christ's divinely foreordained right to reveal light and truth to the Father's children, and he also stripped from Eve the protection from Satan's wiles that Christ's revelations of light and truth always provide. "Light and truth forsake that evil one," the Lord proclaims (D&C 93:37). Thus Eve not only "fell" by submitting to temptation, but she also lost additional vital blessings in the process.

As LDS scholar High Nibley explains this experience, "So into this world, most glorious and beautiful, with everything supplied, come Adam and Eve. And then comes somebody else. Satan's been *lying in wait for them,* as a matter of fact. That's one of the things the word *Satan* actually means, the one who lies in wait, who lurks in ambush, waiting—he was there first, waiting. And so Satan's first act is to offer to Adam and Eve the one gift that has been forbidden them. . . . He has given the fruit to Adam and Eve; it was not his prerogative to do so—regardless of what had been done in other worlds. (When the time comes for such fruit, it will be given us legitimately)" (*Approaching Zion,* pp. 91–92).[1]

Later, after the Father and the Son had made their promised return to give Adam and Eve additional instructions and information—revealed knowledge or light and truth—and had instead received their confessions that they had partaken of the forbidden fruit, God confronted Satan concerning his role in presenting the fruit to Adam and Eve. The devil's response, as we might have guessed, was evasive self-justification. Why? Because he knew he had done that which he had no right to do!

In response, therefore, God said to the devil, "Because *thou* hast done this thou shalt be cursed above all cattle, and above every beast of the field; upon thy belly shalt thou go, and dust shalt thou eat all the days of thy life" (Moses 4:20; italics mine).

Again, why was the devil cursed? Because by lying to Eve and presenting her with knowledge (though not light and truth, because he has none), the devil had usurped or taken unto himself Christ's mission and power, by which he was causing Eve to worship him as the revelator (Moses 1:12) and hoping to destroy the world (Moses 4:6). In other words, the problem was Satan himself rather than the "fruit" he presented.

The devil's plan seemed to be working, too. Because Adam and Eve had transgressed God's commandment, they had become "subject to the will of the devil" (D&C 29:40) and were therefore "spiritually dead" or "cast out from . . . [God's] presence" (D&C 29:41)—which issue was discussed at length much earlier in this volume.

THE MIND OF GOD

Such a tragic triumph surely must have warmed the cockles of Satan's heart. Happily, however, he "knew not the mind of God" (Moses 4:6). And what was God's mind? To the Prophet Joseph the Lord stated, "It must needs be that the devil should tempt the children of men, or they could not be agents unto themselves; for if they never should have bitter they could not know the sweet—Wherefore, it came to pass that the devil tempted Adam, and he partook of the forbidden fruit and transgressed the commandment, wherein he became subject to the will of the devil, because he yielded unto temptation. Wherefore, I, the Lord God, caused that he should be cast out from the Garden of Eden, from my presence, because of his transgression, wherein he became spiritually dead, which is the first death, even that same death which is the last death, which is spiritual, which shall be pronounced upon the wicked when I shall say: Depart, ye cursed.

"But, behold, I say unto you that I, the Lord God, gave unto Adam and unto his seed, that they should not die as to the temporal death, until I, the Lord God, should send forth angels to declare unto them repentance and redemption, through faith on the name of mine Only Begotten Son. And thus did I, the Lord God, appoint unto man the days of his probation—that by his natural death he might be raised in immortality unto eternal life, even as many as would believe" (D&C 29:39–43).

Satan's diabolical intentions, therefore—for Adam and Eve as well as for all the rest of us—were foiled through that same glorious plan of salvation we have been discussing throughout this volume—the plan wherein man, through the laws and ordinances of the gospel, may come unto Christ and through Him be delivered from the bondage of sin or spiritual death unto eternal life.

SATAN AS REVELATOR OF DECEPTION

Despite the wondrous triumph of the Father's plan of salvation, the devil has not for one moment given up his desire to overthrow God and assume the role of Christ. He remains the father of lies and continues in his endeavors to be the revelator to mankind, occasionally even taking on the appearance of an angel of light in his efforts to mislead and destroy (2 Corinthians 11:14; 2 Nephi 9:9). When he tried this with the Prophet Joseph, it took Michael the Archangel to come and detect him (D&C 128:20). Another, with whom he enjoyed much success, was a man named Korihor, to whom Satan also appeared as an angel (Alma 30:53), lying to him and revealing false information or knowledge containing no light and truth (Alma 30:52–53) all of which led to Korihor's destruction (Alma 30:59–60).

Even when Satan does not appear as an angel of light but remains unseen, he continues with his constant barrage of deceptions and lies, seeking to impose his own will upon us as he usurps the roles of Christ and the Holy Ghost. Moreover, it is evident that God has allowed him a certain amount of right or power to do this—which Satan falsely calls his priesthoods. It was because of these rights to tempt and torment man that Jesus, while being tempted of the devil in the wilderness, did not at first rebuke him. Concerning Satan's powers, Joseph Smith stated, "Without attempting to describe . . . the design of God in relation to the human body and spirit, I would just remark . . . that the spirits of good men cannot interfere with the wicked beyond their prescribed bounds, for Michael, the Archangel, dared not bring a railing accusation against the devil, but said, 'The Lord rebuke thee, Satan.' . . . It would seem . . . that wicked spirits have their bounds, limits, and laws by which they are governed or controlled . . . and it is very evident that they possess a power that none but those who have the Priesthood can control" (*Teachings,* p. 208).

Evil spirits, or devils, who follow Lucifer in his cunning plan of afflicting, tormenting, and destroying mortals through the revealing of lies and false knowledge, seem to have been given or assigned, by Satan, specific powers or missions—specific issues with which they are to torment their mortal victims. And interestingly, this seems to be done in the manner of an organized assault, just as Christ's missionary force is an organized assault against these same powers of darkness. As an example of such an assignment we turn again to Korihor, learning that he was possessed of a lying spirit, or a spirit who had been given the specific power or assignment to entice mortals to become liars (Alma 30:42). How well he accomplished his assignment with Korihor!

While in prison in Liberty, Missouri, Joseph Smith identified the evil spirit who was responsible for the woes of the Saints in Missouri. At the same time, he taught some interesting things concerning the character of that spirit—the spirit of confusion—and thus of other spirits under Satan's dominion. He wrote, "It is an imperative duty that we owe to God, to angels, with whom we shall be brought to stand, and also to ourselves, to our wives and children, who have been made to bow down with grief, sorrow, and care, under the most damning hand of *murder, tyranny, and oppression,* supported and urged on and upheld by the influence of that *spirit* which hath so strongly riveted the creeds of the fathers, who have inherited lies, upon the hearts of the children, and [that spirit has] filled the world with *confusion,* and has been growing stronger and stronger, and is now the *very mainspring of all corruption,* and the whole earth groans under the weight of its iniquity. It is an iron yoke, it is a strong band; they are the very handcuffs, and chains, and shackles, and fetters of hell" (D&C 123:7–8; italics mine).

In other words, the spirit Joseph identified as a confusing spirit, or spirit of confusion, had become so powerful in revealing confusion to the minds of men that it was now supporting and upholding other spirits—those with powers or assignments to reveal or engender murder, tyranny, and oppression. Worse, working together—a secret until it was revealed to the Prophet—that secret combination of spirits had become as an iron yoke, a strong band; the very handcuffs, chains, shackles, and fetters of hell, so terrible in their revelatory powers that the whole earth was groaning under the weight of their iniquity!

As we have from the scriptures learned the names or identities of the spirits of lying, confusion, murder, tyranny, and oppression, so by asking we can learn the names of any of Satan's followers and thus enjoy greater power over them. When Christ was ready to cast the unclean spirits[2] from a man of the tombs possessed by them (Mark 5:1–13), He first asked their name. The spirits replied that their name was Legion, for they were many. Because Christ knew their identity, he then acknowledged them, granted their bizarre request to be allowed to possess a herd of swine (He would never have allowed such a request from devils or evil spirits, because in the premortal world they had forfeited the right to a body forever) and then cast them out of the man they had inhabited.

Other Satanic names, assignments, or revelatory powers we read of in the scriptures are:

Infirmity—causing sickness and physical pain (Luke 13:11).

Adultery and *whoremongering*—agitating a person's baser desires until control is lost and adultery is committed (1 Corinthians 6:9).

Divorce—influencing couples to feel more and more alienated until the family unit is finally destroyed (Malachi 2:15–16).

Resistance—influencing a person to be unwilling to listen to or practice righteousness even when it is understood (Zechariah 3:1).

Apostasy—influencing a person to become so emotionally disturbed over some point or other of doctrine, or over the perceived 'unrighteous' actions of another, that the person ignores the rest of the gospel and abandons the entire Church (John 3:20; 2 Nephi 9:46).

Murder—influencing a person to thirst for another's life until at last it is taken (2 Nephi 9:9). Besides working with *confusion,* as pointed out above, these spirits also work hand-in-glove with spirits of apostasy, for so often, such murders occur following apostasy from the truth.

Confusion—influencing a person to lose understanding of a calling, a point of doctrine, or a divinely inspired purpose until failure in that righteous endeavor has occurred (1 Corinthians 14:3; D&C 123:7–8, 10). This spirit of confusion has such power that it is able to support, urge on, and uphold many lesser spirits such as *murder, tyranny,* and *oppression.* Thus, once a spirit of *confusion* obtains power over someone, causing testimony to falter and righteous resolves to disintegrate against the wall of doubt and despair, then many other spirits, most likely including *anger, affliction,* and *apostasy,* are invited to take up their abode within that same person. It is not long, then, before the person is progressing through the three stages of apostasy, identified by Joseph Smith as kicking against the pricks, persecuting the Saints, and ultimately fighting against God (D&C 121:36–38), meanwhile also experiencing the personal consequences of these and all other apostate actions—loss of the Spirit, denying the faith, and fearing (D&C 63:16).

Destruction—causing a person's physical body to deteriorate until physical death occurs (1 Corinthians 5:5).

Contention—influencing a person to argue, quarrel, fight, complain, and otherwise drive away the Spirit of God by his or her inability to get along with others (3 Nephi 11:29).

Anger—associated with the spirits of contention, the spirits of *anger* mentioned by Mormon (Moroni 9:3) seem to have tremendous destructive powers. In fact, Mormon tells his son Moroni that Satan's implanted or "revealed" *anger* led Mormon's people to unbelievable acts of depravity, leaving them without order and without mercy but strong in their *perversions,* and *brutal* (Moroni 9:4, 9, 18–19).

Devourer—causing a person to lose his ability to financially sustain and support his family (Malachi 3:7–12; Revelation 13:1–9).

Fear—influencing a person to fear one thing or another until all ability to have faith in anything at all has been taken away (2 Timothy 1:7). From Moses' experience with this spirit, we can see the danger inherent in allowing ourselves to be subject to fear. Only after Moses submitted to fear did he ever see the bitterness of hell (Moses 1:20).

In fact, the entire litany of satanically revealed qualities or characteristics listed in chapter 4 would also be assigned the powers of Satan's spirit followers.

These spirits, names, tasks, assignments, revelations, characteristics, or whatever we choose to call them are the tragic legacies of misery I so often found myself dealing with as bishop. As we consider them, it is well to note that, first, Satan takes advantage of our own natural weaknesses (the natural man) as he reveals his diabolical will to us; and second, that the focus of some of these satanic revelations is against ourselves—the devil is revealing misinformation to *us* about *us* that will ultimately destroy *us personally.* The rest of this revelatory garbage is directed against others—those of us who listen are being "inspired" by the devil to hurt or destroy loved ones or others who surround us. Either way, of course, Satan triumphs.

One other thing to note—and this may be painful—is that *all* of us have dealt with one or more of these tendencies or inclinations on more than one occasion—and perhaps are doing so now. If for any reason this is the case, and we do not feel an urgency to be rid of them by true repentance and appropriate priesthood action, then it might be well to reconsider the words of Abinadi: "Remember that he that persists in his own carnal nature, and goes on in the ways of sin and rebellion against God, remaineth in his fallen state and the devil hath all power over him. Therefore he is as though there was no redemption made, being an enemy to God; and also is the devil an enemy to God" (Mosiah

16:5). Allied with the devil by receiving and embracing his false revelations, there is no hope of successfully concluding the wilderness journey.

THE AGENCY OF MAN

Returning to Eve's experience with Satan in the Garden of Eden, we know that God, "the same which knoweth all things, for all things are present before [his] eyes" (D&C 38:2), including the past and the future, certainly could have stopped Satan from usurping Christ's divine power. Had He done so, however, He would have thwarted Eve's agency, which He had given her as part of His plan of salvation. Remember His explanation to Joseph Smith: "It must needs be that the devil should tempt the children of men, or they could not be agents unto themselves; for if they never should have bitter they could not know the sweet" (D&C 29:39). Obviously Adam and Eve were in this category, meaning that neither of them was perfect, but they were like us, susceptible to sin and weakness. In fact, all mankind have sinned (Romans 5:12) save one, Jesus Christ, "who did no sin, in whom [the Father was] well pleased" (D&C 45:4).

That being the case, if the fruit of the tree of knowledge of good and evil might have been given legitimately, then why wasn't it? Why did God allow Christ's right to give knowledge to be usurped by Satan? With us being hardly better off than Satan in knowing "the mind of God," we can do little better than reply, "Because that is how God allowed it to happen." Did God know Eve would exercise her agency by receiving the fruit from Satan? Of course, for He is all-knowing (D&C 38:2). And because He is also all-powerful (D&C 20:17; *Lectures on Faith*, p. 9), it is also proper to say that, because He allowed it to happen, the entire event must have been part of His plan.

Elder Dallin H. Oaks puts it this way, "When Adam and Eve received the first commandment [to be fruitful, and multiply and replenish the earth (Moses 2:28)], they were in a transitional state, no longer in the spirit world but with physical bodies not yet subject to death and not yet capable of procreation. They could not fulfill the Father's first commandment without transgressing the barrier between the bliss of the Garden of Eden and the terrible trials and wonderful opportunities of mortal life.

"*For reasons that have not been revealed,* this transition, or 'fall,' could not happen without a transgression—an exercise of moral agency amounting to a willful breaking of a law (see Moses 6:59). This would be a planned offense, a formality to serve an eternal purpose. The Prophet Lehi explained that 'if Adam had not transgressed he would not have fallen' (2 Nephi 2:22), but would have remained in the same state in which he was created.

"'And they would have had no children; wherefore they would have remained in a state of innocence, having no joy, for they knew no misery; doing no good, for they knew no sin' (2 Nephi 2:23). But the fall was planned, Lehi concludes, because 'all things have been done in the wisdom of him who knoweth all things' (2 Nephi 2:24).

"It was Eve who first transgressed the limits of Eden in order to initiate the conditions of mortality. Her act, whatever its nature, was formally a transgression but eternally a glorious necessity to open the doorway toward eternal life. Adam showed his wisdom by doing the same. And thus Eve and 'Adam fell that men might be' (2 Nephi 2:25)" ("The

Great Plan of Happiness," *Ensign*, November 1993, p. 72; italics mine).

President Joseph Fielding Smith taught, "I never speak of the part Eve took in this fall as a sin, nor do I accuse Adam of a sin. . . . Adam's . . . was a transgression of the law, but not a sin . . . for it was something that Adam and Eve had to do" (*Doctrines of Salvation*, 1:114–15).

And the Prophet Joseph adds in conclusion, "Adam did not commit sin in eating the fruit, for God had decreed that he should eat and fall" (*Words*, p. 63; spelling and punctuation standardized).

Finally, the Lord revealed to Moses how our first parents felt once the fall and its consequences had been made clear to them. Adam said, "Blessed be the name of God, for because of my transgression my eyes are opened, and in this life I shall have joy, and again in the flesh I shall see God" (Moses 5:10). And Eve said, "Were it not for our transgression we never should have had seed, and never should have known good and evil, and the joy of our redemption, and the eternal life which God giveth unto all the obedient" (Moses 5:11). Though we don't yet understand all the "whys" of what transpired in the garden, these are joyful outbursts from wonderful people who had done what needed to be done. Surely we have great cause to rejoice with them.

BUT SATAN CONTINUES

Meanwhile, Satan, who must have thought, at least until he was cursed, that he had triumphed completely after beguiling Eve in the garden of Eden, was not giving up, either then or now. Hugh Nibley says, "Acting out of order, the [devil] is denounced and cursed. . . . Nettled by this rebuke and the curse, he flares up in his pride and announces what his program for the economic and political order of the new world is going to be. He will take the resources of the earth, and with precious metals as a medium of exchange he will buy up military and naval might, or rather those who control it, and so will govern the earth—for he is the prince of this world. He does rule: he is king. Here at the outset is the clearest possible statement of a military-industrial complex ruling the earth with violence and ruin. But as we are told, this cannot lead to anything but war, because it has been programmed to do that. It was conceived in the mind of Satan in his determination "to destroy the world" (Moses 4:6). The whole purpose of the program is to produce blood and horror on this earth" (*Approaching Zion*, p. 92).

Said in today's vernacular, Satan is not a good guy!

ALL THINGS WORK TOGETHER FOR GOOD

Nevertheless, to those who are willing to pay the price of complete repentance and righteous living, the Lord has promised that, Adam and Eve-like, our own submissions to the devil, as well as our innocent mistakes and every other "bad thing" we may experience, will all "work together for good" (Romans 8:28; D&C 90:24; 98:3; 100:15; 105:40). This seems to be particularly true for those who are seeking the face of Christ, striving to come unto Him. Every mistake becomes a building block, every "bad thing" a learning experience, every sin and transgression an opportunity, through repentance and mighty prayer, to grow closer to the Lord Jesus Christ.

Moreover, those who seek the presence of God must, as did Adam and Eve, Moses, and Jesus Christ, come face to face with the reality of Satan and his temptations. We may or may not see him; we may or may not hear his voice or experience other obvious manifestations of his presence. Yet, like Moses, we will be required to overcome our fear of him and to confront him "face to face" as we put at defiance his false revelations and evil ways. In doing so we will bear witness to him of our allegiance to Christ and His Father, spurn completely his temptations, and finally, in the name of Christ, command him to depart. Otherwise, we will surely experience at least somewhat the bitterness of hell, for our fear—that which stops most of us from doing these things—is part of what gives Satan his power over us.

TO HAVE POWER OVER SATAN WE MUST COMPREHEND HIM

The youthful Joseph Smith was given a marvelous opportunity to comprehend the devil during his first visit to the hill Cumorah. Oliver Cowdery wrote that after Joseph had tried to take the plates and couldn't, and then had prayerfully repented, the angel Moroni "said, 'Look!' and as he thus spake [Joseph] beheld the prince of darkness, surrounded by his innumerable train of associates. All this passed before him, and the heavenly messenger said, 'All this is shown, the good and the evil, the holy and impure, the glory of God and the power of darkness, that you may know hereafter the two powers and never be influenced or overcome by that wicked one. Behold, whatever entices and leads to good and to do good, is of God, and whatever does not is of the wicked one: *It is he that fills the hearts of men with evil* [gives false revelation], *to walk in darkness and blaspheme God;* and you may learn from henceforth, that his ways are to destruction, but the way of holiness is peace and rest. . . . You have now beheld the power of God manifested and the power of Satan: You see that there is nothing that is desirable in the works of darkness; that they cannot bring happiness; that those who are overcome therewith are miserable, while on the other hand the righteous are blessed with a place in the Kingdom of God where joy unspeakable surrounds them" (*The Papers of Joseph Smith,* 1:87–88; italics mine).

Part of our comprehending Satan is accomplished through the ordinances of the holy temple. As Brigham Young stated, "The Spirit of the Lord and the keys of the priesthood, hold power over all animated beings" (Nibley, *Nibley on the Timely and The Timeless,* p. 88). Joseph Smith discussed this power over animated beings when he said, "I preached in the grove on the keys of the kingdom, charity, etc. The keys are certain signs and words by which false spirits and personages may be detected from true, which cannot be revealed to the elders till the temple is completed. . . . There are signs in heaven, earth and hell; the elders must know them all, to be endowed with power, to finish their work and prevent imposition" (*Discourses of the Prophet Joseph Smith,* p. 152).

Elaborating on this theme, Joseph Smith taught on another occasion, "It is evident from the Apostles' writings, that many false spirits existed in their day, and had 'gone forth into the world,' and that it needed intelligence which God alone could impart to detect false spirits, and to prove what spirits were of God. The world in general have been grossly ignorant in regard to this one thing, and why should they be otherwise—for 'the things of God knoweth no man, but the Spirit of God.'

"There always did, in every age, seem to be a lack of intelligence pertaining to this subject. Spirits of all kinds have been manifested, in every age, and among all people . . . and all contend that their spirits are of God. Who shall solve the mystery? 'Try the spirits,' says John, but who is to do it? The learned, the eloquent, the philosopher, the sage, the divine—all are ignorant.

"'Try the spirits,' but what by? Are we to try them by the creeds of men? What preposterous folly—what sheer ignorance—what madness! Try the motions and actions of an eternal being (for I contend that all spirits are such) by a thing that was conceived in ignorance, and brought forth in folly—a cobweb of yesterday! Angels would hide their faces, and devils would be ashamed and insulted, and would say, 'Paul we know, and Jesus we know, but who are ye?' Let each man of society make a creed and try evil spirits by it, and the devil would shake his sides; it is all that he would ask—all that he would desire. Yet many of them do this, and hence 'many spirits are abroad in the world.'

"One great evil is, that men are ignorant of the nature of spirits; their power, laws, government, intelligence, etc., and imagine that when there is anything like power, revelation or vision manifested, that it must be of God" (*Teachings*, pp. 202–3).

"As we have noticed before, the great difficulty lies in the ignorance of the nature of spirits, of the laws by which they are governed, and the signs by which they may be known; if it requires the Spirit of God to know the things of God; and the spirit of the devil can only be unmasked through that medium, then it follows as a natural consequence that unless some person or persons have a communication, or revelation from God, unfolding to them the operation of the spirit, they must eternally remain ignorant of these principles; for I contend that if one man cannot understand these things but by the Spirit of God, ten thousand men cannot; it is alike out of the reach of the wisdom of the learned, the tongue of the eloquent, the power of the mighty. And we shall at last have to come to this conclusion, whatever we may think of revelation, that without it we can neither know nor understand anything of God, or the devil; and however unwilling the world may be to acknowledge this principle, it is evident from the multifarious creeds and notions concerning this matter that they understand nothing of this principle, and it is equally as plain that without a divine communication they must remain in ignorance. The world always mistook false prophets for true ones, and those that were sent of God, they considered to be false prophets, and hence they killed, stoned, punished and imprisoned the true prophets, and these made to hide themselves in deserts and dens, and caves of the earth, and though the most honorable men of the earth, they banished them from their society as vagabonds, whilst they cherished, honored and supported knaves, vagabonds, hypocrites, impostors, and the basest of men. . . .

"Every one of these professes to be competent to try his neighbor's spirit, but no one can try his own, and what is the reason? Because they have not a key to unlock, no rule wherewith to measure, and no criterion whereby they can test it. Could any one tell the length, breadth or height of a building without a rule? test the quality of metals without a criterion, or point out the movements of the planetary systems, without a knowledge of astronomy? Certainly not; and if such ignorance as this is manifested about a spirit of this kind, who can describe an angel of light? If Satan should appear as one in glory, who can tell his color, his signs, his appearance, his glory?—or what is the manner of his manifestation? Who can detect the spirit of the French prophets with their revelations and their visions, and power of manifestations? Or who can point out the spirit of the Irvingites, with their apostles and prophets, and visions and tongues, and interpretations, &c., &c. *Or who can drag into daylight and develop the hidden mysteries of the false spirits that so frequently are made manifest among the Latter-day Saints? We answer that no man can do this without the Priesthood, and having a knowledge of the laws by which spirits are governed; for as 'no man knows the things of God, but by the Spirit of God,' so no man knows the spirit of the devil, and his power and influence, but by possessing intelligence which is more than human, and having unfolded through the medium of the Priesthood the mysterious operations of his devices;* without knowing the angelic form, the sanctified look and gesture, and the zeal that is frequently manifested by him for the glory of God, together with the prophetic spirit, the gracious influence, the godly appearance, and the holy garb, which are so characteristic of his proceedings and his mysterious windings" (*History of the Church,* 4:573; italics mine).

It is evident that Joseph knew a great deal about the nature and powers of spirits, both those who followed Lucifer and we who followed Christ. Much of this information he has left for us to learn.

HOW EVIL SPIRITS ACT UPON MORTALS

Apparently the pattern of abuse of both an evil and an unclean or false spirit upon a mortal is to come at him repeatedly from the outside, afflicting, tormenting with fears and temptations, wearing at the person in the area of the spirit's assignment or the person's weakness. This continues until the victim finally gets rid of the spirit through righteousness and rebuking, or succumbs to it and partakes of the sin. Once a person has succumbed, the spirit is allowed to gain entry to the person's body (Mosiah 3:6; 3 Nephi 2:2; Mark 5:1–13), where it is able to exert even more power and influence than before (Moses 4:3–4; D&C 93:39). In this manner diseases sometimes occur (*Journal of Discourses*, 4:133–34), marriages are broken up, commandments are not kept, testimonies are lost, missions are abandoned, families are destroyed, callings are not fulfilled, and even peoples' lives are taken before their time (Pratt, *Key to the Science of Theology*, p. 116).

Nephi says, "At that day shall he rage in the hearts of the children of men, and stir them up to anger against that which is good. And others will he pacify, and lull them away into carnal security, that they will say: Al is well in Zion; yea, Zion prospereth, all is well—and thus the devil cheateth their souls, and leadeth them away carefully down to hell. And behold, others he flattereth away, and telleth them there is no hell; and thus he sayeth unto them: I am no devil, for there is none—and thus he whispereth in their ears, until he grasps them with his awful chains, from whence there is no deliverance" (2 Nephi 28:20–22).

Concerning this scripture, Latter-day Saint scholar Dennis L. Largey writes, "A closer look at some of the keys words used in this passage is helpful to broaden our understanding of how Satan operates: First, he *pacifies*, which means he appeases or placates. Second, he *cheats*, swindles, misleads, fools, or practices fraud upon, which means he deceives by trickery. Third, he *flatters,* which means he compliments excessively and insincerely, especially to win favor, to feed vanity, or to persuade that what one wants to believe is the case. Fourth, he *leads* the way by going in advance, by conducting, escorting, or directing, by causing one to follow a certain course of action or line of thought. All of this—the pacifying, the cheating, the flattering, and the leading—is done carefully, which is synonymous with thoroughly, painstakingly, and conscientiously. Satan thus customizes his dishonesty according to the susceptibility of his target. His favorite approach is whatever works. In the pride of his heart, he does not drive from the rear but leads from the front. Knowing only a few would follow him if his true identity and design were manifested, he carefully draws people into the false conclusion of supposing they are winning when, in fact, they are slowly, but nevertheless effectively being destroyed" ("The Enemies of Christ," *The Book of Mormon: Second Nephi, The Doctrinal Approach,* pp. 297–98).

MORTALS HAVE POWER OVER SATAN

According to what the Lord told the Prophet Joseph, "that wicked one cometh and taketh away light and truth, *through disobedience,* from the children of men" (D&C 93:39; italics mine). Therefore, what may be termed the heavenly or eternal law under which Satan and his followers function is *that they are governed by each of us individually, according to how we choose to live.* Satan's power over us *always* hinges upon our obedience or disobedience—our willingness or unwillingness to submit to the mind and will of the Father.

As Joseph Smith taught, "All beings who have bodies

have power over those who have not. The devil has no power over us only as we permit him. The moment we revolt at anything which comes from God, the devil takes power. . . . We came to this earth that we might have a body and present it pure before God in the celestial kingdom. The great principle of happiness consists in having a body. The devil has no body, and herein is his punishment" (*Teachings*, p. 181).

As a caution, the Prophet also said that "'Satan was generally blamed for the evils which we did, but if he was the cause of all our wickedness, men could not be condemned. The devil could not compel mankind to do evil; all was voluntary. Those who resisted the Spirit of God, would be liable to be led into temptation, and then the association of heaven would be withdrawn from those who refused to be made partakers of such great glory. God would not exert any compulsory means, and the devil could not; and such ideas as were [so] entertained . . . were absurd.' What beautiful harmony between the Prophet's doctrine here and that of the Apostle James: 'Let no man say when he is tempted, I am tempted of God: for God cannot be tempted with evil, neither tempteth he any man: But every man is tempted, when he is drawn away of his own lusts, and enticed. Then when lust hath conceived, it bringing forth sin: and sin when it is finished, bringeth forth death' [James 1:13–15]" (*History of the Church*, 4:xli).

And, "In this world, mankind are naturally selfish, ambitious and striving to excel one above another; yet some are willing to build up others as well as themselves. So in the other world there are a variety of spirits. Some seek to excel. And this was the case with Lucifer when he fell. He sought for things which were unlawful. Hence he was sent down, and it is said he drew many away with him; and the greatness of his punishment is that he shall not have a tabernacle. This is his punishment. So the devil, thinking to thwart the decree of God, by going up and down in the earth, seeking whom he may destroy—any person that he can find that will yield to him, he will bind him, and take possession of the body and reign there, glorying in it mightily, not caring that he had got merely a stolen body; and by-and-by some one having authority will come along and cast him out and restore the tabernacle to its rightful owner. The devil steals a tabernacle because he has not one of his own: but if he steals one, he is always liable to be turned out of doors" (*History of the Church,* 5:388).

As he mentions someone with authority casting Satan out, Joseph Smith is speaking of the fact that anyone who has taken upon himself or herself the name of Christ through proper baptism has the right to rebuke the devil in Christ's name and command him to depart. This action becomes even more effective or powerful after one has been endowed in the temple. Those who hold the priesthood are given even greater powers—for instance, to release from their holds upon mortals all unclean or false spirits and then to cast them out. But we must remember that rebuking Satan or his evil followers under any condition is not a prayer, for we neither kneel before Satan nor pray to him. Nevertheless, rebuking may appropriately be done during or immediately following prayer or a priesthood blessing.

HOW TO DETECT SATAN

Satan, therefore, is *always* subject to the authority of Christ as manifested through his *righteous* mortal servants.

Occasionally, however, if he appears pretending to be an angel of light—a messenger from God—other measures may need to be taken. Joseph Smith taught, "When a messenger comes saying he has a message from God, offer him your hand and request him to shake hands with you. If he be an angel he will do so, and you will feel his hand. If he be the spirit of a just man made perfect he will come in his glory; for that is the only way he can appear—Ask him to shake hands with you, but he will not move, because it is contrary to the order of heaven for a just man to deceive; but he will still deliver his message. If it be the devil as an angel of light, when you ask him to shake hands he will offer you his hand, and you will not feel anything; you may therefore detect him" (D&C 129:4–8).

And, "The devil may appear as an angel of light. Ask God to reveal it; if it be of the devil, he will flee from you; if of God, He will manifest Himself, or make it manifest" (*Teachings*, p. 162).

OUR SAFETY

In conclusion, the Prophet gave us the key for avoiding the destruction the devil has planned for each of our souls. "[Joseph] said he did not care how fast we run in the path of virtue; resist evil, and there is no danger; God, men, and angels will not condemn those that resist everything that is evil, and devils cannot; as well might the devil seek to dethrone Jehovah, as overthrow an innocent soul that resists everything which is evil" (*Teachings*, p. 226).

By learning to recognize Satan and his spirit followers, to rebuke them appropriately, and then to do our level best to resist evil from day to day, we who travel through the wilderness of the Lord will have the power to overcome the devil in our lives, and he will be bound. And according to President Spencer W. Kimball, "When Satan is bound in a single home—when Satan is bound in a single life—the Millennium has already begun in that home, in that life" (*The Teachings of Spencer W. Kimball*, p. 172).

It surely seems worth the effort, doesn't it?

NOTES

1. Examining Brother Nibley's comment concerning "what had been done in other worlds," we know very little about them beyond the fact that they exist, "worlds without number" (Moses 1:33). All of them were created or "organized" (Abraham 4:1) by the Only Begotten Son for God's "own purpose" (Moses 1:33). We also know that "there are many worlds that have passed away by the word of my power. And there are many that now stand, and innumerable are they unto man; but all things are numbered unto me, for they are mine and I know them" (Moses 1:35). It is also likely that, while these worlds are in many ways similar, no two will be exactly alike. Brother Nibley explains: "What is creation? An endless procession of worlds rolling off the assembly line? No, creation never duplicates; it is never mere production after a set mold" (*Approaching Zion*, pp. 270–71). Nevertheless, we know that on each of God's worlds that has been so organized, there has, does, or will dwell an "Adam, which is many" (Moses 1:34), and an "Eve," so named "because she is the mother of all living" (Moses 4:26). We also know that these "Adams" and "Eves" and their posterity are spirit children of our eternal Father, created in the image of the Only Begotten (Moses 2:27). We know that: "in the language of Adam, Man of Holiness is [the Father's] name, and the name of his Only Begotten is the Son of Man, even Jesus

Christ" (Moses 6:57). The remainder of the Father's posterity (us), therefore, are also sons and daughters of Man—or mankind—no matter in which world they (or we) have been placed (D&C 76:24). And just as do we, they too have need of Christ's atonement. "He is the Lamb slain from the foundation of the world," said Brigham Young. "Is it so on any other earth? [Yes.] On every earth" (*Journal of Discourses*, 14:71). Therefore the inhabitants of all worlds must also be susceptible to the wiles and temptations of the (or *a*) devil, for they must also succumb and "fall." Elder Orson Pratt taught: "Notwithstanding the unnumbered worlds which have been created . . . all these creations [are] fallen worlds" (*Journal of Discourses* 19:293). As Lehi explained: "Wherefore, all mankind [are] in a lost and in a fallen state, and ever would be save they should rely on this Redeemer" (1 Nephi 10:6). Finally, we know that the Lord, at least for now, intends to give us no further information regarding these other worlds or their inhabitants. To Moses He simply said: "But only an account of this earth, and the inhabitants thereof, give I unto you" (Moses 1:35).

2. When a spirit is called unclean or false, it means that the spirit has been born into mortality, chosen to live falsely or in wickedness, and then died in an unrepentant or unclean state. When a spirit is referred to as a devil or evil spirit, it is one who followed Lucifer from the premortal world and has therefore been denied the privilege of ever possessing a mortal tabernacle. Christ and others of His followers cast out both these types of spirits (1 Nephi 11:31, 3 Nephi 7:19), so it is obvious that both devils and unclean spirits have power to afflict and torment mankind (See Pratt, *Key to the Science of Theology*, p. 116, and Brigham Young in *Journal of Discourses*, 4:133–34).

Chapter Twenty-One

THE HOLY TEMPLE

The temple is the doorway along the straight and narrow path through which all wilderness travelers must pass in order to reenter the presence of the Lord. Having lost that presence through spiritual death and our own subsequent carnality, still we yearn after the perfect love we once felt. Thus, in the midst of our adversity and affliction in this turbulent world, we are drawn to the temple, where by most sacred ordinances the Lord seals us to Him and empowers us to overcome all things and make our way back into His presence. As President Joseph Fielding Smith put it, "You cannot receive an exaltation until you have made covenants in the House of the Lord and received the keys and authorities that are there bestowed and which cannot be given in any other place on the earth today" (*Doctrines of Salvation,* 2:253).

Elder Robert D. Hales adds, "In our day, the steadying arm of the Lord reaches us through the ordinances of His holy temples. Said the Prophet Joseph to the early Saints in Nauvoo, 'You need an endowment, brethren, in order that you may be prepared and able to overcome all things' (*History of the Church,* 2:309). How right he was! Being blessed with the temple covenants and endowed with power [makes] it possible for the Latter-day Saints to endure tribulation with faith" (*Ensign,* May 2003, p. 17).

A PERSONAL EXPERIENCE

I will never forget the night a recently deceased ward member "spoke" to me, pleading so forcefully and with such anguish that it awakened me from a deep sleep, his message remaining firmly implanted in my mind. "Bishop," he had pleaded, "I need your help! I can see now how wrong I have been! Please, if you will help get my wife ready and take her to the temple for her own endowment, I have been promised that in one year from now I will also be ready for our son to do my work. That is the only way my wife and I with our children can be an eternal family and be able to dwell in the presence of the Lord." Then he had added, almost as an afterthought: "Oh, yes, and please tell her that I have never seen such exquisitely beautiful flowers as these where I am!"

It should be noted that this brother and his wife were renowned for their lovely yard. More important, he was also known far and wide as a wonderful man, kind, tender, and gentle to his wife and family; generous, thoughtful, and loving to his neighbors; and absolutely adored by all the children in our neighborhood. All his own children had married in the temple, and his wife had a firm testimony of the gospel's truthfulness, though in their later years she had deferred to him in terms of her church activity. Nevertheless, in every way but one he lived as righteous a life as his sweetheart, even attending every Church meeting where any of his children or grandchildren were participating. Only, for some reason, despite literally dozens of frequently intense though always amiable conversations with me, he simply couldn't accept the idea that there would be a life after death or that families could be made eternal. Now, of course, after his "leap into the darkness" of death, he was seeing things more clearly, and he was desperate that an eternal sealing exist between him and his beloved wife, children, and grandchildren.

When I shared with this brother's wife my nighttime experience, she wept—both in sorrow that her sealing to him hadn't happened while he had lived at her side in mortality, and in joy that it was finally going to happen anyway. Several months later she was endowed, and exactly a year to the day following her husband's death, she, with her son's help, was sealed to him in an eternal family unit. That day in the temple, through the power of the Holy Ghost, this brother "spoke" to my mind again—a sweetly simple "Thank you, Bishop" that flooded my emotions and thrilled me to the core. Soon thereafter his wife had become an avid family history researcher as well as a set-apart temple ordinance worker, no doubt laboring at his side despite the fact that he was on the other side of the veil. And both of these sweet people remain a testimony to me of the eternal force and power of temple ordinances—that those ordinances truly do provide the power by which, and the gateway through which, righteous people may behold the face of Christ and obtain His presence!

FROM THE ANCIENT PROPHETS

Adam, cast into the lone and dreary world, searched diligently until true messengers delivered to him the keys or ordinances that opened the doorway behind which the Lord was waiting. Abraham, seeking all the blessings of the fathers, embarked on the same quest through the powers of the holy priesthood (Abraham 1:2–4) until at last and in triumph he exclaimed, "Thy servant has sought thee earnestly; now I have found thee" (Abraham 2:12).

Isaac and Jacob at their sacred altars, Moses on Mount Horeb, Lehi at the Tree, Nephi on the mountain top, the brother of Jared on the mount Shelem—all these wilderness travelers conducted the search that is outlined and empowered for each of us in the temple, gradually increasing the hold, the seal, between themselves and their Lord, until in reality they had, through Christ, brought themselves back into His presence. This was the very quest for which they had sought and obtained a remission of their sins, and for which they had entered the Lord's wilderness—to rend the veil of unbelief, come unto Christ, and thereafter behold His face (See D&C 101:38), to stand in His presence (JST Genesis 14:30–31; D&C 84:19; 107:19) and be encircled eternally in the arms of His pure and perfect love (D&C 6:20; 2 Nephi 1:15).

ON THE MOUNTAINTOP

Most of us are familiar with the fact that Isaiah spoke of the temple as the Lord's mountain, pointing out that it was a place of spiritual education and empowerment. "In the last days, . . . the mountain of the Lord's house shall be established in the top of the mountains, and shall be exalted above the hills; and all nations shall flow unto it. And many people shall go and say, Come ye, and let us go up to the mountain of the Lord, to the house of the God of Jacob; and *he will teach us of his ways, and we will walk in his paths*" (Isaiah 2:2–3; italics mine). And Nephi wrote, "I, Nephi, did go into the mount oft, and I did pray oft unto the Lord; wherefore *the Lord showed unto me great things*" (1 Nephi 18:3; italics mine). It is obvious that these two prophets thought of the Lord's mountain as a place where people might obtain spiritual empowerment—a place where they might learn for themselves from the very mouth of God. Mountains, therefore, were their temples. As the Prophet Joseph put it, "The rich can only get . . . certain signs and words . . . in the Temple, the poor may get them on the mountain top as did Moses" (*History of the Church,* 4:608; italics mine).

AN ETERNAL JOURNEY

And what sorts of "great things" where shown these ancient sojourners in their lofty, cloud-shrouded temples? The same exact things we can see and learn today. As Elder John A. Widtsoe wrote, "The temple endowment relates the story of man's eternal journey; sets forth the conditions upon which progress in the eternal journey depends; requires covenants or agreements of those participating, to accept and use the laws of progress; gives tests by which our willingness and fitness for righteousness may be known, and finally points out the ultimate destiny of those who love truth and live by it" (*Program of the Church*, p. 78). Elder James E. Talmage adds, "The ordinances of the endowment embody certain obligations on the part of the individual, such as covenant and promise to observe the law of strict virtue and chastity, to be charitable and benevolent, tolerant and pure; to devote both talent and material means to the spread of truth and the uplifting of [mankind]; to maintain devotion to the cause of truth; and to seek in every way to contribute to the great preparation that the earth may be made ready to receive her King—the Lord Jesus Christ. With the taking of each covenant and the assuming of each obligation a promised blessing is pronounced, contingent upon the faithful observance of the conditions" (*The House of the Lord*, p. 100).

THE TEMPLE IS ZION

According to Hugh Nibley, "Ancient writers assure us repeatedly that the temple is the earthly type of Zion, a holy place removed from contact with the outer world, set apart for ordinances from which the world is excluded; while it is in the world, the temple presents a forbidding front of high gates, formidable walls, narrow doors, and frowning battlements, dramatizing the total withdrawal of Zion from the world and its defensive position over against it" (*Approaching Zion*, pp. 27–28).

Since Zion cannot be built up "unless it is by the principles of the law of the celestial kingdom" (D&C 105:5), and since it must at all times be holy enough to be the Lord's home ("The Lord hath chosen Zion; he hath desired it for his habitation" [Psalm 132:13] and "mine abode forever" [Moses 7:21]), it only makes sense that the temple is the earthly place where the righteous, such as those great men described above, may, as did they, behold the face of God.

ALL VERY REAL

All this is much more real than most of us realize. As the scripture says of the brother of Jared, "The Lord showed himself unto him, and said: Because thou knowest these things ye are redeemed from the fall; therefore ye are brought back into my presence; therefore I show myself unto you" (Ether 3:13).

Therefore, what Mahonri Moriancumer had beheld for so long with the eye of faith was now visually confirmed. He had rent "the veil of unbelief" (Ether 4:15) with his persistent efforts, and now he had beheld the face of the Lord. Rather than seeing in order to believe, which is the way of the world, he had believed in order to see, and so on the mountain of the Lord's temple, God rewarded his righteous faith and efforts.

AWED BY THE LORD'S PRESENCE

The "temple" prayer of the brother of Jared is also instructive, for though he was in actuality seeking light for his people's barges, he seems much more concerned about his own and his people's inadequacy before the Lord. Probably because of his three-hour chastisement, he feared the anger of the Lord exceedingly. Yet he pressed on past his fear because he knew he had been commanded to do what he was doing, and he obtained (Ether 3:2–6).

Isaiah, another wilderness traveler, also reported great fear when he realized that he was actually in the presence of the Lord. He cried, "Woe is me! for I am undone; because I am a man of unclean lips, and I dwell in the midst of a people of unclean lips: for mine eyes have seen the King, the Lord of hosts" (Isaiah 6:5).

As we seekers after the face of Christ draw closer and closer to the presence of the Lord, even though we have been born again, we see ever more clearly the great contrast between God and our own carnal or mortal natures. We may, therefore, be sorely tempted to shrink back and give up our quest. Many, such as the children of Israel, do shrink, and they spend the remainder of their lives wandering in the wilderness. But those who are determined press boldly on, exercising mighty faith and constant repentance as they penetrate the veil until they are brought at last into the presence of the Lord.

Thus, as had the brother of Jared, the great Isaiah pressed on until one of the Lord's seraphim or angels left the altar of the Lord's temple and, coming to Isaiah, declared, "Lo, this hath touched thy lips; and thine iniquity is taken away, and thy sin purged" (Isaiah 6:7).

TEMPLES IN THIS DISPENSATION

Though we have already shown the significance of the temple in the lives of the early Kirtland Saints, it should be helpful to examine the scriptural history of temple ordinances in this dispensation—and thus we will discover why temple ordinances and worship empower us to obtain God's presence.

In 1823 Moroni declared to the youthful Joseph Smith, speaking for the Lord, "Behold, I will reveal unto you the Priesthood, by the hand of Elijah the prophet, before the coming of the great and dreadful day of the Lord" (D&C 2:1).

One definition of the word *reveal* means "to explain or empower." So, Elijah's mission was to reveal or make available specific powers to Latter-day Saints so that they would be enabled to more effectively use the priesthood they held. President Ezra Taft Benson states, "Even though the Aaronic Priesthood and Melchizedek Priesthood had been restored to the earth, the Lord urged the Saints to build a temple to receive the keys by which this order of priesthood could be administered on the earth again, 'for there (was) not a place found on earth that he may come to and restore again that which was lost . . . even the fulness of the priesthood' (D&C 124:28). Again, the Prophet Joseph said: 'If a man gets a fullness of the priesthood of God he has to get it in the same way that Jesus Christ obtained it, and that was by keeping all the commandments and obeying all the ordinances of the house of the Lord' (*Teachings*, p. 308)" (*The Teachings of Ezra Taft Benson*, p. 249).

And how eternal are these ordinances? Again we turn to the Prophet Joseph, who said, "God purposed in Himself that there should not be an eternal fullness until every dispensation should be fulfilled and gathered together in one, and that all things whatsoever, that should be gathered together in one in those dispensations unto the same fullness and eternal glory, should be in Christ Jesus; *therefore He set the ordinances to be the same forever and ever,* and set Adam to watch over them, to reveal them from heaven to man, or to send angels to reveal them" (*History of the Church,* 4:208; italics mine).

Because His ordinances are eternally vital, the Lord

declared to the tiny Church in New York, "That ye might escape the power of the enemy, and be gathered unto me a righteous people, without spot and blameless—Wherefore, for this cause I gave unto you the commandment that ye should go to the Ohio, and there I will give unto you my law; and there *you shall be endowed with power from on high*" (D&C 38:31–32; italics mine). Again He says, "I gave unto you a commandment that you should build a house, in the which house *I design to endow those whom I have chosen with power from on high*" (D&C 95:8; italics mine). In Nauvoo the Lord said to the Saints, "Build a house to my name, for the Most High to dwell therein. For there is not a place found on earth that he may come to and *restore again that which was lost unto you, or which he hath taken away. . . . For therein are the keys of the holy priesthood ordained, that you may receive honor and glory*" (D&C 124:27–28, 34; italics mine). And, in a revelatory letter concerning temple work and the sealing powers of the priesthood, Joseph Smith wrote, "The great and grand secret of the whole matter, and the *summum bonum* of the whole subject that is lying before us, consists in obtaining the powers of the Holy Priesthood. For him to whom these keys are given there is no difficulty in obtaining a knowledge of facts in relation to the salvation of the children of men, both as well for the dead as for the living" (D&C 128:11).

The Lord declares, "This greater priesthood administereth the gospel and holdeth the key of the mysteries of the kingdom, even the key of the knowledge of God. Therefore, in the ordinances thereof [and where are most of our ordinances found?], the power of godliness is manifest. And without the ordinances thereof, and the authority of the priesthood, the power of godliness is not manifest unto men in the flesh; for without this no man can see the face of God, even the Father, and live" (D&C 84:19–22).

Thus President Harold B. Lee declares, "When you enter a holy temple, you are by that course gaining fellowship with the saints in God's eternal Kingdom where time is no more. . . . In the temples of your God you are endowed not with a rich legacy of worldly treasure, but with a wealth of eternal riches that are above price" (*Decisions for Successful Living,* p. 141).

THE MYSTERIES OF GODLINESS AND PEACEABLE THINGS OF THE KINGDOM

Such temple ordinances (or keys) of priesthood empowerment as we have been discussing, which reveal "the mysteries of Godliness," are often called the "peaceable things of the kingdom." According to scripture, these mysteries and peaceable things are taught by the Holy Ghost through personal revelation (D&C 36:2). The Lord says, "If thou shalt ask, thou shalt receive revelation upon revelation, knowledge upon knowledge, that thou mayest know the mysteries and peaceable things—that which bringeth joy, that which bringeth life eternal" (D&C 42:61).

Some wilderness travelers might balk at the thought of "delving into the mysteries" of godliness, but that is because they don't understand the difference between them and the mysteries of man. Where the latter lead to confusion, endless arguments, and contention, the former actually lead to God. Thus Joseph Smith said, "I advise all to go on to perfection, and to search deeper and deeper into the mysteries of Godliness" (*Teachings*, p. 364). Why? Because we come unto Christ as we gain knowledge of Him and His gospel. The great prophet Nephi adds, "He that diligently seeketh shall find; and the mysteries of God shall be unfolded unto them, by the power of the Holy Ghost, as well in these times as in times of old, and as well in times of old as in times to come; wherefore, the course of the Lord is one eternal round" (1 Nephi 10:19). Alma continues, "Yea, he that repenteth and exerciseth faith, and bringeth forth good works, and prayeth continually without ceasing—unto such it is given to know the mysteries of God; yea, unto such it shall be given to reveal things which never have been revealed" (Alma 26:22).

But, as Alma explained to Zeezrom, "It is given unto many to know the mysteries of God; nevertheless they are laid under a strict command that they shall not impart only according to the portion of his word which he doth grant unto the children of men, according to the heed and diligence which they give unto him" (Alma 12:9). And how is the amount of knowledge imparted to be determined? Again Alma answers, "He that will harden his heart . . . receiveth the lesser portion of the word . . . until they know nothing concerning his mysteries . . . and he that will not harden his heart, to him is given the greater portion of the word, until it is given unto him to know the mysteries of God until he know them in full" (Alma 12:10–11).

There are at least a dozen additional scriptural references stating the same thing: each Latter-day Saint, if he wants to come unto Christ during mortality, must seek to know and understand the mysteries of Godliness (for instance, Matthew 13:11; Luke 8:10; 1 Nephi 1:1; 2:16; Jacob 4:8; Mosiah 1:5; 2:9; Alma 10:5; 12:9–11; D&C 6:7; 8:11;

63:22–23; 76:5–10). For those who want to successfully seek the face of Christ, such understanding is imperative.

President Ezra Taft Benson states, "The temple ceremony was given by a wise Heavenly Father to help us become more Christ-like. The endowment was revealed by revelation and can be understood only by revelation. The instruction is given in symbolic language. The late Apostle John A. Widtsoe taught, 'No man or woman can come out of the temple endowed as he should be, unless he has seen, beyond the symbol, the mighty realities for which the temple stands' ("Temple Worship," an address given in Salt lake City, 12 October 1920)" (*The Teachings of Ezra Taft Benson*, pp. 250–51).

President Harold B. Lee adds, "The temple ceremonies are designed by a wise Heavenly Father, who has revealed them to us in these last days as a guide and a protection throughout our lives, that you and I might not fail of an exaltation in the celestial kingdom where God and Christ dwell. . . . We talk of security in this day, and yet we fail to understand that here on this temple block we have standing the holy temple wherein we may find the symbols by which power might be generated that will save this nation from destruction. Therein may be found the fulness of the blessings of the priesthood" (*Teachings of Harold B. Lee*, p. 574).

President Lee also noted, "As early as 1841, the Lord revealed to Joseph Smith that 'there is not a place found on earth that he may come to and restore again that which was lost unto you, or which he hath taken away, even the fulness of the priesthood. For I deign to reveal unto my church things which have been kept hid from before the foundation of the world, things that pertain to the dispensation of the fulness of times.' (D&C 124:28, 41).

"These revelations, which are reserved for and taught only to the faithful Church members in sacred temples, constitute what are called the 'mysteries of godliness.' The Lord said He had given to Joseph 'the keys of the mysteries, and the revelations which are sealed' (D&C 28:7). As a reward to the faithful, the Lord promised: 'And to them will I reveal all mysteries, yea, all the hidden mysteries of my kingdom from days of old.' (D&C 76:7). In this sense, then, a mystery may be defined as a truth which cannot be known except by revelation" (*Teachings of Harold B. Lee*, p. 575).

KEYS OF THE PRIESTHOOD

By now it should have been noted that the Lord, His modern prophets, and others who have been closely associated with them frequently refer to the ordinances of the priesthood, as administered in the temple, as "keys" or "keys of the priesthood." In our day, however, such usage has become more narrowly or carefully defined. Now the word "keys" and the phrase "keys of the priesthood," reiterated each time a temple recommend is issued, refer specifically to the powers and authority held in fullness by the president of the Church and passed down from him by ordination or setting apart through specific lines of priesthood authority.

Nevertheless, we know that Joseph Smith and others, as they used the word "keys" or the phrase "keys of the priesthood," were often referring to some or all of the ordinances of the priesthood as administered in the temple. These ordinances were first administered by the Prophet to Church members on May 4, 1842. On that date he recorded, "I spent the day in the upper part of the store, that is my private office (so called because in that room I keep my sacred writings, translate ancient records, and receive revelations) and in my general business office . . . in council with General James Adams, of Springfield, Patriarch Hyrum Smith, Bishops Newell K. Whitney and George Miller, and President Brigham Young and Elders Heber C. Kimball and Willard Richards, instructing them in the principles and order of the Priesthood, *attending to washings, anointings, endowments and the communication of keys pertaining to the Aaronic Priesthood, and so on to the highest order of the Melchizedek Priesthood,* setting forth the order pertaining to the Ancient of Days, and all those plans and principles by which anyone is enabled to secure the fulness of those blessings which have been prepared for the Church of the First Born and come up and abide in the presence of the Eloheim in the eternal worlds. In this council was instituted the ancient order of things for the first time in these last days. And the communication I made to this council were of things spiritual and to be received only by the spiritually minded; and *there was nothing made known to these men but what will be made known to all the Saints of the last days, so soon as they are prepared to receive, and a proper place is prepared to communicate them, even to the weakest of the Saints;*. . . . [So let them] wait their time with patience in all meekness, faith, perseverance unto the end, knowing assuredly that all these things referred to in this council are always governed by the principle of revelation" (*History of the Church,* 5:1–2; italics mine).

Three days before that, on May 1, he gave this public explanation: "The keys are certain signs and words by which false spirits and personages may be detected from true, which cannot be revealed to the Elders till the Temple is completed" (*History of the Church,* 4:608).

And two days before that, on April 28, 1842, apostle George A. Smith, recording Joseph's remarks to the Relief Society, reported that he "spoke of delivering the keys of the Priesthood to the Church, and said that the faithful members of the Relief Society should receive them with their husbands, that the Saints whose integrity has been tried and proved faithful, might know how to ask the Lord and receive an answer" (*Teachings,* p. 226).

Bathsheba W. Smith, wife of George A. Smith, spoke of the fulfillment of this when she reported of Joseph, "When speaking in one of our general fast meetings, he said that we did not know how to pray to have our prayers answered. But when I and my husband had our endowments . . . Joseph Smith presiding, he taught us the order of prayer" (*Juvenile Instructor,* June 1, 1892, p. 345; also *Words,* p. 54, footnote 19).

GOD'S LANGUAGE OF POWER

As was pointed out earlier in this volume, Enoch and other ancient prophets were given by the Lord His "language" of priesthood power (Moses 7:13), a language related directly to temple worship (Moses 7:17). Through that language they were enabled to overcome spiritual death and be brought back into the presence of the Lord (Moses 7:16), where they might ask and rcceive (D&C 124:95, 97).

Through the Prophet Joseph the Lord has revealed this same priesthood "language" of power to the Latter-day Saints. However, the question might appropriately be asked,

Power to do what? The answer at first glance is multifaceted: "that the Saints whose integrity has been tried and proved faithful, might know how to ask the Lord and receive an answer" (*Teachings*, p. 226); that "false spirits and personages may be detected from true" (*History of the Church,* 4:608); that the Saints might "get a blessing that will be worth remembering, if we should live as long as John the Revelator" (*Discourses of the Prophet Joseph Smith*, p. 113); that we might "become more Christ-like" (*The Teachings of Ezra Taft Benson,* 250–51); that we might receive "that which bringeth joy, that which bringeth life eternal" (D&C 42:61); that we might learn "of his ways, and . . . walk in his paths" (Isaiah 2: 3); that He might show unto us "great things" (1 Nephi 18:3); that "the mysteries of God shall be unfolded unto [us], by the power of the Holy Ghost" (1 Nephi 10:19); that we might be taught "the peaceable things of the kingdom" (D&C 36:2); that we might receive "the fulness of the priesthood" (D&C 124:28); that we might receive "the key of the mysteries of the kingdom, even the key of the knowledge of God" (D&C 84:19); and finally, that we might, like the brother of Jared, "see the face of God, even the Father, and live" (D&C 84:22).

On the occasion of the dedication of the southeast cornerstone of the Salt Lake Temple, on April 6, 1853, Brigham Young declared, "Let me give you the definition of . . . your endowment . . . in brief. . . . It is, to receive all those ordinances in the House of the Lord, which are necessary for you, after you have departed this life, to enable you to walk back to the presence of the Father, passing the angels who stand as sentinels, being enabled to give them the key words, the signs and tokens, pertaining to the Holy Priesthood, and gain your eternal exaltation in spite of earth and hell!" (*Journal of Discourses,* 2:31).

In summary, then, this God-given language of priesthood power—ordinances administered by proper authority in our holy temples—gives every worthy Latter-day Saint power to overcome the devil and be taught concerning, and thereafter obtain for himself or herself, ever-increasing righteousness. As that is accomplished, this same power enables us to obtain charity, or Christ's pure love, to open the heavens, to behold the face of Christ and enjoy the second comforter, to come back into God's actual presence upon our mortal death, and thereafter to be granted, as a joint-heir with the beloved Christ, all that the Father hath (see D&C 84:38).

TO GAIN AN UNDERSTANDING

And how do we gain an understanding of how to do this? As Joseph Smith explained, "The endowment you are so anxious about, you cannot comprehend now, nor could Gabriel explain it to the understanding of your dark minds; but strive to be prepared in your hearts, be faithful in all things, [and] be clean every whit. Let us be faithful and silent, brethren, and if God gives you a manifestation, keep it to yourselves; be watchful and prayerful . . . do not watch for iniquity in each other, if you do you will not get an endowment, for God will not bestow it on such. But if we are faithful, and live by every word that proceeds forth from the mouth of God, I will venture to prophesy that we shall get a blessing that will be worth remembering, if we should live as long as John the Revelator" (*Discourses of the Prophet Joseph Smith,* p. 113).

President Heber C. Kimball, addressing this same topic,

said, "This is why you are required to be sober, to be honest, that you could ask and receive, knock and it should be opened, and that when you sought for things you should find them. [The endowment] is putting you in possession of those keys by which you can ask for things you need and obtain them. This is the key by which to obtain all the glory and felicity of eternal life. It is the key by which you approach God . . . and be recognized. . . . Now you have been taught how to pray. . . . The principles which have been opened to you are the things which ought to occupy your attention all of your lives. They are not second to anything. You have the key by which, if you are faithful, you will claim on your posterity all the blessings of the priesthood" (*Scenes in Nauvoo, and Incidents from Heber C. Kimball's Journal,* Helen Mar Whitney, in "Women's Exponent," July 15, 1883, p. 26).

IF WE ARE FAITHFUL

To me, the most important phrase in Heber C. Kimball's journal quoted above is, "if you are faithful." Brigham Young obviously agreed, saying, "The Gospel has brought to us the holy Priesthood. . . . The keys of that Priesthood are here; we have them in our possession; we can unlock, and we can shut up. We can obtain salvation, and we can administer it. . . . But the Lord has so ordained that no man shall receive the benefits of the everlasting priesthood without humbling himself before him, and giving him the glory for teaching him, that he may be able to witness to every man of the truth, and not depend upon the words of any individual on the earth, but know for himself, live 'by every word that proceedeth out of the mouth of God,' love the Lord Jesus Christ and the institutions of his kingdom, and finally enter into his glory. Every man and woman may be a revelator, and have . . . the spirit of prophecy, and foresee the mind and will of God concerning them. . . . The Priesthood is given to the people and the keys thereof, and, when properly understood, they may actually unlock the treasury of the Lord, and receive to their fullest satisfaction. But through our own weaknesses, through the frailty of human nature, [many] are not capable of doing so" (*Discourses of Brigham Young*, pp. 202–3).

Of course, this human frailty is why the Lord encourages us with this wise counsel, which applies to both temples and our own homes: "Organize yourselves; prepare every needful thing; and establish a house, even a house of prayer, a house of fasting, a house of faith, a house of learning, a house of glory, a house of order, a house of God; that your incomings may be in the name of the Lord; that your outgoings may be in the name of the Lord; that all your salutations may be in the name of the Lord, with uplifted hands unto the Most High.

"Therefore, cease from all your light speeches, from all laughter, from all your lustful desires, from all your pride and light-mindedness, and from all your wicked doings. . . . See that ye love one another; cease to be covetous; learn to impart one to another as the gospel requires. Cease to be idle; cease to be unclean; cease to find fault one with another; cease to sleep longer than is needful; retire to thy bed early, that ye may not be weary; arise early, that your bodies and your minds may be invigorated. And above all things, clothe yourselves with the bond of charity, as with a mantle, which is the bond of perfectness and peace. Pray always, that ye may not faint" (D&C 88:119–21, 123–26).

THIS IS SERIOUS BUSINESS

All we who sojourn through the Lord's wilderness must recognize the eternal significance and seriousness of temple ordinances. This may be difficult for some of us, however, for we have not been very well prepared. This troubled President George Q. Cannon, who declared, "I believe that our endowments are too easily obtained. Men and women go to the temples who do not understand the value of the precious blessings that are bestowed upon them. . . . These blessings become so common that many people do not value them or know how to use them.

"When the Prophet Joseph first communicated that the Lord had revealed to him the keys of the endowment, I can remember the great desire there was on every hand to understand something about them. When the Prophet would speak about his desire to complete the temple in order that he might impart unto his fellow servants that which God had delivered to him, a thrill went through the congregation and a great desire for this filled their hearts. . . .

"Then, when he did communicate the endowments to a few persons before the temple was completed, the whole people were moved with desire to complete the temple in order that they might receive these great blessings therein. They were valued beyond price. A man that could go in and get his endowments was looked upon as though he had received some extraordinary blessing—something akin to that which the angels received—and it was estimated and valued in that way.

"[But] how is it now? There is a complete indifference, it may be said, in relation to it. Young people go there . . . with no particular desire only to get married, without realizing the character of the obligations that they take upon themselves or the covenants that they make and the promises involved in the taking of these covenants. The result is, hundreds among us go to the house of the Lord and receive these blessings and come away without having any particular impression made upon them.

"I think that this is deplorable. When men have gifts and blessings bestowed upon them and they do not value them, they become a cause of condemnation rather than blessing" (*Gospel Truth,* p. 179).

That we not be so condemned, it is imperative that we understand that our endowment is literally a gift of power from God to us, for therein He gives to each worthy individual, male as well as female, the eternal ordinances of His holy priesthood. Once these are obtained, then through strict obedience and faithful temple attendance, each Saint can obtain knowledge and power sufficient "to overcome all things" (*Discourses of the Prophet Joseph Smith,* p. 113; D&C 38:32; 95:8; 128:11; 124:95, 97). Brigham Young adds, "Go on and build the temples of the Lord, that you may receive the endowments in store for you, and possess the keys of the eternal Priesthood, that you may receive every word, sign, and token, and be made acquainted with the laws of angels, and of the kingdom of our Father and our God, and know how to pass from one degree to another, and enter fully into the joy of your Lord" (*Discourses of Brigham Young,* pp. 395–96).

An understanding of these things makes regular and frequent temple attendance a highly desirable experience for all modern wilderness travelers.

Part Four

THE BLESSINGS OF ZION

Chapter Twenty-Two

"OH! I BESEECH YOU!"

On Friday morning, May 12, 1844, the Prophet Joseph stood on the stand in front of the unfinished Nauvoo Temple, preaching one of his last sermons in mortality. As he spoke of some of the eternal blessings that come to the Saints through the priesthood, he suddenly pleaded with the congregation, "Oh! I beseech you to go forward, go forward and make your calling and your election sure" (*Words*, p. 368; *Teachings*, p. 366). What we seekers after Christ must ask ourselves today is, first, What did the Prophet mean by this emphatic admonition? What calling and what election was Joseph Smith pleading that the Saints make sure? And second, What are we to do about it today?

CALLING AND ELECTION

Inextricably linked by both the Lord and His mortal prophets, the *calling* and *election* spoken of by Joseph actually began with a person's exceeding faith and good works in the premortal world (Alma 13:3–10), wherein he or she became "noble and great" (Abraham 3:22–28). It is also interwoven with the covenant God made with Abraham and his posterity (Abraham 2:6–11; D&C 132:29–50), including Isaac (Genesis 24:60; 26:1–4, 24) and Jacob (Genesis 28; 35:9–13; 48:3–4).

This great covenant was made when the Lord appeared to Abraham in Haran, in response to his deep-set faith, saying, "My name is Jehovah, and I know the end from the beginning; therefore my hand shall be over thee. And I will make of thee a great nation, and I will bless thee above measure, and make thy name great among all nations, and thou shalt be a blessing unto thy seed after thee, that in their hands they shall bear this ministry and Priesthood unto all nations; and I will bless them through thy name; for as many as receive this Gospel shall be called after thy name, and shall be accounted thy seed, and shall rise up and bless thee, as their father; and I will bless them that bless thee, and curse them that curse thee; and in thee (that is, in thy Priesthood) and in thy seed (that is, thy Priesthood), for I give unto thee a promise that this right shall continue in thee, and in thy seed after thee (that is to say, the literal seed, or the seed of the body) shall all the families of the earth be blessed, even with the blessings of the Gospel, which are the blessings of salvation, even of life eternal" (Abraham 2:8–11).

Those among God's spirit children who, like Abraham, achieved such exceeding righteousness as to be classified as "noble and great" received the premortal promise or foreordination to come to earth through the lineage of Abraham, thereby receiving the right to the same priesthood covenants and blessings as the Lord had pronounced upon him—they were called and elected by God to receive those promises. The *calling* and *election* referred to, therefore, is reserved for members of the house of Israel, which membership our patriarchal blessings confirm upon us either through birthright or adoption.

Referring specifically to the *calling,* such people as have been described above, after being born into mortality and suffering a spiritual death through submitting to the will of Satan, are then reborn of both the water and the Spirit and receive a complete remission of sins. They thus undergo the mighty change of heart because of their covenant to thereafter keep God's commandments (Mosiah 5:7), and so they are "*called* unto the fellowship of his Son Jesus Christ our Lord" (1 Corinthians 1:9; italics mine; see also verses 26–27; Hebrews 3:1). The prophet Alma adds that these people are "*called and prepared from the foundation of the world* according to the foreknowledge of God, on account of their exceeding faith and good works; in the first place being left to choose good or evil; therefore they having chosen good, and exercising exceedingly great faith, are *called with a holy calling,* yea, with that holy calling which was prepared with, and according to, a preparatory redemption for such. And thus they have been *called to this holy calling on account of their faith . . . this holy calling being prepared from the foundation of the world for such as would not harden their hearts, being in and through the atonement of the Only Begotten Son*" (Alma 13:3–5; italics mine).

But what holy calling have we been called to? As was explained in chapter eight of this volume, we have been called (foreordained) to become children in the family of Jesus Christ. After we have fully repented and have been found worthy, and after we have demonstrated an intractable commitment to Jesus Christ, we are called by God to fellowship with Christ, an "adoption of children by Jesus Christ to himself" (Ephesians 1:3–5), thus becoming Christ's sons or daughters—members of His high and holy family. Remember the words of King Benjamin: "Because of the covenant which ye have made ye shall be *called* the children of Christ, his sons, and his daughters; for behold, this day he hath spiritually begotten you; for ye say that your hearts are changed through faith on his name; therefore, ye are born of him and have become his sons and his daughters" (Mosiah 5:7; italics mine).

This is the *calling.*

The *election* is part and parcel of the same doctrine and process. To Joseph Smith the Lord revealed the sublime words of a millennial song in which He referred to the election, or election of grace. The song begins:

> *The Lord hath brought again Zion;*
> *The Lord hath redeemed his people, Israel,*
> *According to the election of grace,*
> *Which was brought to pass by the faith*
> *And covenant of their fathers.*
> (D&C 84:99)

Those who through foreordination are made participants in this faith and covenant of our fathers, which began at least in this context with Abraham, become through personal righteousness the recipients of this "election of grace" as provided through Christ's atonement. To Joseph Smith the Lord said, "Whoso is faithful unto the obtaining these two priesthoods of which I have spoken, and the magnifying their calling, are sanctified by the Spirit unto the renewing of their bodies. They become the sons of Moses and of Aaron [holders of both the Aaronic and Melchizedek priesthoods] and *the seed of Abraham,* and the church and kingdom, *and the elect* of God" (D&C 84:33–34; italics mine).

The *election* or *election of grace* has its first phase, as did the *calling,* with the privilege of being elected or chosen by God to enter into mortality through the lineage of Abraham—becoming his seed—and of obtaining all the blessings of the priesthood that he was promised. Elder Bruce R. McConkie writes, "This election of grace is a very fundamental, logical, and important part of God's dealings with men through the ages. To bring to pass the salvation of the greatest possible number of his spirit children, the Lord, in general, sends the most righteous and worthy spirits to earth through the lineage of Abraham and Jacob. This course is a manifestation of his grace or in other words his love, mercy, and condescension toward his children.

"This election to a chosen lineage is based on preexistent worthiness and is thus made 'according to the foreknowledge of God' (1 Peter 1:2). Those so grouped together during their mortal probation have more abundant opportunities to make and keep the covenants of salvation, a right they earned by pre-existent devotion to the cause of righteousness. As part of this election, Abraham and others of the noble and great spirits were chosen before they were born for the particular missions assigned them in this life (Abraham 3:22–24; Rom. 9:1)" (*Mormon Doctrine,* p. 216).

Continuing this explanation, the Prophet Joseph, after

reading the 9th chapter of Romans, said, "The election . . . here spoken of . . . ha[s] reference to the seed of Abraham, according to the promise God made to Abraham, saying, 'In thee, and in thy seed, all the families of the earth shall be blessed.' To them belonged the adoption [into the family of Christ] and the covenants [pertaining to priesthood ordinances and lineage as promised to Abraham], &c. . . . The election of the promised seed still continues, and in the last day, they shall have the Priesthood restored unto them, and they shall be the 'saviors on Mount Zion,' the ministers of our God. . . . The whole of the chapter [Romans 9] ha[s] reference to the Priesthood and the House of Israel" (*Teachings*, p. 189).

As did the *calling,* the second phase, being *elected*—remember, the first phase took place in the premortal world—takes place here in mortality, and it also begins with baptism and confirmation in the Lord's true Church (D&C 53:1). Thereafter the election process moves forward as we grow in the gospel—receiving "grace for grace" (D&C 93:20)—until, as with our *calling,* we are born of the Spirit, thereby being granted a complete remission of sins and undergoing the mighty change of heart because of our covenant to hereafter keep God's commandments. Thus we become "the seed of Abraham, and the church and kingdom, and the *elect* of God" (D&C 84:33–34; italics mine).

According to Elder McConkie, "The elect of God comprise a very select group, an inner circle of faithful members of The Church of Jesus Christ of Latter-day Saints. They are the portion of church members who are striving with all their hearts to keep the fulness of the gospel law in this life, so they can become inheritors of the fulness of gospel rewards in the life to come. . . . To gain this elect status, they must be endowed in the temple of the Lord (D&C 95:8), enter into that 'order of the priesthood' named 'the new and everlasting covenant of marriage' (D&C 131:1–4), and overcome by faith until, as the sons of God, they merit membership in the Church of the Firstborn (D&C 76:50–70, 94–96). The elect of God are the chosen of God; and he has said: 'There are many who have been ordained among you, whom I have called but few of them are chosen.' (D&C 95:5; D&C 121:34–40)" (*Mormon Doctrine*, pp. 217–18).

This is the *election*.

"MADE SURE"

With an understanding, now, of why the prophets linked *calling* and *election* together as one phrase and doctrine, it remains for those who seek the face of the Lord to make those promised covenants and blessings a sure or divinely guaranteed thing, never-ending or eternally in force. As Peter declared, "*Give diligence to make your calling and election sure:* for if ye do these things, *ye shall never fall:* For so an entrance shall be ministered unto you abundantly into the everlasting kingdom of our Lord and Saviour Jesus Christ" (2 Peter 1:10–11; italics mine).

Elder McConkie goes on to explain, "All blessings promised in connection with the callings of God are conditional; they are offered to men provided they obey the laws upon which their receipt is predicated (D&C 130:20–21). 'For all who will have a blessing at my hands,' the Lord says, 'shall abide the law which was appointed for that blessing, and the conditions thereof, as were instituted from before the foundation of the world' (D&C 132:5).

"It follows, then, that when the law has been lived to the full, the promised blessing is guaranteed. 'I, the Lord, am bound when ye do what I say; but when ye do not what I say, ye have no promise' (D&C 82:10). Accordingly, when a man lives the law that qualifies him for eternal life, the Lord is bound by his own law to confer that greatest of all gifts upon him. *And if by a long course of trial and obedience, while yet in this life, a man proves to the Lord that he has and will abide in the truth,* the Lord accepts the exhibited devotion and issues his decree that the promised blessings shall be received. The calling [and election], which up to that time [have been] provisional, [are] then made sure. The receipt of the promised blessings are no longer conditional; they are guaranteed. Announcement is made that every gospel blessing shall be inherited.

"To have one's calling and election made sure is to be sealed up unto eternal life; it is to have the unconditional guarantee of exaltation in the highest heaven of the celestial world; it is to receive the assurance of godhood; it is, in effect, to have the day of judgment advanced, so that an inheritance of all the glory and honor of the Father's kingdom is assured prior to the day when the faithful actually enter into the divine presence to sit with Christ in his throne, even as he is 'set down' with his 'Father in his throne' (Revelation 3:21)" (*Doctrinal New Testament Commentary,* 3:329–31; italics mine).

It is no wonder that "the Prophet Joseph Smith used to repeatedly urge the brethren to make their calling and election sure" (Marion G. Romney, Conference Report, October 1960, pp. 73–78).

A CAUTION ABOUT INTEGRITY

Before we can actually progress in this highly spiritual area, however, we must thoroughly understand the issue of integrity. Brigham Young taught, "There is one principle that I wish the people would understand and lay to heart. Just as fast as you will prove before your God that you are worthy to receive the mysteries, if you please to call them so, of the kingdom of heaven—that you are full of confidence in God—that you will never betray a thing that God tells you—that you will never reveal to your neighbor that which ought not to be revealed, as quick as you prepare to be entrusted with the things of God, there is an eternity of them to bestow upon you. Instead of pleading with the Lord to bestow more upon you, plead with yourselves to have confidence in yourselves, to have integrity in yourselves, and know when to speak and what to speak, what to reveal, and how to carry yourselves and walk before the Lord. And just as fast as you prove to Him that you will preserve everything secret that ought to be—that you will deal out to your neighbors all which you ought, and no more, and learn how to dispense your knowledge to your families, friends, neighbors, and brethren, the Lord will bestow upon you, and give to you, and bestow upon you, until finally he will say to you, 'You shall never fall; your salvation is sealed unto you; you are sealed up unto eternal life and salvation, through your integrity'" (*Journal of Discourses*, 4:371–72).

TWO WAYS

An appropriate question at this point might be, "How does one know when this has happened?" Scriptural evidence seems to indicate that one's calling and election can be made sure in either of two ways, though it seems likely that both are interrelated. They are (1) receiving the voice of God in a personal revelation wherein the promise of exaltation is given; and (2) receiving by ordinance the fulness of the priesthood through the more sure word of prophecy by "him who is anointed" (D&C 132:7).

THE VOICE OF GOD

Throughout history, even when the blessings of receiving the fullness of the priesthood have not been readily available, righteous men and women who have progressed spiritually to the fullest extent possible have obtained the voice of God declaring their callings and elections to be sure. Thus Moses taught, "[The approval of God] was delivered unto men by *the calling of his own voice,* according to his own will, unto as many as believed on his name" (JST Genesis 14:29). In our day the Lord has declared, "Wo unto all those who come not unto this priesthood which ye have received, which I now confirm upon you who are present this day, by *mine own voice out of the heavens*" (D&C 84:42; italics mine).

Joseph the Prophet declared, "There are three grand secrets . . . which no man can dig out, unless by the light of revelation. . . . I am going to take up this subject by virtue of the knowledge of God in me, which I have received from heaven" (*Teachings,* p. 304). "These are the three secrets: '1st key: Knowledge is the power of salvation. 2nd key: Make your calling and election sure. 3rd key: It is one thing to be on the mount and hear the excellent voice [bearing witness of the Son], and another to hear the voice [of God] declare to you, You have a part and lot in that kingdom'" (*Teachings,* p. 306).

Thus did Peter teach: "[Christ] received from God the

Father honour and glory, when there came such a voice to him from the excellent glory, This is my beloved Son, in whom I am well pleased. And *this voice which came from heaven we heard,* when we were with him in the holy mount. *[But] We have also a more sure word of prophecy;* whereunto ye do well that ye take heed, as unto a light that shineth in a dark place, until the day dawn, and the day star arise in your hearts" (2 Peter 1:17–19; italics mine).

While we will examine the nature of this more sure word of prophecy a little later, we see that both Peter and the Prophet Joseph are telling us that receiving the voice of God, by revelation, must be a specific promise of our exaltation; otherwise, it will not do. Some individuals who obtained this voice declaring their exaltation are Adam (Moses 6:51, 66–67), Abraham (Abraham 1:16–19), Isaac (Genesis 26:2–4, 24–25), Jacob (Genesis 32:24–30), Moses (Moses 1:1–5), the brother of Jared (Ether 3:13), Nephi (1 Nephi 11:6–7, 11), his brother Jacob (2 Nephi 2:2–4, 33:6), Moroni (Ether 12:37–39), and our Savior, the Lord Jesus Christ (D&C 93:11–22; *Teachings,* p. 308), a company of venerable persons whose righteousness we continue to memorialize centuries after they made their journey through mortality.

As an additional example of one who obtained his promise of exaltation in this manner, consider the experience of Nephi the son of Helaman. "As he was thus pondering—being much cast down because of the wickedness of the people of the Nephites, their secret works of darkness, and their murderings, and their plunderings, and all manner of iniquities—and it came to pass as he was thus pondering in his heart, behold, a voice came unto him saying: Blessed art thou, Nephi, for those things which thou hast done; for I have beheld how thou hast with unwearyingness declared the word, which I have given unto thee, unto this people. And thou hast not feared them, and hast not sought thine own life, but hast sought my will, and to keep my commandments. And now, because thou hast done this with such unwearyingness, *behold, I will bless thee forever; and I will make thee mighty in word and in deed, in faith and in works; yea, even that all things shall be done unto thee according to thy word, for thou shalt not ask that which is contrary to my will. Behold, thou art Nephi, and I am God. Behold, I declare it unto thee in the presence of mine angels*" (Helaman 10:3–6; italics mine).

In our day, the Prophet Joseph Smith is the classic example of one who was sealed up unto eternal life by obtaining the voice of God out of the heavens. Of him the scripture states, "I am the Lord thy God, and will be with thee even unto the end of the world, and through all eternity; for verily *I seal upon you your exaltation,* and prepare a throne for you in the kingdom of my Father, with Abraham your father" (D&C 132:49; italics mine). This revelation was given in 1832, a full decade before Nauvoo Temple ordinances began being administered to Joseph and others.

Another in this dispensation whose experience is worthy of note is Heber C. Kimball. In his published journal, under date of Far West, April 6, 1839, he recorded, "I returned to Far West April 5th, and remained a few days. My family having been gone about two months (during which time I heard nothing from them), our brethren being in prison, and death and destruction following us wherever we went, I felt very sorrowful and lonely. While in this condition, the following words came to my mind, and the Spirit said unto me, 'Write.' I obeyed by taking a piece of paper and writing on my knee, as follows: 'Verily, I say unto my servant Heber, thou art my son in whom I am well pleased; for thou art careful to hearken to my words, and not transgress my law nor rebel against my servant Joseph Smith; for thou hast a respect to the words of mine anointed, even from the least to the greatest of them; *therefore, thy name is written in heaven, no more to be blotted out forever,* because of these things; and this spirit and blessing shall rest down upon thy posterity for ever and ever" (*President Heber C. Kimball's Journal,* p. 70; italics mine).

As a final example, Mary Elizabeth Rollins Lightner related that in an 1831 meeting she attended, "Joseph looked around very solemnly. It was the first time some of them had ever seen him. Said he, 'There are enough here to hold a little meeting.' They got a board and put it across two chairs to make seats. Martin Harris sat on a little box at Joseph's feet. They sang and prayed. Joseph got up and began to speak to us. As he began to speak very solemnly and very earnestly, all at once his countenance changed and he stood mute. Those who looked at him that day said there was a search light within him, over every part of his body. I never saw anything like it on the earth. I could not take my eyes off him; he got so white that anyone who saw him would have thought he was transparent. I remember I thought I could almost see the cheek bones through the flesh. I have been through many changes since but that is photographed on my brain. I shall remember it and see in my mind's eye as long as I remain upon the earth.

"He stood some moments. He looked over the congregation as if to pierce every heart. He said, 'Do you know who has been in your midst?' One of the Smiths said an angel of the Lord. Martin Harris said, 'It was our Lord and Savior,

Jesus Christ.' Joseph put his hand down on Martin and said: 'God revealed that to you. Brethren and sisters, the Spirit of God has been here. The Savior has been in your midst this night and I want you to remember it. There is a veil over your eyes for you could not endure to look upon Him. You must be fed with milk, not with strong meat. I want you to remember this as if it were the last thing that escaped my lips. He has given all of you to me and has *sealed you up to everlasting life that where he is, you may be also.* And if you are tempted of Satan say, 'Get behind me, Satan.'

"These words are figured upon my brain and I never took my eye off his countenance. Then he knelt down and prayed. I have never heard anything like it before or since. I felt that he was talking to the Lord and that power rested down upon the congregation. Every soul felt it. The spirit rested upon us in every fiber of our bodies" (Mary Elizabeth Lightner, "Address at Brigham Young University," April 14, 1905, typescript, BYU, p. 1; italics mine).

Brigham Young felt so strongly about members of the Church obtaining this and similar experiences that he declared, "Any person knowing and understanding the Scriptures as they are, and understanding the mind and will of God can understand at once that when he is shut out from the presence of the Lord, *when he does not hear his voice,* sees not his face, receives not the ministering of his angels or ministering spirits, and has no messenger from the heavens to visit him, he must surely be in hell" (*Journal of Discourses,* 2:137; italics mine).

Thus we see that no matter the conditions of the world in which we may find ourselves, we should and will be allowed to progress spiritually as far as we wish to go.

THE HOLY SPIRIT OF PROMISE

In the above examples, the voice of God was made manifest to those involved through the power of the Holy Ghost acting in His capacity as the Holy Spirit of Promise. As Elder McConkie explains, "This name-title is used in connection with the sealing and ratifying power of the Holy Ghost, that is, the power given him to ratify and approve the righteous acts of men so that those acts will be binding on earth and in heaven. 'All covenants, contracts, bonds, obligations, oaths, vows, performances, connections, associations, or expectations,' must be sealed by the Holy Spirit of Promise, if they are to have 'efficacy, virtue, or force in and after the resurrection from the dead; for all contracts that are not made unto this end have an end when men are dead.' (D&C 132:7)" (*Mormon Doctrine,* p. 361).

For such to occur, of course, requires great worthiness. That is why wilderness travelers have been required to repent of all their sins and go out of Babylon, always maintaining a spirit of humility and repentance as they strive to heed, trust, do, and accomplish all that has been commanded by way of the additional light and knowledge they receive from the Lord. As the Savior said to Joseph Smith, these are they "who overcome by faith, and are sealed by the Holy Spirit of promise, which the Father sheds forth upon *all those who are just and true*" (D&C 76:53; italics mine).

THE FULLNESS OF THE PRIESTHOOD

Sister Mary Lightner's 1831 experience quoted above illustrates another aspect of receiving this heavenly voice and promise: at first it may not be heard personally, but it may be spoken by God through the mouth of one of his worthy, duly ordained mortal servants. As Joseph Smith put it, "Abraham's was a more exalted power or priesthood (for he could talk and walk with God), and yet consider how great this man (Melchizedek) was when even this patriarch Abraham gave a tenth part of all his spoils and then received a blessing under the hands of Melchizedek, even the last law or a fulness of the law or priesthood, which constituted Abraham a king and a priest after the order of Melchizedek or an endless life" (*Words,* p. 246). "Melchizedek had power of an endless life, of which [the type] was our Lord Jesus Christ, which Abraham also obtained by the offering of his son Isaac. . . . [This was] not the power of a Prophet nor apostle nor patriarch only, but of King and Priest to God, to open the windows of heaven and pour out the peace and law of endless life to man. . . . No man can attain to this Joint Heirship with Jesus Christ without being administered to by one having the same power and authority of Melchizedek" (*Words,* p. 245).

"Now for the secret and grand key," Joseph declared. "Though they might hear the voice of God and know that Jesus was the Son of God, this would be no evidence that their election and calling was made sure, that they had part with Christ, and were joint heirs with him. They then would want that more sure word of prophecy, that they were sealed in the heavens and had the promise of eternal life in the kingdom of God. Then, having this promise sealed unto them, it was an anchor to the soul, sure and steadfast" (*Teachings,* p. 298).

Thus the Lord declared, "All covenants, contracts, bonds, obligations, oaths, vows, performances, connections, associations, or expectations, that are not made and entered into and sealed by the Holy Spirit of promise, of him who is anointed, both as well for time and for all eternity, and that too most holy, by revelation and commandment through the medium of mine anointed, whom I have appointed on the earth to hold this power (and I have appointed unto my servant Joseph to hold this power in the last days, and there is never but one on the earth at a time on whom this power and the keys of this priesthood are conferred), are of no efficacy, virtue, or force in and after the resurrection from the dead; for all contracts that are not made unto this end have an end when men are dead" (D&C 132:7).

From the foregoing it is apparent that he whom the Lord calls His "anointed"—the president of the Church—is alone responsible for the bestowal of all priesthood blessings throughout the Church. He alone "possesses and is authorized to exercise all priesthood keys," we learn in temple recommend interviews. So it is with what the Lord calls "the fulness of the priesthood." In explaining to the Prophet Joseph the importance of building the Nauvoo Temple, the Lord declared, "There is not a place found on earth that he may come to and restore again that which was lost unto you, or which he hath taken away, even *the fulness of the priesthood*" (D&C 124:28; italics mine). Peter calls this ordinance, which was to be restored to the earth through priesthood authority in the Nauvoo Temple, "the more sure word of prophecy" (2 Peter 1:19); Elder McConkie calls it "the fulness of the sealing power" (*Mormon Doctrine,* p. 217); and the Prophet Joseph referred to it as both "the patriarchal power" and "the keys of knowledge and power" (*Teachings,* p. 325). It is all the same—the sealing up of individuals to eternal life through the authorized priesthood ministrations of the Lord's mortal mouthpiece or those he may have appointed. The president of the Church, therefore, is responsible for its administration. Thus the Lord says, "The keys of the kingdom . . . belong always unto the Presidency of the High Priesthood" (D&C 81:2), and only one man on earth at a time, the president of the Church, can exercise them in their fullness (see D&C 132:7).

THE SIGNIFICANCE OF THE TEMPLE

Since the fullness of the priesthood could not be restored until a proper temple had been erected (D&C 124:28), the temple must also be significant in its administration. During April conference in 1844, Joseph declared: "The declaration this morning is, that as soon as the Temple and baptismal font are prepared, we calculate to give the Elders of Israel their washings and anointings, *and attend to those last and more impressive ordinances, without which we cannot obtain celestial thrones*. But there must be a holy place prepared for that purpose. There was a proclamation made during the time that the foundation of the Temple was laid to that effect, and there are provisions made until the work is completed, so that men may receive their endowments *and be made kings and priests unto the Most High God* . . . There must, however, be a place built expressly for that purpose, and for men to be baptized for their dead" (*Teachings*, pp. 362–63; italics mine).

Elder McConkie adds, "The Blessed Jesus, who is the Christ, is our prototype, pattern, and model. As he gained glory and exaltation, so shall we if we do as he did. In all things—in word, in deed, in belief, in doctrine, in faith, in ordinances, in personal righteousness—in all things he says, 'Follow thou me.' (2 Ne. 31:10). As he obtained the fullness of the Melchizedek Priesthood in order to gain exaltation, so must we" (*A New Witness for the Articles of Faith,* p. 315). The Prophet Joseph continues, "If a man gets a fullness of the priesthood of God he has to get it in the same way that Jesus Christ obtained it, and that was by keeping all the commandments and *obeying all the ordinances of the house of the Lord.* . . . All men who become heirs of God and joint-heirs with Jesus Christ will have to receive the fulness of the ordinances of his kingdom; and those who will not receive all the ordinances will come short of the fulness of that glory, if they do not lose the whole" (*Teachings,* pp. 308–9; italics mine).

"In setting forth as much as can, with propriety, be spoken outside of the temple," Elder McConkie concludes, "the Lord says that 'the fulness of the priesthood' is received only in the temple itself. This fulness is received through washings, anointings, solemn assemblies, oracles in holy places, conversations, ordinances, endowments, and sealings (D&C 124:40). It is in the temple that we enter into the patriarchal order, the order of priesthood that bears the name 'the new and everlasting covenant of marriage'" (*A New Witness for the Articles of Faith,* p. 315).

However, as Elder McConkie reminds us, "It should be clearly understood that these high blessings are not part of celestial marriage. 'Blessings pronounced upon couples in connection with celestial marriage are conditioned upon the subsequent faithfulness of the participating parties.' (*Doctrines of Salvation,* 2:46–47)" (*Mormon Doctrine,* p. 110).

THE MORE SURE WORD OF PROPHECY

When the president of the Church is instructed "by revelation and commandment" to exercise these keys of sealing power in their fulness in behalf of worthy Church members, his blessing or pronouncement of the fullness of the priesthood is called in scripture "the more sure word of prophecy"; that is, it is a prophetic declaration as if from the mouth of God that will not fail, for, as the Lord says, "Whether by mine own voice or by the voice of my servants, it is the same" (D&C 1:38). The Lord declares, "The more sure word of prophecy means a man's *knowing* that he is sealed up unto eternal life, by revelation and the spirit of prophecy through the power of the Holy Priesthood" (D&C 131:5; italics mine). Thus Joseph said, "I anointed [Judge James Adams] to the patriarchal power—to receive the keys of knowledge and power, by revelation to himself" (*Teachings*, p. 326).

Speaking of the power and authority of the Prophet Joseph to do this work, President George Q. Cannon stated that "when he spoke by the power of God, it was the word of God to this people. When he sealed a man up to eternal life, he bestowed upon him the blessings pertaining to eternity, and to the Godhead, or when he delegated others to do it in his stead, God in the eternal world recorded the act; the blessings that were sealed upon that man or that woman, they were sealed to be binding in this life, and in that life which is to come; they became part of the records of eternity, and would be fulfilled to the very letter upon the heads of those upon whom they were pronounced. . . . There is no doubt about it" (*Journal of Discourses*, 24:274).

Though the Holy Ghost acting as the Holy Spirit of Promise first ratifies all priesthood ordinances conditionally, in this one instance—receiving the fullness of the priesthood by the more sure word of prophecy—the ratification and seal are final. Elder McConkie explains, "When the Holy Spirit of Promise places his ratifying seal upon . . . someone whose calling and election is thereby made sure—because there are no more conditions to be met by the obedient person—this act of being sealed up unto eternal life is of such transcendent import that of itself it is called being sealed by the Holy Spirit of Promise, which means that in this crowning sense, being so sealed is the same as having one's calling and election made sure. Thus, to be sealed by the Holy Spirit of Promise is to be sealed up unto eternal life; and to be sealed up unto eternal life is to be sealed by the Holy Spirit of Promise" (*Doctrinal New Testament Commentary,* 3:334–36).

Thus the Lord declares, "If a man marry a wife by my word, which is my law, and by the new and everlasting covenant, and it is sealed unto them by the Holy Spirit of promise, *by him who is anointed, unto whom I have appointed this power and the keys of this priesthood;* and it shall be said unto them—Ye shall come forth in the first resurrection; and if it be after the first resurrection, in the next resurrection; and shall inherit thrones, kingdoms, principalities, and powers, dominions, all heights and depths—then shall it be written in the Lamb's Book of Life, that he shall commit no murder whereby to shed innocent blood, and if ye abide in my covenant, and commit no murder whereby to shed innocent blood, it shall be done unto them in all things whatsoever my servant hath put upon them, in time, and through all eternity; and shall be of full force when they are out of the world; and they shall pass by the angels, and the gods, which are set there, to their exaltation and glory in all things, as hath been sealed upon their heads, which glory shall be a fulness and a continuation of the seeds forever and ever" (D&C 132:19; italics mine).

THE KEYS OF ELIJAH

These sealing powers we have been speaking of are the keys restored by Elijah to Joseph Smith and Oliver Cowdery in the Kirtland Temple (D&C 110:13–16). Joseph taught, "The spirit, power, and calling of Elijah is, that ye have power to hold the key of the revelations, ordinances, oracles, powers and endowments of *the fulness of the Melchizedek Priesthood* and of the kingdom of God on the earth; and to receive, obtain, and *perform all the ordinances* belonging to the kingdom of God" (*Teachings*, p. 337; italics mine).

Therefore, "the power of Elijah is sufficient to make our callings and elections sure" (*Words*, p. 330). "To be sealed by the Holy Spirit of Promise is to be sealed by the spirit and power of Elijah (*Words*, p. 335). "God . . . shall send Elijah . . . to reveal the covenants to seal the hearts of the fathers to the children and the children to the fathers—anointing and sealing—*called, elected and made sure*—without father &c, [which is] a priesthood which holds [power] by right from the eternal Gods—and not descent from father and mother" (*Words*, p. 244; italics mine).

THE SPIRIT OF ELIJAH

In addition to the above, in the chapter of this book dealing with the ministering of angels, the Prophet Joseph was quoted concerning Elias, Elijah, and Messiah. The full quotation is, "The spirit of Elias is first, Elijah second, and Messiah last. Elias is a forerunner to prepare the way, and the spirit and power of Elijah is to come after, holding the keys of power, building the Temple to the capstone, placing the seals of the Melchizedek Priesthood upon the house of Israel, and making all things ready; then Messiah comes to His Temple, which is last of all. . . . Messiah is above the spirit and power of Elijah, for He made the world, and was the spiritual rock unto Moses in the wilderness. Elijah was to come and prepare the way and build up the kingdom before the coming of the great day of the Lord, although the spirit of Elias might begin it" (*Teachings*, p. 340).

It should now be more evident why Joseph declared the visitation of these three personages to be broader than their appearance in the Kirtland Temple. All angelic ministrants act in the role of Elias as they labor with those who have been born again, serving as forerunners in preparing their charges for the higher sealing blessings of Elijah. And when these people are sealed up unto eternal life by having their calling and election made sure through the more sure word of prophecy, then they have received the ministration and sealing powers of Elijah.

Long after the Kirtland Temple appearances of Elias and Elijah, Elder Orson Pratt taught, "We need never look for the coming of the Son of God—for the day when he shall suddenly come to his temple and sit like a refiner of silver, and with fuller's soap to purify and purge the sons of Levi, &c., until Elijah the Prophet is sent. . . . [When] he is sent . . . he will be sent with power and authority, like other angels sent from heaven, to bestow the same authority that is upon himself on some individuals upon the earth, that they may go forth holding that same authority that Elijah himself held, having the same keys, receiving the same instructions, in regard to the Latter-day dispensation,—*a mission, in other words, sent from heaven by Elijah as a ministering angel to seek out the chosen vessels, and ordain them,* and send them to administer to the inhabitants of the earth" (*Journal of Discourses,* 7:78; italics mine).

PRIESTS AND KINGS

One of the honors given to those who have received the fullness of the priesthood is that they are made priests and kings to God. It was not enough that Joseph be a king and a priest to the Most High, but he insisted that his people be a society of priests 'as in Paul's day, as in Enoch's day,' through the full ordinances of the temple (*Words,* pp. 54–55). As he put it, "Those holding the fulness of the Melchizedek Priesthood are kings and priests of the Most High God, holding the keys of power and blessing." And, "What was the power of Melchizedek? 'Twas not the Priesthood of Aaron which administers in outward ordinances, and the offering of sacrifices. Those holding the fulness of the Melchizedek Priesthood are kings and priests of the Most High God, holding the keys of power and blessings" (*Teachings,* p. 322).

Elder McConkie elaborates: "Holders of the Melchizedek Priesthood have power to press forward in righteousness, living by every word that proceedeth forth from the mouth of God, magnifying their callings, going from grace to grace, until through *the fulness of* the ordinances of the temple they receive the fulness of the priesthood and are ordained kings and priests. Those so attaining shall have exaltation and be kings, priests, rulers, and lords in their respective spheres in the eternal kingdoms of the great King who is God our Father (Rev. 1:6; 5:10)" (*Mormon Doctrine,* p. 425; italics mine).

It was ever Joseph's intention that these priests and kings act in their office in communing with God. Speaking to the Twelve on February 23, 1844, Joseph Smith said, "I want every man that goes [west to explore for a new home for the Saints] to be a king and a priest. When he gets on the mountains [the Lord's temple] he may want to talk with his God" (*History of the Church,* 6:244).

THE ORDER OF THE SON OF GOD

Those who have received the fullness of the priesthood are also brought into the order of the Son of God. President Ezra Taft Benson says, "To enter into the order of the Son of God is the equivalent today of entering into the fulness of the Melchizedek Priesthood, which is only received in the house of the Lord" ("What I Hope You Will Teach Your Children About the Temple," *Ensign,* August 1985, p. 8).

Alma wrote, "Now, as I said concerning the holy order, or this high priesthood, there were many who were ordained and became high priests of God; and it was on account of their exceeding faith and repentance, and their righteousness before God, they choosing to repent and work righteousness rather than to perish; *therefore they were called after this holy order,* and were sanctified, and their garments were washed white through the blood of the Lamb. Now they, after being sanctified by the Holy Ghost, having their garments made white, being pure and spotless before God, could not look upon sin save it were with abhorrence; and there were many, exceedingly great many, who were made pure and entered into the rest of the Lord their God" (Alma 13:10–12; italics mine).

Among a host of others, Alma was a member of this

order (Alma 4:20), as was Jacob the son of Lehi (2 Nephi 6:2), Melchizedek, and Enoch. Of these latter two prophets Moses wrote, "Melchizedek lifted up his voice and blessed Abram. Now Melchizedek was a man of faith, who wrought righteousness; and when a child he feared God, and stopped the mouths of lions, and quenched the violence of fire. And thus, having been approved of God, he was ordained an high priest after the order of the covenant which God made with Enoch, *it being after the order of the Son of God;* which order came, not by man, nor the will of man; neither by father nor mother; neither by beginning of days nor end of years; but of God; and it was delivered unto men by the calling of his own voice, according to his own will, unto as many as believed on his name" (JST Genesis 14:25–29; italics mine).

President Benson says, "Because Adam and Eve complied with these requirements, God said to them, 'Thou art after the order of him who was without beginning of days or end of years, from all eternity to all eternity' (Moses 6:67). Three years before Adam's death, a great event occurred. He took his son Seth, his grandson Enos, and other high priests who were direct-line descendants, with others of his righteous posterity, into a valley called Adam-ondi-Ahman. There Adam gave to these righteous descendants his last blessing. The Lord then appeared to them. The vast congregation rose up and blessed Adam and called him Michael, the prince and archangel. The Lord himself declared Adam to be a prince forever over his own posterity. Then Adam, in his aged condition, rose up and, being filled with the spirit of prophecy, 'predicted whatsoever should befall his posterity unto the latest generation'" (D&C 107:53–65).

"The Prophet Joseph Smith said that Adam blessed his

posterity because 'he wanted to bring them into the presence of God' (*Teachings*, p. 159). [In this] illuminating passage from section 107 of the Doctrine and Covenants [we are told] how Adam was able to bring himself and his righteous posterity into God's presence: 'The order of this priesthood was confirmed to be handed down from father to son, and rightly belongs to the literal descendants of the chosen seed, to whom the promises were made. This order was instituted in the days of Adam, and came down by lineage [in order] . . . that his posterity should be the *chosen of the Lord*, and that *they should be preserved unto the end of the earth*' (D&C 107:40–42; italics mine).

"How did Adam bring his descendants into the presence of the Lord? By entering into the priesthood order of God [and then bringing them in after him]. Today we would say they went to the house of the Lord and received their blessings.

"The order of priesthood spoken of in the scriptures is sometimes referred to as the patriarchal order because it came down from father to son. But this order is otherwise described in modern revelation as an order of family government where a man and a woman enter into a covenant with God—just as did Adam and Eve—to be sealed for eternity, to have posterity, and to do the will and work of God throughout their mortality. . . .

"Adam followed this order and brought his posterity into the presence of God. He is the great example for us to follow. Enoch followed this pattern and brought the saints of his day into the presence of God. Noah and his son Shem likewise followed the same pattern after the flood.

"Abraham, a righteous servant of God, desiring, as he

said, 'to be a greater follower of righteousness,' sought for these same blessings. Speaking of the order of the priesthood, he said, 'It was conferred upon me from the fathers; it came down from the fathers, from the beginning of time, . . . even the right of the firstborn, or the first man, who is Adam, or first father, through the fathers unto me.' So Abraham declared, 'I sought for mine appointment unto the Priesthood according to the appointment of God unto the fathers' (Abraham 1:2–4)" ("What I Hope You Will Teach Your Children about the Temple," *Ensign* August 1985, pp. 8–9).

As was pointed out in chapters 2 and 3 of this volume, Moses also attempted to bring his people into the same holy order of the Son of God so they might have power to see His face, but they hardened their hearts against such an opportunity, and so the Lord would not allow them into His rest, "which rest is the fulness of his glory" (see D&C 84:23–25). An interesting detail of the Lord's action against the children of Israel was revealed to Joseph Smith, who recorded the Lord's words: "I will take away the priesthood out of their midst; *therefore my holy order, and the ordinances thereof shall not go before them; for my presence shall not go up in their midst*" (JST Exodus 34:1; italics mine).

We know of one significant group yet to appear who will be ordained to this sacred order. Joseph Smith wrote in response to a question, "What are we to understand by sealing the one hundred and forty-four thousand, out of all the tribes of Israel—twelve thousand out of every tribe? We are to understand that those who are sealed are high priests, *ordained unto the holy order of God,* to administer the everlasting gospel; for they are they who are ordained out of every nation, kindred, tongue, and people, by the angels to whom is given power over the nations of the earth, to bring as many as will come to the church of the Firstborn" (D&C 77:11; italics mine).

POWER IN THE PRIESTHOOD

Such righteous individuals as are anointed and sealed unto this holy order are given powers commensurate with the spiritual position they have obtained before the Lord. As Moses proclaimed, "God having sworn unto Enoch and unto his seed with an oath by himself; that every one being ordained after this order and calling should have power, by faith, to break mountains, to divide the seas, to dry up waters, to turn them out of their course; to put at defiance the armies of nations, to divide the earth, to break every band, to stand in the presence of God; to do all things according to his will, according to his command, subdue principalities and powers; and this by the will of the Son of God which was from before the foundation of the world. And men having this faith, coming up unto this order of God, were translated and taken up into heaven.

"And now, Melchizedek was a priest of this order; therefore he obtained peace in Salem, and was called the Prince of peace. And his people wrought righteousness, and obtained heaven, and sought for the city of Enoch which God had before taken, separating it from the earth, having reserved it unto the latter days, or the end of the world" (JST Genesis 14:30–34).

Enoch used this power with great effectiveness. In the writings of Moses as revealed to Joseph Smith we read, "So great was the faith of Enoch that he led the people of God, and their enemies came to battle against them; and he spake the word of the Lord, and the earth trembled, and the mountains fled, even according to his command; and the rivers of water were turned out of their course; and the roar of the lions was heard out of the wilderness; and all nations feared greatly, so powerful was the word of Enoch, and so great was the power of the language which God had given him" (Moses 7:13).

The scriptures contain other accounts of the remarkable powers that accompany the granting of the fullness of this patriarchal order of the priesthood. For instance, we know that the Lord said to Nephi, the son of Helaman, "Thou art Nephi, and I am God. Behold, I declare it unto thee in the presence of mine angels, that ye shall have power over this people, and shall smite the earth with famine, and with pestilence, and destruction, according to the wickedness of this people. Behold, I give unto you power, that whatsoever ye shall seal on earth shall be sealed in heaven; and whatsoever ye shall loose on earth shall be loosed in heaven; and thus shall ye have power among this people. And thus, if ye shall say unto this temple it shall be rent in twain, it shall be done. And if ye shall say unto this mountain, Be thou cast down and become smooth, it shall be done. And behold, if ye shall say that God shall smite this people, it shall come to pass" (Helaman 10:6–10).

A final example of someone blessed with this power is the brother of Jared, whose faith enabled him to pierce the veil and see the finger of the Lord. As Moroni wrote, "There were many whose faith was so exceedingly strong, even before Christ came, who could not be kept from within the veil, but truly saw with their eyes the things which they had beheld with an eye of faith, and they were glad. And behold, we have seen in this record that one of these was the brother of Jared; for so great was his faith in God, that when God put forth his finger he could not hide it from the sight of the brother of Jared, because of his word which he had spoken unto him, which word he had obtained by faith. And after the brother of Jared had beheld the finger of the Lord, because of the promise which the brother of Jared had obtained by faith, the Lord could not withhold anything from his sight; wherefore he showed him all things, for he could no longer be kept without the veil" (Ether 12:19–21).

Thereafter the brother of Jared ordered the mountain Zerin to remove, and it was removed (Ether 12:30). But he was given another power that is even more remarkable, one that was almost the envy of the great Moroni, who wrote in prayer, "Thou hast not made us mighty in writing like unto the brother of Jared, for thou madest him that the things which he wrote were mighty even as thou art, unto the overpowering of man to read them" (Ether 12:24). Wouldn't *that* be a wonderful power!

A JOYOUS PROMISE TO PARENTS WHO RECEIVE THIS BLESSING

Joseph Smith declared, "A measure of this sealing is to confirm upon their head in common with Elijah the doctrine of election or the covenant with Abraham . . . where it says they shall seal the servants of God in their foreheads &c it means to seal the blessing on their heads meaning the everlasting covenant thereby making their calling and election sure . . . which when a father and mother of a family have entered into, their children . . . are secured by the seal wherewith the parents have been sealed [and such children] cannot be lost . . . And this is the oath of God unto our Father Abraham, and this doctrine shall stand forever" (*Words*, pp. 241–42).

And "the doctrine or sealing power of Elijah is . . . that degree of power which holds the sealing power of the Kingdom. . . . Make your calling and election sure. Go from grace to grace until you obtain a promise from God for yourselves that you shall have eternal life. This is eternal life, to know God and his son Jesus Christ—it is to be sealed up unto eternal life and obtain a promise for our posterity. Whatever you shall bind on earth shall be bound in heaven. This is the power of Elijah" (*Words*, pp. 331, 34).

AT ALL HAZARDS

The Prophet also taught, "After a person hath faith in Christ . . . then let him continue to humble himself before God, hungering & thirsting after righteousness & living by every word of God & the Lord will soon say unto him Son thou shalt be exalted. &c When the Lord has thoroughly proved him and finds that the man is determined to serve him *at all hazards*, then the man will find his calling and election made sure" (*Words*, p. 5; italics mine).

Those wilderness wanderers who have given up every worldly thing, and who have waded uncomplainingly through every trial and adversity until they have accomplished this, have become patriarchs over their own families in the full and complete sense of the word. Having the fullness of the priesthood and reigning as kings and priests unto God, they have received all the blessings of the sealing power, or keys, of Elijah, which is also called the Patriarchal

Priesthood. They have fulfilled the declaration of Joseph Smith, who said, "The Bible says 'I will send you Elijah . . . that he turn the hearts of the fathers to the children & the hearts of the children to their fathers. . . . Now the word 'turn' here should be translated bind or seal. But what is the object of this important mission or how is it to be fulfilled? The keys are to be delivered, the Spirit of Elijah is to come, the gospel to be established, the Saints of God gathered, Zion built up, and the Saints to come up as Saviors on Mount Zion. But how are they to become Saviors on Mount Zion? By building their temples, erecting their baptismal fonts, and going forth and receiving all the ordinances, baptisms, confirmations, washings, anointings, ordinations and sealing powers upon [their] heads" (*Words,* p. 318).

FOR SISTERS AS WELL AS BRETHREN

Lest the foregoing imply that such blessings are for men only, consider the following words from Elder James E. Talmage: "In the restored Church of Jesus Christ . . . in accordance with divine requirement . . . it is not given to woman to exercise the authority of the Priesthood independently; nevertheless, in the sacred endowments associated with the ordinances pertaining to the House of the Lord, woman shares with man the blessings of the Priesthood. When the frailties and imperfections of mortality are left behind, in the glorified state of the blessed hereafter, husband and wife will administer in their respective stations, seeing and understanding alike, and co-operating to the full in the government of their family kingdom. Then shall woman be recompensed in rich measure for all the injustice that womanhood has endured in mortality. Then shall woman reign by Divine right, a queen [and priestess] in the resplendent realm of her glorified state, even as exalted man shall stand, priest and king unto the Most High God. Mortal eye cannot see nor mind comprehend the beauty, glory and majesty of a righteous woman made perfect in the celestial kingdom of God" ("The Eternity of Sex," *Young Woman's Journal,* October 1914, pp. 602–3).

PEACE IN THE LORD JESUS CHRIST

A final reward for those who have made their calling and election sure is that from time to time they can be filled with perfect peace, no matter what they are called upon to endure, no matter what is transpiring in the world around them. That is why the Prophet Joseph called this divine promise "an anchor to the soul, sure and steadfast." He then elaborated, "Though the thunders might roll and lightnings flash, and earthquakes bellow, and war gather thick around, yet this hope and knowledge would support the soul in every hour of trial, trouble and tribulation" (*Teachings,* p. 298).

Not only can such people's inner peace become an amazing but comforting beacon and example to those around them in this troubled world, friends and loved ones included, but it will flow eternally "as a river, and [their] righteousness as the waves of the sea" (Isaiah 48:18), not only in this life but in the world to come. Elder McConkie taught, "Those who gain this peace in this life shall die in peace (D&C 45:46), continue in peace in the paradise of God (Alma 40:12), and then rise in the resurrection to inherit eternal peace in the kingdom of God. 'Learn that he who doeth the works of righteousness shall receive his reward, even peace in this world, and eternal life in the world to come' (D&C 59:23)" (*Mormon Doctrine*, p. 562).

It is to these righteous individuals, therefore, that Christ proclaims, "Peace I leave with you, my peace I give unto you: not as the world giveth, give I unto you. Let not your heart be troubled, neither let it be afraid." (John 14:27; see also 16:33).

A REMINDER

Finally, it is vital that we remember that this is a process that may consume our entire mortal lives. As Elder B. H. Roberts puts it, the children of Christ "are not fully developed men and women in the things of God. It is expected that they will have to 'grow in grace and in the knowledge of God.' . . .

"The new-born saints will find themselves in a new atmosphere, sensitive to new forces operating upon them, new powers developing within them; and as the young child staggers in its first attempts to walk, and has many a fall before it will obtain complete control over its muscles—so the newborn member of Christ's Church will make many mistakes and perhaps blunders in the days of his infancy. . . .

"There is no one great thing that man can do and then do no more and obtain salvation. After entering into the kingdom of God, . . . it is by learning 'precept upon precept; line upon line; here a little and there a little,' that salvation will be made secure. It is by resisting temptation today, overcoming a weakness tomorrow, forsaking evil associations the next day, and thus day by day, month after month, year after year, pruning, restraining and weeding out that which is evil in the disposition, that the character is purged of its imperfections. Salvation is a matter of character-building under the Gospel laws and ordinances, and more especially with the direct aid of the Holy Spirit.

"Nor is it enough that one get rid of evil. He must do good. He must surround himself with circumstances congenial to the sensitive nature of the Holy Ghost, that he may not be offended, and withdraw himself; for if he does so, amen to the man's spiritual or moral development. He must cultivate noble sentiments by performing noble deeds—not great ones, necessarily, for opportunity to do what the world esteems great things, comes but seldom to men in the ordinary walks of life; but noble deeds may be done every day; and every such deed performed with an eye single to the glory of God, draws one that much nearer into harmony with Deity. . . .

"Thus by refusing to follow the evil inclinations of the disposition on the one hand, and cultivating noble sentiments on the other, a character may be formed that shall be godlike in its attributes, and consequently its possessor will be fitted to dwell with God, and if so prepared, there is no question but his calling and election are sure" (*Gospel and Man's Relationship to Deity*, pp. 196–98, as quoted in: Robert L. Millet, *Alive in Christ: The Miracle of Spiritual Rebirth*, p. 183).

AND SHOULD WE DIE

Whether an individual has his calling and election made sure by receiving the promise of exaltation by the direct voice of God out of the heavens, or if he receives it through the voice and priesthood of the Lord's authorized mortal administrator, does not seem to matter. Neither does it matter whether the latter (the highest priesthood blessings or fullness of the priesthood) are received in this life or the next. Though mortal death may come upon us, yet "even so in Christ shall [we] all be made alive" (1 Corinthians 15:22) and be made "partakers of the inheritance of the saints" (Colossians 1:12) or "the heavenly gift" (4 Nephi 1:3). Why? Because "all ordinances of the temple that are done for the living, including marriage for time and eternity and *the fulness of the priesthood,* can also be done for the dead" (*Words,* p. 385, note 8; italics mine. For further information, see *Teachings,* pp. 362–63; James E. Talmage, *The House of the Lord,* pp. 163, 211; and B. H. Roberts, *A Comprehensive History of The Church of Jesus Christ of Latter-day Saints—Century 1,* 6:495).

Because these highest ordinances cannot be sought after in the same way we do our endowments or sealings of husbands and wives, but come only through direct revelation to the Lord's mortal mouthpiece, in which the Lord indicates both our identity and readiness, this matter must be left *entirely* in His hands. Our waiting on the Lord, therefore, that "in patience [we] may possess [our] souls" (D&C 101:38) becomes a vital part of the trust in God that is required of all true wilderness travelers.

Nevertheless, this understanding is why Elder McConkie could declare: "This is a true gospel verity—that everyone in the Church who is on the straight and narrow path, who is striving and struggling and desiring to do what is right, though far from perfect in this life; if he passes out of this life while he's on the straight and narrow, he's going to go on to an eternal reward in his Father's kingdom.

"You don't need to get a complex or get a feeling that you

have to be perfect to be saved. You don't. There's only been one perfect person, and that's the Lord Jesus, but in order to be saved in the Kingdom of God and in order to pass the test of mortality, what you have to do is get on the straight and narrow path—thus charting a course leading to eternal life—and then, being on that path, pass out of this life in full fellowship. I'm not saying that you don't have to keep the commandments. I'm saying you don't have to be perfect to be saved. The way it operates is this: you get on the path that's named the 'straight and narrow.' You do it by entering the gate of repentance and baptism. The straight and narrow path leads from the gate of repentance and baptism, a very great distance, to a reward that's called eternal life. If you're on that path and pressing forward, and you die, you'll never get off the path. There is no such thing as falling off the straight and narrow path in the life to come, and the reason is that this life is the time that is given to men to prepare for eternity. Now is the time and the day of your salvation, so if you're working zealously in this life—though you haven't fully overcome the world and you haven't done all you hoped you might do—you're still going to be saved. You don't have to do what Jacob said, 'Go beyond the mark.' You don't have to live a life that's truer than true. You don't have to have an excessive zeal that becomes fanatical and unbalancing. What you have to do is stay in the mainstream of the Church and live as upright and decent people in the Church—keeping the commandments, paying your tithing, serving in the organizations of the Church, loving the Lord, staying on the straight and narrow path. If you're on that path when death comes—because this is the time and day appointed, this is the probationary estate—you'll never fall off from it, and, for all practical purposes, your calling and election is made sure" ("The Probationary Test of Mortality," address given at the University of Utah, January 10, 1982, p. 11).

Our challenge, therefore, is to live so that we become fully worthy of receiving the fullness of the priesthood and to endure in that worthy state or condition to whatever end the Lord might require of us.

And all this, of course, is preparatory to receiving the Messiah as Second Comforter, the ultimate blessing available to man.

Chapter Twenty-Three

ZION—THE PURE IN HEART

By now it should be obvious that the Lord's purpose in allowing Babylon's ex-patriots an admittance into His wilderness school is to burn out of their hearts "like a refiner's fire, and like fullers' soap" (Malachi 3:2) their last vestiges of pride, vanity, and worldliness. Thus purged and purified "as gold and silver" (Malachi 3:3), such righteous individuals, who have neither faltered nor turned back but instead trusted in the Lord with all their hearts, leaning not upon their own understanding (Proverbs 3:5), have miraculously (because it is accomplished only through the grace and merits of the Lord) become sufficiently righteous (D&C 97:21) that their callings and elections have been made sure. By such exceeding purity of heart, therefore, they are blessed "to bring forth . . . Zion at that day" (1 Nephi 13:37); by being obedient they have been given "power after many days to accomplish all things pertaining to Zion" (D&C 105:37); and having been "tried in all things" they are now "prepared to receive the glory . . . of Zion" (D&C 136:31).

ZION IN ALL WORLDS

Elder Orson Pratt made an interesting point concerning such righteous individuals. First he quoted part of the revelation God gave to Enoch, which reads as follows: "And Enoch said unto the Lord: How is it that thou canst weep, seeing thou art holy, and from all eternity to all eternity? And were it possible that man could number the particles of the earth, yea, millions of earths like this, it would not be a beginning to the number of thy creations; and thy curtains are stretched out still; and yet thou art there, and thy bosom is there; and also thou art just; thou art merciful and kind forever; and *thou hast taken Zion to thine own bosom, from all thy creations, from all eternity to all eternity;* and naught but peace, justice, and truth is the habitation of thy throne; and mercy shall go before thy face and have no end; how is it thou canst weep?" (Moses 7:29–31; italics mine).

Elder Pratt then said, "There is one thing connected with this same revelation, to which I wish also to call your attention. . . . Notwithstanding the unnumbered worlds which have been created, out of each one of these creations the Lord had taken Zion (in other words a people called Zion who have become or been made pure in heart) to his own bosom. What does this signify? Are we not to understand that all these creations were fallen worlds. Why did he not take them all? Because they were not all worthy, because being fallen, they did not keep his commandments, because they did not exercise their agency to worship God; for that reason he did not take them all to himself. He did not qualify them and make them one in him, as Jesus is one with the Father; he did not make them like him in all respects, to go forth and make new creations and people them. I mention these things to show that we have, in the revelations that God has given, many indications, that there are worlds beside our own that are fallen; also that we may see that the Lord has one grand method, for the salvation of the righteous of all worlds—that Zion is selected and taken from all of them" (*Journal of Discourses*, 19:293).

TWO ASPECTS OF ZION

For our purposes, however, we will deal with the two aspects of Zion as it exists in this world. First, it is an actual, physical place, of which Enoch's city (Moses 7:16–18, 68) was the perfect prototype, but it is also (or will be) "the whole of America . . . from north to south" (*Teachings*, p. 362). Second, it is a spiritual place of refuge (D&C 45:66–67) no matter the physical surroundings, a pure and righteous state of being (D&C 97:21) where one enjoys all the blessings of a city where Christ has His permanent abode (Moses 7:64); an eternal city that has not at this time been built up by the Lord, or brought down from its place in heaven (Revelation 3:17), but soon will be, and it will be known both as Zion and the New Jerusalem (Revelation 21:2).

According to the Prophet Joseph, "Now many will feel disposed to say, that this New Jerusalem spoken of, is the Jerusalem that was built by the Jews on the eastern continent. But you will see, from Revelation 21:2, there was a New Jerusalem coming down from God out of heaven, adorned as a bride for her husband; that after this, the Revelator was caught away in the Spirit, to a great and high mountain, and saw the great and holy city descending out of heaven from God" (*Teachings*, p. 86).

Holy Zion is, in every particular, the exact opposite of Babylon, its "inverse image." Zion, like Babylon, "is a type. If . . . Babylon is the culmination of the worldly power wherever it happens . . . [then] Zion is wherever the celestial order prevails" (Nibley, *Approaching Zion*, pp. 14, 16).

THE ZIONS OF ADAM AND ENOCH

The Lord has established several Zions on this earth, perhaps one in every prophetic dispensation. For Adam and Eve, in addition to the garden, which we are told was a part of God's heaven (Genesis 13:10), our first parents attained a Zion of their own. Therefore, "the Holy One of Zion . . . established the foundations of Adam-ondi-Ahman" (D&C 78:15). Several generations later Enoch gathered his righteous followers together in the name of the Lord, whereupon "the Lord called his people ZION" and Enoch "built a city that was called the City of Holiness, even ZION" (Moses 7:18–19). But then "it came to pass that Zion was not, for God received it up into his own bosom; and from thence went forth the saying, ZION IS FLED" (Moses 7:69). Nevertheless, as individuals continued to exercise faith sufficient to come up into Enoch's holy order of God, they "were translated and taken up into heaven" (JST Genesis 14:32).

THE ZION OF MELCHIZEDEK

The great high priest Melchizedek was this sort of man, "therefore he obtained peace in Salem, and was called the

Prince of peace. And his people wrought righteousness, and obtained heaven [became a Zion people], and sought for the city of Enoch which God had before taken, separating it from the earth, having reserved it unto the latter days, or the end of the world. . . . And this Melchizedek, having thus established righteousness, was called the king of heaven by his people, or, in other words, the King of peace" (JST Genesis 14:33–34, 36).

ZION IN ANCIENT AMERICA

Another Zion was established by the resurrected Christ when He visited ancient America, His disciples literally obtaining heaven (3 Nephi 28:13) before gradually bringing all the people of that generation into the Lord's true and living Church (3 Nephi 28:23; 4 Nephi 1:1–2). Thereafter "there were no contentions and disputations among them, and every man did deal justly one with another. And they had all things common among them; therefore there were not rich and poor, bond and free, but they were all made free, and partakers of the heavenly gift. . . . And the Lord did prosper them exceedingly in the land . . . and [they] became an exceedingly fair and delightsome people . . . [and] they did walk after the commandments which they had received from their Lord and their God, continuing in fasting and prayer, and in meeting together oft both to pray and to hear the word of the Lord . . . [and] there were mighty miracles wrought among [them] . . . [and] there was no contention in the land, because of the love of God which did dwell in the hearts of the people. And there were no envyings, nor strifes, nor tumults, nor whoredoms, nor lyings, nor murders, nor any manner of lasciviousness; and surely there could not be a happier people among all the people who had been created by the hand of God. There were no robbers, nor murderers, neither were there Lamanites, nor any manner of -ites; but they were in one, the children of Christ, and heirs to the Kingdom of God" (4 Nephi 1:2–3, 7, 10, 12–13, 15–17). "And [the Lord] did show himself unto them oft, and did break bread oft, and bless it, and give it unto them" (3 Nephi 26:13).

But as Brother Nibley writes, Zion, including that enjoyed by the Nephites, comes and goes. "When the world cannot support Zion, Zion is not destroyed but taken back home. 'And thou hast taken Zion to thine own bosom, from all thy creations,' says Moses 7:31" (*Approaching Zion,* p. 6). Then are the wicked destroyed who have been left behind, the case of the Nephites being a prime example.[1]

PROPHETS LONG FOR ZION

"When the world is qualified to receive Zion," Brother Nibley continues, "'there shall be mine abode, and it shall be Zion, which shall come forth out of all the creations which I have made' (Moses 7:64). Accordingly, the ancient prophets of Israel yearned for the time when Zion would be restored again. Jeremiah and Isaiah hoped to see Zion restored in their time. They certainly knew it would come in a later day. Typical of their attitude is the prophecy of the Psalmist: 'My days are like a shadow that declineth, and I am withered like grass. But thou, O Lord, . . . shalt arise, and have mercy upon Zion: for the time to favour her, yea, the set time, is come. . . . When the Lord shall build up Zion, he shall appear in his glory.' And then he adds, 'This shall be written for the generation to come' (Psalms 102:11–18). After all the calamities, said Jeremiah, 'there shall be a day, that the watchmen upon the mount Ephraim shall cry, Arise ye, and let us go up to Zion unto the Lord our God' (Jeremiah 31:6). And of course we all know the prophecy of Micah 4:1–2: 'But in the last days . . . the mountain of the house of the Lord shall be established in the top of the mountains, and it shall be exalted above the hills; and people shall flow unto it. And many nations shall come. . . . For the law shall go forth of Zion, and the word of the Lord from Jerusalem.' This was the hope of the prophets. It was also anticipated in the days of the ancient apostles that 'ye are come unto mount Sion, and unto the city of the living God, the heavenly Jerusalem, and to an innumerable company of angels,' as Paul describes the Church (Heb. 12:22).

"But it's in the last days that the fulfillment will really get underway with the restoration and the steps approaching the establishment of Zion. In every age, though, as the Doctrine and Covenants tells us, the saints are 'they who are come unto Mount Zion, and unto the city of the living God, the heavenly place, the holiest of all, . . . the general assembly and church of Enoch, and of the First-born' (D&C 76:66–67). That is the eternal order of Zion, and the saints have been at work for many years, supposedly preparing to receive it."

THE IDEAL ZION

Brother Nibley continues, "What is this ideal Zion like? In the last days, we are told, it will be a place of refuge in a doomed world. 'It shall be called the New Jerusalem, a land of peace, a city of refuge, a place of safety for the saints of the Most High God; . . . and the terror of the Lord also shall be there, . . . and it shall be called Zion' (D&C 45:66–67). At that time, 'every man that will not take his sword against his neighbor must needs flee unto Zion for safety' (D&C 45:68). And the wicked shall say that Zion is terrible. Terrible because it is indestructible. Her invulnerability makes her an object of awe and terror. As Enoch said, 'Surely Zion shall dwell in safety forever. But the Lord said unto Enoch: Zion have I blessed, but the residue of the people have I cursed' (Moses 7:20). So Zion was taken away and the rest destroyed. Zion itself is never in danger; on the contrary, it alone offers safety to the world, 'that the gathering together upon the land of Zion, and upon her stakes, may be for a defense, and for a refuge from the storm, and from wrath when it shall be poured out without mixture upon the whole earth' (D&C 115:6). It would seem that Zion enjoys the complete security of a bit of the celestial world and that nothing can touch it as long as it retains the character. But celestial order it *must* be. As we have seen, Zion cannot be built up 'Unless it is by the principles of the law of the celestial kingdom' (D&C 105:5). It must at all times be holy enough to receive the Lord himself in person. 'For the Lord hath chosen Zion; he hath desired it for his habitation' (Psalm 132:13); 'Behold mine abode forever' (Moses 7:21). Zion is heaven. It is where God lives. A bit of heaven indeed. . . .

"The two words most commonly used to describe Zion are *beauty* and *joy*, and the same two words most often relate to heaven and paradise. Beauty comes first, for beauty is whatever gives joy. Now we approach the question of what Zion looks like: 'The city of our God. . . . Beautiful for situation, the joy of the whole earth, is mount

Zion. . . . Let mount Zion rejoice, let the daughters of Judah be glad. . . . Walk about Zion and go round about her' (Psalm 48:1–2, 11–12). An eminently delightful place. 'Out of Zion, the perfection of beauty, God hath shined' (Psalm 50:2). 'For Zion must increase in beauty, and in holiness; . . . Zion must arise and put on her beautiful garments' (D&C 82:14). 'And blessed are they who shall seek to bring forth my Zion at that day; . . . and whoso shall publish peace, . . . how beautiful upon the mountains shall they be' (1 Ne. 13:37). These are more than figures of speech. As President Joseph F. Smith put it, 'Things upon the earth, so far as they have not been perverted by wickedness, are typical of things in heaven. Heaven was the prototype of this beautiful creation when it came from the hand of the Creator, and was pronounced good.' (*Journal of Discourses*, 23:175). There you have the environment of Zion; and for a foretaste of it, all we have to do is go to the canyons and look around us. For the earth comes from the hand of the Creator most glorious and beautiful, with great rivers, small streams, and mountains and hills to give variety and beauty to the scene, designed by God as a place of beauty and delight. That is the way we must keep it" (*Approaching Zion*, pp. 6–7).[2]

PERFECT PEACE FOUND IN ZION

For those who are weary of dwelling in a troubled world such as ours, Zion is the preeminent place of peace and refuge from the storm (D&C 45:66–67). Why is that? Because in Zion Satan is "bound, that he . . . have no place in the hearts of the children of men. . . . For they that are wise and have received the truth, and have taken the Holy

Spirit for their guide, and have not been deceived—verily I say unto you, they [have not been] hewn down and cast into the fire, but [have abided] the day. And the earth [is] given unto them for an inheritance; and they shall multiply and wax strong, and their children shall grow up without sin unto salvation. For the Lord [is] in their midst, and his glory [is] upon them, and he [is] their king and their lawgiver" (D&C 45:55, 57–59).

Can it possibly be questioned that perfect peace exists only in Zion? And since "the temple is the earthly type of Zion, a holy place removed from contact with the outer world" (*Approaching Zion*, pp. 27–28), it is easy to understand why we feel and enjoy such peace when we attend the temple and "stand . . . in holy places" (D&C 87:8).

THE TRUE JOY OF ZION

For those who have prevailed in all things by going out of Babylon and patiently enduring the Lord's wilderness school until their callings and elections have been made sure, true joy is a fullness of the perfect "peace of God, which passeth all understanding" (Philippians 4:7). A fullness of this perfect peace is found only in Zion because it is the eternal abode of the Lord. There He reveals Himself in perfect love or charity to all the inhabitants thereof, making His true peace the reward of all the pure in heart. "Naught but peace, justice, and truth is the habitation of [His] throne, and mercy shall go before [His] face and have no end," Enoch fervently declared. Christ is "Messiah, the King of Zion, the Rock of Heaven, which is broad as eternity" (Moses 7:31, 53).

Because such peace as the Lord gives "passeth all understanding," it cannot be made known to the world, "Neither is man capable to make [it] known, for [it is] only to be seen and understood by the power of the Holy Spirit, which God bestows on those who love him, and purify themselves before him; to whom he grants this privilege of seeing and knowing for themselves; that through the power and manifestation of the Spirit, *while in the flesh,* they may be able to bear his presence [behold His face] in the world of glory. And to God and the Lamb be glory, and honor, and dominion forever and ever. Amen" (D&C 76:116–19; italics mine).

NOTES

1. "When the Nephites decided to give up that order [of Zion]," Brother Nibley writes, "they went the other way. They didn't slowly subside into the more relaxed economy of Israel. They went right to the other extreme, in a quick transition to the telestial. Israel's economy has a strong appeal. (If you don't believe it, spend a few nights before the telestial economy of television fare.) 'Now, in this two hundred and first year there began to be among them those who were lifted up in pride' (4 Ne. 1:24) (the Nephites had to work all the time to preserve the order—eating, fasting, praying, and doing all the other things). They couldn't tolerate the righteous pace, [however], so they were lifted up in pride, such things as wearing costly apparel and seeking the fine things of the world. 'And from that time forth they did have their goods and their substance no more common among them. And they began to be divided into classes' (4 Nephi 1:25–26). They did not dwindle in unbelief but willfully rebelled against the gospel of Christ. They didn't just subside imperceptibly into a more relaxed way of life. Not at all. They didn't dwindle. 'They did wilfully rebel against the gospel of Christ' (4 Ne. 1:38). Even as it was in the

beginning, they went back to their old vices: 'As a dog returneth to his vomit, so a fool returneth to his folly' (Proverbs 26:11). They actually taught their children to hate the children of God, even as the Lamanites were taught to hate the children of Nephi from the beginning. It was the old order—the same old hatreds and tribal warfare—and they actively promoted it. The teaching was deliberate: 'And also the people . . . of Nephi began to be proud in their hearts [fighting fire with fire], because of their exceeding riches, and become vain like unto their brethren, the Lamanites. And from this time the disciples began to sorrow for the sins of the world. And . . . both the people of Nephi and the Lamanites had become exceedingly wicked one like unto another' (4 Ne. 1:43–45). In a few verses and a few decades, they had deliberately pushed themselves all the way from a celestial order (there couldn't be a happier people ever created by the hand of the Lord on the earth; 4 Ne. 1:16) to the other extreme; the prophets mourned and withdrew, for the people of Nephi and the Lamanites had become equally wicked (4 Ne. 1:45). This is the state described by Samuel the Lamanite: 'Ye are cursed because of your riches, . . . because ye have set your hearts upon them, and have not hearkened unto the words of him who gave them unto you. Ye do not remember the Lord your God, . . . but ye do always remember your riches' (Helaman 13:21–22). Always the economy, the economy—as if that were the solution to anything. 'For this cause hath the Lord God caused that a curse should come upon . . . your riches . . . Yea, wo unto this people . . . And behold, the time cometh that he curseth your riches, that they become slippery, that ye cannot hold them' (Helaman 13:23–24, 31)" (*Approaching Zion*, pp. 325–26).

2. "We're not making Zion here," Brother Nibley says, "but we're preparing the ground to receive it. As the Lord says, 'My people must be tried in all things, that they may be prepared to receive the glory that I have for them, even the glory of Zion; and

he that will not bear chastisement is not worthy of my kingdom' (D&C 136:31). We must be prepared to receive this glory; we don't produce it ourselves. We must be ready, [though], so that we won't die of shock when we get it" (*Approaching Zion*, p. 4).

Chapter Twenty-Four

THE CROWNING BLESSING OF LIFE

To obtain the ultimate blessing of seeing the face of Christ and partaking directly of His divine love and approbation, righteous individuals must progress steadily forward in the spirit, clinging steadfastly to every word that proceeds forth out of the mouth of God, and fulfilling the other requirements outlined by the Lord: "Strip yourselves from jealousies and fears, and humble yourselves before me . . . let[ting] not your minds turn back" (D&C 67:10, 14); "seek the face of the Lord always, that in patience ye may possess your souls, and ye shall have eternal life" (D&C 101:38). Then, "in mine own due time, . . ." the Lord promises, "the veil shall be rent and you shall see me and know that I am" (D&C 67:14, 10).

Elder Bruce R. McConkie declares, "What greater personal revelation could anyone receive than to see the face of his Maker? Is not this the crowning blessing of life? Can all the wealth of the earth, all of the powers of the world, and all of the honors of men compare with it? And is it an unseemly or unrighteous desire on man's part to hope and live and pray, all in such a way as to qualify for so great a manifestation?

"There is a true doctrine on these points, a doctrine unknown to many and unbelieved by more, a doctrine that is spelled out as specifically and extensively in the revealed word as are any of the other great revealed truths. There is no need for uncertainty or misunderstanding; and surely, if the Lord reveals a doctrine, we should seek to learn its principles and strive to apply them in our lives. This doctrine is that mortal man, while in the flesh, has it in his power to see the Lord, to stand in his presence, to feel the nail marks in his hands and feet, and to receive from him such blessings as are reserved for those only who keep all his commandments and who are qualified for that eternal life which includes being in his presence forever. Let us . . . [believe] what the Lord has promised as to seeing his face and being in his presence while we are yet pilgrims far removed from our heavenly home" (*A New Witness for the Articles of Faith,* p. 492).

Such diligent, patient seeking, then, permits qualified, pure-hearted men and women to "have the privilege of receiving the mysteries of the kingdom of heaven, to have the heavens opened unto them, to commune with the general assembly and church of the Firstborn, and to enjoy the communion and presence of God the Father, and Jesus the mediator of the new covenant" (D&C 107:18–19). "This greater priesthood administereth the gospel and holdeth the key of the mysteries of the kingdom, even the key of the knowledge of God" (D&C 84:19).

As a further explanation of this, Joseph Smith wrote that "the keys of this priesthood consisted in [Noah] obtaining the voice of Jehovah, that [Jehovah] talked with him in a familiar and friendly manner, that he continued to him the Keys, the Covenants, the power and the glory with which [Jehovah] blessed Adam at the beginning. . . . Elijah was the last prophet that held the keys of this priesthood, and who will, before the last dispensation, restore the authority and deliver the keys of this priesthood in order that all the ordinances may be attended to in righteousness" (*Words*, pp. 42–43).

According to Joseph Smith, therefore, these keys of access to God, held in fullness by the president of the Church, enable or empower the least members in the church to also bring themselves into the presence of God (*Teachings*, p. 137). As we have pointed out, this is called beholding the face of Christ. "Verily, thus saith the Lord: It shall come to pass that *every soul* who forsaketh his sins and cometh unto me, and calleth on my name, and obeyeth my voice, and keepeth my commandments, *shall see my face and know that I am*" (D&C 93:1; italics mine). This experience, of course, is true worship, and according to Moses, it occurs when calling upon God through the name of His Only Begotten in mighty prayer (Moses 1:17), which for the pure in heart is accomplished with greatest effectiveness through worship in God's holy temples.

The crowning blessing granted through the priesthood keys revealed or delivered by Elijah, then, is to see and know personally, God the Father and His Beloved Son, Jesus

Christ. As Elder McConkie says, "The purpose of the endowment in the house of the Lord is to prepare and sanctify his saints so they will be able to see his face, here and now, as well as to bear the glory of his presence in the eternal worlds" (*The Promised Messiah,* p. 583).

Ultimately, therefore, if we are to successfully conclude the Lord's wilderness school, whether in this life or the next, we must see Christ face to face as one person sees another, speak with Him in like manner, and feel the wounds in His hands and feet. This is called receiving the Second Comforter.

ALL MEN ARE TO KNOW THE LORD

"I am going on in my progress for eternal life," Joseph Smith said of himself; and then in fervent pleading to all the Saints, he exclaimed, "Oh! I beseech you to go forward, go forward and make your calling and your election sure" (*Words,* p. 368; *Teachings,* p. 366). Why? Because "this principle ought (in its proper place) to be taught," the Prophet responded, "for God hath not revealed anything to Joseph, but what he will make known unto the Twelve, and even the least saint may know all things as fast as he is able to bear them, for the day must come when no man need say to his neighbor, know ye the Lord; for *all shall know him (who remain) from the least to the greatest.* How is this to be done? It is to be done by this sealing power, and the other Comforter spoken of, *which will be manifest by revelation*" (*Teachings,* p. 149; italics mine).

The Prophet continues, "The other Comforter spoken of is a subject of great interest, and perhaps understood by few of this generation. After a person has faith in Christ, repents of his sins, and is baptized for the remission of his sins and receives the Holy Ghost, (by the laying on of hands), which is the first Comforter, then let him continue to humble himself before God, hungering and thirsting after righteousness, and living by every word of God, and the Lord will soon say unto him, Son, thou shalt be exalted. When the Lord has thoroughly proved him, and finds that the man is determined to serve him at all hazards, then the man will find his calling and his election made sure, then it will be his privilege to receive the other Comforter, which the Lord hath promised the saints, as is recorded in the testimony of St. John, in the 14th chapter, from the 12th to the 27th verses" (*Teachings*, pp. 149–50).

In a portion of this scriptural passage mentioned by Joseph Smith, the apostles were told by Jesus, "If ye love me, keep my commandments. And I will pray the Father, and he shall give you another Comforter, that he may abide with you for ever; *even* the Spirit of truth; whom the world cannot receive, because it seeth him not, neither knoweth him: but ye know him; for he dwelleth with you, and shall be in you. *I will not leave you comfortless: I will come to you.* Yet a little while, and the world seeth me no more; but ye see me: because I live, ye shall live also. At that day ye shall know that I *am* in my Father, and ye in me, and I in you. He that hath my commandments, and keepeth them, he it is that loveth me: and he that loveth me shall be loved of my Father, and I will love him, and *will manifest myself to him.*

"Judas saith unto him, not Iscariot, Lord, how is it that thou wilt manifest thyself unto us, and not unto the world? Jesus answered and said unto him, If a man love me, he will keep my words: and my Father will love him, and *we will come unto him, and make our abode with him*" (John 14:15–23; italics mine).

In a revelation to a group of Latter-day Saints in December 1832, the Lord said that the alms of their prayers were "recorded in the book of the names of the sanctified, even them of the celestial world" (D&C 88:2). This meant they had "overcome by faith" and were "sealed by the Holy Spirit of promise, which the Father sheds forth upon all those who are just and true" (D&C 76:53). "Wherefore," the Lord said to them, "I now send upon you another Comforter, even upon you my friends, that it may abide in your hearts, even the Holy Spirit of promise; which other Comforter is the same that I promised unto my disciples, as is recorded in the testimony of John. This Comforter is the promise which I give unto you of eternal life, even the glory of the celestial kingdom; which glory is that of the church of the Firstborn, even of God, the holiest of all, through Jesus Christ his Son" (D&C 88:3–5).

SEEING AND KNOWING GOD

In this volume we have discussed many individuals who have experienced the Second Comforter and have seen and known God. While not wishing to be repetitious, perhaps it would be worthwhile to reconsider a few of them.

Enoch was one of the first to record his remarkable experience, declaring, "I saw the Lord; and he stood before my face, and he talked with me, even as a man talketh with another, face to face; and he said unto me: Look, and I will show unto thee the world for the space of many generations" (Moses 7:4).

Abraham records his relief upon finally obtaining this

grand blessing by declaring, "After the Lord had withdrawn from speaking to me, and withdrawn his face from me, I said in my heart: Thy servant has sought thee earnestly; now I have found thee" (Abraham 2:12). So will we all feel that great relief, if we are faithful in our quest. Later Abraham recorded another visit by the Lord, during which He once again spoke with him "face to face" (Abraham 3:11).

Mahonri Moriancumer, the brother of Jared, was also able to attain to this remarkable spiritual experience while dwelling in the wilderness. His account is interesting because of the amount of knowledge the Lord was willing to impart once the veil had been opened. Moroni, in recording the event, states that "the veil was taken from off the eyes of the brother of Jared, and he saw the finger of the Lord; and it was as the finger of a man, like unto flesh and blood; and the brother of Jared fell down before the Lord, for he was struck with fear. And the Lord saw that the brother of Jared had fallen to the earth; and the Lord said unto him: Arise, why hast thou fallen? And he saith unto the Lord: I saw the finger of the Lord, and I feared lest he should smite me; for I knew not that the Lord had flesh and blood.

"And the Lord said unto him: Because of thy faith thou hast seen that I shall take upon me flesh and blood; and never has man come before me with such exceeding faith as thou hast; for were it not so ye could not have seen my finger. Sawest thou more than this? And he answered: Nay; Lord, show thyself unto me. And the Lord said unto him: Believest thou the words which I shall speak? And he answered: Yea, Lord, I know that thou speakest the truth, for thou art a God of truth, and canst not lie.

"And when he had said these words, behold, the Lord

showed himself unto him, and said: Because thou knowest these things ye are redeemed from the fall; therefore ye are brought back into my presence; therefore I show myself unto you. Behold, I am he who was prepared from the foundation of the world to redeem my people. Behold, I am Jesus Christ. I am the Father and the Son. In me shall all mankind have life, and that eternally, even they who shall believe on my name; and they shall become my sons and my daughters. And never have I showed myself unto man whom I have created, for never has man believed in me as thou hast. Seest thou that ye are created after mine own image? Yea, even all men were created in the beginning after mine own image. Behold, this body, which ye now behold, is the body of my spirit; and man have I created after the body of my spirit; and even as I appear unto thee to be in the spirit will I appear unto my people in the flesh. . . .

"Therefore," Moroni concludes, "it sufficeth me to say that Jesus showed himself unto this man in the spirit, even after the manner and in the likeness of the same body even as he showed himself unto the Nephites. And he ministered unto him even as he ministered unto the Nephites; and all this, that this man might know that he was God, because of the many great works which the Lord had showed unto him. And because of the knowledge of this man he could not be kept from beholding within the veil; and he saw the finger of Jesus, which, when he saw, he fell with fear; for he knew that it was the finger of the Lord; and he had faith no longer, for he knew, nothing doubting. Wherefore, having this perfect knowledge of God, he could not be kept from within the veil; therefore he saw Jesus; and he did minister unto him" (Ether 3:6–20).

To Joseph Smith the Lord bore personal witness of this man's righteousness and calling, stating that he gave to the brother of Jared the Urim and Thummim when he was upon the mount, "when he talked with the Lord face to face" (D&C 17:1).

Nephi, who also saw the Lord in His premortal state, tells us that this marvelous blessing was accomplished not because of age or ecclesiastical experience but through intense desire, great diligence, and lowliness of heart. He declares, "I, Nephi, being exceedingly young, nevertheless being large in stature, and also having great desires to know of the mysteries of God, wherefore, I did cry unto the Lord; and behold he did visit me, and did soften my heart that I did believe all the words which had been spoken by my father; wherefore, I did not rebel against him like unto my brothers. And I spake unto Sam, making known unto him the things which the Lord had manifested unto me by his Holy Spirit. And it came to pass that he believed in my words. But, behold, Laman and Lemuel would not hearken unto my words; and being grieved because of the hardness of their hearts I cried unto the Lord for them. And it came to pass that the Lord spake unto me, saying: Blessed art thou, Nephi, because of thy faith, for thou hast sought me diligently, with lowliness of heart" (1 Nephi 2:16–19). And "*I spake unto him as a man speaketh; for I beheld that he was in the form of a man; yet nevertheless, I knew that it was the Spirit of the Lord; and he spake unto me as a man speaketh with another*" (1 Nephi 11:11; italics mine).

To Nephi's younger brother, Jacob, their father, Lehi, spoke by way of priesthood blessing, "Thy soul shall be blessed, and thou shalt dwell safely with thy brother, Nephi;

and thy days shall be spent in the service of thy God. Wherefore, I know that thou art redeemed, because of the righteousness of thy Redeemer; for thou hast beheld that in the fulness of time he cometh to bring salvation unto men. And *thou hast beheld in thy youth his glory;* wherefore, thou art blessed even as they unto whom he shall minister in the flesh; for the Spirit is the same, yesterday, today, and forever. And the way is prepared from the fall of man, and salvation is free" (2 Nephi 2:3–4; italics mine).

Speaking of himself in the third person, Moses recorded, "He saw God face to face, and he talked with him, and the glory of God was upon Moses; therefore Moses could endure his presence" (Moses 1:2).

Later on Moses led Nadab, Abihu, and seventy of the elders of Israel to see the Lord's face on the top of the mount, thus obtaining the Second Comforter (Exodus 24:9–10). Unfortunately, most of the Israelites did not receive that blessing—because they *chose* not to receive it. This angered the Lord, and because of their rebelliousness that entire generation was never allowed to see the face of God and "enter into his rest" (D&C 84:24). Therefore "the children of Israel walked forty years in the wilderness, till all the people that were men of war, which came out of Egypt, were consumed, because they obeyed not the voice of the Lord: unto whom the Lord sware that he would not shew them the land, which the Lord sware unto their fathers that he would give us, a land that floweth with milk and honey" (Joshua 5:6).

JESUS AMONG THE NEPHITES

One of the most supernal instances of Christ appearing to mortals occurred in the Land Bountiful almost a year after the Savior's crucifixion and resurrection in Jerusalem (3 Nephi 8:5; 10:18). At the temple, once the people had exercised sufficient faith (Ether 12:7), the resurrected Lord made himself physically manifest to upwards of 2,500 of them (see 3 Nephi 17:25).

The record states that they twice heard a voice out of heaven but did not understand it. "And again the third time they did hear the voice, and did open their ears to hear it; and their eyes were towards the sound thereof; and they did look steadfastly towards heaven, from whence the sound came. And behold, the third time they did understand the voice which they heard; and it said unto them: Behold my Beloved Son, in whom I am well pleased, in whom I have glorified my name—hear ye him. And it came to pass, as they understood they cast their eyes up again towards heaven; and behold, they saw a Man descending out of heaven; and he was clothed in a white robe; and he came down and stood in the midst of them; and the eyes of the whole multitude were turned upon him, and they durst not open their mouths, even one to another, and wist not what it meant, for they thought it was an angel that had appeared unto them.

"And it came to pass that he stretched forth his hand and spake unto the people, saying: Behold, I am Jesus Christ, whom the prophets testified shall come into the world. . . . And it came to pass that when Jesus had spoken these words the whole multitude fell to the earth; for they remembered that it had been prophesied among them that Christ should show himself unto them after his ascension into heaven" (3 Nephi 11:5–10, 12).

In the days, months, and years that followed, the number

of Nephite people who saw the resurrected Lord swelled to unknown thousands as He "did show himself unto them oft" (3 Nephi 26:13), commanding, "Thrust your hands into my side, and also that ye may feel the prints of the nails in my hands and in my feet" (3 Nephi 11:14). And Jesus continued to manifest himself unto the righteous among them until, as was pointed out earlier, the last prophet, Moroni, was visited by Him more than 400 years later (Ether 12:39).

AGAIN A PROCESS

It is likely that most wilderness travelers who are blessed to receive the Second Comforter will be granted that sublime experience as a consequence of a series of relatively small but increasingly significant events, such as the brother of Jared experienced, who first heard the voice of the Lord (Ether 1:40–43; 2:14), saw the Lord's finger (Ether 3:6), and finally was admitted fully into His divine presence (Ether 3:13). Moroni, who had obtained this fullness, testified of his experience: "I, Moroni, bid farewell unto the Gentiles, yea, and also unto my brethren whom I love, until we shall meet before the judgment-seat of Christ, where all men shall know that my garments are not spotted with your blood. And then shall ye know that *I have seen Jesus, and that he hath talked with me face to face,* and that he told me in plain humility, even as a man telleth another in mine own language, concerning these things" (Ether 12:37–39; italics mine).

THE FULLNESS OF GOD'S GLORY

When one who has prepared himself through diligent obedience in all things receives such an experience, it is said that he or she has received "the fulness of His glory" (D&C

76:20; 84:24; *Journal of Discourses,* 13:241). Joseph Smith taught, "All those who keep [the Father's] commandments shall grow up from grace to grace, and become heirs of the heavenly kingdom, and joint-heirs with Jesus Christ; possessing the same mind, being transformed into the same image or likeness, even the express image of him who fills all in all; *being filled with the fulness of his glory,* and become one in him, even as the Father, Son and Holy Spirit are one.

"As the Son partakes of the fulness of the Father through the Spirit, so the saints are, by the same Spirit, to be partakers of the same fulness, to enjoy the same glory; for as the Father and the Son are one, so, in like manner, the saints are to be one in them. Through the love of the Father, the mediation of Jesus Christ, and the gift of the Holy Spirit, they are to be heirs of God, and joint-heirs with Jesus Christ" (*Lectures on Faith,* pp. 50–52; 3 Nephi 28:10–11; italics mine).

MEMBERSHIP IN THE CHURCH OF THE FIRSTBORN

By way of further explanation, Elder Joseph Fielding Smith taught, "As sons and daughters [of Christ] then, we are heirs of his kingdom and shall receive by right the fulness of the glory and be entitled to the great blessings and privileges which the Lord in his mercy has revealed to us in the dispensation of the fulness of times. 'For as many as are led by the Spirit of God,' Paul has written, 'they are the sons of God. . . . . The Spirit itself beareth witness with our spirit, that we are the children of God: And if children, then heirs; heirs of God, and joint-heirs with Christ; if so be that we suffer with him, that we may be also glorified together'"

(*Doctrines of Salvation,* 2:38–39). Elder Smith also wrote, "The Lord has made it possible for us to become members of the Church of the Firstborn, by receiving the blessings of the house of the Lord and overcoming all things. Thus we become heirs, 'priests and kings, who have received of his fulness, and of his glory,' who shall 'dwell in the presence of God and his Christ forever and ever,' with full exaltation. Are such blessings worth having?" (*Doctrines of Salvation,* 2:42).

It is this promise of sharing in the same glory with Christ that is intended by the words of the revelation that states, in part, "I, John, bear record that I beheld his glory, as the glory of the Only Begotten of the Father, full of grace and truth, even the Spirit of truth, which came and dwelt in the flesh, and dwelt among us. And I, John, saw that *he received not of the fulness at the first,* but received grace for grace; and he received not of the fulness at first, but continued from grace to grace, until he received a fulness; and thus he was called the Son of God, because he received not of the fulness at the first. And I, John, bear record, and lo, the heavens were opened, and the Holy Ghost descended upon him in the form of a dove, and sat upon him, and there came a voice out of heaven saying: This is my beloved Son. And I, John, bear record that *he received a fulness of the glory of the Father; and he received all power, both in heaven and on earth,* and the glory of the Father was with him, for he dwelt in him." Christ himself then declares: "I give unto you these sayings that you may understand and know how to worship, and know what you worship, that *you may come unto the Father in my name, and in due time receive of his fulness. For if you keep my commandments you shall receive of his fulness, and be glorified in me as I am in the Father;* therefore, I say unto you, you shall receive grace for grace" (D&C 93:11–20; italics mine).

A JOINT-HEIR WITH CHRIST

Remembering the sequence of visitations Joseph taught—Elias, Elijah, and then Messiah, it is now clear that the mission of Messiah, or the Lord Jesus Christ, as he fully manifests himself to an individual through the true veil as the Second Comforter, is to present to the individual all power—everything He Himself has received from the Father. As Joseph taught, "The Spirit of Messiah is all power in Heaven and in Earth—Enthroned in the Heavens as King of Kings and Lord of Lords" (*Words*, p. 336). In a personal visitation in which the Messiah "comes to his Temple which is last of all" (*Words*, p. 332), the Messiah's mission is to confirm power equal to His own upon the righteous, temple-oriented individual. That individual then becomes a joint-heir with Christ, in very deed a priest and a king to the Most High God, to rule and reign with Christ forever.

For example, "Thus I, Abraham, talked with the Lord, face to face, as one man talketh with another; and he told me of the works which his hands had made. . . . [And the Lord declared:] I dwell in the midst of them all [the intelligences and spirits]; *I now, therefore, have come down unto thee to declare unto thee the works which my hands have made,* wherein my wisdom excelleth them all, for I rule in the heavens above, and in the earth beneath, in all wisdom and prudence, over all the intelligences thine eyes have seen from the beginning; I came down in the beginning in the midst of all the intelligences thou hast seen" (Abraham 3:11, 21; italics mine).

In other words, the purpose of this divine visit or mission, called obtaining the fullness of Christ's glory, is to make the individual equal with the Lord in all things—a joint-heir with Christ of all that the Father has. As Bruce R. McConkie puts it, "As the literal Son of God—the Firstborn in the spirit, the Only Begotten in the flesh—Christ is the natural heir of his Father. It thus became his right to inherit, receive, and possess all that his Father had. (John 16:15). And his Father is possessor of all things: the universe; all power, wisdom, and goodness; the fulness of truth and knowledge; and an infinity of all good attributes. By heirship and by obedience, going from grace to grace, the Son attained these same things (D&C 93:5–17)" (*Mormon Doctrine,* p. 394).

Christ, therefore, has "gained every endowment, quality, attribute, perfection, power, and possession so that 'in him dwelleth all the fulness of the Godhead bodily' (Col. 2:9). He has received the 'fulness of the glory of the Father' (D&C 93:4–20; Col. 1:19)" (*Mormon Doctrine,* p. 349).

"By obedience to the fulness of gospel law, righteous men are adopted into the family of God so that they also become heirs, *joint-heirs with Christ* (Rom. 8:14–18; Gal. 3:26–29; Gal. 4:1–7), inheritors of all that the Father hath. (D. & C. 84:33–41.)" (*Mormon Doctrine,* p. 394).

During the April conference in 1844, while speaking of those who would be "heirs of God and joint-heirs with Jesus Christ," Joseph Smith first asked for a definition of the phrase and then answered himself. "What is it? [It is] to inherit the same power, the same glory and the same exaltation, until you arrive at the station of a God, and ascend the throne of eternal power, the same as those who have gone before" (*Teachings,* p. 347).

Elder McConkie says, "A joint-heir is one who inherits equally with all other heirs including the Chief Heir who is the Son. Each joint-heir has an equal and an undivided portion of the whole of everything. If one knows all things, so do all others. If one has all power, so do all those who inherit jointly with him. If the universe belongs to one, so it does equally to the total of all upon whom the joint inheritances are bestowed.

"Joint-heirs are possessors of all things. (D&C 50:26–28). All things are theirs for they have exaltation. (D&C 76:50–60). They are made 'equal' with their Lord. (D&C 88:107). They gain all power both in heaven and on earth and receive the fullness of the Father, and all knowledge and truth are theirs. (D&C 93:15–30). They are gods. (D&C 132:20). Celestial marriage is the gate to this high state of exaltation. (*Doctrines of Salvation,* 2:24, 35–39; D&C 131:1–4; D&C 132:1)" (*Mormon Doctrine, p.* 395).

THE REST OF THE LORD

In the revelation on priesthood, the Lord told the Prophet Joseph that the Lord's rest was the fullness of his glory (D&C 84:24). The Lord's rest, therefore, is to stand in His glorious presence and behold His face. As Alma declared, "There were many who were ordained and became high priests of God; and it was on account of their exceeding faith and repentance, and their righteousness before God, they choosing to repent and work righteousness rather than to perish; therefore they were . . . sanctified, and their garments were washed white through the blood of the Lamb. Now they, after being sanctified by the Holy Ghost, having their garments made white, being pure and spotless before

God, could not look upon sin save it were with abhorrence; and there were many, exceedingly great many, who were made pure and *entered into the rest of the Lord their God.* And now, my brethren, I would that ye should humble yourselves before God, and bring forth fruit meet for repentance, that *ye may also enter into that rest*" (Alma 13:10–13; italics mine).

Clearly, the Lord desires His sons and daughters to attain to this glorious experience during mortality. As the Prophet Joseph put it, "Great and marvelous are the works of the Lord, and the mysteries of his kingdom which he showed unto us, which surpass all understanding in glory, and in might, and in dominion; which he commanded us we should not write while we were yet in the Spirit, and are not lawful for man to utter; neither is man capable to make them known, for they are only to be seen and understood by the power of the Holy Spirit, *which God bestows on those who love him, and purify themselves* before him; to whom *he grants this privilege of seeing and knowing for themselves;* that through the power and manifestation of the Spirit, *while in the flesh,* they may be able to bear his presence in the world of glory" (D&C 76:114–18; italics mine).

Elder McConkie adds, "True saints enter into the *rest of the Lord* while in this life, and by abiding in the truth, they continue in that blessed state until they rest with the Lord in heaven" (*Mormon Doctrine,* p. 633). As Mormon puts it, "I would speak unto you that are of the church, that are the peaceable followers of Christ, and that have obtained a sufficient hope by which ye can enter into the rest of the Lord, from this time henceforth until ye shall rest with him in heaven" (Moroni 7:3; D&C 84:17–25; Matthew 11:28–30; Hebrews 3:7–19). "For he that is entered into [God's] rest, he also hath ceased from his own works. . . . Let us labour therefore to enter into that rest" (Hebrews 4:10–11).

FEELING THE SAVIOR'S WOUNDS

When the Savior appeared to his disciples in the upper room shortly after his resurrection, one of his first actions was to invite them to step forward and feel for themselves the wounds in his hands and feet. Luke records, "And as they thus spake, Jesus himself stood in the midst of them, and saith unto them, Peace be unto you. But they were terrified and affrighted, and supposed that they had seen a spirit. And he said unto them, Why are ye troubled? and why do thoughts arise in your hearts? Behold my hands and my feet, that it is I myself: *handle me, and see;* for a spirit hath not flesh and bones, as ye see me have. And when he had thus spoken, he showed them his hands and his feet" (Luke 24:36–40; italics mine).

To the Nephites at the temple in Bountiful the message was the same: "Arise and come forth unto me," the resurrected Lord declared, "that ye may thrust your hands into my side, and also that *ye may feel the prints of the nails in my hands and in my feet,* that ye may know that I am the God of Israel, and the God of the whole earth, and have been slain for the sins of the world. And it came to pass that the multitude went forth, and thrust their hands into his side, and did feel the prints of the nails in his hands and in his feet; and this they did do, going forth one by one until they had all gone forth, and did see with their eyes and did feel with their hands, and did know of a surety and did bear record, that it was he, of whom it was written by the prophets, that should come" (3 Nephi 11:14–15; italics mine).

To make rock-solid their testimonies of His literal resurrection and eternal divinity, the risen Lord granted these blessed individuals the privilege of actually handling his glorified body. It seems reasonable that he might do the same for those in our day who have gone forth at all hazards and have overcome all things and demonstrated their constancy.

THE VISION OF ALL

The Prophet taught that "when any man obtains this last Comforter he will have the personage of Jesus Christ to attend him or appear unto him from time to time. & even he will manifest the Father unto him & they will take up their abode with him, & the visions of the heavens will be opened unto him & the Lord will teach him face to face & he may have a perfect knowledge of the mysteries of God, & this is the state and place the Ancient Saints arrived at when they had such glorious visions Isaiah, Ezekiel, John upon the Isle of Patmos, St. Paul in the third heavens, & all the Saints who held communion with the general assembly & Church of the First Born" (*Words*, p. 5).

"While the Prophet stated there were things they received that were unlawful to utter (2 Corinthians 12:4 [1–4]; 3 Nephi 17:17; 19:34 [32–34]; 28:12–14; D&C 76:11–50), yet there was a general theme revealed to all. That theme pertained to the future destiny of man before and during the earth's millennial state" (*Words*, p. 311, footnote 4).

Thus Moses beheld every particle of the earth, "and he beheld also the inhabitants thereof, and there was not a soul which he beheld not; and he discerned them by the Spirit of God; and their numbers were great, even numberless as the sand upon the sea shore. And he beheld many lands; and each land was called earth, and there were inhabitants on the face thereof" (Moses 1:28–29).

Nephi was shown what was most likely the same vision, and he recorded by commandment that portion of it pertaining to the doings of mankind up through the expedition of Christopher Columbus (1 Nephi 11–14). From that point forward the vision was to be recorded by John, known as the Revelator (1 Nephi 14:25). His record is the book of Revelation in the New Testament.

The brother of Jared was also shown this magnificent vision. The scripture relates, "The Lord . . . showed unto the brother of Jared all the inhabitants of the earth which had been, and also all that would be; and he withheld them not from his sight, even unto the ends of the earth. For he had said unto him in times before, that if he would believe in him that he could show unto him all things—it should be shown unto him; therefore the Lord could not withhold anything from him, for he knew that the Lord could show him all things. And the Lord said unto him: Write these things and seal them up; and I will show them in mine own due time unto the children of men" (Ether 3:25–27).

Following the Lord's visit to the Nephites, this vision, recorded millennia earlier by the brother of Jared, was made available to the people (Ether 4:2). However, once they had dwindled again in unbelief, the Lord commanded Moroni to hide up the vision in the earth. Moroni then says, "I have written upon these plates the very things which the brother of Jared saw; and there never were greater things made manifest than those which were made manifest unto the brother of Jared. Wherefore the Lord hath commanded me to write them; and I have written them. And he commanded me that I should seal them up; and he also hath commanded that I should seal up the interpretation thereof; wherefore I have sealed up the interpreters, according to the commandment of the Lord" (Ether 4:4–5). This vision, therefore, is what is contained in the sealed portion of the gold plates, of which Moroni instructed Joseph Smith, "Touch them not in order that ye may translate" (Ether 5:1).

However, this glorious vision is not always to remain sealed. Moroni promises, "The Lord said unto me: [this vision] shall not go forth unto the Gentiles until the day that *they shall repent of their iniquity, and become clean before the Lord.* And in that day that *they shall exercise faith in me,* saith the Lord, even as the brother of Jared did, that they may become sanctified in me, *then will I manifest unto them the things which the brother of Jared saw, even to the unfolding unto them all my revelations,* saith Jesus Christ, the Son of God, the Father of the heavens and of the earth, and all things that in them are.

"And he that will contend against the word of the Lord, let him be accursed; and he that shall deny these things, let him be accursed; for unto them will I show no greater things, saith Jesus Christ; for I am he who speaketh. . . . But he that believeth these things which I have spoken, him will I visit with the manifestations of my Spirit, and he shall know and bear record" (Ether 4:6–8, 11; italics mine).

This promise appears to be directed to individuals as much as it is directed to the Church as a whole, for the only way for the Church as a whole to repent of their iniquity is for the individual members to do so. Therefore, once our repentance has been accepted by the Lord because of our exceeding faith, and we have become clean and sanctified, or in other words, made completely pure of heart, then will the Lord "manifest unto [us] the things which the brother of Jared saw, even to the unfolding unto [us] all [His] revelations . . . [that we] shall know and bear record" (Ether 4:7, 11).

CHARITY—THE PURE LOVE OF CHRIST

Finally we return to the theme with which this volume opened—the commandment to pray that we might obtain for ourselves charity, Christ's pure love. Remember the words of the prophet Mormon: "If ye have not charity, ye are nothing, for *charity never faileth.* Wherefore, cleave unto charity, *which is the greatest of all,* for all things must fail—but charity is the pure love of Christ, and *it endureth forever;* and whoso is found possessed of it at the last day, it shall be well with him. Wherefore, my beloved brethren, pray unto the Father with all the energy of heart, that ye may be filled with this love, which he hath bestowed upon all who are true followers of his Son, Jesus Christ; that *ye may become the sons of God;* that *when he shall appear* we shall be like him, for *we shall see him as he is;* that we may have this hope; that we may be purified even as he is pure" (Moroni 7:46–48; italics mine).

In its fullest sense, then, Christ's bestowal of charity or love is His "appearing" and taking up His abode with us, His sons and His daughters, so that we may "see him as he is" and "be purified even as he is pure"—this after granting us through His love or atonement, first, a spiritual rebirth, and second, the glorious promise of exaltation—making our calling and election sure—which manifestation of His love "is the greatest of all . . . for it endureth forever."

These are the unimaginable, incomprehensible blessings we may anticipate as we obtain the divinely promised presence of the Second Comforter—even the fullness of God's glory—the incredible conclusion of our quest to "seek always the face of the Lord."

Part Five

FINAL THOUGHTS

Chapter Twenty-Five

WHO WE REALLY ARE

We have now come full circle, from a discussion concerning understanding and then praying for the pure love of Christ and seeking the face of the Lord always, through analysis of the fact that Joseph Smith and many of his Kirtland Saints accomplished this, and on through some of what we must do if we expect to receive these sublime blessings in our own journey through mortality—a journey that has been perfectly calculated by God to provide peace in this life and eternal life hereafter (see D&C 59:23). And when that glorious journey is successfully completed, we can joyfully anticipate being numbered among those to whom the Prophet referred when he said, "Many of us have gone at the command of the Lord in defiance of everything evil, and obtained blessings unspeakable, in consequence of which our names are sealed in the Lamb's book of life, for the Lord has spoken it" (*Teachings*, p. 8).

IN DEFIANCE OF EVERYTHING EVIL

This phrase from the Prophet's statement underlies an extremely significant aspect of our coming unto Christ that was mentioned earlier but bears repetition. The journey will be fraught with difficulty, for we must defy or forsake *everything* that is evil! As we go out of Babylon, we are putting at defiance the world and *all* its attendant evils, and we had better expect trials and satanic opposition fully commensurate with the high and heavenly blessings we are seeking! As the wise Peter explained to the Saints, "Beloved, think it not strange concerning the fiery trial which is to try you, as though some strange thing happened unto you: but rejoice, inasmuch as ye are partakers of Christ's sufferings; that, when his glory shall be revealed, ye may be glad also with exceeding joy. If ye be reproached for the name of Christ, happy are ye; for the spirit of glory and of God resteth upon you: on their part he is evil spoken of, but on your part he is glorified. But let none of you suffer as a murderer, or as a thief, or as an evildoer, or as a busybody in other men's matters. Yet if any man suffer as a Christian, let him not be ashamed; but let him glorify God on this behalf. For the time is come that judgment must begin at the house of God: and if it first begin at us, what shall the end be of them that obey not the gospel of God? And if the righteous scarcely be saved, where shall the ungodly and the sinner appear? Wherefore let them that suffer according to the will of God commit the keeping of their souls to him in well doing, as unto a faithful Creator" (1 Peter 4:12–19).

Moreover, history confirms that the world will *never* applaud our efforts at purity and righteousness, no matter how heroic they may be. Peter continues, "Forasmuch then as Christ hath suffered for us in the flesh, arm yourselves likewise with the same mind: for he that hath suffered in the flesh hath ceased from sin; that he no longer should live the rest of his time in the flesh to the lusts of men, but to the will of God. For the time past of our life may suffice us to have wrought the will of the Gentiles, when we walked in lasciviousness, lusts, excess of wine, revellings, banquetings, and abominable idolatries: Wherein they think it strange that ye run not with them to the same excess of riot, speaking evil of you" (1 Peter 4:1–4).

SATAN'S DESIGN

Such difficulties are not overly appealing to any of us, particularly when the evil allure of Babylon is displayed with ever-increasing intensity and appeal in every conceivable direction. The straightness of the Lord's way, therefore, may appear narrower, more intimidating, and more frightening than it actually is. This is exactly according to Satan's design, for he knows full well the blessings that await us if we press ever forward—the very blessings he has eternally forfeited! "Be fearful of this," he whispers hopefully as he launches into his ever-present lies. "You can't do it! It will be too hard! Too painful!" Or, "You can never repent! You are far too evil or stupid or insignificant or [you fill in this space] to think that Christ will ever manifest Himself to you! Surely you don't think He will fill such a failure as you with His perfect love! Or allow you to see His face!" Or he might whisper, "Come on! If you will temporarily put your energies into seeking after money, fame, power, and so forth, look at all the *things* I can give you! The *stuff!* Once you have just a little more *things* and *stuff,* you will finally be settled or content or secure or happy or able to serve! *Then* will be the time for your great spiritual journey! Meanwhile, there's still *plenty* of time, so don't worry about putting your spiritual journey off a little longer!"

And so the devil's lies go on, made even more effective because we know somewhat of our own carnal natures—the natural man we inherited at birth and thereafter—and we fear that we cannot put this behind us. Sin comes too easily to us, too persistently! As a bishop, what made this truly interesting to me, and what I continually endeavored to teach my ward members, is that our momentous determination concerning whether or not to forsake Babylon and come to Christ and Mount Zion is never completed in one gigantic leap—one huge moment. Rather, it is made through thousands of tiny choices, seemingly insignificant, that we make every single day. These choices involve friends; activities; conversations; language; humor; food and beverage consumption; entertainment; leisure activity; leisure inactivity; prayer or the lack thereof; willing participation in family home evenings, scripture study and Church activities or the opposite; joyful and wholehearted service to others or being a self-absorbed idler; partaking of the Lord's proffered ordinances, including not only baptism and the temple but the weekly offered sacrament of the Lord's Supper; and so forth. The longer I served as bishop, the more I became convinced that there is *nothing* any of us knowingly does, day or night, that does not somehow affect the direction our own spiritual life is going. Significantly, through this same *minutiae* of decisions, we bring upon ourselves our own supernal joy and happiness or our own unmitigated misery.

And even when we actually overcome the natural man by forsaking our sins and being born again, too many of us, like Laman and Lemuel, continue to fear that the Lord will make no such glorious things known to us as He has promised (1 Nephi 15:8–10). I have pondered long on this, and I believe that such spiritual paralysis stems in large measure from a lack of understanding our own true eternal natures and identities. More, I believe a great many of the difficulties we experience in mortality could be avoided, or at least made lighter, if we could only come to such an eternal understanding more quickly. That squares with what Brigham Young taught: "This is the reason why we are here, and kicked and cuffed round, and hated and despised, by the world. The reason why we do not live in peace is because we are not prepared for it. We are tempted and tried, driven, mobbed, and robbed; apostates are in our midst, which cause trouble and vexation of spirit, and it is all to keep down our pride and learn us to honor the God of Jacob in all things *and to make us appear [who] we really are*" (*Times and Seasons*, 6:1100–1101; italics mine).

WHO WE REALLY ARE

Who we really are, as well as the course of spiritual growth we can pursue through and beyond the Lord's wilderness school, was shown in vision to Joseph Smith. He wrote under the spirit of revelation, "They are they who received the testimony of Jesus, and believed on his name and were baptized after the manner of his burial, being buried in the water in his name, and this according to the commandment which he has given—that by keeping the commandments they might be washed and cleansed from all their sins, and receive the Holy Spirit by the laying on of the hands of him who is ordained and sealed unto this power; and who overcome by faith, and are sealed by the Holy Spirit of promise, which the Father sheds forth upon all those who are just and true. They are they who are the church of the Firstborn. They are they into whose hands the Father has given all things—they are they who are priests and kings, who have received of his fulness, and of his glory; and are priests of the Most High, after the order of Melchizedek, which was after the order of Enoch, which was after the order of the Only Begotten Son. Wherefore, as it is written, they are gods, even the sons of God—wherefore, all things are theirs, whether life or death, or things present, or things to come, all are theirs and they are Christ's, and Christ is God's. . . . These shall dwell in the presence of God and his Christ forever and ever. These are they whom he shall bring with him, when he shall come in the clouds of heaven to reign on the earth over his people. These are they who shall have part in the first resurrection. These are they who shall come forth in the resurrection of the just. . . . These are they who are just men made perfect through Jesus the mediator of the new covenant, who wrought out this perfect atonement through the shedding of his own blood. These are they whose bodies are celestial, whose glory is that of the sun, even the glory of God, the highest of all, whose glory the sun of the firmament is written of as being typical" (D&C 76:51–70).

AN INTRIGUING VIEW

But even knowing all this, it is remarkable how many of us will continue singing perfectly to Satan's lying tune: "But that isn't me God is talking about. It can't be! I know myself too well, and I'll never make it that far—at least not in this life."

If we find ourselves entertaining such thoughts, then let us consider the following. On Christmas day in 1844, William W. Phelps wrote a letter that was published to the Church (see *Times and Seasons* 5:758). In that epistle Brother Phelps referred to what he had learned from Joseph Smith regarding the meaning of "from eternity" or "from everlasting." Brother Phelps wrote, "And that eternity [the one during which Christ's doings have been known], agreeable to the records found in the catacombs of Egypt, has been going on in this system [not this world], almost two thousand five hundred and fifty-five millions of years."

Elder Bruce R. McConkie, who quotes a small portion of Phelps's letter, adds, "That is to say, the papyrus from which the Prophet Joseph translated the Book of Abraham, to whom the Lord gave a knowledge of his infinite creations, also contained this expression relative to what apparently is the universe in which we live, which universe has been created by the Father through the instrumentality of his Son" (*The Mortal Messiah, Book I*, pp. 32–33, endnote 7).

If we correctly understand what the Prophet was saying, the earliest events referred to in our scriptures—"The head of the Gods" calling "a council of the Gods" to arrange for the creation and peopling of the earth (D&C 121:30–32; *Teachings*, pp. 348–49), as well as of "the grand council of heaven" in which those destined "to minister to the inhabitants of the world" were "ordained" to their respective callings (*Teachings*, p. 365)—took place some two and a half billion years ago. It was then that Jehovah offered himself as the one to go down to earth and bring to pass the Father's plan of salvation through His own life, death, and resurrection (Abraham 3:27; Moses 4:1–2; Isaiah 14:13–14; *The Promised Messiah,* p. 48).

It is nearly impossible for our finite minds to comprehend such an expanse of time. Suffice it to say, Jehovah assumed responsibility for this world and its future inhabitants a long, long time ago.

What astounds me is that each of us was numbered in the heavenly host who participated in at least one of those long-ago councils, offering a sustaining vote in support of Jehovah, rejecting Lucifer's counterfeit plan, and being absolutely certain of our own individual identities as we did so. And once Jehovah had been sustained as God and Christ the Redeemer, we who had thus kept our first estates were foreordained to our own future mortal assignments and presumably set about learning how to accomplish the tasks we would be given. Elder McConkie writes, "Since men are foreordained to gain exaltation, and since no man can be exalted without the priesthood, it is almost self-evident that worthy brethren were foreordained to receive the priesthood. And so we find Alma teaching that those who hold the Melchizedek Priesthood in this life were 'called and prepared from the foundation of the world according to the foreknowledge of God' (Alma 13:1–12). And Joseph Smith said, 'Every man who has a calling to minister to the inhabitants of the world,' and this includes all who hold the Melchizedek Priesthood [as well as the sisters], 'was ordained to that very purpose in the Grand Council of heaven before this world was. I suppose that I was ordained to this very office in that

Grand Council' (*Teachings*, p. 365)" (*Doctrinal New Testament Commentary*, 3:328–29).

VERY ANCIENT BEINGS

That ought to provide us with a new perspective on who we are. Contrary to the fairly negative image most of us have of ourselves as weak and struggling mortals who are prone to failure more than success (which imaage is based entirely on either satanically inspired doubts or an incredibly brief span of time here on earth), we are all, in reality, almost inconceivably ancient beings, filled with glory, light, knowledge, and enormous potential. And we acquired these godly traits by exercising "exceeding faith and good works" (Alma 13:3) a long, long time ago. With that mind-boggling fact before us, consider five questions that you might ask yourself:

1. Since I know I had a premortal identity separate from who I am today, and since I also know that I had enough "exceeding faith and good works" to be "called and elected" by God to be of the house of Israel and to become a son or daughter of Christ, then who or what do I suppose my identity was during that lengthy first estate?

2. Is not that glorious and ancient identity more properly the "true" me than the one I now know, which is at most no more than a few decades old?

3. Is two and a half billion years sufficient time for me to have become acquainted not only with Christ and our Father but also with all the holy angels such as Gabriel, Raphael, and Michael?

4. Isn't it possible that I not only knew such great beings but that I also mingled with them as a valued associate, who was entrusted with similar assignments?

5. Since I successfully kept my first estate, which lasted eons of time, isn't it a little foolish and shortsighted for me to doubt my ability to keep my present second estate for a mere seventy or eighty years?

It is no wonder that Satan, who has an intimate knowledge of our true age and identity, tries so hard to convince us that we are without spiritual merit or worth. If he can't, then he knows he has lost in his declared quest to ensure "that all men might be miserable like unto himself" (2 Nephi 2:27).

A MORE CHARITABLE VIEW

Thankfully, through the experiences I have had while serving as bishop and while trying to carry to the best of my ability Christ's mantle of pure love, I have found myself seeing people in a more positive and hopeful way—more the way I firmly believe that Christ sees us *all the time.* In spite of the failures I have personally experienced and the failures experienced by others as we have worked together to keep the commandments and live the gospel, the Spirit has constantly filled me with the greatest of hope!

One morning in our daily scripture study, while I was wrestling with a particularly discouraging ward situation, my wife selected and then read to me from 3 Nephi 22, where the resurrected Christ quotes Isaiah's tender and joyful rhapsody of Jesus' own premortal words, which He spoke as the Lord God Jehovah. Beginning with verse seven, the passage reads, "For a small moment have I forsaken thee, but with great mercies will I gather thee. In a little wrath I hid my face from thee for a moment, but with everlasting kindness will I have mercy on thee, saith the Lord thy Redeemer. For . . . as

I have sworn that the waters of Noah should no more go over the earth, so have I sworn that I would not be wroth with thee. For the mountains shall depart and the hills be removed, but my kindness shall not depart from thee, neither shall the covenant of my peace be removed, saith the Lord that hath mercy on thee. O thou afflicted, tossed with tempest, and not comforted! Behold, I will lay thy stones with fair colors, and lay thy foundations with sapphires. And I will make thy windows of agates, and thy gates of carbuncles, and all thy borders of pleasant stones. And all thy children shall be taught of the Lord; and great shall be the peace of thy children. In righteousness shalt thou be established; thou shalt be far from oppression for thou shalt not fear, and from terror for it shall not come near thee. Behold, they shall surely gather together against thee, not by me; whosoever shall gather together against thee shall fall for thy sake. Behold, I have created the smith that bloweth the coals in the fire, and that bringeth forth an instrument for his work; and I have created the waster to destroy. No weapon that is formed against thee shall prosper; and every tongue that shall revile against thee in judgment thou shalt condemn. This is the heritage of the servants of the Lord, and their righteousness is of me, saith the Lord" (3 Nephi 22:7–17; Isaiah 54).

How can such promises fail to fill us with hope? Surely, in spite of the sorrow and suffering we are called upon to experience or witness, the Lord has not departed from us, either collectively or individually! Neither indeed will He! And the sweet and lovely evidence of this is all around us.

Throughout the Church dwell men, women, and young people who are loving, serving, and instructing each other, both on their own and through all sorts of Church callings and programs.

These individuals are learning the joys and rewards of happily paying their tithes and offerings, which includes offering to the Lord a broken heart and contrite spirit (D&C 59:8).

Being meek and lowly in heart, these wonderful people "never . . . weary of good works" (Alma 37:34) but quietly and without fanfare go the extra mile as they serve God and Christ by serving and blessing the rest of us (Mosiah 2:17).

These admirable souls are anxiously and prayerfully endeavoring to repent of the sins and weaknesses that have kept them from Christ, and through humble confessions to their bishops, the Lord's common judges, to make certain their hearts are indeed broken with Godly sorrow and their spirits are truly contrite or humbly teachable—and therefore acceptable before the Lord.

Such are coming to cherish with all their hearts the sweet peace given by the Holy Ghost because they have been giving back to Christ *all* their burdens of sorrow, filthiness, and sin.

They are climbing back to their feet no matter how many times they may slip and fall, finally recognizing that Christ's love for them is never conditioned on their goodness or perfection, and that He is always and forever willing to forgive, to assist, and to bless.

They are doing their best to put into effect, in their homes and in their lives, those basic laws of the gospel that the prophets have given them—personal, companionship, and family prayer; personal, companionship, and family scripture study; family home evening; regular church attendance and frequent visits to the temple, and so on.

They are both studying and prayerfully pondering the words of Christ and his mortal servants, at home with their families as well as in Church settings.

They are recognizing that they are like everyone else in the Lord's Church—learning, struggling, and growing in the Lord *one day at a time.*

They are coming to understand that absolutely none of us is immune to the stumblings, temptations, trials, and vicissitudes of mortal life, and that only through the grace, merits, and mercy of Christ will any of us endure or come through with eternal success.

And finally, they are allowing their hearts to fill with an earnest desire to come to Christ and be filled with His love, realizing that this fervent desire, granted them through the glorious power of the Holy Ghost, will lead them to spiritual rebirth and ultimate victory over this world and all its destructive elements.

To see the light of Christ growing ever brighter in the countenances of the sweet people whom I have been blessed to know personally in my own little ward, those who are truly coming to Him despite the satanic opposition they have and are encountering, fills my soul with the most exquisite joy I am capable of imagining. That is a great part of how I know that the Church is true—God's only true and living Church on the earth today. It is part of how I know that Christ's atonement was and is a real and living miracle, and that He himself lives and labors among us constantly, through the medium of the Holy Spirit, though until He is ready we "see him not." It is part of how I know that Satan cannot prevail and that Christ and His righteousness will ultimately triumph!

As I conclude this volume, which for me has been a tremendous exercise in understanding and pressing forward with my own spiritual quest, I bear solemn witness of two things: First, that virtually any one of us, no matter our station in mortality, has the capacity to achieve all the spiritual possibilities and triumphs the Lord holds out to us through His scriptures and His prophets. And second, that Jesus Christ lives and stands waiting with outstretched arms to "take up his abode with us," and that He will do so as quickly as we are willing to put aside the world and surrender our hearts and lives wholly to Him.

"Behold," He declares with words that fairly ring through the eternities, "that which you hear is as the voice of one crying in the wilderness—in the wilderness, because you cannot see him—my voice, because my voice is Spirit; my Spirit is truth; truth abideth and hath no end; and if it be in you it shall abound. And if your eye be single to my glory, your whole bodies shall be filled with light, and there shall be no darkness in you; and that body which is filled with light comprehendeth all things. Therefore, sanctify yourselves that your minds become single to God, and the days will come that you shall see him; for he will unveil his face unto you, and it shall be in his own time, and in his own way, and according to his own will" (D&C 88:66–68).

That such will be so, I humbly testify in His holy name. Amen.

BIBLIOGRAPHY

Backman, Milton V., Jr. *The Heavens Resound: A History of Latter-day Saints in Ohio, 1830–1838.* Salt Lake City: Deseret Book, 1983.

Benson, Ezra Taft. *The Teachings of Ezra Taft Benson.* Salt Lake City: Bookcraft, 1988.

Boss, R. Wayne, and Leslee S. Boss. "Single Parents." N.p., 2003.

Cannon, George Q. *Gospel Truth: Discourses and Writings of President George Q. Cannon.* Compiled by Jerreld L. Newquist. Salt Lake City: Deseret Book, 1987.

Carter, Kate B., comp. *Our Pioneer Heritage.* 20 vols. Salt Lake City: Daughters of the Utah Pioneers, 1958–77.

Church History in the Fulness of Times. Salt Lake City: The Church of Jesus Christ of Latter-day Saints, 1989.

Fay, Jim, and Charles Fay. *Love and Logic Magic: When Kids Leave You Speechless.* Golden, Colo.: Love and Logic Press, 2000.

Godfrey, Kenneth W., Audrey M. Godfrey, and Jill Mulvay Derr. *Women's Voices: An Untold History of the Latter-day Saints, 1830–1900.* Salt Lake City: Deseret Book, 1982.

Hinckley, Gordon B. *Be Thou an Example.* Salt Lake City: Deseret Book, 1981.

———. *Teachings of Gordon B. Hinckley.* Salt Lake City: Deseret Book, 1997.

Journal of Discourses. 26 vols. London: Latter-day Saints' Book Depot, 1854–86.

Kimball, Heber C. *President Heber C. Kimball's Journal, Seventh Book of the Faith-Promoting Series.* Salt Lake City: Juvenile Instructor Office, 1882.

Kimball, Spencer W. *The Miracle of Forgiveness.* Salt Lake City: Bookcraft, 1969.

———. *Teachings of Spencer W. Kimball.* Edited by Edward L. Kimball. Salt Lake City: Bookcraft, 1982.

Largey, Dennis L. "The Enemies of Christ," in *The Book of Mormon: Second Nephi, The Doctrinal Approach.* Provo, Utah: Brigham Young University Religious Studies Center, 1989.

Lee, Harold B. *Decisions for Successful Living.* Salt Lake City: Deseret Book, 1973.

———. *Stand Ye in Holy Places.* Salt Lake City: Deseret Book, 1974.

———. *Teachings of Harold B. Lee.* Compiled by Clyde J. Williams. Salt Lake City: Bookcraft, 1996.

Maxwell, Neal A. *All These Things Shall Give Thee Experience.* Salt Lake City: Deseret Book, 1979.

———. *Even As I Am.* Salt Lake City: Deseret Book, 1982.

———. *The Promise of Discipleship.* Salt Lake City: Deseret Book, 2001.

McConkie, Bruce R. *Doctrinal New Testament Commentary.* 3 vols. Salt Lake City: Bookcraft, 1965–73.

———. *Doctrines of the Restoration: Sermons and Writings of Bruce R. McConkie.* Edited by Mark L. McConkie. Salt Lake City: Bookcraft, 1989.

———. *Mormon Doctrine.* 2d ed. rev. Salt Lake City: Bookcraft, 1966.

———. *The Mortal Messiah.* 4 vols. Salt Lake City: Deseret Book, 1979–81.

———. *A New Witness for the Articles of Faith.* Salt Lake City: Deseret Book, 1985.

———. *The Promised Messiah.* Salt Lake City: Deseret Book, 1978.

Millet, Robert L. *Alive in Christ: The Miracle of Spiritual Rebirth.* Salt Lake City: Deseret Book, 1997.

Nibley, Hugh. *An Approach to the Book of Mormon.* Provo, Utah, and Salt Lake City: Foundation for Ancient Research and Mormon Studies and Deseret Book, 1988.

———. *Approaching Zion.* Provo, Utah, and Salt Lake City: Foundation for Ancient Research and Mormon Studies and Deseret Book, 1989.

———. *Nibley on the Timely and the Timeless.* Provo, Utah: Brigham Young University Religious Studies Center, 1978.

———. *The Prophetic Book of Mormon.* Provo, Utah, and Salt Lake City: Foundation for Ancient Research and Mormon Studies and Deseret Book, 1989.

———. *Temple and Cosmos.* Provo, Utah, and Salt Lake City: Foundation for Ancient Research and Mormon Studies and Deseret Book, 1992.

Nibley, Preston. *Exodus to Greatness.* Salt Lake City: Deseret News Press, 1947.

Olsen, Joseph William. "Biography of Erastus Snow." Master's thesis. Provo, Utah: Brigham Young University, 1935.

Pratt, Parley P. *Key to the Science of Theology.* Salt Lake City: Deseret Book, 1948.

Program of the Church. Salt Lake City: LDS Department of Education, 1936.

Roberts, B. H. *The Gospel and Man's Relationship to Deity.* Salt Lake City: Deseret Book, 1966.

Smith, Joseph. *Discourses of the Prophet Joseph Smith.* Edited by Alma P. Burton. Salt Lake City: Deseret Book, 1965.

———. *History of The Church of Jesus Christ of Latter-day Saints.* 7 vols. Edited by B. H. Roberts. Salt Lake City: The Church of Jesus Christ of Latter-day Saints, 1932–51.

———. *Lectures on Faith.* Compiled by N. B. Lundwall. Salt Lake City: Bookcraft, n.d.

———. *The Papers of Joseph Smith.* 2 vols. Edited by Dean C. Jessee. Salt Lake City: Deseret Book, 1984–92.

———. *Teachings of the Prophet Joseph Smith.* Compiled by Joseph Fielding Smith. Salt Lake City: Deseret Book, 1976.

———. *The Words of Joseph Smith.* Edited by Andrew F. Ehat and Lyndon W. Cook. Provo, Utah: Brigham Young University Religious Studies Center, 1980.

Smith, Joseph F. *Gospel Doctrine: Selections from the Sermons and Writings of Joseph F. Smith.* Compiled by John A. Widtsoe. Salt Lake City: Deseret Book, 1939.

Smith, Joseph Fielding. *Doctrines of Salvation: Sermons and Writings of Joseph Fielding Smith.* 3 vols. Compiled by Bruce R. McConkie. Salt Lake City: Bookcraft, 1954–56.

Talmage, James E. *The Articles of Faith.* Salt Lake City: Deseret Book, 1981.

———. *The House of the Lord.* Salt Lake City: Deseret Book, 1968.

Taylor, John. *The Gospel Kingdom: Selections from the Writings and Discourses of John Taylor.* Compiled by G. Homer Durham. Salt Lake City: Bookcraft, 1943.

Tullidge, Edward W. *The Women of Mormondom.* New York: Tullidge & Crandall, 1877.

Whitney, Orson F. *Life of Heber C. Kimball.* Salt Lake City: Bookcraft, 1945.

Young, Brigham. *Discourses of Brigham Young.* Compiled by John A. Widtsoe. Salt Lake City: Deseret Book, 1954.

INDEX

INDEX